The King of Children

THE
KING *of*
CHILDREN

The Life and Death of Janusz Korczak

B E T T Y   J E A N   L I F T O N

St. Martin's Griffin ✹ New York

Grateful acknowledgment is made to Holocaust Library for permission to reprint excerpts from *Ghetto Diary* by Janusz Korczak, translated by Jerzy Bachrach and Barbara Krzywicka (Vedder), copyright © 1978 by Holocaust Library; and to the late Martin Wolins for permission to reprint excerpts from *Selected Works of Janusz Korczak*, selection by Martin Wolins, translated by Jerzy Bachrach, published for the National Science Foundation, Washington, D.C., by the Scientific Publications Foreign Cooperation Center of the Central Institute for Scientific, Technical and Economic Information, Warsaw, Poland, 1967

All photographs not otherwise credited are reprinted courtesy of Beit Lohami Haghetaot/Ghetto Fighters House, Israel, and the Janusz Korczak Workshop Archives, Warsaw

Frontispiece: Janusz Korczak, 1933

ISBN 0-312-15560-3

First published in the United States of America by Farrar, Straus & Giroux

First St. Martin's Griffin Edition: April 1997

10   9   8   7   6   5   4   3   2   1

For my children
Natasha Karen and Kenneth Jay
and
the children
of Janusz Korczak
and
the children of the world

Contents

Reformers come to a bad end. Only after their death do people see that they were right and erect monuments in their memory.

—JANUSZ KORCZAK, *King Matt the First*

Introduction

Children, Jewish children, were always the first to suffer, the first to be subjected to hunger and thirst; they were the first to go off to the unknown. Wherever Jews suffered, their children suffered more. But under the Nazis, more than ever, and more than others, they knew a fate that, even today, breaks one's heart.

In *The King of Children*, Betty Jean Lifton has re-created, with passion and generosity, the life of an extraordinary man who, until the end of his life, dreamed and worked only for unfortunate children, and who lost his life hand-in-hand with the Jewish children he had tried to protect.

Henryk Goldszmit, better known as Janusz Korczak, will remain in Jewish and Polish history, and in universal history, a symbol at once troubling and reassuring. That one individual like him was able to accomplish so many daily miracles is, to be sure, encouraging. But there were not many like him, and that is alarming.

Janusz Korczak was a physician, educator and writer who lived only for others. An assimilated Jew, he practiced a universal humanism. He hardly distinguished between Jewish and Polish children: He loved them and was involved in their well-being, feeling and wanting to feel as close to one as to the other. His was total, absolute love, which no doubt isolated him from the adult world. He remained a bachelor; children alone had a right to his time, to his life.

The public at large knows Korczak only through his death, or rather through his march toward death, and it's a pity. The whole man deserves to be studied. His disturbed childhood and anguished adolescence (his father was confined to a mental institution and ultimately died there), his military service, his war memories, his first works on behalf of unfortunate children, his feelings and ambivalent attitudes toward religious Judaism and Jewish identity, his trips to Palestine, his complex and ambivalent relationships with women, his profound ties to Polish culture and nationalism—this is the story Lifton has told.

Of course, it is his period in the ghetto that fascinates us the most. How did he manage to build, inside the walls of the Warsaw Ghetto, in the heart of ugliness, a little separate kingdom where the child was prince? In 1930, at age 61, Korczak put his international prestige as an author of fine children's books to use protecting deserted, abandoned and orphaned children. No longer having the right to take care of Christian children, he concentrated on Jewish children—some 200–300 of them—for whom he became guide and father, supplier and protector. He got them to sing, to dream, to hope; he spoke to them of Palestine, but also of the Hindu writer Rabindranath Tagore;

he gave them a Jewish education, but a Polish one as well. For he believed, at least in the beginning, that they would survive the war, they and he, and that the world would become normal again.

Unfortunately, Korczak's children—like all the others—were protected by no one. On the morning of Aug. 6, 1942, their turn came.

Later, in certain circles, he was reproached for not having scattered his children. The fact is that he discouraged parents and friends who wanted to take children out of the orphanage in order to hide them somewhere else—in Christian homes, perhaps. Children needed to be together, he said. In this way, they are less afraid. And then, the danger seemed greater outside than in the orphanage. At what moment did he realize that he had been mistaken?

With times deteriorating and persecutions intensifying, and oppression becoming heavier and more inhuman, sometimes Korczak appeared to have shown signs of weariness. He seemed tired. He drank vodka. And, in his personal journal, it is his childhood that dominated. Was he fleeing the present? Was he plunging himself into his childhood so as to turn away from that of his children driven to the brink of despair? Christian friends tried to persuade him to leave the ghetto; the documents were ready. He refused. He was committed to remain with his children.

He always thought that the Germans wouldn't dare to attack an institution whose reputation extended beyond the borders of Poland. Naivete? Pride? Perhaps both? It was out of pride that, until the end, he refused to wear the Jewish star. There was nothing astonishing about the fact that the respect he generated was widespread.

He had entrée to the Jewish Council of Elders. Adam Czerniakov, the President, was his friend, as was the influential advisor, Abraham Gepner. And Korczak never hesitated to solicit assistance and protection from his friends in high places. But, on July 22, 1942 Czerniakov committed suicide so as not to have to deport the orphans.

At that moment, the fate of those in the orphanage was sealed. Fifteen days later "the king of children" and his young subjects went to their deaths with a dignity that impressed the ghetto. It impressed even the Jewish police who, the moment they saw them get into the wagons that were to lead them to Treblinka, stood at attention and rendered them honors.

Lifton tells the following with a moving simplicity that takes your breath away: In his arms, old Korczak carries a little girl, while he takes a little boy's hand. At one point, the children begin singing. Korczak himself walks in silence.

—Elie Wiesel

Who Was
Janusz Korczak?

"The lives of great men are like legends—difficult but beautiful," Janusz Korczak once wrote, and it was true of his. Yet most Americans have never heard of Korczak, a Polish–Jewish children's writer and educator who is as well known in Europe as Anne Frank. Like her, he died in the Holocaust and left behind a diary; unlike her, he had a chance to escape that fate—a chance he chose not to take.

His legend began on August 6, 1942, during the early stages of the Nazi liquidation of the Warsaw Ghetto—though his dedication to destitute children was legendary long before the war. When the Germans ordered his famous orphanage evacuated, Korczak was forced to gather together the two hundred children in his care. He led them with quiet dignity on that final march through the ghetto streets to the train that would take them to "resettlement in the East"—the Nazi euphemism for the death camp Treblinka. He was to die as Henryk Goldszmit, the name he was born with, but it was by his pseudonym that he would be remembered.

It was Janusz Korczak who introduced progressive orphanages designed as just communities into Poland, founded the first national children's newspaper, trained teachers in what we now call moral education, and worked in juvenile courts defending children's rights. His books *How to Love a Child* and *The Child's Right to Respect* gave parents and teachers new insights into child psychology. Generations of young people had grown up on his books, especially the classic *King Matt the First*, which tells of the adventures and tribulations of a boy king who aspires to bring reforms to his subjects. It was as beloved in Poland as *Peter Pan* and *Alice in Wonderland* were in the English-speaking world. During the mid-1930s, he had his own radio program, in which, as the "Old Doctor," he dispensed homey wisdom and wry humor. Somehow, listening to his deceptively simple words made his listeners feel like better people.

At the end, Korczak, who had directed a Catholic as well as a Jewish orphanage before the war, had refused all offers of help for his own safety from his Gentile colleagues and friends. "You do not leave a sick child in the night, and you do not leave children at a time like this," he said.

I first heard of Janusz Korczak in the summer of 1978 when friends who had left Poland during the war stopped by my home on Cape Cod with a theater director who had just arrived from Warsaw. As she was describing what it had been like for her troupe to perform in Janusz Korczak's ghetto orphanage, I interrupted to ask who Korczak was. I couldn't tell if she was more shocked at my ignorance or at my mispronunciation of his name, but she spent a few moments teaching me to say *Kor-chock* before answering my question.

As we spoke about him that afternoon on Cape Cod, Korczak emerged as a utopian and yet pragmatic figure preoccupied with creating a better world through the education of children. I could also see him belonging to that unique group of writers, along with Lewis Carroll and James Barrie, who were most at home in the company of the children for whom they created their stories. With a difference. Korczak's children did not romp with their nannies on the manicured lawns of Kensington Gardens but languished in the dark slums of Warsaw. He set up orphanages and lived among children in real life, not just in the imagination, for he saw them as the salvation of the world.

It wasn't that Korczak glorified children, as did Rousseau, whom he considered naïve. Korczak felt that within each child there burned a moral spark that could vanquish the darkness at the core of human nature. To prevent that spark from being extinguished, one had to love and nurture the young, make it possible for them to believe in truth and justice. When the Nazis materialized out of that darkness with their swastikas, polished boots, and leather whips, Korczak was prepared to shield his Jewish children, as he always had, from the injustices of the adult world. He went with them into the ghetto, although he had been offered refuge on the Aryan side of occupied Warsaw, and spent the last two-odd years of his life protecting them and other orphans from starvation and disease.

The theater director described how she had watched with others from behind shuttered windows in the Warsaw Ghetto as Korczak, head held high, marched by with his little band on that last day. It seemed to her then that this man, who behaved as if he had a divine calling to save children, had failed, much as his fictional King Matt had failed in his attempt to make the world a better place. And yet, by remaining true to his principles and not abandoning the children when they needed him most, he had achieved his own kind of victory.

Korczak wrote of life as a strange dream, and sometimes my own life seemed just that as I began learning about his. Until 1978 I had been neither personally nor professionally involved with the Holocaust, but in the fall of that year my thirteen-year-old daughter and I went to live in Munich with my husband, who was beginning his study of the psychology of Nazi doctors. It wasn't long before our small apartment was filled with books on the Third Reich and I was foraging through this grim library.

Plunging into Holocaust literature, especially in Germany, was like plunging into an abyss. I seemed to be living in two time frames at once, with the past often taking on more reality than the present. Waking up in the middle of the night, I would transform the smoke stacks of the neighboring brewery into crematoria; the local train would become a cattle car; and Bavarian men parading in colorful costumes would metamorphose into the SS goose-stepping through the streets in full regalia. As an assimilated American Jew who had never dwelt on my Jewish identity, I was now confronted with what it meant to be a Jew during the Third Reich in Europe—and, for that matter, through all of history.

Often, in the volumes describing the murderous behavior of Nazi doctors, I would find references to Janusz Korczak's last march with the children. I wanted to know more about this man—a good doctor—who had chosen to die rather than compromise the principles by which he lived. What had given him the strength to uphold those principles in a world gone mad?

But something else drew me to Janusz Korczak. I identified with him as a writer—as one who has written fantasies for children, and working as a journalist in the Far East, reported on war-wounded, orphaned, and displaced children in Hiroshima, Korea, and Vietnam. Many of my books are concerned with the right of all children to know their heritage and to grow up in a world unthreatened by war.

Yet I might not have pursued my interest in Janusz Korczak any

further had my husband and I not been injured in a car crash in Paris
and gone to the Sinai to recuperate. On our return trip by way of Jerusalem, I heard that some of the orphans Korczak had raised and the
teachers he had trained were living in Israel. And in that city of strange
dreams I made a sudden decision to remain for a few months with my
daughter in order to interview them.

I rented a small stone house overlooking the walls of the Old City
and went about with an interpreter to interview Korczakians, as they call
themselves. They ranged in age from the fifties to the eighties, all having
lived or taught in his Jewish orphanage during different periods after its
founding in 1912. Many were alive because as Zionists they had emigrated
to Palestine in the nineteen-thirties; a few had survived ghettos and
concentration camps or had spent the war years in remote towns in Siberia. Others had come to Israel following the 1967 Six-Day War in the
wake of the "anti-Zionist purge" that essentially swept Poland of its remaining Jews.

"I don't want to talk about the dead Korczak, but the living one,"
they would begin, disturbed at his being remembered for the way he
died rather than for the way he had lived. It was not the martyr whom
they had known and revered, but the vital, fallible father and teacher.

Listening to them, I could envision Korczak as a modest, disciplined
man who dismissed with an ironic quip problems that would have overwhelmed others. Traveling to the kibbutzim and the cities he had visited
during the two brief trips he made to Palestine in the mid-thirties, I tried
to understand his state of mind then. Although not a Zionist, Korczak
had been forced, like so many acculturated Jewish writers in prewar
Europe, to keep one step ahead of the malevolent thrusts of history.
When the rise of extreme nationalism in Poland caused him to despair
about the future of his work, he turned to Palestine but was deeply
ambivalent about whether or not to settle there. Believing that, to avoid
being a deserter, "one has to remain at one's post till the very last moment," he was still in Warsaw on September 1, 1939, when the Nazi
invasion of Poland settled the issue for him.

Who was Janusz Korczak? I have on my desk his two best-known
photographs: one of himself as a young boy that he used as the frontispiece
of his book *King Matt the First* so that his readers could see him as he
was when he was small and vulnerable like them; the other of a man
whose eyes are intense and sad and whose bald head disappears into white

space because an impulsive orphan ripped the photograph out of the developer before it was ready.

These are the two Janusz Korczaks—the young utopian King Matt who dreamed of making a better world for children, and the skeptical Old Doctor who knew that one always falls short of attaining the dream.

"It will be hard to describe Korczak to Americans," the Korczakians had told me in Israel. I was to hear the same sentiments from Korczakians in Poland—but for different reasons. "He was very Polish," Igor Newerly, Korczak's former secretary and now a prominent writer, told me. "But at the same time that he was part of the Polish intelligentsia of his period, he was alone. A man with his own individualistic style and beliefs. He was warm and witty, but he was also lonely and sad. He was everything, and you have to capture that."

To capture everything, I soon realized, meant to see Korczak as both a Pole *and* a Jew; to be both—in the words of the novelist Tadeusz Konwicki—is more difficult than to be just a Pole or just a Jew. The problem is revealed in the semantics of the issue: a Polish Catholic is called a Pole, but a Polish Jew is called a Jew, not a Pole.

Perhaps because Korczak was determined to live as both a Pole and a Jew in prewar Poland, he was not above criticism in his lifetime: many Jews saw him as a renegade who wrote in Polish rather than Yiddish or Hebrew, while no amount of acculturation could make the right-wing Poles forget that he was a Jew. The radical socialists and the communists of the interwar period saw him as a conservative because he was not politically active, and the conservatives saw him as a radical because of his socialist sympathies. There were those who considered him an eccentric, even as they sang his praises and supported his causes: unmarried, asocial, he was as intolerant of pompous and self-aggrandizing adults as he was tolerant and forgiving of mischievous children.

As I talked with people in Warsaw, I pondered how to write this book about Janusz Korczak. Those who do not want their biographies written burn their papers; history had done that for Korczak. The Warsaw Ghetto, where he was confined from late 1940 until mid-1942, was destroyed by the Germans during the uprising there a year after his death. Consumed in the flames were the notebooks in which Korczak had jotted down his thoughts in his microscopic handwriting; his letters and memorabilia; his observations on children's sleep patterns, and the weight and height charts collected over thirty years that were to comprise a book on child development; his library of both literary and scientific books in French, German, and Russian, as well as Polish; and his drafts of books he planned to write. The relatives and childhood friends who would have been able to fill in the details of Korczak's early life and provide some portrait of his parents and sister died in the camps.

To go in search of Janusz Korczak, as I did, was to seek a man who was no longer there in a place that was no longer there. His multi-ethnic world no longer exists. Warsaw, once called the Paris of the East, vibrant with cafés, fine restaurants, and cabarets, was leveled by the Germans during the uprising of the Poles in 1944. Rebuilt after the war (with the baroque Palace of Culture, an unwelcome gift from the Russians, dominating the skyline), the city resonates with economic and political discontent.

During my four trips to Poland and my two trips to Israel between 1979 and 1986, the Korczakians were always generous enough to delve into their memories for one more detail about their experiences with Korczak. In the sparse archives in Warsaw and Israel I was able to find a few books of reminiscences by people who had known Korczak in one capacity or another. There were also copies of his twenty-four published fiction and nonfiction books—many of them autobiographical—as well as the newspaper and magazine articles, numbering over one thousand, that he wrote throughout his life. Other than the six dozen letters written in the late twenties and thirties that were saved by their recipients in Palestine, all that remains of Korczak's private papers is the diary that he wrote in the last desperate months of his life. Smuggled out of the ghetto after his death, it was sealed up in the walls of his Catholic orphanage in the Warsaw suburb of Bielany and retrieved after the war ended.

Although Korczak died a year before the Warsaw Ghetto Uprising, many of his surviving Jewish orphans and teachers returned to Poland from all over the world to honor him during the commemoration of the Uprising's fortieth anniversary in April of 1983. They came reluctantly, some because of the imposition of martial law in 1981 and the disbanding of Solidarity, but most because of the pain of reliving the past and of seeing how little remained of the world they had known.

It is this lost world of Janusz Korczak, and of Warsaw's 350,000 Jews, that one encounters when one visits the former site of the Jewish quarter. It had been walled in by the Nazis to make the ghetto, and then burned by them to make the barren stretch of rubble that for many years after the war the Poles referred to as the "Wild West." New buildings have gradually risen over the ashes and rubble. The Ghetto Fighters Monument sits in the center of this unnatural landscape, reminding one of the unnatural cruelties which were committed there.

The International Janusz Korczak Association, based in Warsaw, invited its members to an unveiling of his bust that now commands the front courtyard of the former Jewish orphanage. The irony would not be lost on the Old Doctor that the four-storied white building, gutted during the war, was restored in the mid-fifties without the garret room that had served as his study. The stretch of roof is no longer broken by the graceful arc of the three-paned window through which he had peered at the children playing below and fed the wild sparrows who kept him company. When the unveiling ceremony was over, the Korczakians wandered through the orphanage, looking—for what? Themselves as children or apprentice teachers? For the Old Doctor? For Stefa Wilczynska, who had been his codirector for thirty years?

The Polish orphans who live there now moved like phantoms through the halls, making room for the old phantoms who had come back. They invited us to sit in the large recreation room, which had also served for dining and studying in Korczak's day, to watch them perform two short plays: one a humorous skit based on a scene from *King Matt;* the other a reenactment of the march by Korczak and the Jewish orphans to the train that transported them to Treblinka. The Polish children became the ill-fated Jewish ones they had heard so much about, walking slowly with Korczak to their unknown destination, even climbing up into an imaginary cattle car and gathering in a circle around him, swaying with the movement of the train, as he told them one last story in which good prevails over evil.

On the chartered bus that was taking us back to our lodgings, I sat next to Michal (Misha) Wroblewski, a teacher who was the last among the survivors to have seen Korczak alive. He had been working on the other side of the wall—at a job Korczak had managed to find for him—and returned to the ghetto orphanage late that afternoon to find everyone gone.

Misha was silent for some time, and then he leaned over to me: "You know, everyone makes so much of Korczak's last decision to go with the children to the train. But his whole life was made up of moral decisions. The decision to become a children's doctor. The decision to give up medicine and his writing career to take care of poor orphans. The decision to go with the Jewish orphans into the ghetto. As for that last decision to go with the children to Treblinka, it was part of his nature. It was who he was. He wouldn't understand why we are making so much of it today."

As I worked on this book back in New York City and Cape Cod, I came to see Korczak as a man who walked without fear over what the Hasidim call the narrow bridge of life, making at each stage the moral decisions that would inform his actions.

PART ONE

1878-1918

1

Child of
the Drawing Room

He made his first moral decision at the age of five.

Peering down at the courtyard around which his fashionable Warsaw building was wrapped like a fortress, Henryk Goldszmit confided to his maternal grandmother, the only one who understood him, his "bold scheme to remake the world." He would do away with all money, but how to do it and what to do next, he had no idea. The problem was perplexingly difficult, but the goal was clear: to fix things so that there would be no more dirty or hungry children like the janitor's son and the gang down below with whom he was forbidden to play.

"My little philosopher," said his grandmother, slipping him a raisin.

He never knew the exact year he was born—July 22, 1878, or 1879—because his father, Jozef Goldszmit, a prominent lawyer in Warsaw, delayed registering his birth. "I suffered a few difficult moments over that," Korczak was to write. "Mother called it gross negligence."

Jozef may already have been showing signs of the instability that would eventually erupt into mental illness, or his procrastination may have been deliberate. Warsaw was then part of the Czarist empire (Poland having been partitioned over a century before by Austria, Prussia, and Russia), and many parents falsified their sons' ages with the hope of postponing, even avoiding, their induction into the Czar's army. But though he hadn't officially registered the birth of his first, and only, son, Jozef sent announcements to friends at home and abroad. He was extremely proud of a letter of blessing from the Chief Rabbi of Paris: "Your son will be a great man of Israel." Korczak kept the letter throughout his life, although he was aware that there had been little in his early behavior to give his father confidence that he was raising a great man.

He was a dreamy child who could play for hours on his own. The large household was dominated by women: besides his mother, there were his younger sister and maternal grandmother, a cook, a maid, and a series of French governesses. Outside was a world where men had power, but in this elegant apartment of ornately carved chests and tables, plush sofas, and oriental rugs, "that stern regiment of women" held sway.

In those days there were few places a child could play. Saxon Garden, in the heart of the city and not far from his home on Senatorska Street behind the National Theater, had no playgrounds with swings or soccer fields where a child could stretch his legs and work off his energy. Janitors took a broom to anyone who dared bounce a ball near their gates, and the police chased those children who made a sport of jumping on and off the red horse-drawn tramcars that clanged through the streets. Because it was considered bad manners for a child of good family to play in the courtyards, a sensitive, overprotected boy like Henryk could do nothing except sit indoors and "harbor secrets," or press his nose against the dining-room window and envy the janitor's son and the other roughnecks in the courtyard below.

The boy heard repeatedly from his mother that poor children were dirty, used bad language, and had lice in their hair. They fought, threw stones, got their eyes poked out, and caught terrible diseases. But he saw nothing wrong with the janitor's son and his friends. They ran about merrily all day, drank water from the well, and bought delicious candy from the hawkers whom he wasn't allowed to go near. Their bad words were actually funny, and it was a hundred times more inviting to be down there with them than in that boring apartment with his French governess and his little sister Anna. "A child is someone who needs to move," he would write one day; to forbid this is "to strangle him, put a gag in his mouth, crush his will, burn his strength, leaving only the smell of smoke."

"That boy has no ambition," his mother said when she saw him playing hide-and-seek with his sister's doll. She didn't understand that while searching for the doll, he moved into dimensions beyond the narrow confines of his apartment. "The doll wasn't merely a doll, but the ransom in a crime, a hidden body which had to be tracked down."

"Children's games aren't frivolous," he would write. "Uncovering a secret, finding a hidden object, proving that there is nothing that cannot be found—that's the whole point."

His father flew into a rage, calling him "a clod, fool, or an idiot," when he saw him sitting for hours with his building blocks. He didn't understand that Henryk was constructing the solitary towers that would appear in *King Matt the First* and other books as a symbol of refuge for the orphaned and the lost. "Feelings that have no outlet become daydreams," he wrote. "And daydreams become the internal script of life. If we knew how to interpret them, we would find they come true. But not always in the way we expect."

It was also considered bad manners for a child to hang around the kitchen, but sometimes when his parents were out Henryk would sneak in to ask the cook to tell him a story. This imaginative woman would set him up on a high stool by the table where she was working—as if he were "a human being and not a lapdog on a silk cushion."

"So it is to be a fairy tale? Well, all right. What was I going to say? Oh, yes, it was like this. Just a moment, let me see." She seemed to know he needed time to make himself comfortable before she started.

"So she is going through the forest," the cook might begin, as if continuing where she had left off before. "It is very dark, nothing can be seen, neither trees nor animals, not even a stone. It is pitch black. And she is so afraid. Well, she crosses herself once, and that helps a little. She makes the sign of the cross once more and goes on . . ."

She knew when to pause to let him catch his breath, when to rush on. He never forgot the warmth of her style, the dramatic suspense, as natural to her as the rhythm of her fingers kneading the dough. He would always be grateful for her patience when he interrupted with a question, the respect she had for both the tale and the listener; it was she, he knew, who was responsible for the magical ingredients that went into his own talent as a storyteller.

Not all of his experiences with the household staff were positive. One night when his parents had gone to the theater, Catherine, his French governess, had a visitor in the kitchen, a strange man with high boots. When Henryk started to cry that he wanted him to go away, his governess told him to apologize. The boy refused. "If you don't, we'll leave you here alone," the governess threatened. "I will turn out the light, and you'll be in the dark. An old beggar will come and grab you, and put you in a large bag."

He stood there helplessly until his parents came home. "Why isn't my son sleeping?" his mother asked the governess. And then to him: "Were you crying? Your eyes are red." He shook his head no, and kissed her.

The drawing room was another place that was off-limits to children. During the day the gauze curtains filtered out the rays of the sun but not the clip-clop sounds of the horse-drawn carriages passing over the cobblestone street below: like all fashionable drawing rooms, it faced the front rather than the dark courtyard. Only at night when there were guests did the room come to life under the candlelit chandeliers.

Sometimes Henryk was summoned to meet the guests and recite the Romantic ballad by Adam Mickiewicz that all good Polish children were required to memorize for such occasions: "The Return of Daddy." He would stand pale and awkward as he began: "Daddy is not coming back! Daddy is not coming back!"—becoming as he spoke the child who feared his father would be killed by bandits on his way home from a business trip. The father was eventually spared by the bandits, who were moved that a child was waiting for him. But little Henryk was never spared the "false smiles" of the men with prickly beards who blew cigar smoke in his face, and the strong perfume of the women who tried to draw him onto their laps. (Until he was reprimanded for it, he wiped his face thoroughly after each kiss.) He was embarrassed by the senseless questions and hollow laughter: Whom did he resemble? Oh, he was such a big boy! Just look how he'd grown! Didn't they know that children don't want to be touched or kissed by strangers? Even his mother and father seemed like strangers at such moments.

His father had already become unpredictable. He tweaked Henryk's ears quite hard despite the most emphatic protests from the boy's mother and grandmother. "If the child goes deaf, it'll be your doing," his mother would say. Once, when the boy had an exciting piece of news, he ran into his father's study and tugged at his sleeve. Jozef exploded at him for causing an inkblot on an important piece of paper. Yet at other times his father would act like a friend, especially during the Christmas season, when he would take Henryk and his sister to a Nativity play. His mother was always nervous when the children were out with Jozef. Sometimes it seemed to the boy that his charming, mercurial father was as dangerous as the janitor's son. He exuded a reckless male sense of freedom that was both exciting and terrifying.

Something in Henryk knew that there was reason for his mother's concern. "Mama was right to be reluctant about entrusting her children to the care of her husband," he would say when looking back on that time, "but just as rightly my sister and I would welcome such excursions with whoops of delight and remember fondly even the most strenuous and disastrous pleasures sought with an amazing intuition by that not particularly reliable pedagogue—my father."

One year when he went with his father to a Nativity play in the long, overheated hall of an orphanage, his father agreed with "a mysterious, strange lady" that his son would see better if he sat with the other children in the front row. Already overwhelmed by the air of mystery in the packed house, the boy panicked at the thought of being separated from his father. He also remembered that he was always terrified when the Devil and Death came prancing out.

He called out helplessly as he was being led away: "Daddy!"

His father, not comprehending, replied only: "Go along, silly boy."

On the way to his seat, he kept asking the woman whether Herod and the Devil would appear, but she was as unaware of his anguish as his father. "Wait and see," was all she said. It was not by chance that the future educator would instruct teachers: "Don't force surprises on children if they don't want them."

Preparations dragged on and on before the curtain went up, and the faint sounds and whispers coming from behind it set his nerves on edge. The lamps were smoking. The children pushed and shoved each other: "Move over! Take that hand away! Keep your legs to yourself! Don't lean on me!" A bell rang, and then, after what seemed a very long time, it sounded again.

Writing about the incident years later, Korczak could not recall if the Devil was red or black, but he knew that never before had he heard such a laugh or seen such leaps, such a pitchfork, such a very long tail. "I even suspected, which may well be true, that hell really does exist." Somehow, he managed to survive the experience and even felt a pang of regret when the lights went up, revealing an ordinary room in Warsaw filled with cigarette smoke that made him cough.

He had his father's hand in his again, but could not remember if they stopped to have ice cream or chipped ice with pineapple juice. He did recall that he lost his scarf, and developed a low fever for which he was kept in bed for three days. His mother let his father know that he was not to bring ice cream home until spring, and admonished him sternly when he tried to approach his son's bed on the third day: "Your hands are cold, don't go near him!"

Jozef withdrew meekly, but threw his son a "conspiratorial glance." The boy answered with a "cunning, knowing grin." At that moment, Korczak would write, father and son were as close as they would ever be: "I think we both felt that in the end it was we men who held the upper hand . . . We were the masters, but we had to give in for the sake of peace."

There was another event during the Christmas season that Henryk both looked forward to and dreaded—the Nativity puppet show that the unemployed construction workers from Miodowa Street brought around the neighborhood. His father always invited them in over his mother's objections that they would track in mud. While the men made their way to the kitchen entrance, the maid rushed about hiding small valuables, convinced that these yearly visitors were the reason for two missing spoons.

The "regiment of women" was always in a high state of agitation as the puppeteers set up their little wooden stage in the kitchen. He watched from the doorway. It was not Death or the Devil prancing about to the accompaniment of an accordion or barrel organ that he had been dreading all year, but rather that moment at the end of the performance when the curtains closed and an old man appeared from behind the set with a sack to take up a collection.

The boy had already changed all the money he had into tiny two-penny coins as his father had instructed; trembling with excitement, he tossed them into the sack. But as usual, after peering inside, the old man said, "Not enough, young gentleman, not enough! A bit more!"

He had scrimped all year to avoid this terrible confrontation, even refusing street beggars their expected allotment so that he'd have extra coins. But the old man was as insatiable as his sack was bottomless: "It managed to devour every last penny. I gave and gave, always trying to see if finally he'd say enough."

It was never enough. The old man with the sack was teaching him "the hopelessness of defense against persistent requests and unbounded demands that are impossible to meet."

Henryk did not know that the puppet shows and Nativity plays had religious as well as cultural significance. By stressing the ethical rather than the ritual part of their Jewish heritage, his parents had not yet made him aware of that "mysterious question of religion." It took the janitor's son and the death of his canary to do that.

The canary had been the boy's closest friend, caged in as they both were, neither allowed to fly free. (The bird might perish from the cold outside, just as Henryk might perish from some terrible disease.) But one day he found the canary lying stiff on the bottom of the cage. He picked up the little body, put the beak in his mouth, and tried to breathe life into it. It was too late. His sister Anna helped him wrap the dead bird in cotton and put it into an empty candy box. There was no place to bury it except under the chestnut tree in the forbidden courtyard below. With great care he constructed a little wooden cross to put over the grave.

"You can't do that!" the maid told him. "It's only a lowly bird, lower than man." When tears streamed down his face, she added, "It's a sin to cry over it."

But Henryk was stubborn, even then. He marched down to the courtyard with his box, his sister tagging behind him, and began digging the little grave. Then the janitor's son came along, took in the scene shrewdly, and objected to the cross for a different reason: the canary was Jewish. And, what was worse, so was Henryk.

It was a moment of revelation he never forgot: "I, too, was a Jew, and he—a Pole, a Catholic. It was certain paradise for him, but as for me, even if I did not call him dirty names, and never failed to steal sugar for him from my house—I would end up when I died in a place which, though not hell, was nevertheless dark. And I was scared of the dark . . .

"Death—Jew—Hell. A black Jewish paradise. Certainly plenty to think about."

2

Heritage

Henryk had stumbled upon a problem—the Jewish problem—that confronted all Polish Jews at some time in their lives. He would learn that his paternal grandfather, Hirsh Goldszmit, after whom he was named, had spent his life trying to solve it. Hirsh died at the age of sixty-nine in 1874, just a few years before his grandson was born, in the provincial town of Hrubieszow, southeast of Lublin.

Hirsh was a dreamer and a man of action, much as his grandson would be. In the early nineteenth century he joined the Haskalah, the Jewish Enlightenment movement that encouraged Jews to become part of the secular world. The Jews had been welcomed into Poland by the Polish kings in the Middle Ages, but they had remained isolated in the society. Hirsh and his fellow *maskilim* tried to convince them that if they cut off their beards and sidelocks, exchanged their long caftans for Western suits, and made Polish rather than Yiddish their primary language, they could still retain their spiritual values. It was an arduous task. Centuries of discrimination in the diaspora had made them suspicious of Gentiles and comfortable only among themselves. "Build a fence around the Torah, and don't get mixed up with anything from the outside" was a popular saying.

Somehow Hirsh, whose father was a glazier and trader in rabbit skins, managed to leap over the fence and make his way to medical school. After receiving his degree, he married Chana Ejser, two years his junior, and became the first doctor in Hrubieszow's small Jewish hospital. In true

Haskalah spirit, Hirsh gave his three sons and two daughters Christian as well as Hebrew names, and as a leader in the Jewish community—whose three thousand Jews made up half the town's population—he took advantage of any chance to praise ways in which Poles and Jews worked together. Soliciting funds for his small hospital in the regional Hebrew newspaper, Hirsh commended the two rabbis who had gone about like "beggars" collecting donations in spite of advanced age, poor health, and little means of their own, as well as the Gentile on the charity board who "spared no effort" in helping them.

But Hirsh's claim that a secular education would not lead one's children away from their own faith and into the dreaded jaws of conversion was weakened in 1849 when his eldest son, eighteen-year-old Ludwik, converted. Although conversion was not an uncommon occurrence in that impassioned period of Polish uprisings against the Russians, Hirsh himself remained a Jew, continuing to exhaust himself with projects that would build bridges between his people and the Poles.

It was not only the intransigence of his own people that made Hirsh's task so frustrating, but the fact that a good many Poles did not consider a Jew, no matter how enlightened, a Pole. When Korczak's father, Jozef, was born in 1844, Hirsh had to go to the Office of Non-Christian Religions with two Jewish witnesses to register him. He took the capmaker and the innkeeper. Four years later, he asked the synagogue caretaker and the ritual slaughterer to testify to the birth of his next boy, Jakub. Rather than converting like their older brother, Jozef and Jakub would carry on their father's assimilationist mission by dedicating their lives to projects that would lift poor Jews into the mainstream of Polish society.

When he was a small boy, Jozef went to Hebrew school in Hrubie-szow, for the *maskilim* believed in giving their boys a grounding in Torah before their secular schooling. He was attending a Polish *gymnasium* in Lublin during the failed uprising of 1863, reciting with the rest of his classmates the patriotic poems of Poland's three great nineteenth-century Romantic poets, Adam Mickiewicz, Juliusz Slowacki, and Zygmunt Krasinski—poems he would pass on to his son, along with a yearning for national liberation from the Russians.

Little of Jozef Goldszmit in his healthy, productive years has come down to us except through his own articles and books. We haven't even a photograph to divulge whether he was responsible for his son's fair complexion and baldness as well as his patriotic fervor. In the *Ghetto*

Diary Korczak writes: "I should devote a great deal of space to my father. I tried to put into practice the goals he strove for, and which my grandfather pursued with such pain." But Korczak was never to fill in his complex feelings about this father who, like him, had literary aspirations as a young man.

Jozef was twenty when he wrote his first article for the *Israelite* (a progressive Polish-language bimonthly which had just begun publication), describing his nervousness on arriving in the big city to study law. In those days Warsaw was a bustling tree-lined capital of half a million people, one in six of whom were Jews who, except for a small assimilated circle, lived in squalid poverty. With its Royal Palace, occupied by the Czar's Viceroy, its skyline dominated by the onion-shaped domes of the huge Russian church, and its cobblestone streets teeming with droshkies, wagons, porters, and vendors, Warsaw could easily overwhelm an impressionable newcomer. Seeking a quiet place in which to gather his thoughts, Jozef wandered into the synagogue on Danilowiczowska Street, which, like everything else in this city, seemed grand compared to what he had known in the provinces, only to have loud clanging from the nail factory next door drown out the music and prayers. "Such things should not be allowed to happen in a House of God," he reported indignantly. It was his first crusade, but not his last.

Like so many of his generation who had become disillusioned with armed struggle after the failed insurrections against the Czar, Jozef believed that the only way to create a strong Polish nation was to build its economy from within. Wanting the Jewish people to be part of this vision, he took time from his law studies to raise money for Polish-language craft schools in both Lublin and Warsaw, where poor Jewish boys and girls could learn skills that would equip them to enter the Polish work force. Both he and his younger brother Jakub, who would follow him in law, wrote articles promoting those schools.

Jozef also collaborated with Jakub on a series of monographs called *Portraits of Famous Jews*, in which they hoped to enlighten the public about remarkable Jews of high moral character. (They later expanded this project to include famous Poles.) The first volume was on Moses Montefiore, the exuberant philanthropist and financial advisor to Queen Victoria, who traveled the globe with his carriage, wife, and doctor in tow, distributing large sums of money to poor Jews for hospitals and orphanages, never neglecting to slip something to the sultans and czars of those lands for their own poor.

"Sir Montefiore is a Jew and he never forgets it. But he is also an Englishman, and an exemplary citizen of his country who fights not with the sword but with the force of virtue," Jozef expounded in his flowery nineteenth-century Polish. This message was one that both he and his brother would stress in all their writings: it was possible to be both a loyal Jew and a loyal citizen of one's country. At the age of eighty-four, in failing health, Montefiore had not hesitated to make a strenuous trip to Jerusalem when he heard his fellow Jews were once again in dire need. "Even though the journey is dangerous, nothing will stop me," Jozef quotes him. "Having devoted my entire life to my people, I will not desert them now."

Known as the "Brothers Goldszmit," Jozef and Jakub used writing as a tool to educate and raise both Polish and Jewish consciousness. They wrote numerous articles on the need to secularize Jewish education and upgrade Jewish orphanages, and even turned their hand to fiction to address burning social issues. One has only to read their stilted novels— Jozef's on the need for medical planning for poor Jews; Jakub's on the plight of women driven to prostitution—to understand why their dream of helping to create a genre of books about Jewish life that would become part of Polish literature was doomed to failure.

The Goldszmit brothers moved easily in the narrow stratum of society made up of Polish and Jewish liberal intelligentsia. Their friends included the most famous Polish writers of that period, many of whom created Jewish characters in their novels with whom Polish readers could empathize. When Jakub became editor of the Polish-language Jewish *Kalendar*, his Polish friends contributed articles affirming their brotherhood with the Jews. The *Kalendar*'s purpose, Jakub wrote, was to "enlighten Christians concerning Jews and Judaism and to help bridge the gulf that still keeps the Jews separate." But Jakub infuriated the wealthy leaders of the small but influential assimilated Jewish community with an article in the *Kalendar* criticizing their "spiritual poverty." Labeling them a "class of religious hypocrites who do not believe in anything," he accused them of shirking their responsibility toward the poor Jewish masses.

Jozef's last major publication, in 1871, was his dissertation on Talmudic divorce law, a subject in which he specialized. Praised in an introduction by his Warsaw University law professor for being the first to make this esoteric topic accessible to the Polish people, Jozef was clearly intent on demythologizing the Talmud, which many Poles blamed for the strange and even "evil" behavior of the Jews. Unlike other assimilated

Jews who joined the Poles in criticizing the holy book as a backward influence on their people, Jozef gives an erudite overview of Jewish law (quoting both German and Hebrew sources) as it operated in Poland from the eleventh century to the nineteenth.

There are no records as to when and how Jozef Goldszmit met his wife, Cecylia Gebicka, but it may have been in 1874 when he lectured on Jewish marriage law in Kalisz, an old industrial town in western Poland. He was thirty, and she seventeen. It is probable that Jozef had introductions to the leading Jewish families in Kalisz, among whom was Cecylia's father, Adolf Gebicki. A successful textile manufacturer active in both Jewish and Polish circles, Adolf, who himself was the son of a doctor, had an assimilated background and moral fervor similar to Jozef's. (He was even something of a folk hero to the poor Jews of Kalisz whom he saved from homelessness by persuading the Governor to spare their dilapidated tenements marked for demolition.) The following year, when he was fifty-three, Adolf was "felled like an oak and paralyzed" (as his obituary would read). He, his wife Emilia, and his son moved to Warsaw, perhaps to be near his daughter, who was by then either married or engaged to Jozef. When he died two years later, Emilia moved in with the newly married couple.

Although Korczak wrote with deep affection in the *Ghetto Diary* of his "Grannie" (the only grandparent he knew, and the only person in his household who "understood" him), he was more reticent about his complex relationship with his mother, whose picture he kept on his desk all his life. "My mother. Later about that," he noted. But there was to be no later.

3

Confessions of
a Butterfly

*I am a butterfly drunk with life. I don't know where to soar,
but I won't allow life to clip my colorful wings.*
—Confessions of a Butterfly

Henryk was tutored at home by governesses until he was seven,
as was the custom in educated circles, and then sent to a "strict, boring,
and oppressive" Russian elementary school where Polish language and
history were forbidden subjects. Punitive teachers pulled children by the
ears and beat them with rulers or a cat-o'-nine-tails.

He never forgot the way a boy who urinated on the blackboard eraser
as a prank was spread out on a desk by the janitor, who held his legs
while the composition teacher stood over him with a switch. "I was terrified. It seemed to me that when they finished with him, I would be
next. I was ashamed, too, because they beat him on his bare bottom.
They unbuttoned everything—in front of the whole class."

He became so nervous at the very thought of going to school that
his parents withdrew him after a few months. But one lesson he learned
there remained with him: Children are not respected by adults. He would
notice how children were trampled in the streetcar, yelled at for nothing,
slapped for accidentally bumping into someone. They were always being
threatened: "I'll give you to a wicked old man!" "You'll be put in a bag!"
"A beggar will take you away!" He would write of children as a powerless,
suppressed class, a little people subjugated by a race of big people: "The
adult world revolves around the sensitive child at a dizzying speed. Nothing, no one can be trusted. Grownups and children cannot understand
each other. It is as if they are different species."

*   *   *

Henryk was eleven in 1889 when his father suffered the first of the breakdowns that would take him in and out of mental hospitals for the next seven years and drain the financial resources of the family. To escape the tensions in his troubled household, the boy disappeared even deeper into the world of his imagination. At thirteen he was writing poetry and expanding his horizons—he would learn foreign languages, travel, be a naturalist, a writer.

When he was fourteen his grandmother died, and there was no longer anyone with whom to share those dreams. For a time he sought solace at her grave, which was next to his grandfather's in the Jewish cemetery. The Jews, like the Poles, regarded the cemetery as a gathering place, almost an extension of their own home, where one's loved ones were always available to listen to problems and often endowed with a wisdom they hadn't had in life.

Bored by his strict Russian *gymnasium* in Praga, a suburb on the right bank of the Vistula (probably the only school the family could afford by then), reading became his salvation. "The world vanished, only the book existed." He began writing a journal, which he would one day rework into a novel titled *Confessions of a Butterfly*: it was a slim volume with much of the romantic weltschmerz of *The Sorrows of Young Werther*, which Henryk, like so many Polish students, had read avidly.

Both the sorrows and the loves seem to be those of young Henryk Goldszmit from his thirteenth to his sixteenth year, although the narrator describes himself as a cold Slav from the North who is puzzled by his attraction to a dark-eyed Jewish beauty he passes on the street. She rouses his curiosity about the mysterious Jewish people—the "Sphinx of Nations." But rather than romance, it is reconciliation that he yearns for: reconciliation between the Poles and the Jews. Even at that early age it seems that Henryk was beginning to experience the inner division that was part of the process of assimilation in this Roman Catholic society. By making his narrator Polish, and viewing Jewishness through his eyes, he was experimenting with his two identities—Pole and Jew.

Like Henryk, the narrator has to cope not only with a mentally unstable father but also with strange and confusing sexual stirrings. He has erections and wet dreams that "degrade" his dignity as a man, and fears for his own sanity because masturbating was believed to cause madness. Reassured by his doctor that masturbation is not a disease, only a shortcoming, he is warned to avoid it, as well as everything else that might overstimulate him—"nicotine, alcohol, daydreams, and prostitutes, eighty percent of whom are infected." (Retaining his belief in the harmfulness of masturbation, Korczak would write about his efforts to break the boys in his orphanage of the habit. "If you overcome nature, you overcome yourself," he told them.)

The narrator resolves to work on controlling himself, but cannot save a friend who has "succumbed" to a servant girl. "I can boldly say he is standing at the edge of an abyss." (It may be that Henryk connected sex, which was "dangerous, unhealthy, and undignified," with his father's condition. A part of him may have suspected that the illness might be syphilis: the disease was rampant then and known to affect the brain.)

There is one person, a boy his own age named Stash, toward whom he feels "not friendship but a kind of love one can feel only toward girls." Stash has a girlish delicacy because of a heart ailment. He puts his arm around Stash's shoulder during recess; holds his hand as they walk about the city. Watching a sunset together, they both have tears in their eyes. "Why can't one exchange tears like wedding rings? . . . Our souls were joined together in silence. There were no candles burning before the altar, only the sun. No priest to bless us, only the sky. No wedding guests to give us hypocritical congratulations, only the fir, birch, and oak trees. No organs playing, only the wind. . . . I experienced the most beautiful hour of my life. Why did I want to cry?" In his *Ghetto Diary* Korczak would recall the strong feelings he had for this boy: "Fourteen . . . friendship (love) for Stash."

As his father's condition worsens, the narrator has to spend more time at home with him. He is becoming the father, while his sick father is assuming the role of the son. In the middle of the night he is awakened by the beating of his own heart, and feels as if he were "crying over the grave of his childhood."

One day he lets his father win at cards because it seems to make him happy. "Oh, my God," he prays that night, "let him survive to an old age. And give me the strength to help him." He knows that his father must have once had dreams like his. But "now there is nothing left."

Sometime in the early 1890s, Jozef Goldszmit's behavior became unmanageable at home. He was committed to a "madhouse," probably the newly built brick asylum in Tworki, twenty miles south of Warsaw. Built at great expense by the Czar, Tworki housed four hundred and twenty patients from all over the Russian Empire; it even had a separate walled-off compound for criminals awaiting trial. A treeless, desolate place, whose high red-brick walls were surrounded by unhealthy swamps, it was the most advanced mental hospital in the Empire—the first to be lit by electricity. A large Russian Orthodox church together with a small Roman Catholic chapel dominated the grounds. The wards were filled with people suffering from syphilis, alcoholism, schizophrenia, and manic-depressive psychosis. Treatment, modeled on the European system, stressed work projects such as carpentry. There was little in the way of medicine other than herbs, chemicals, or barbiturates. Distinguished patients like Jozef were quartered in a special walled-off compound, given small plots to garden, and encouraged to read and spend time in the carpentry shop. Those who became uncontrollable were put into straitjackets and tied down in bed.

To visit Tworki, one had to take the Warsaw–Vienna train to the small town of Pruszkow and then hire a horse and wagon for the remaining two miles over muddy, rutted roads. The nurses were kindly Polish nuns, but Henryk seems to have been mortified by the "condescending" smile of the psychiatrist attending his father. The boy could not understand why his father couldn't pull himself together and return home to his family.

Over the years that Jozef was institutionalized, the medical bills piled up faster than his wife could find the means to pay them. One by one the paintings and fine china began to disappear to the pawnshop. Everything that had stood firm in the drawing room—that spoke of eternity—was now up for sale. Once, Henryk and his sister saw their father's cloak in a pawnshop window. It looked so familiar as it hung there that it might have been in the hall of their apartment waiting for its owner to come along and take it to the courthouse or on a stroll to the café. They decided to say nothing to their mother, but to save their pennies and buy it back as a surprise. But by the time they had scraped together enough money, the coat was gone. "The pawnshop is life," Korczak would write. "What you pawn—ideals or honor for comfort or security—you'll never retrieve again." He would make it a point to possess only the essentials, and to arrange life so that he could hold on to those few things he needed.

In order to help support his family, Henryk began tutoring the children of wealthy friends and acquaintances. He never forgot the humiliation of being addressed by some of the mothers in language reserved for servants or his surprise at seeing himself in many of those overprotected rich boys who were pale from being indoors all day and flabby

from lack of exercise. He soon devised a technique for putting them at
ease. He would arrive with a briefcase and unpack it slowly, letting them
examine each object and ask questions about it. Then he would mesmerize
them with a fairy tale or two before leading them into less enchanting
realms of grammar, history, and geography. He discovered in the process
that he liked working with children—and that he was able to forget his
own anxieties while he concentrated on theirs.

Henryk's efforts to develop himself as a tutor inspired his first
pedagogical article, a feuilleton titled "The Gordian Knot," which was
published in the popular illustrated weekly *Thorns* when he was only
eighteen. Writing in the first person, he describes "wandering the world"
looking for someone to answer his question: Will the day come when
mothers stop thinking about clothes and strolls through the park and
fathers about cycling and playing cards and begin raising and educating
the children they have turned over to governesses and tutors? The dignified old man to whom he poses this question replies that he has seen
the "miracles" of the nineteenth century produce gasoline, electricity,
and railroads and people like Edison and Dreyfus, and so surely that day
will come, bringing with it a new breed of mothers who will prefer books
on pedagogy to the latest novels. After asking the old man precisely when
this great day will arrive, the author gives the reader the choice of two
endings: that the old man will fall down dead before he can answer, or
that he will put out his hand and ask for three rubles.

The fledgling writer was already displaying his penchant for injecting
irony and wit into the discussion of serious questions: how to motivate
parents to take a leading role in shaping their children's minds and character, and how to develop a pedagogic strategy that would seize the
imagination of adults and help children to "see, understand, and love, as
well as to read and write." Seeing his article in print encouraged the
young author to submit more. The editor of *Thorns* remembered Henryk
as a shy young man in a school uniform who would enter the office
tentatively, place an unsolicited feuilleton signed *Hen* on his desk, and
leave without a word. Amazed at the talent in those pieces, the editor
gave him a special column.

Jozef Goldszmit died at the age of fifty-two on August 25, 1896, under
mysterious circumstances—possibly by his own hand. A large procession
of colleagues and friends, both Catholics and Jews, representing the publications and philanthropies he had once been associated with, accom-

panied the immediate family in walking behind the horse-drawn wagon that carried his coffin to the Jewish cemetery. He was buried along the main aisle reserved for the Jewish community's most prominent citizens. The tombstone, a tall, narrow slab (now riddled with bullets from the fighting that took place in the cemetery during the Warsaw Uprising of 1944), was engraved in Polish rather than Hebrew, as was the custom for many assimilated Jews. It was adorned only with an embossed wreath.

Soon after her husband's death, Henryk's mother obtained a license from the Board of Education to take in student boarders—a socially accepted solution for widows in her position. Placing a notice in the *Israelite*, she offered tutoring for those who needed it, but did not specify that it would be done by her eighteen-year-old son, who was now the man in the family.

Between school and his tutoring, Henryk had few spare moments, but alone in his room, his only refuge in an apartment now filled with boarders, he was haunted by the thought that he, too, might end up in an asylum. He was the "son of a madman, a hereditary affliction." He poured out his anguish in a novel called *Suicide* in which the hero "hated life out of fear of insanity." He wrote poems with the same dark sentiments until a well-known editor responded to one that began "Ah, let me die / Ah, don't let me live! / Ah, let me descend into my dark grave!" with an unsympathetic "Go ahead!"

"To wound a poet's heart is like treading on a butterfly," he confided to his journal. "I won't be a writer, but a doctor. Literature is just words, while medicine is deeds."

4

Which Way?

Two years later, in the fall of 1898, Henryk—by then an intense young medical student of twenty with vivid blue-green eyes and reddish hair already thinning at the crown—seemed to have forgotten his determination to abandon writing. Hearing of a playwriting contest under the patronage of the famous pianist Ignacy Paderewski, he submitted a four-act play entitled *Which Way?*, about a deranged man whose madness destroyed his family. It won honorable mention (despite the judges' reservations about its somber mood and lack of dramatic tension), but the play would not concern us did it not bear the pseudonym Janusz Korczak.

Legend has it that Henryk learned at the last moment that he needed a pen name for the contest and took it hastily from the first book he saw on his desk: *The Story of Janasz Korczak and the Swordbearer's Daughter*, by Poland's most prolific historical novelist, Jozef Ignacy Kraszewski. The printer (it is said) made a mistake, and the name came out Janusz rather than Janasz. But, in reality, pseudonyms were not a contest requirement, and Henryk's decision to take the name of a Kraszewski character could not have been random chance. Uncle Jakub Goldszmit had dedicated his novel *The Family Drama* to Kraszewski with the emotional supplication: "Take me under your wing, Master, like an eagle protecting a fledgling bird!" The young playwright seems also to have been seeking shelter under the Master's wing.

The noble character and courage of the fictional Janasz Korczak, a poor orphan of gentry lineage, must have appealed to Henryk, if not the contrived plot. A broken leg prevents Janasz from serving in the Battle of Vienna in 1863, but he does not let it prevent him from rescuing his beloved cousin, Jadwiga, and his uncle, the King's swordbearer, from the enemy. Denied Jadwiga's hand in marriage because he is only a poor relative, Janasz turns his fate around by patience, honesty, and self-control, eventually winning Jadwiga and a place in the king's court.

Henryk might have assumed a pen name to protect the anonymity of his family—possibly even to change his luck. ("I escaped from my youth as from a lunatic asylum," he would tell an interviewer.) But it was also not chance that he chose a Polish one. In a country where one's surname reveals one's religious affiliation, Goldszmit was unmistakably a Jew, the outsider. With an old gentry name such as Janusz Korczak, Henryk could re-create himself as an insider, linked to a heroic Polish past.

Still, it was not an easy transition. For the next six years, he did not sign Janusz Korczak to the hundreds of articles and feuilletons that flowed from his pen—some of them humorous observations on human behavior, others earnest essays on land reform, health insurance, pedagogy, women's rights, the plight of poor children, and travel articles from Switzerland and France. Instead, he used fragments of his two selves: Hen, Ryk, Hen-Ryk, G., Janusz, or K.—as if he needed time to fully integrate his new identity. Only his medical articles in professional journals were consistently signed Henryk Goldszmit, as they would be for the rest of his life.

Henryk's friends wondered why he wanted to be a doctor when his literary career was going so well. When Leon Rygier, a fellow writer, encountered him in his blue medical uniform watching some children playing quietly near their nursemaids in Saxon Garden, he asked him just that.

"Being a doctor didn't interfere with Chekhov's becoming a great writer," Henryk replied. "It deepened his creative work. To write anything of value, one has to be a diagnostician." (Much later he would say he owed most to Chekhov—a great social diagnostician and clinician.) "Medicine will give me insight into human personality, even into the nature of children's play," he continued. "See those children over there. Each one plays differently. I want to know why."

In response to Rygier's comment that not all great writers were doctors, he conceded wryly that his decision might have been influenced by the fact that a literary career was too risky when one had a mother and sister to support. (He didn't mention that both his paternal grandfather and his maternal great-grandfather were doctors.)

Henryk had committed himself to a medical career, but he was impatient with his training. He considered most of his professors pompous, insensitive men who seemed detached from the suffering of their patients. As far as he could see, medical schools dehumanized doctors. Students were taught little more than "dull facts from dead pages," and when they finally received their degrees, they didn't know how to cope with sick people. His critical attitude toward the system did not go unnoticed by his professors, one of whom told him: "Hair will grow on the palm of my hand before you become a doctor."

Because of his extracurricular activities as a journalist and the mandatory hours of military training he had to put in over a two-year period, it took Henryk six years instead of the usual five to graduate. Even that was an achievement given that, like so many of his generation, he was caught up in the revolutionary fervor of the time. Poland was in transition from an agricultural society to an industrialized one, and Warsaw was rapidly changing as new factories were built and tens of thousands of peasants crowded into the slums in search of jobs that only a few would find. Successful writers devoted much of their time to championing the cause of workers and peasants. Stefan Zeromski's novel *Homeless People* became a bible for Henryk and his friends; its protagonist, Dr. Judym, gave up love and personal happiness to serve the poor: "I am responsible!" he cried. "If I, a doctor, will not do it, who will?"

Henryk was equally ready to sacrifice himself for the impoverished children he observed in the Warsaw streets. He saw them as the most disadvantaged proletariat of all because they had no one to represent them: "Unkempt boys in run-down shoes, shiny frayed pants, caps thrown carelessly on shorn hair, agile, slight, undisciplined, practically unnoticeable. Not yet burned out by the heat of life, not yet sucked dry by exploitation, no one knows where they manage to find strength, these active, silent, numerous, poor little workers of tomorrow."

The roguish little street beggars soon flocked to the medical student who was willing to listen to them. They besieged him with sad tales of hunger and abuse, while holding out their hands for whatever they could get. Other passersby brushed them off, but they knew that he would always have something for them, if only a piece of candy, an encouraging word, or a kiss on the forehead.

A friend with whom Henryk was walking one day was amazed by an urchin who came running after them, shouting that he wanted to return the twenty kopecks he had received two years before.

"I lied when I told you my father would kill me if I didn't come home with the money I'd lost," the boy confessed. "I've been looking for you a long time so I could give your money back."

As the child counted out the kopecks with his grubby little fingers, Henryk asked how many times he'd used that trick:

"A lot."

"Did it work?"

"Most of the time."

"Have you given the money back to the others, too?"

"No."

"Then why are you giving it back to me?"

"Because you kissed me on the forehead. It made me feel sorry for what I did."

"Was it so strange to have someone kiss you?"

"Yes, my mother is dead. I don't have anyone to kiss me anymore."

"But didn't anyone tell you that it's not good to lie and beg?"

"The priest told me it's not good to lie, but he says that to everyone."

"And was there no one else who cared enough to guide you?"

"No one," says the boy, no longer able to hold back his tears. "I have no one."

Henryk set down his encounters with these urchins, driven to lying and stealing by poverty and neglect, in a novel, *Children of the Street.* His message was that they could be saved only if they were reached through education in their early years. But who was to educate them? Certainly not their drunken, debauched parents, for no one had educated *them.* If the process weren't interrupted, the evil would be passed on.

Not everyone appreciated his lofty ideas. When he wrote in *Thorns:* "I am a person concerned above all else with the problem of uplifting the lives of children," the editor (who was concerned above all else with entertaining his readers) suggested he find another outlet for this preoccupation. From then on, Henryk published in *Voice* magazine, a sounding board for intellectuals who congregated around the Flying University.

Henryk had met the editor of *Voice,* Jan Wladyslaw Dawid, Poland's first experimental psychologist, when he attended his course at the Flying

University. This underground college, so named because students and professors had to keep moving from one location to another to escape surveillance by the police, attracted the finest minds in the country. Though divided into two socialist factions—one advocating national independence and the other an international socialist alliance within the Russian empire—they were united in their determination to keep alive Polish history and culture, which the Czar was determined to stamp out. Those who were caught spent a few weeks, months, or even years in a prison cell, or in exile in Siberia.

Henryk had been taken to his first lecture in Dawid's apartment by his friend Leon Rygier. There were so many coats in the entrance hall they had trouble finding hooks for their own. Once inside the candlelit living room, whose shades were drawn to avoid detection by the police, he was introduced to other students and accepted tea from Dawid's wife, Jadwiga Szczawinska, who presided over the samovar with the same energy she expended on all the projects in which she and her husband were involved.

It was Jadwiga, a woman of formidable organizational ability, who, while still single, had started the Flying University in her small apartment to provide education for young women in Polish language and literature. When word spread about this remarkable clandestine venture, men clamored to be included; and by the mid-1880s there were over a thousand young students of both sexes enrolled in courses at various underground locations in Warsaw. Jadwiga even managed to set up an extensive scientific library for the university, but her domineering personality alienated many of the faculty. Her husband, who was known to "fight like David with Goliath" over issues he believed in, was said to be powerless when it came to Jadwiga.

The secret gatherings of the Flying University provided social as well as academic opportunities. Zofia Nalkowska, a precocious fifteen-year-old who wanted to be an emancipated woman (and who would become a well-known novelist), kept a diary of the sessions at the Dawids' apartment during the time that Korczak was there. In one entry she notes that the girls were really dressed up, but that she looked as attractive as any of them in her brown dress, which gave her a good figure. She tried to concentrate on what Dawid was saying, but sometimes found herself glancing over at the boy with the nice smile who had asked to borrow her notes.

Zofia was not alone in her criticism of the "wise and clever" professor's dry, factual delivery, yet Dawid's reputation as a mumbler who wrote much better than he spoke did not prevent students from flocking to his courses. He had studied in Leipzig with the founder of experimental psychology, Wilhelm Wundt, and his lectures were filled with the radical ideas in education that were sweeping both sides of the Atlantic at the time: ideas that called for liberating the child from the conventional restraints of the past. Rousseau had paved the way for this pedagogical breakthrough in 1762 with his fictional Emile, a boy who was encouraged to grow and develop naturally. And Johann Pestalozzi, working with real children in his famous boarding school set up in 1805 in Yverdon, laid the foundation for progressive education.

Korczak considered Pestalozzi one of the greatest scientists of the nineteenth century. Many of his later ideas on education, the dignity of work, and the importance of observing clearly in order to think clearly, reflect the influence of that dedicated Swiss educator. But it was Dawid's experiments with measuring the psychological responses of children at different ages—work that anticipated the field of child development—that made Henryk decide to do scientific research on the child that would exclude everything that "smacked of subjectivity." Already the two sides of Henryk's character were jockeying for position: the scientist would always be suspicious of the artist, keeping him in check by compiling height and weight charts—material that the artist would seldom find time to correlate.

Another strong influence on the young medical student was Zofia's father, Waclaw Nalkowski, a fiercely outspoken social activist, who developed the field of modern geography. "Who knows famous Poles?" Korczak would ask when writing of Nalkowski. He saw the geographer as a "blazing star in a small firmament," who, had he been born in a country where there was no Russian censor, would have been internationally famous.

Henryk also became a lifelong friend of the imposing Stefania Sempolowska (her trademark a broad-brimmed hat with two ostrich feathers, and a long black dress with a stylish train), who wrote on natural history and supported the rights of Jews, peasants, and workers. Her concern about educating the illiterate masses led her to become a driving force behind the Free Lending Library, where Henryk gave his Saturdays to inspiring unruly children to read. The Russian authorities, convinced that the library was spreading atheism and other subversive ideas, conducted constant roundups. Between raids on the Flying University and the library, Henryk spent "enough time in the cooler" to have his "rough edges" taken off.

Turn-of-the-century liberals like the Dawids, Nalkowski, and Sempolowska—who stood for a democratic socialism that refused to recognize class or ethnic divisions—set the moral standards of their time; one did not compromise one's principles no matter the consequences. Living modestly, without affectation or false ambition, they became Henryk's "tutors in the social sphere." Much of the strength he needed to draw on in later life can be traced to their uncompromising ethical character. The Poland he felt part of was the one they represented.

5

Muzzle on the Soul

Life bites like a dog.
—*Child of the Drawing Room*

There were few who knew that Henryk Goldszmit was leading a double life. The medical student lived dutifully at home with his widowed mother, but his other self, Janusz Korczak, the tortured writer, prowled through the roughest slums of the city alone or in the company of Ludwik Licinski, a friend from the Flying University.

Four years Henryk's senior, Licinski, a poet and ethnographer, was always on the road, giving as his full address: Warsaw. Like other writers in the Young Poland movement—as this *fin de siècle* literary group was called—he delighted in attacking the materialism of the bourgeoisie, whom they looked on as philistines. Licinski would succumb at an early age to tuberculosis contracted during exile in Siberia, but at this time in his brief life, he was a good companion for Henryk, who "felt he was dying in his tiny apartment with his overprotective mother." At night they wandered the sandy banks of the Vistula River, celebrated the name days of prostitutes, and got drunk on "stinking" vodka. "He could play on those people's heartstrings in the most subtle way," Licinski recalled. "The murderer Lichtarz told him: 'I would give my soul for you.'"

Zofia Nalkowska came along one night during her "last fling" before marriage to Leon Rygier. She drank vodka from the bottle, kissed the mistress of a laundry owner, and enjoyed flirting with Licinski, who was hopelessly in love with her. Henryk felt a sense of liberation in this rough quarter too—but of a different kind. His soul, which was "howling like a dog," was being unleashed.

"I dreamed I was a poodle," Janek (a diminutive of Janusz) begins the semi-autobiographical novel that Henryk was writing at this time. "My coat was shaved. I felt somewhat cold in that attire, but knowing my master was pleased with me, I wagged my tail merrily and gazed devotedly into his eyes. . . . I had no fleas, worries or responsibilities. However, I had to be obedient and faithful while demonstrating the intelligence that is expected of a poodle."

The poodle is undone when a passerby looks at him with pity instead of admiration, his eyes saying: "This dog has a muzzle on his soul." Totally demoralized, the poodle can neither eat nor sleep, and reaches a point of such disorientation that he bites his master's hand. He is about to be shot when the author wakes up from his dream.

The book, *Child of the Drawing Room*, is about awakening. Janek realizes he has slept through his life trying to conform to his parents' idea of what he should be. Feeling suicidal, as if he has "lost his soul," he leaves home with a snarl at his mother and father: "Get off my back! Get off—or I'll bite!"

He manages to sublet the tenth bed in a room already occupied by the families of a factory locksmith and horse-carriage driver, spends his last kopeck at a bar, panhandles on the street, and follows a prostitute home. But he has no interest in seducing her. "Tell me a story," he asks, as they lie together in bed. "You're boring," is her response. "I feel sorry for you," he says, hogging all the covers as he relates the plan that he and his friend Stash once had to rehabilitate prostitutes.

It is the neglected and abused children of this poor district to whom Janek is drawn. He finds them in the shadows of buildings, "their pale skin stretched like thin parchment over their crooked bones." Under the bridges he gives them candy and medicine, and, he hopes, a belief in human kindness. He goes with them into their squalid dwellings to tell stories and give lessons in reading. The order intrinsic in grammar may help order their thoughts.

On a Christmas Eve, dressed like St. Nicholas, Janek goes from room to room in his tenement house dispensing gifts to the children: a little ball, an apple, candies. He hangs a cross on the neck of a small red-haired boy known only as Carrot Top, whom he finds sitting all alone in the dark. When the child asks him if he is really a saint, he responds "Yes," struck that it is a child who should ask him that question.

At that moment Janek is aware that he has changed, that "new invisible powers" are gathering inside him, powers that from then on will "illuminate" his way. He is transformed from a self-absorbed writer gathering material for a book into a man of spiritual faith who is responsible for his fellow human beings.

All the themes of the author's life are in this novel: his constricted childhood, his fear of suicide and madness, his avoidance of sex, his determination to be a social reformer, his dedication to children. As the book ends, Janek has lost most of his illusions, but not his rage at discovering that two orphaned girls have been sexually abused by their uncle. When the night watchman in the slum tells him to go home, he shouts, as he once had at his parents, "Get out of here! Or I'll bite! I'll b-i-i-t-e!"—his syllables blurring into incomprehensibility.

While *Child of the Drawing Room* was being serialized in *Voice* magazine under the byline of Janusz Korczak, Henryk Goldszmit began a residency at the Jewish Children's Hospital. But no sooner had he received his medical diploma in March 1905, than he was conscripted as a doctor into the Czar's Imperial Army to serve in the Russo-Japanese War. Torn abruptly out of his life "like a slave puppet," the new lieutenant found himself stationed on a hospital train on the Trans-Siberian Railroad, shuttling back and forth between Harbin and Mukden. Japan, emerging as a modern nation after centuries of isolation, was proving victorious in both land and sea battles over the demoralized Russian forces riddled with corruption, badly led, and inefficiently supplied.

The young doctor quickly learned that "war helps you see the illness of the whole body." He viewed the patients lined up that first rainy day at the station as "prisoners" waiting for treatment of enteritis, gastritis, venereal disease, or chronic illnesses. Their diseases, like the international conflict over markets in Manchuria and Korea, had "unseen roots in the past" for which there was no quick cure.

The most seriously ill were taken aboard. "The train is full of mad people," he wrote to his *Voice* readers. "One of them doesn't even know his name, how old he is, or where he is going. Another, equally oblivious to what is going on, broods about why his wife took his pipe. A third, called the Idiot, sings dirty songs."

They were not soldiers anymore, but "sick people" from whom he was learning about the malignancies festering in Russian society. He moved among his patients—barely literate Russian, Ukrainian, and Polish peasants, fierce Cossacks, and poor Jews—dispensing medicine for both body and soul. Discovering that they responded well to stories, he told them Russian tales. He was not unaware of the irony that he, a Polish-Jewish doctor, was comforting them in the language of his oppressor: the perfect Russian that had been drilled into him at his Czarist *gymnasium*.

Every spare moment the young lieutenant spent exploring the devastated Chinese towns and villages. "It was not that I came to China, China came to me," he wrote in another article. "Chinese famine, Chinese orphan misery, Chinese mass mortality. War is an abomination. Especially because no one reports how many children are hungry, ill-treated, and left without protection."

After meeting four-year-old Iuo-ya, who "was extraordinarily patient in teaching Chinese to an inept pupil," he decided that not only should there be institutes of Oriental languages, but everyone should have to spend a year in a village in the Orient studying under a four-year-old. Iuo-ya made him realize that young children who have not yet become "too conscious of grammar and too influenced by novels, textbooks, and school," can convey the spirit of a language.

Visiting a village school, he was shocked to see a teacher, reeking of vodka and opium, beating his pupils on their heels with a thick yardstick. On one side was written in black ink: "He who refuses to learn is deserving of punishment"; and on the other: "He who studies will be wise." Lieutenant Goldszmit managed to buy the yardstick, though he knew that after a few days the teacher would make a new one. When the war was over, he would show his orphans how to play ball (*palant*) with the stick. He would tell them that, though Chinese children look different and use a different alphabet, all children are the same.

As the hospital train steamed back and forth in that turbulent year 1905, the illnesses that had "lain dormant" in the huge empire of the Czar were exacerbated by news of Japanese victories. Workers' strikes and student demonstrations continued to erupt in industrial centers. The very word "revolution" was a stimulant to the staff and patients on the train, who voted to join the railway workers' strike. When a military delegation arrived to punish the rebellious soldiers, they asked Lieutenant Goldszmit to represent them. He was reluctant to become involved—it was neither his country nor his war—but the men pleaded so persuasively that he agreed. However, as he stood on the speaker's crate, he did not talk of the strike or of the revolution but rather of the suffering of children.

"Before you go to war for any purpose," he told the amazed delegation, "you should stop to think of the innocent children who will be injured, killed, or orphaned." He was beginning to articulate what would become his philosophy for life: no cause, no war, was worth depriving children of their natural right to happiness. Children should come before politics of any kind.

6

Little Hospital

Children, being small and weak, have little market value.
—The Child's Right to Respect

When he returned to Warsaw in early 1906, Lieutenant Henryk Goldszmit was amazed to find that during his absence he had become famous as Janusz Korczak, the author of *Child of the Drawing Room*. Critics proclaimed him a new voice in Polish literature that had found "the color of poverty, its stench, its cry, and its hunger." The public was anxious to meet the audacious young writer who had been called away to war just when his star was rising and was now back to illuminate their drawing rooms.

However, the renowned Janusz Korczak was no more accessible than the unknown Henryk Goldszmit had been. Warsaw was still in a state of revolutionary ferment and there was a lot of catching up to do on what had happened in his absence. *Voice* magazine had been closed down three months earlier and Jan Dawid, along with many other intellectuals, was in exile in Cracow. But there had been some victories: the school boycott, far from over, had at least forced the demoralized Russian government to allow the opening of private schools, which, though not accredited, were permitted to teach in the Polish language. The Flying University, now operating in the open as the Society for Scientific Courses (later to become the Free Polish University), was sanctioned to give courses in Polish, as were some departments at Warsaw University.

Declining all invitations except from intimate friends, Korczak reclaimed the position he had left as resident doctor ("general drudge") in the Children's Hospital on Sliska Street. The pride of the Jewish community, this tree-shaded one-story stucco hospital, built by the wealthy Bersohn and Bauman families, had seven wards, forty-three beds, an operating room, a lab, and an outpatient clinic that was open without charge to children of all faiths.

He settled into a routine that included everything from battling scarlet fever, typhus, measles, dysentery, and tuberculosis to cataloguing the 1,400-volume medical library. His mother, "a good old soul," ran the apartment that came with the job on fifteen rubles a month. He supplemented his annual salary of two hundred rubles (about one hundred dollars) with another hundred from private practice and odd sums from his articles. His mother was shocked at how often he took horse carriages to see patients: "A droshky to go to Zlota Street? Twenty kopecks? Spendthrift!"

Although it was unusual for any but the most wealthy Jewish doctors to have Gentile patients, Korczak's private practice was soon studded with the names of Warsaw's most prominent families. A number of social hostesses began to realize that the only way to lure Janusz Korczak to their homes was through a sick child. He tried to make time to respond to their calls, but whenever he suspected it was Korczak the author, rather than Goldszmit the doctor, who was being summoned, he could be very rude. In one case, having been asked to come immediately to attend two young brothers, he arrived to find the mother in a hostess gown.

"Please wait a moment, Doctor. I'll send for the boys."

"Are they out?"

"Not far. They're playing in the park. Meanwhile—a cup of tea?"

"I can't spare the time to wait."

"But Dr. Julian always . . . Have you been writing anything lately?"

"Unfortunately, only prescriptions!"

And he stormed out. The next day a colleague phoned: "For God's sake, my friend! They're furious. You've made enemies!"

"I don't give a damn!"

He was equally impatient with middle-class Jewish mothers, who must have reminded him of his own. To one who insisted her child should have tea, he snapped: "If your child needed to drink tea, God would have given you milk in one breast, and tea in the other." And to another whose little darling was clearly overweight, he observed: "Even Rothschild doesn't give his child more than five meals a day."

Only to the poor was he unfailingly compassionate, paying calls late at night to the basement at 52 Sliska Street or the attic at 17 Panska. He was a medical Robin Hood, taking fees from the rich so that he could afford to give medicine to the poor. But even the poor he charged twenty kopecks because "it is written in the Talmud that an unpaid doctor is no help to a sick man." And he was always available to the children of "socialists, teachers, newspapermen, young lawyers, even doctors." This idealistic young doctor was considered a mad, dangerous lunatic by certain doctors and wholesale pharmacists who were threatened by his night calls, low fees, and habit of dispensing free medicine.

The children never questioned his sanity or his antics. One mother entered the sickroom to find both her child and the doctor missing; when she cried out in alarm, they both poked their heads out from under the bed. Another knew that her sick daughter would never fall asleep until Dr. Goldszmit came. Like a sorcerer he would wave everyone from the room, and then, sitting by the child's bed, he would caress her hands and tell her stories about each finger, blowing on it to make it drowsy. When he got to number ten, she was always asleep.

A former patient, Henryk Grynberg, who became a doctor himself, said that Korczak's hands were cold when he made house calls, and that it felt good when he put them on your brow. If you didn't have a fever, he'd try to warm them before coming into the room. He always had some playful banter in this kosher home. "You see, you had your secret sausage, and God punished you. Because of this, your mother will have to make tea and put in a few drops of cognac, as further punishment."

Korczak may have endeared himself to his patients, but he infuriated Russian hospital administrators with his indignant articles calling for basic hospital reforms, not the least of which was that management should be turned over to the Poles. He criticized doctors ("unethical tradesmen") who made distinctions in the treatment of wealthy and nonpaying patients and who categorized patients according to their disease, rather than viewing them as individuals with a whole range of life problems. The only group that merited his praise were midwives, whom he felt were not appreciated enough for their important role in assisting human beings into the world. He was an advocate of breast feeding, in an era of wet nurses. "The breast does not belong to the mother, but to the baby," he said.

Even at his own hospital, Korczak had to fight for "intelligent" treatment of the young patients, overruling doctors and nurses who forbade parents to bring toys because they might carry germs. The children—whom the city was casting his way "like seashells"—had so little to make them smile, and he was painfully aware of his lack of resources.

"Little hospital. I remember winter, cold, the horse and carriage arrives," he would write. "They carefully carry a bundle with a sick child inside. Bell rings. Calling for the doctor to come down. I am coming. One blanket belongs to the family, one to a neighbor, sometimes three blankets from two neighbors. Clothes, flannels, petticoats, mufflers, bundle of odiferous infection. Finally, the patient. Scarlet fever. The unit for infectious diseases has no more room. Pointless begging. Please, on the floor, in the corridor—anywhere. Doctor, I'll give you a ruble. Sometimes—trapped. I will leave the child here. You'll have to take her. Sometimes a curse."

He had to be firm, to hide the sorrow he felt for the children who had nowhere to go and those he knew would not survive. Yet he was impressed by how "dignified, mature, and sensible a child could be when face to face with death." He was to place the right of the child to die at the top of his Magna Carta of Children's Rights. No matter how much a mother loved her child, she had to allow him the right to premature death. It was possible, he wrote, that a child had a destiny other than being his mother's child. "The naturalist knows that not every seed produces an ear of corn, not every chick is born fit to live, not every sapling grows into a tree."

Still, inveterate actor that he was, Korczak did not easily admit the harsh reality of hospital life. When the daughter of a colleague exclaimed: "How terrible it must be to wake up in a strange hospital with no mommy or daddy," he replied: "Oh, we know how to cope with that. Every child has a pillow made of chocolate and whipped cream. If she wakes up and feels unhappy, she breaks off a piece, and feels much better."

The truth of the matter was that the frightened child would wake and see the twinkling eyes of the doctor trying to put her at ease. It was apparent to everyone at the hospital, from the director to the lowliest orderly, that it was not so much the medicine as the magic of Dr. Goldszmit's way with children that made them well. When a girl named Zofia, who was becoming weak from not eating, refused her mug of broth, he told her how sad the mug was at being rejected. If she did not drink the broth, it would roll right out of the hospital into the street and be run over by a tramcar. Zofia clasped the mug, then drank the broth right down.

Henryk Goldszmit, the doctor, would stay at the Children's Hospital for seven years, but Janusz Korczak, the writer and future educator, was restless. The doctor saw a feverish child through the dramatic crises of his illness, but the educator was aware that when the child was released, he disappeared back into a dark, sunless world that the doctor could neither enter nor alter. "When the devil will we stop prescribing aspirin for poverty, exploitation, lawlessness, and crime?" he would complain to his colleagues. But what could he prescribe to change his patients' lives?

It was the same frustration the five-year-old reformer had felt—how could he remake the world so that there would be no more hungry or dirty children? Complaining about injustice wasn't enough. As a schoolboy he had once been rebuked by a tram conductor whom he had criticized for cracking a whip on the horses to make them pull the tramcars more quickly: "If you are so full of pity, get down yourself and pull, young man. It will be nicer for the horses." He had taken the message to heart: "Keep your mouth shut if you're not helping. Don't criticize if you don't know a better way."

Thinking back to that tramcar incident, he had to admit to himself that for all of his dissatisfaction about social inequities, he had not yet found the means to offer a better way of life to deprived children.

7

Summer Camps

They start to laugh with a different laugh than the one they had in the city.

—*Moshki, Joski, and Srule*

One summer day in 1907, Janusz Korczak, dressed in sports clothes, stood in the large courtyard of the Summer Camps Society and watched as one hundred and fifty poor Jewish boys arrived for what would be their first trip to the country. He noted the boys who came with families and those who straggled in alone, the ones who were clean and those who were neglected; he noted their apprehensiveness as they said final good-byes for three weeks, and their fearfulness and shyness as they lined up in pairs. He knew they were wondering what kind of counselor he'd be—one who was strict or one they could hoodwink.

Having volunteered his services to the camp society while in medical school, he valued the opportunity it offered to work with children outside of a hospital environment. The camp to which he was assigned, about eighty miles from Warsaw, had been funded by an assimilated Jewish philanthropist, with the stipulation that only Polish be spoken. Forbidden Polish music and patriotic songs were played on the gramophone as a way of exposing the children to the Polish national culture and history that the Russians were still trying to obliterate.

In the humorous and moving book he wrote about his experiences with those ten-year-old boys, *Moshki, Joski, and Srule* (diminutives of typical Jewish names), Korczak portrayed himself as a bungling Gulliver in the land of streetwise Lilliputians who taught him everything he knew about the young: "There for the first time I came in touch with a com-

munity of children and learned the alphabet of educational practice. Rich
in illusions, lacking in experience, sentimental, and young, I believed
that the mere fact that I wanted to achieve something with children was
enough." The thirty children assigned to him had seemed a reasonable
number because he did not as yet understand the skill he would need to
keep the "menacing mob" under control. Having complete freedom to
create his own program of games, swimming, excursions, and storytelling,
he had blithely concentrated on locating a gramophone, a magic lantern,
fireworks, checkers, and dominoes.

"There I was, like someone wearing kid gloves and a carnation in
his buttonhole, setting out in search of enchanting impressions and warm
memories to be got from the hungry, abused, and disinherited," he wrote.
"I wanted to discharge my duties at the cost of little more than a few
smiles and cheap fireworks . . . I expected their friendliness and was
unprepared for their shortcomings bred in the dark alleys of city life."

When the boys made a wild dash from the train to the horse-drawn
carts waiting to take them to the camp, the new counselor had his first
moment of panic. The most aggressive ones claimed the best seats, the
most awkward lost their bags, prayer books, and toothbrushes, and there
was pandemonium before everyone was finally accounted for. It was then
he learned that keeping order depends entirely upon the ability to anticipate—"having foreseen, it is possible to prevent." His nerves were on
edge that first night. One of the boys who was unaccustomed to sleeping
alone on a narrow bed slid with a thud off his freshly filled hay mattress
onto the floor. Others moaned or talked in their sleep. The next day was
no better. When the boys weren't squabbling over seating at the tables
or who slept where, or attacking each other with belt buckles, they were
baiting him with noises in the semidark dormitory to see what he would
do. Flustered by his inability to maintain either discipline or order, he
announced he would punish the next one who made a noise. Grabbing
"the bold whistler" who took up the challenge, Korczak pulled his ears,
and even threatened to lock him out on the veranda, where a fierce
watchdog was loose.

It was his lowest moment: "I was not a novice in the educational
field; I had been tutoring for years and had read numerous books on child
psychology. Yet there I was helpless, confounded by the mystery of the
collective soul of a children's community." He had come filled with "ideals,"
but the boys' sharp ears had caught the "ring of a counterfeit coin."
Conspiracy, rebellion, treachery, reprisals were life's reply to his "rev-

eries." As he struggled to win the confidence of the campers, he knew he would never again be naïvely romantic about children.

By the end of the first week, the most unlikely boys had emerged as leaders and the most unruly ones began to show consideration for others. Aaron, who had weak lungs and lived with his mother, a factory worker, was in his glory recounting the fairy tales he had heard while convalescing in the courtyard of his tenement. Weintraub, who lost a leg after being shot on the street, had learned to play checkers in the hospital and organized some tournaments. Chaim, the biggest troublemaker, always defended Mordko, who had sad black eyes, was awkward at games, and conversed with a cuckoo in the woods. Ugly Anzel came to be accepted as someone who had become nasty and fat because of the mean way he had been treated by other children. And the gentle nature of twelve-year-old Kruk, who already worked in a factory and looked after his incorrigible eight-year-old brother at camp, won him the title of Prince among the boys.

"In life there are two kingdoms," Korczak wrote. "There is the kingdom of pleasure, balls, salons, and beautiful clothes, where for centuries the richest, happiest, and laziest have been called princes. But there is also that other kingdom of hunger, troubles, and hard work. Its princes know from early childhood how much a pound of bread costs, how to take care of younger brothers and sisters, how to work. Kruk and his friends are princes in the kingdom of sad thoughts and black bread—hereditary princes."

Korczak was gratified to see how rapidly his young princes blossomed in that wholesome environment: "Yesterday—a caveman; today—a good sport. Yesterday—timid, fearful, solemn; a week later—bold, lively, bursting with initiative and song."

One morning, as the children were on their way to a distant forest, they stopped to eat by a railroad track. The cinders stirred up by the wind fell into their breakfast. A peasant passing by said: "Children, don't sit where it's so dusty. My field is much nicer."

"But if we walk on your land, we'll trample whatever is growing there," one child replied.

"Oh, how much harm can you do if you're barefoot? Go along. It's my field, I give you permission."

Korczak, the counselor, was moved by the offer. He was thinking: "Oh, Polish peasant, look at those boys more closely. They are not the children you think they are. They are Jewish bastards who are not allowed to play in the city parks. Coachmen hit them with their whips, pedestrians push them off the sidewalks, superintendents chase them from their courtyards with brooms. These are not children, these are Moshkis— little Jews, yes. And not only aren't you chasing them from under your trees, you are inviting them into your field."

"What kind of things do you do in Warsaw?" the peasant asked the boys. And he told them where they could find the best berries.

Such encounters helped the young campers' Polish as well as their spirits. They may have heard only Polish curses in Warsaw—"Jewish bastards!" "Drop dead!"—but in the country, Korczak wrote, "the Polish language smiles at the children with the greenness of the trees and the gold of the wheat. It is mixed with birdsong, starlight, and fresh river breezes. Polish words, like wild flowers, rearrange themselves into meadows." The same was true for Yiddish—"so noisy and full of curses on the streets of Warsaw"—which became softer, even poetic, as the children played together in the countryside.

The campers were amazed when a Warsaw newspaper arrived with news about them on the first page: "Mamelok climbed up to the window and looked into the kitchen; Hawelkie and Szekielewski don't want to eat kasha; Boruch had a fight with his brother Mordko; Butterman forgave Yemen for hitting him; the new dog escaped his chain, but Franek grabbed him." There were also articles about the joys of going barefoot in the country, and the history of summer camps.

The older boys caught on that the counselors had written the paper, but the little ones were very impressed that their activities were being reported in Warsaw. And Janusz Korczak, whose idea it was, had his first chance to test the effectiveness of a children's newspaper.

He also tried out a system in which, once a week, the boys were to grade their own and each other's conduct, rather than being graded by their counselor. When Korczak asked everyone what grades they thought they deserved—on a scale from one to five—some tried to be honest, but Mort, who had thrown stones at the camp's dog, demanded a five. The other boys decided he could get a five only if the dog forgave him. But how could they know?

"The dog is on a chain, so Mort should go up to him with a piece of meat," one said. "If the dog takes the meat instead of biting him, it means he is willing to forgive and forget."

Everyone agreed it was a fine plan. Luckily for Mort, the dog was in a "wonderful" mood. It wagged its tail as he approached, and took the meat from him. Satisfied that the dog had forgiven him, the boys gave Mort a five. But Mort felt guilty. The next day he asked for a lower number.

Setting up a children's court was to prove a more difficult challenge. While still a child, Korczak may well have imagined himself going off to court to defend workers' rights, as his father had; he may have heard his father complain about the injustices of the legal system. Now he had a chance to create a children's court in which there would be true justice: a boy who was pestered by a bully could sue him, and other boys, acting as judges, would decide the case. He expected the campers to be as enthusiastic as he was about their court of peers, but it didn't turn out that way. They couldn't grasp the concept that suing someone was more effective than punching him in the nose, and they didn't like tattling on each other. It wasn't until Korczak himself sued some rule breakers that the court could begin to function.

Choosing judges was a random process at first. Korczak announced that anyone who wanted to be a judge should meet on the veranda at 1 p.m. He was deliberately half an hour late, and most of the boys had wandered off by the time he arrived. The ones who had the patience to remain became the judges.

Civil and criminal cases were heard once a week on the veranda or in a clearing in the forest. One counselor acted as prosecutor, another as defense lawyer, and three campers as judges. The most serious infractions were: going alone into the woods ("Forbidden because a bull might attack you") and not responding to bells ("We cannot go out and drag everyone by the nose to the table").

In the Case of Picking Flowers, two boys charged with being late to breakfast after they wandered off to pick flowers, were acquitted because it was taken into account that they did not have such an opportunity in the city, and it was their first offense. The judges were not so lenient in the Pinecone Case because Fishbein showed no remorse over throwing pinecones with small stones in them at another boy. The prosecutor had a difficult time getting him to admit his motive.

"Why did you do it?"

"Because I had a lot of pinecones and didn't know what to do with them."

"Why didn't you throw them away?"

"Because it would have been wasteful."

This got a laugh from the spectators.

"Are you sure there weren't small stones among the pinecones?"

"I don't know."

Because Fishbein was one of the younger boys, he was sentenced to only ten minutes of detention.

Korczak carefully recorded the trials and the children's response. He was improvising as he went along, though he must have been familiar with the early experiments in children's courts in Poland at the end of the eighteenth century. The National Commission of Education (the first such ministry in Europe) had recommended "Courts of Arbitration" in which students could settle their own arguments—punishments included not being allowed to wear one's sword with a senior uniform during holy days—but the courts were in operation for only a short period after the partitions. It took a half century before the famous educator Bronislaw Trentowski rediscovered them: "If any one of your students breaks the rules, get some pupils of his own age to judge him. Everyone wants to be judged by his equals. Kings by kings, scientists by scientists, and children by children. The verdict will infuriate him less than if it comes from you, and will exert a greater influence." Trentowski's court was short-lived like those earlier ones, and, in truth, Korczak's court had not made much progress by the end of the camp season.

On the day before the boys were to return to Warsaw, Oscar, the camp poet, wrote:

> *The children celebrate because they are going home.*
> *They will exchange the green forests for the dank walls.*
> *The flowers laugh in the sun now,*
> *But when winter comes, they will fade.*

That night the boys surprised their counselor by presenting him with a stork's nest. Then they all sat around a campfire watching their last sunset. Tomorrow in Warsaw they would not see such a beautiful sight, Korczak reminded them, only the ugly yellow lanterns that lined the streets. It was the lamplighter who changed day into night in the city, while in their camp it was the sun itself that turned off the light and turned on the night.

As the sun dipped into the horizon, disappearing little by little, a few boys cried out, "It's gone!"

"No, there's still a little left," others shouted.

"And now we should take each other by the hand, sing our song, wave our flag over our heads, and begin walking," Korczak told them. "But not back to Warsaw."

"Where? Where should we walk?" the boys wanted to know.

"To the sun."

Everyone was surprised.

"It will be a long journey but we can do it. We'll sleep in the fields and earn money along the way."

The boys entered into the spirit. Gerson could play his violin in exchange for some milk, Oscar could recite one of his poems and Aaron one of his tales in exchange for bread.

"We will walk, walk, walk for a very long time," their counselor told them. "If Weintraub gets tired, we'll make a wheelchair and take turns pushing him."

"And then what?" asked the boys.

The bell rang, calling them to supper before he could answer. The next day they made their way by train back to Warsaw, and shortly after that Korczak left for almost a year in Europe.

In going to Berlin that fall to do advanced work in pediatric medicine, Korczak was following in the tradition of Jan Dawid and other Polish intellectuals who had looked to Germany for "light and knowledge." Berlin, the capital of the prosperous German Empire, had one of the best medical systems on the continent: it was known for its highly developed program in community hygiene and its infant and orphan services. While deciding whether or not to make the trip—it meant taking a leave from the Children's Hospital and from his mother as well—Korczak discussed the pros and cons with his colleagues, some of whom felt he would benefit from study there, and others that he would be disappointed. Of all the suggestions given him about how to behave with the Germans, he chose to take only two seriously: not to indulge his penchant for shaking hands indiscriminately with everyone regardless of rank, and to change his collar twice a day.

Korczak did not arrive in the capital city as a famous writer but as a poor student. He found a modest room that was clean and offered a regular change of towels—breakfast was included, but some nights he had only enough money for two glasses of milk and bread.

He admired Berlin's good bus system (which Warsaw lacked) and its many free libraries, open twelve hours a day, but the city seemed "in-

different" to his presence. From August to September he took vacation
refresher courses for doctors sponsored by the Berlin Medical Association.
He was impressed that the professors, like the buses, were always on
time, but he hated the idea of having to pay for lectures. Selling knowledge
made the university into a "marketplace." Nevertheless, he chose special
courses, along with other foreigners, in neurology and electrocardiogra-
phy, and studied the latest findings on tuberculosis and other childhood
illnesses. Watching how the Germans checked urine and took blood, he
couldn't help comparing their advanced medical techniques with the less
developed ones in Poland. Yet, by the end of two months, he felt he was
in a "factory." Reading over his notes, he wasn't certain that he had learned
very much that would help him in his own practice; they only confirmed
what he already knew: that he had to rely on his own observations, and
not accept any theory that he had not tested himself.

Korczak also spent two months each studying under the world-famous
German-Jewish pediatricians Heinrich Finkelstein and Adolf Baginski,
one month in a home for the retarded and another in Theodor Ziehen's
psychiatric clinic at the Charité. He made shorter visits to insane asylums
and detention centers for so-called juvenile delinquents. Leaving Germany in the late spring of 1908, he stopped off in Switzerland, where he
interned for one month in a neurological clinic in Zurich. When he returned to Warsaw in the early summer of 1908, he was struck by how
poor and provincial the city was.

Before resuming work at the Children's Hospital on Sliska Street,
Korczak treated himself to four weeks at a camp for one hundred and
fifty Polish boys, where there was "no lack of authentic rascals." In the
book he wrote about this experience, *Jozki, Jaski, and Franki,* his readers
were once again charmed by the adventures of the awkward, bespectacled
counselor trying to reach street urchins set loose in nature for the first
time. But though he was playing the buffoon in print, he was still trying
to develop the strategies he had worked out the year before at the Jewish
camp. These children of poverty, many with drunken fathers and invalid
mothers who could not care for them, also set snares for him, but this
time he was prepared. He carefully memorized everyone's name and
made notes on his initial impressions, spotting the most aggressive boys,
who were certain to be troublemakers. On the second day, when the
boys became raucous in the dormitory before dawn, he heard one pro-
claim: "I am the Minister in the Blue Shirt!" Instead of being angry,

Korczak stomped in dramatically and asked: "All right, who is the Minister in the Blue Shirt?" The tension lifted as he burst out laughing. "Like Napoleon winning a battle with one successful attack," he had won the trust of the children—a trust "without which it would not only be impossible to write a book about children, but also impossible to love, rear, or even observe them."

Experimenting further with his court, he noted that when three of the meanest boys were outrageous enough to steal berries from little Jasiek, who was weak and stuttered, the judges acquitted them because they had already been punished by the other campers who refused to play with thieves. Two of the culprits became friendly and kind right after that, but the third didn't until he heard "the forest's prayer"—that moment when the trees speak and the sky answers. Whoever hears it "feels funny in his soul" and bursts into tears although he's not sad, and doesn't know why. And the next day he wakes up much better than he was before he heard the prayer.

As he worked to help his Jozkis overcome their problems, he was reminded of the struggles of his Moshkis. Years later, when the *Jewish Monthly* asked him to compare Jewish and Polish children, he quoted John Ruskin's opinion that one should look for the similarities and not the differences in children. With wry self-mockery, he contrasted himself to the "true scientist" who would test 32,000 mice to the eighth generation to find out the influence of alcohol on the mouse, while he had access to only two hundred children a year. And even if he believed in psychological tests, how could he trust the results? True, he had heard it said that Jewish children were more emotional than Polish, but he had seen tears of joy and sorrow in both groups watching the same movie—and without counting the tears one by one, he would not feel qualified to verify the emotional superiority of either group. He preferred answers based on personal experience.

Back at his post at the Children's Hospital that September, Korczak found his old despair waiting for him. What was he doing there? What good was it to cure sick children when they only returned to their unhealthy surroundings? When a colleague, Izaak Eliasberg, a highly respected diagnostician in dermatitis and venereal disease, told him about the Orphans Aid Society, to which he and his wife, Stella, belonged, Korczak listened carefully. The Society was holding a fund-raising party for a shelter it supported. They could draw some wealthy philanthropists if he were able to come.

Korczak accepted, little knowing how fortuitous the occasion would be. He was to meet Stefania (Stefa) Wilczynska, a woman who would not only share his dream of creating an ideal haven for poor children, but would help make it possible.

8

The Decision

By the time Korczak arrived at the shelter in the dilapidated former nunnery on Franciskanska Street, the program in honor of Maria Konopnicka, a poet and children's writer, had already begun. He stood in the back watching the pale, spindly performers with their shaven heads, their clean but ill-fitting clothes, reciting the poems they had been rehearsing all week. He was so moved by their shy smiles, he could hardly hold back his tears.

They were not all full orphans. Most of their fathers had died of consumption, malnutrition, and overwork; their widowed mothers, unable to manage, were forced to put them in shelters like this while they went out to work. The older ones were already streetwise and tough, with the same sorrow in their sunken eyes, in their uneasy high-pitched laughter, that Korczak had observed in the Polish waifs of the Warsaw slums—"rare children who bear not only the weight of their ten years, but deep in their souls the burden of many generations."

Korczak noticed Stefa standing to one side coaching them, her lips moving with theirs. Whenever a child finished, he ran to her for a hug, and then stayed close, clinging with the others like magnets to her long skirt.

No one would have called Stefa a beauty, even then. At the age of twenty-three, she was eight years younger than Korczak and a good head taller. Her dark, serious eyes—the best feature in her broad, plain face—revealed both warmth and strength. In a picture of her taken at the time, a short functional hairdo frames an intense, no-nonsense expression, which already suggests the woman who is destined to carry responsibility for hundreds of children on her shoulders for thirty years. A white Peter Pan collar rests without artifice on a black sweater that covers a plump figure bordering on the matronly.

Stefa's acculturated background was in many ways similar to Korczak's. She spoke no Yiddish and had little knowledge of Jewish ritual. She, her older sister Julia, and her younger brother Stanislaw (Stash) occupied a six-room apartment with their parents in a building that had been part of her mother's dowry. The two oldest daughters had already married and moved out. Stefa's father, the owner of a textile factory, was in fragile health, and left much of the responsibility for raising the children to his wife. In a period when few women received a higher education, Stefa's mother, an ardent Polish patriot, saw to it that her two youngest daughters went to Mlle Jadwiga Sikorska's exclusive private school for girls—where Polish culture was taught surreptitiously—and then to the University of Liège in Belgium rather than to the Russian university in Warsaw. While they were away, she busied herself adding to their trousseaus, which she kept in large hope chests in her bedroom, little imagining that neither of them would ever marry. Everything was fastidiously prepared, down to the last properly sewn button; she judged the character of a person by how tightly his buttons were secured. Tied to home by her young son and her husband, this energetic woman who loved to travel contented herself with touring remote areas of the city by tramcar. She would come back refreshed, as from a long adventure. It was from this unconventional mother that Stefa absorbed many of her values and her organizational ability.

Stefa's degree was in natural science, but her real interest lay in education. When she returned to Warsaw and noticed the small Jewish shelter near her home run by the Orphans Aid Society, she immediately volunteered her services. Before long, she became so indispensable that Stella Eliasberg put her in charge. (The director who ran the shelter before the Society took over had used its meager funds for her own purposes, dressing and eating well, while the emaciated children, clad in rags, crawled about the filthy floor grabbing at rotten potatoes that had been thrown to them.) Stefa's only assistant was an energetic thirteen-year-old ward of another orphanage, Esterka Weintraub, who had become like a daughter.

Stefa had also become very close to the Eliasbergs in the course of her work. When they told her that Janusz Korczak was going to attend the shelter's party, she had no doubt that this famous advocate of children's welfare would be interested in their project—but how interested she could not have anticipated. Korczak began stopping by the shelter at odd moments to chat with her and play with the children. The orphans would scream with delight at the sight of the slim, modest, balding doctor whose pockets were always filled with candy and magic tricks, and whose repertoire of riddles and fairy tales was limitless. They made an effective team: Stefa with her ability to bring order to the dark, ramshackle quarters, and he with his natural way with children. His love, which he would one day call "pedagogical love" (not sentimental, but based on mutual respect), embraced them all, and especially little Esterka Weintraub, whose sweet, helpful disposition made her as appealing to him as to Stefa. When they talked of sending her someday to Stefa's university in Belgium, it was almost as if they were discussing the future of their own daughter.

Life in the shelter became more important to Korczak as life outside became more harassed. On July 22, 1909, which happened to be his birthday, Korczak's sister's husband, Jozef Lui, died at the age of thirty-nine. (Nothing is known of Lui—whose odd name adds to the mystery—or of his marriage to Anna, who by then was a French legal translator.)

It was a bad period for everyone. In a new wave of Czarist repression, thousands of the elite of Polish society—among them intellectuals, socialists, and members of the revolutionary party—were either imprisoned or sent to Siberia. The universities were closed, and most of the reforms won in the abortive revolution of 1905 were abolished. *Society* magazine, which Jadwiga Dawid had started when *Voice* was closed by the police four years earlier, was itself forced to stop operating. Whatever the cause, political pressure or Dawid's involvement with another woman—or a combination of both—Jadwiga had a nervous breakdown. She would throw herself into a well the following year, at the age of forty-six.

Korczak was rounded up with many other writers and incarcerated in Spokojna prison. He was relieved to find himself in the same cell with Ludwik Krzywicki, the renowned sociologist, whom he knew from Flying University days. A radical socialist who had translated Marx into Polish, Krzywicki was as acquainted with jail cells as he was with classrooms, where he was known for his dazzling lectures—many of them prepared behind bars. Going in and out of prison had become an accepted way of life for him, one that he didn't question, unlike Jan Dawid and Waclaw

Nalkowski, who had long felt the futility of political activity as a means of solving Poland's internal problems.

Krzywicki had learned to endure life in cramped windowless cells where his "longest walk" was seven paces and his only companion a fly (about whom he wrote long letters to his son). Korczak was amazed at how the professor was able to shut out the irritations of the environment and to concentrate on keeping his inner self intact. He spent each day as if he were in his own study, spreading his papers and maps over the grimy floor and tracing the migrations of ancient tribes. During the two months they spent together, it is believed that Krzywicki encouraged his young friend to pursue his goals. (Korczak was to draw upon the discipline he learned from Krzywicki when he was incarcerated, years later, by the Nazis.)

Released from prison through the intercessions of a highly placed Polish family whose child he had treated, Korczak once again spent as much time as he could with Stefa and the children at the shelter. Eliasberg and his wife confided to him their dream of moving the children from that inadequate building into a large, modern orphanage. Stefa had agreed to assume general management, they said, and if someone like Korczak was involved, they were sure that the Orphans Aid Society could attract more patrons and raise the large amount of money needed. The Eliasbergs had caught Korczak at the right moment; discouraged by the political situation and still restless at the hospital, he was ready to make a radical change in his life.

In 1910, Warsaw society learned, with some surprise, that Janusz Korczak intended to give up a successful medical practice and literary career to become the director of an orphanage for Jewish children. Few people understood that medicine alone was no longer enough for this visionary pediatrician—that it did not, as Erik Erikson said of Gandhi's law practice, "feed his reformatory zeal." The orphanage would give him a chance to put some of his educational ideas into practice, and though it might appear he was making a sacrifice in taking it over, it did not seem so to him. "The reason I became an educator was that I always felt best when I was among children," he told a young interviewer many years later. But the decision had not been easy. "The road I have chosen toward my goal is neither the shortest nor the most convenient," he was to write. "But it is the best for me—because it is my own. I found it not without effort or pain, and only when I had come to understand that all the books I read, and all the experiences and opinions of others, were misleading."

Part of the difficulty in making his decision lay in assuring himself that he was not betraying medicine by leaving the hospital for the orphanage. (It was a conflict he never fully resolved.) He wanted to believe that rather than renouncing medicine for pedagogy, he could combine the two disciplines. Using the orphanage as a laboratory for clinical observation, he wanted to work out an educational diagnostic system based on tangible symptoms. Just as a doctor diagnosed disease by the complaints of the patient, so the teacher had to be aware of the moods of his pupil: "What a fever, a cough, or nausea is for the physician, so a smile, a tear, or a blush should be for the educator." Medicine was concerned only with curing the sick child, but pedagogy could nurture the whole child. As an educator, he could be the "sculptor of the child's soul."

His little republic would not be as ambitious as the School of Life he had once envisioned on the shores of the Vistula—a utopian center with shelters for the homeless, a hospital to provide knowledge of the suffering of the body "without which there is no education," a bank for practical instruction on handling money, and a pawnshop to teach "the transience of unessential things." But it would still be a just community whose young citizens would run their own parliament, court of peers, and newspaper. In the process of working together, they would learn consideration and fair play, and develop a sense of responsibility toward others, which they would carry with them into the adult world. In helping his orphans to respect others, a first step toward gaining self-respect, Korczak was a pioneer in what we now call "moral education." He was concerned not with teaching children their ABC's—they would go to public school for that—but with the grammar of ethics.

The underlying philosophy of the children's republic was: children are not the people of tomorrow, but people today. They are entitled to be taken seriously. They have a right to be treated by adults with tenderness and respect, as equals, not as masters and slaves. They should be allowed to grow into whoever they were meant to be: the "unknown person" inside each of them is the hope for the future.

Had Korczak been given a choice, the little republic would have comprised an integrated group of Jewish and Catholic children, but that was not possible. Each religious denomination was responsible for its own, and the Orphans Aid Society was a Jewish philanthropy. Still, Korczak hoped to bridge the religious gap by being active in the Polish Teachers Union and presenting his work as a possible model for all boarding homes, Polish and Jewish alike.

A plot of land was purchased in a poor, mixed Catholic and Jewish working-class neighborhood at 92 Krochmalna Street. Like so many Warsaw streets that reflected the haphazard way the Jews and Poles had accommodated to each other over the centuries, Krochmalna had a split personality. (Isaac Bashevis Singer, who grew up at No. 10, called Krochmalna "a deep stratum of an archaeological dig which I could never uncover.") The sprawling tenement houses at the notorious lower end indiscriminately harbored thieves, racketeers, and prostitutes along with poor Hasidic rabbis (such as Singer's father), pious housewives, and more than its share of Warsaw's three hundred thousand impoverished Jewish porters, shoemakers, and artisans.

The upper end of Krochmalna, by contrast, was less populated. There was even a small orchard on the orphanage's piece of land, which was bordered by small factories, shops, and wooden houses, and in the midst of them a simple Catholic church.

The planning of the orphanage was a "momentous experience" for Korczak, who met a few evenings a week with the two architects at the Eliasberg home. For the first time he understood "the prayer of work and the beauty of real activity." He was not merely designing a building with walls and windows; he was creating a spiritual space. He wanted to get as far away as possible from "the cages of city apartments" and the unhygienic boarding houses that "combined the defects of the convent and the barracks." His goal was a spacious, light, and airy structure that satisfied the individual need of every child. He marveled that "a square on the blueprint today becomes a hall, a room, a passageway tomorrow." But he learned to be cautious in his enthusiasm: "Every snap decision was a directive to the artisan, who gave it permanent form." Every idea had to be weighed in terms of money, feasibility, and utility. He decided that a teacher is not entirely proficient unless he or she understands building materials: "A small shelf, a metal plate, a nail in the right place, each may solve an acute problem."

The eldest of the Eliasbergs' four daughters, Helena, remembered how she and her sisters looked forward to the nights the funny doctor came to work with the architects: "We had never seen a grownup like him. He kissed our hands when he arrived as if we were ladies, and came over to us from time to time to laugh and joke. He even let us draw on his bald head with the colored pencils he was using on the blueprints."

While waiting for the orphanage to be built, Korczak spent about half a year in Paris, training with pediatric specialists and looking at orphanages and detention centers, much as he had done in Berlin three years earlier. Paris had a long history of sheltering émigré Polish writers and artists, and one can imagine that Korczak visited with some of them. He would tell friends later of his walks along the Seine and visits to the galleries and museums. He came away from his experience realizing that he felt temperamentally closer to the French than to the Germans. Berlin had taught him "to simplify and be inventive in small matters, to concentrate on what he knew step by step, and, systematically, to go forward from that," but Paris taught him "to think of whatever we do not know, but should like to know, must and will know." Berlin was a workday filled with small worries and efforts, but Paris was the festive tomorrow with brilliant premonition, powerful hope, and unexpected triumph. In Paris he pored over the "wondrous" books of the French clinicians and, flushed with excitement, dreamed of writing the definitive book on the child.

The death of Stefa Wilczynska's father in January 1911 probably brought Korczak back to Warsaw. It was an inauspicious beginning for the new year. Then, in February, Waclaw Nalkowski, Korczak's mentor from the Flying University, collapsed on the street at the age of fifty-five and died a few days later in the hospital. The loss of Nalkowski sent shock waves through Warsaw's intellectual community, or what was left of it. Dawid was in Cracow, a lonely man after Jadwiga's suicide, writing on the psychology of religious experience. And now Nalkowski, with his uncompromising principles that made him foes as well as friends, could no longer give Korczak sustenance. In his eulogy at the funeral, Korczak sought to console the large crowd of Polish patriots.

A happy man died—a man who lived the way he wanted, and died the way he wanted, in a hospital bed. He was not killed by those who today, like cowards, sing his praise. He was not killed by those who lived and got fat eating the crumbs of his thought. He was not killed by those who could not see his greatness. He did not fight any of them. He merely dismissed them with a toss of his head. It was Death who felled Nalkowski. Let us rejoice that he lived on Polish soil.

Helping Nalkowski's widow, herself a geologist, organize his papers and seeing to last-minute details of the orphanage plans did not lift Korczak's spirits. Right after the cornerstone of the building was laid on June 14, 1911, he left for England to visit orphanages there—but also, one suspects, to shake his depression. He was to have an experience there that appears to have given him a clearer sense of the direction his personal life was to take.

It began with a refreshing ride from London to the suburb of Forest Hill to visit an orphanage. He was struck by the large windows and wide benches of the trolley, the smoothness of the ride. He was equally impressed at finding Forest Hill an affluent suburb with rolling green lawns as far as the eye could see. He felt like a country bumpkin as he admired the clippers on long poles which the gardeners were using to cut hedges, and paused for a while to see how a lawn mower worked.

But the biggest surprise was the orphanage, "two little one-story houses sitting together like twins, thirty boys in one, thirty girls in the other." Why would an affluent area like Forest Hill have orphans? he wondered. What do the people die of in a place like this? The director greeted him politely and showed him around "with no trace of German arrogance or French formality." He saw the carpentry shop where the boys trained, and the laundry, sewing room, and embroidery workshop for the girls. Every child had his or her own garden plot, and kept rabbits, doves, or guinea pigs. There was even a museum next to the school that held, among other treasures, one small mummy.

On leaving, he signed the visitor's book—*Janusz Korczak, Warsaw*. He didn't need language to know what everyone had been thinking as he was shown around: "Warsaw? A strange guest from far away. Why is he looking at everything with such interest? The school? But there are children, so there must be a school. The orphanage? But there are orphans, so they must have someplace to stay. Swimming pool? Playground? But all of this is necessary."

He was conscious of his threadbare clothes and worn shoes and felt like a beggar who had wandered in by chance. Walking back to the trolley stop, he was again overwhelmed by the luxuriant green lawns, the manicured parks, and the large community swimming pool. Suddenly perceiving his life as "disordered, lonely, and cold," he saw himself as a shabby stranger, alienated and alone. And it came to him with sudden clarity that the son of a madman, "a slave who is a Polish Jew under Russian occupation," had no right to bring a child into the world.

This realization "cut through him like a knife," he would write, and immediately he felt as if he had "committed suicide." The child he might have fathered died with him at that moment, but there emerged a "revitalized" man who took for a son "the idea of serving the child and his rights." He who was ambivalent about so many things had now settled once and for all on remaining childless. He was giving up the responsibilities of marriage and family at which his father had failed—and for which, in truth, he, Janusz Korczak, had never shown any inclination. Though he could not remain a child, he would inhabit the world of childhood, but as the "responsible pedagogue" his father was not. He was thirty-three: almost the same age his father had been when he was born.

"Out of a mad soul we forge a sane deed," he wrote in later years. The deed was "a vow to uphold the child and defend his rights." No religious order had asked him for such a vow—but he was to uphold it as conscientiously as any priest.

9

The Children's Republic

*The child—a skilled actor with a hundred masks: a different
one for his mother, father, grandmother or grandfather, for
a stern or lenient teacher, for the cook or maid, for his own
friends, for the rich and poor. Naïve and cunning, humble and
haughty, gentle and vengeful, well behaved and willful, he
disguises himself so well that he can lead us by the nose.*
—*How to Love a Child*

Because the orphanage wasn't completed on schedule, the children
were unable to move in until October of 1912. They had already vacated
their former shelter and were forced to wait in temporary quarters in the
countryside long after it had been deserted by summer vacationers. Used
to the bustle of the crowded city slums, they were filled with anxiety,
imagining the surrounding woods to be full of cannibals and wild animals.
When "those noisy, frozen, excited, impudent" boys and girls finally
arrived at 92 Krochmalna one rainy afternoon, they were still carrying
sticks and clubs from their woodland games and looked a little wild themselves.

The four-storied white house, one of the first in Warsaw to have
central heating and electricity, loomed before the orphans like something
out of a fairy tale. They wandered breathlessly through the huge first-
floor room, with its tall windows and two-story cathedral ceiling, that was
to serve as a dining hall, study, and play area, and stared in disbelief at
the tiled bathrooms with toilets that flushed, and with gleaming porcelain
sinks equipped with both hot and cold running water, all so unlike the
foul, rat-infested outhouses they had known. Everything, even the tiled

kitchen, was clean and beautiful, as if designed for very important people.

After dinner, the children were bathed in the large porcelain tubs. Then, dressed in warm nightclothes, they were shown to their assigned beds in the boys' and girls' dormitories, which were separated by a small glassed-in room from which Korczak planned to observe and reassure them.

The smallest children were given iron cots separated by wooden partitions, which Korczak had designed with a wide hole in the middle in case they woke in the night and needed to reach out for someone. But still they were scared, large and small alike. One of the girls, who had never slept without her two sisters huddled against her on their dirty straw pallet, burst into tears. And a boy who had never seen a bed with white sheets before crawled under it. Korczak and Stefa went from cot to cot, touching the children, kissing them, comforting them, until everyone was asleep.

Setting up their little republic was to prove a sixteen-hour-a-day job—without breaks, holidays, or weekends, Korczak would say. And Stefa would recall that for the first few years she was so busy she couldn't take part in the real life of Warsaw; she might as well have been living in a provincial town. But for both of them all that mattered was that this shared experiment not fail.

As it turned out, Korczak would refer to that first year of the Orphans Home as the worst year of his life. He had believed that after his camp experiences he could never again be taken by surprise, but he was wrong. Rather than appreciating their new accommodations and accepting the rules of communal life, the children had "declared war" even before he realized what was going on. For the second time he was confronted by a menacing community before whom he stood helpless. Overwhelmed by all his regulations, the children adopted a position of absolute resistance that no cajoling could overcome. Coercion produced resentment. The new home they had been waiting for so eagerly had become hateful.

Only later did Korczak realize how difficult it was for the children to give up their old way of life. Shabby and imperfect as their former shelter had been, lacking light and adequate furnishings, they actually missed it. They were "dwarfed by the magnificence" of this new setting. The "impersonal necessity" of a regular routine seemed to "erase" them. Those children who had been leaders wilted and failed; those who had been cooperative now balked at every turn. They were unmoved by

Korczak's lofty sentiments about the dignity of work. ("A clean polished table is as important as a neatly written page.") They watched skeptically as he placed the mop and broom, which he proclaimed noble works of art, in a place of honor by the dormitory door.

Refusing to bow down to a mop and a broom, they rebelled, became conspiratorial. They put pebbles down the washbasins, disconnected the bell, scribbled on the walls. They spread rumors at lunch that a worm had been found in the soup, and refused to eat. They took bread from the table, which was forbidden, and hid it under their pillows and mattresses. Things would get irretrievably lost or misplaced. Who did it? No one knew. Who spilled it? Who broke it? Silence.

Sometimes, when Korczak was shouting—"Stealing again! I'm not going to waste my energy on the education of crooks!"—he found his voice breaking and his eyes smarting with tears of frustration. He consoled himself that every new teacher must experience this difficult testing hour. But he knew that, no matter how harassed he felt, he had to give the impression that he was in control of the community. He learned not to "fly off the handle," even when one of the biggest rascals broke an expensive china urinal while cleaning it, and not long after a jar containing more than a gallon of cod-liver oil. His restraint paid off; it won him "an ally." Slowly the "collective conscience" was aroused. Day by day a few more children came over to his side.

After six months, when everyone was finally beginning to settle in, fifty new children were admitted. Once again the little community was in turmoil as the newcomers rebelled and defied authority.

The new staff also caused problems. A school had been organized in the home by the philanthropists, but the teachers they hired walked about like "aristocrats," creating an "abyss" between themselves and the cook, janitor, and washerwoman, to whom they felt superior. Hating pedantry of any kind (he often said he would rather leave a child in the care of an old woman who had bred chickens for five years than with a newly graduated nurse), Korczak dismissed the teachers, who he truly did believe were less essential than the menial workers who kept the orphanage functioning. He sent the children off to schools in the area, retaining only one instructor to help with homework.

It was almost a year before Korczak and Stefa felt they had established a firm base for the little republic. ("For want of a foundation, the roof fell in," became one of his favorite expressions.) They were exhausted but triumphant at finding themselves free of the troublesome personnel. The child could now become the "patron, the worker, and the head of the home."

Not all of the orphans were from poor families. Grigori Schmukler, a violin prodigy, was admitted at the age of twelve after the death of his father, a doctor. Korczak, who loved music, arranged for Grigori to give small fund-raising concerts in the salons of some of the orphanage's patrons. And at night, before the children went to sleep, he sometimes invited Grigori into the glassed-in cubicle between the two dormitories to play Gluck and Polish folksongs for everyone. After the lights were out, Korczak would sit in the semidarkness of the cubicle writing, like a pilot in a cockpit responsible for the well-being of his crew. He enjoyed the murmur of muffled voices that wafted in, for he understood "the deep, warm, spiritual yearnings of children for softly whispered confidences, melancholic reminiscences, and heartfelt advice."

And he was curious. "What were you talking about in the dormitory last night?" he might ask the next day.

The children were unselfconscious in their replies:

"I was telling him what it was like when my dad was alive."

"I asked him why Poles don't like Jews."

"I told him if he tried harder, you wouldn't be angry with him."

"I said when I grow up, I want to take a trip to the Eskimos and teach them to read and build houses like ours."

Korczak responded warmly as the orphans spoke of their innermost feelings. No one knew more than he how paradoxical life was: he wanted them to have brave dreams, but he also wanted them to be realistic about the chances of those dreams coming true. "Dare to dream," he wrote in a book called *Glory*, about three children with high but unrealistic goals. "Something will always come of it." In *The Unlucky Week*, an imaginative boy, very much like Henryk Goldszmit, can't do anything right in school or at home because his teacher and parents are incapable of understanding his feelings. The stories caught the fancy of the public. Korczak was the first in Polish literature to create a child as hero, one who spoke colloquially rather than in the stilted language that fictional children, always peripheral to the plot, had been burdened with in the past.

While Korczak was recording his orphans' patois, he was aware that they expressed their deepest feelings while asleep, releasing emotions that they managed to repress during the day. Walking among the beds listening to the "symphony of children's breathing," observing the grace or torment of the dreamers' positions—even as he fretted over whether a cough was bronchial or just caused by nerves—he took notes for a "major book" on sleeping children and the night. Yet the thought crossed his mind: Did he have the right to observe these children when they were most vulnerable? "Why pry?" he asked himself. "Let Nature keep her secrets." But the scientist had to pry, even as the educator brooded about the morality involved.

Sometimes he would sit tormented in his cubicle, knowing there was nothing he could do to reassure a child who was mourning a dead parent or lonely for his brothers and sisters. Tears were inevitable, but he could never get used to the choked, hopeless, tragic sobs, which must have reminded him of his own at that age when he grieved over his sick father. He knew that there are as many kinds of sobs as there are children: from the "quiet and private, to the capricious and insincere, to the uncontrolled and shamelessly naked." "It is not the child, but the centuries weeping," he wrote in his notebook.

An eight-year-old boy woke with a toothache. Grabbing Korczak's hand, he spilled out his anguish: ". . . then my mother died. Then I was sent to my grandmother, but she also died. Then I was taken to my aunt's but she wasn't home. It was cold. My uncle took me in. Very poor. I was hungry. His children were sick. He put me in the storage room so I wouldn't catch anything. My teeth always hurt at night. Then a woman took me for a short time, but she walked me to a square and left me. It was dark. I was afraid. Boys started to push me. Then a policeman took me to the station. Everyone was Poles. They sent me to my aunt. She shouted at me, and made me swear not to tell you everything that's happened to me. Can I stay here? I can? Aren't you cross with me for throwing the ball on the grass? I didn't know it was forbidden."

"He fell asleep," Korczak noted. "It was strange, but for a brief moment I definitely saw an aura of light around his tired eight-year-old head. I had seen such a phenomenon only once before." And he added: "Even as I write this, I know that no one will understand. It is impossible unless one has been in a large orphanage dormitory in the still of night."

The worst ruffians, who had tried his patience all day, might break down at night. When he heard Moishe sob, he rushed to his bed. "Don't cry. You'll wake the others." Then, kneeling beside him, he whispered: "You know I love you. But I can't let you get away with everything. The wind didn't break the windowpane. You did. You tried to ruin everyone's games, didn't eat your supper, and started a fight in the dorm. I'm not angry . . ."

It didn't surprise Korczak that his words only produced a fresh flow of tears: "Sometimes consolation has the opposite effect—it can aggravate rather than soothe the child's feelings." But although Moishe's sobbing was of an even greater intensity than before, it was briefer.

"Maybe you're hungry. Shall I get you a roll?"

The boy refused.

"Sleep now, sleep, son," Korczak whispered. Then he touched Moishe lightly. "Sleep."

Korczak felt humble at this moment. If only he could shield his children from danger, "keep them in storage" until they became strong enough for independent flight: "An easy enough job for a hawk or hen to warm chicks with her own body. For me, a man and teacher of children not my own, a more complex task. I long to see my little community soar, dream of them flying high. Yearning for their perfection is my sad, secret prayer. But when I am realistic, I know that as soon as they are able they will take off—prowl, stray, or plunder—in search of nourishment and pleasure."

Some of the children did stray off the property for short excursions: several girls went back to the old shelter on Franciszkanska Street just to see it again, and three brothers walked out of town to visit their old house and the forest where they had played. They had to appear before the children's court (which operated irregularly those two years before World War I) for breaking the rule about not leaving the grounds without permission and being late to supper. The judges were lenient, and Korczak noted that "even children have nostalgia, a longing for that which once was and will not return."

Predicting that, in the future, teachers colleges would offer courses in educational journalism, Korczak launched the orphanage newspaper, which he called the "alphabet of life" because it linked one week to another and bound the children together. "With a paper, we'll be able to know everything that's happening," he said. "It doesn't matter that we begin with a small handwritten one. Someday we'll type it, maybe even print it."

The children waited eagerly for Saturday mornings when it was Korczak's custom to read his special column in the paper aloud. (Generations of children would recall the vividness of his style and the warmth of his voice.) "Do you remember," he wrote in one column, "how you didn't have any close friend when you arrived here, and you felt sad and lonely? Do you remember who pushed or hit you and told you to give him something and you had to obey? . . . Now there are new children who feel the same way you did, and don't know their way around. We hope you will take care of your new comrades." And in another: "We waited for it to happen. And it is happening. Children are bringing gifts to their families from our home. We wondered what sort of presents they would be: maybe needles, pencils, a bar of soap? But, no, they are very different! One girl told her brother a fairy tale she heard here, a boy sang a song he had just learned, another demonstrated how he could wash dishes, and a few reported what they had read in our newspaper."

The children delivered their "gifts" every Saturday afternoon after lunch when they were permitted to visit whatever family members they had left. Korczak felt strongly that they should not lose contact with their relatives. "Children without a family feel handicapped," he said. "Even a bad family is better than none." However, as a health precaution, children were not allowed to stay overnight. When they returned at seven in the evening, they were checked for lice.

There were rumblings in the Warsaw Jewish community that the Orphans Home was "too Polish." Korczak was accused of running an "assimilationist factory," even though the orphanage kept kosher and observed the Sabbath and every Jewish holiday. It even invited many of its supporters to its annual Passover seders. Grigori Schmukler remembers the rabbi who conducted the first seder, and how disappointed he and the other children were when they dashed out the door that had been opened for Elijah and didn't find anyone. But they did find the matzoh which had been hidden in a locker in the dining hall and were given candy as a prize.

The children looked forward to Sabbath dinner each Friday night, not only because of the importance it had had in their own homes, but because Korczak made it so much fun. After their baths, after he had led them in a long line snaking up and down the stairs through the house, after the Sabbath candles were lit and they had a festive dinner, after they played lotto and won little candies, after they had put on their pajamas and were in bed, Korczak would come up to either the boys' or the girls' dormitory, depending on whose turn it was, to tell a story.

He could easily have made up a new one each time, but he favored the old fairy tales, especially "Puss in Boots." He never tired of recounting the pranks of that seemingly worthless cat who managed by cunning and ingenuity to win his poor master a princess and a kingdom. Korczak knew that children who feel worthless in a society that doesn't value them, who feel angry and powerless because their parents, due to death or poverty, can no longer protect them, need to believe that there are magic forces that can help them overcome their difficulties.

"I always thought in terms of obstacles," he wrote. "If I'm traveling somewhere by ship, then there's a storm. If I'm in charge of some project, I have trouble at first, and only in the end do I succeed. Because it's boring if things go well from the start . . ." Fairy tales, with their obstacles that the hero or heroine must overcome through perseverance and strength of will, appealed to him because they were so close to life.

"Is it true?" he once heard a child ask while he was telling a story that involved a wizard, a dragon, fairies, and a princess under a spell. Another child answered in a superior voice: "Didn't you hear him say it was a fairy tale?" Faced with the question of how children perceive reality, Korczak decided: "The story lacks reality for the child only because we have told him that fairy tales are not true."

Korczak was drawn to the implicit moral of these tales—that simple, good people are ultimately rewarded for their virtuous nature while the wicked are punished. He reveled in his role of storyteller, describing Puss in his elegant breeches and high boots, the feather tucked jauntily in his cap, the tension when the King's chariot appears with the Princess who will eventually marry Puss's poor master. And no matter where he was in the plot, he wasn't offended when the youngest dropped off to sleep, because, as he liked to say, he had learned a "lesson in humility" from a flock of sheep at summer camp. It happened during an outing after he gave in to the boys' clamor for a fairy tale. They had pulled him to the ground, fought over who would sit next to him, and hung breathlessly on his every word. Just as he was getting to the most exciting part, a flock of sheep ambled by, bleating and kicking up dust, and Bromberg (who was always losing things, like his buttons) jumped up, shouting: "Look, sheep!" All the boys immediately leapt up and ran toward the flock, forgetting the storyteller. At first, sitting there alone, Korczak had been upset, but later he realized that he had the sheep to thank for making him "less arrogant, even modest."

When news of the progressive Warsaw orphanage experimenting with self-government spread beyond Poland to other countries, Korczak found that, along with everything else, he had to cope with a constant parade of foreign officials and educators, including a team of Russian architects who spent days copying the layout of the house. Yet, despite its fame, the little republic was not immune to the "evil whisper of the street seeping in under the door."

In 1910, while the home was under construction, there had been explosive outbursts of anti-Semitism, fueled by politicians like Roman Dmowski, the leader of the right-wing national democratic movement. "There is not room for two races on the banks of the Vistula," Dmowski preached, alluding to the fact that Warsaw's three hundred thousand Jews made up one-third of the city's population. The Jews were a foreign element in Polish society, Dmowski contended, and unsympathetic to national liberation. A militant nationalist told Korczak in a despairing tone over coffee: "Tell me, what is one to do? The Jews are digging our grave." And another Polish acquaintance lamented: "Your virtues are a death sentence to us."

As if reasoned words might have the power to stem the tide of rising anti-Semitism, Korczak wrote an article, "Three Currents," for a major Polish journal. Acknowledging that a complex relationship had always existed between the Poles and the Jews, and that the antagonisms came from both sides, he called for faith in the shared history that bound them together.

There were three distinct currents running through Polish society, he pointed out. The first one, made up of aristocratic Poles whose names ended in "-ski and -icz," had always wanted to live separately from those whose names ended in "-berg, -sohn, and -stein." The second current, made up of "the heirs of Solomon, David, Isaiah, the Maccabees, the Halevis and Spinozas—lawgivers, thinkers, poets—the oldest aristocracy in Europe, with the Ten Commandments as their coat of arms," also preferred to live apart.

But then there was the third current, whose members had always declared: "We are sons of the same clay. Ages of mutual suffering and success link us on the same chain. The same sun shines upon us, the same hail destroys our fields, the same earth hides the bones of our ancestors. There have been more tears than smiles in our history, but that was neither of our faults. Let us light a common fire together . . ." He ended the article with his own personal avowal: "I am in the third current."

Anti-Semitism continued to grow like a fungus in the shadow of Polish nationalism. Shortly after Korczak and Stefa moved the children into the orphanage in 1912, there were rumors that a group of Russian laborers working on the bridges over the Vistula would start a pogrom. The lights in the Jewish quarter would be knocked out, and the Russians would come disguised in old Jewish robes, which, it was said, they were busily procuring from second-hand dealers. Korczak kept the small gate in the side wall unlocked for a fast exit should there be any violence.

In 1913, anti-Semitic hysteria was kindled further by the Beilis trial then in progress in Kiev. Mendel Beilis, a minor clerk, was accused of killing a Christian in order to use his blood for a Passover ceremony. Similar accusations had been leveled at Jews for centuries in Eastern and Central Europe, but word of this one spread across Poland like brushfire. Grigori Schmukler remembers that some children threw stones at him and other orphans as they went to and from school, shouting: "Beilis! Beilis!" Even when Beilis was acquitted by the Kiev jury, the children continued their taunts: "Set the dogs on the Jews!"

Korczak tried to keep good relations with the neighboring children by inviting them over to play after school with his orphans. The eminent German philosopher Hermann Cohen, paying a visit on the last stop.of his tour of East European Jewish communities in 1914, was amazed at what was being accomplished at the orphanage in such trying conditions. Unlike other assimilated Western Jews who looked with condescension on their Eastern brethren as being scarcely out of the Dark Ages, Cohen wrote glowingly in Martin Buber's newspaper *Der Jude:* "I was deeply moved by my visits to exemplary orphan asylums, especially the one directed with ineffable love and modern understanding by Dr. Goldszmit of Warsaw."

As rumors of impending war filled the cafés that spring and summer, Korczak tried a new kind of diplomacy. He persuaded the Orphans Aid Society to buy two hundred pots of flowers for the children to distribute to their neighbors. The rest of Warsaw might be preoccupied with the possibility of world conflict, but up and down their end of Krochmalna red geraniums would blaze in the sun.

10

How to
Love a Child

The outbreak of the Great War put an end to the geranium plan. All of Warsaw was in a state of chaos that August of 1914: refugees crowded into the city from outlying areas and people rushed to hoard food and supplies. The Orthodox Jews at the lower end of Krochmalna were certain that this was the final battle between Gog and Magog, after which the Messiah would come. Expressing a secular version of the same sentiment, Korczak hoped that a pure world would emerge from this conflict. He could not know when he was conscripted once again for medical duty with the Czar's Imperial Army that it would be four long, bloody years before he would see either a new world or his orphans again.

It was a tragic war for the Poles. Mobilized by all three occupying powers—800,000 in the Russian army, 400,000 in the Austrian, and 200,000 in the German—they were put in the intolerable position of fighting against each other. Even their leaders were divided as to which was the greatest enemy: Russia, Germany, or Austria. Those who joked cynically that the only way for Poland to be reunited would be for all three countries to be defeated did not really believe that this was exactly what would happen.

Korczak rushed about as frantically as everyone else, trying to make arrangements for Stefa and the orphans while he was away. Izaak Eliasberg, also conscripted, would not be there to raise funds. Donations to the home had fallen off, while the number of children needing care had increased. When the bank refused to give him more than two hundred

and fifty of the five thousand rubles in his private account, Korczak sought
out his publisher, Jakub Mortkowicz, for the hundred rubles he had left
with him "for a rainy day." In happier times he had often joined Warsaw's
cultural elite in the room behind the bookstore in Mortkowicz's office
and had cappuccino and cream cake with them at the Zemianska, a popular
literary café which shared the same courtyard on Mazowiecka Street.
Mortkowicz, an assimilated Jew, attracted the finest writers to his firm
because of his high standards in publishing. His wife, Janina (as talkative
as her husband was taciturn), published Korczak's stories in the children's
journal, *In the Sunshine*, that she edited with Stefania Sempolowska It
was a tightly connected literary world, and Mortkowicz, unlike the bank,
did not hesitate to give his celebrated author the hundred rubles he
needed. He even offered to look in on his mother during his absence.

Korczak did not find it easy to say goodbye to the orphans. Until
then, it had been they who left him when they were old enough to go
out into the world. He had braced himself for those farewells, and turned
his attention to the newcomers. But now he was the one leaving, and at
a time when they needed him most.

While Korczak reassured the orphans, Stefa reassured him, even
though she felt overwhelmed at being left with complete responsibility
for the children, whose numbers had swelled to one hundred and fifty.
A few months before the outbreak of the war, she had fulfilled her dream
of sending her beloved Esterka Weintraub to college in Belgium, and she
would not consider Korczak's suggestion that Esterka be asked to return.
But before he left Warsaw, Korczak took it upon himself to write Esterka
of his concern about Stefa. As he hoped, she interrupted her studies to
rush back. She stayed at Stefa's side for the next two years, working night
and day under the difficult conditions of the German occupation, even
carrying sick children on her back to the hospital. When she caught typhus
and died during the epidemic of 1916, Stefa felt as if she had lost her
own daughter. Crazed with grief, she even thought of giving up her work,
but because there were so many children dependent on her, she forced
herself to carry on. But never again would Stefa allow herself to become
so deeply attached to any of the orphans.

Korczak was assigned to a divisional field hospital on the Eastern
front. This brutal war, through which he slogged in his heavy Russian
uniform and high military boots as the armies of Russia and the Austro-
Hungarian Empire swept back and forth across the defenseless villages

of Eastern Europe, was to impress on him that men march to "a clock with only one hand—the sword." Not even men, but "an orgy of devils in intoxicated procession." And for what?

While camping overnight in a deserted village, he was riveted by the sight of a blind old Jew groping his way with his stick through the infantry unit's convoy of horses and wagons. The man's family and friends had tried to persuade him to leave with them, but he had insisted on remaining behind to watch over the synagogue and cemetery. (Twenty-five years later, when Korczak chose to remain in the Warsaw Ghetto with his orphans, he would liken himself to that blind old Jew.)

Yet he tried to see everything in universal terms. "It is not only the Jews who suffer," he wrote. "All the world is submerged in blood and fire, in tears and mourning. And suffering does not make men noble, not even the Jews."

Perhaps to keep himself from falling into despair as the field hospital moved back and forth with the troops across the battlefields of Eastern Europe, he began writing the book which would become *How to Love a Child*. It was to be no less than the "synthesis of the child" he had dreamed of during his half year in Paris, distilled from his experiences as a pediatrician, camp counselor, and educator. He wrote in the field station to the deafening cacophony of artillery fire, on a tree stump in a forest where the troops were resting, in a meadow under a pine tree. Everything seemed important—he was constantly pausing to jot things down so that he wouldn't forget. "It would be an irretrievable loss to mankind," he would jest ironically to his orderly.

The orderly, whom we know only as Walenty, was given the task of typing each day's segment. He must have been a long-suffering aide: typing a manuscript on child development is not the usual military assignment. He rebelled only once during a brief respite in their schedule: Korczak quotes him fondly as grumbling, "Is it worth it for just a half hour?" There were times when Korczak would be forced to interrupt his work on the book for as long as a month. During those periods, he would be filled with self-doubt. Why make a fool of himself? "That which is wise is known to a hundred men."

How to Love a Child was originally to be only a short pamphlet for parents and teachers, but perhaps because it was a long war the manuscript grew to hundreds of pages. One of its main theses is that you cannot possibly love a child—your own, or another's—until you see him as a separate being with the inalienable right to grow into the person he was meant to be. You cannot even understand a child until you achieve self-knowledge: "You yourself are the child whom you must learn to know, rear, and above all, enlighten."

Because he was an artist by temperament and not a theorist, Korczak did not produce a systematic tract, but rather images of the child in each fleeting time frame of its development. Feigning modesty, he admits that to most questions the reader may have, he can only answer "I don't know." (But he adds slyly that this seemingly empty phrase contains limitless possibilities of "new breakthroughs.")

"It is impossible to tell parents unknown to me how to rear a child also unknown to me under conditions unknown to me," he writes. The mother must learn to trust her own perceptions; no one can know her child as she does: "To demand that others should provide you textbook prognoses is like asking a strange woman to give birth to your baby. There are insights that can be born only of your own pain, and they are the most precious."

Korczak, the artist, speaks mystically, comparing the child to a piece of parchment covered with hieroglyphs, only some of which the parents will ever be able to decipher: "Seek in that stranger who is your child the undiscovered part of yourself." The pediatrician urges common sense, warning that a baby's development cannot be measured like other things in society: "When is the proper time for a child to start walking and talking? When he does. When should his teeth start cutting? When they do. How many hours should a baby sleep? As long as it needs to."

Behind all of Korczak's assertions are the honed reflections of a child psychologist who was one of the first of his time to recognize the importance of infancy in human development. While Freud was still gathering information on childhood from his adult patients, Korczak already understood the necessity for direct observation of the baby. "Napoleon suffered from tetanus, Bismarck had rickets, each was an infant before he became a man. If we wish to probe the source of thought, emotions, and ambition, we must turn to the infant."

He found in the infant a "well-defined personality composed of innate temperament, strength, and intellect." Bending over a hundred cribs, he could pick out the "trusting and suspicious, the steady and capricious, the cheerful and gloomy, the wavering, the frightened, and the hostile." But though their temperaments might be different, each was attempting to prevail over unknown powers, to probe the secret of the mysterious world which was delivering both good and bad messages. "The infant runs its affairs within the scope of its available knowledge and means—both of which are meager. . . . It does not know yet that the breast, the face, and the hands comprise a unit—the mother."

The mother has only to observe her infant selflessly to receive its message, for what is its intense gaze if not one of inquiry? The baby may not have mastered words yet, but it speaks in "the language of facial expressions, the language of images and emotional recollections." Its every new movement is "like that of a pianist for whom the proper frame of mind and absolute self-control are essential to be able to play."

The child emerges as both the benefactor and the victim of its mother's love, with the author intervening like a guardian angel on its behalf. He is equally wary of teachers, whom he consoles one moment—"You will always make mistakes because you are a human being, not a machine"—and chastises the next—"Children love laughter, movement, playing tricks. Teacher, if life is a graveyard to you, leave the children free to see it as a pasture."

It was one thing to write about how to love a child and another not to have a child to love. When, in February 1917, the field hospital dug in for an indefinite stay on a hill overlooking the town of Tarnopol in Galicia, Korczak was particularly vulnerable. It was almost three years since he had left his orphans in Warsaw, and six months since a short, crumpled letter had somehow got through "the tight ring of bayonets, censors, and spies." At night, when he was finished with his duties, he would sit outside the hospital and watch as one by one the lights went out in the town below. A feeling of homesickness would overwhelm him as he remembered lights-out at the orphanage and the deep silence that fell over everything.

As soon as he had a few free hours, Korczak visited a shelter for homeless children set up in Tarnopol by the municipal authorities. He was shocked by the conditions there. Rather than serving as sanctuaries, places like this were "dustbins into which children were cast as the refuse of war, the waste products of dysentery, typhoid fever, or cholera that had destroyed their parents—or rather their mothers. Their fathers were off fighting for a better world."

How did he happen to notice Stefan? Perhaps the boy was standing apart from the others. Perhaps their eyes met in an unexpected glance of sympathy. Soon they were deep in conversation. When Stefan mentioned that he would like to learn a craft of some kind, Korczak told him about the carpentry shop in his hospital compound. No sooner had he asked the boy if he would like to come along with him, to learn carpentry and how to read, than he regretted it. He had violated his own dictum that one should never spring anything suddenly on a child. "Not today. I'll come for you on Monday," he quickly added. "Ask your brother about it. Think it over." As if there was much for a displaced boy like Stefan Zagrodnik to think over—it was Korczak who had some thinking to do.

As he had noted in his journal, he was used to working with children in groups of one hundred. His every word influenced a hundred minds, his every step was watched by a hundred pair of vigilant eyes. If he failed with some, there were always a few he had reached. He never had to fear "utter defeat." He used to say that working with only one child was a game not worth the candle; he spoke contemptuously of teachers who left group projects to work privately, dismissing them as being in it only for the money or for better personal conditions. But now he was about to offer "the hours, the days, and the months" of his life to one child.

Stefan was waiting eagerly when Korczak came with Walenty and a sledge to pick him up that Monday night. The orderly had been disgruntled from the moment he heard about the plan. First he had had to take on typing manuscripts, and now he was expected to cook and clean for some vagrant Ukrainian boy. To add insult to injury, Stefan was hardly in Walenty's company two minutes before he was calling him by his first name. But Stefan was aware only of his first moonlit ride through the snow as they passed the church, the railway station, carriages and trucks, and the bridge on their way to the field hospital.

Korczak asked little of the boy the first few days, although he made a mental note to have him address Walenty respectfully. He knew from similar incidents at the Warsaw orphanage that the janitor, cook, and washerwoman resented it when the children didn't give "a handle" to their names. But he wanted Stefan to have a chance to feel his way around, test the situation, develop some trust.

Stefan's mother had died when he was seven. He couldn't even remember her name—only that blood came out of her mouth when she coughed and that she didn't come back from the hospital. As for his father, he might have been killed in action by now—or he might still be at the front, or in a POW camp. For a while Stefan had lived with his seventeen-year-old brother in Tarnopol, and then with some soldiers until he was taken off to the municipal shelter where Korczak found him.

At first, it looked as if Walenty were right about his misgivings. Stefan was there only a day when he had a terrible stomachache, brought on by the combination of cold sausage from the soldiers' canteen and the jam cakes and candies he had bought with the fifty kopecks his brother gave him as a send-off.

In the orphanage, sickness often meant extra trouble and could cause tension in the house, but Korczak noted that Stefan's discomfort drew them together, as it does a family. He propped the boy up in bed like the king of the roost. To enable Stefan to do his writing exercises, Korczak carefully secured the inkpot in an old can that Walenty had previously converted into an ashtray. Then, balancing the can in a large box that he emptied for this purpose, he put a supporting pillow on one side and another box on the other side. As Stefan thanked him with a smile, it occurred to Korczak that a boarding home could not afford such a luxury. He also realized that when he was with a large group of children, a smile was too subtle a signal to notice. Only now did he see it as an important signal deserving study.

Korczak held to his pedagogic intent to teach Stefan to read, recording each day's progress in minute detail. It was as if initiating Stefan into the intricacies of Polish grammar would restore the universe to both of them. As Stefan tried to correct his own sentences, without quite knowing how to get them right, Korczak was struck with the thought that a child is endowed with a "grammatical conscience" that may be hindered by the teacher's complex explanations:

> The child's mind—a forest in which the tops of trees gently sway, the branches mingle, and the shivering leaves touch. Sometimes a tree grazes its neighbor and receives the vibrations of a hundred or a thousand trees—of the whole forest. Whenever any of us says "right—wrong—pay attention—do it again," it is like a gust of wind that plays havoc with the child.

Stefan stumbled along awkwardly the first week, but then it was as if he felt the "vibrations." He glided over the book as smoothly as he tobogganed outdoors, negotiating the obstacles with a determination that he had not shown before. He had managed to "transfer the risk of sport to learning." Yet the boy was sly—he knew how to manipulate his mentor. He tried to cheat at checkers, to avoid some of his lessons. He took a cannon shell to the workshop without asking permission and resorted to lying when questioned about it.

The pedagogue was as defenseless as any father. He had to be on guard. "If I let the child get the better of me, then an attitude of disdain is bound to creep in. One must fight back, work toward maintaining authority, by demonstration, without scolding of any kind." As if to further convince himself, he added: "Children like a certain amount of coercion. It helps them to fight their own inner resistance. It spares them the intellectual effort of having to make a choice."

Stefan worked in the carpentry shop while Korczak made his rounds among the two hundred and seventeen patients in the wards, some of them suffering from contagious diseases, others fresh casualties from the front. When Korczak dropped by the carpentry shop, the instructor praised the boy, saying he was hardworking. But it was painful for Korczak to watch Stefan struggling to saw a wobbly plank. He had to force himself not to warn the boy to be careful of his fingers. Already his admonitions— "Don't go out barefoot!" "Don't drink unboiled water!" "Aren't you cold?" "Are you sure you don't have a stomachache?"—were making him sound like those overanxious mothers he had ridiculed in his books.

Even Walenty (who still muttered about all the trouble and that no good would come of all this) was growing protective of Stefan. He went outside more than once to call the boy in from tobogganing when he was late for his evening lesson—"as in a family."

Korczak hoped that Stefan would see the child in the man who sided with him, but he knew that the boy saw a balding thirty-nine-year-old medical officer who, in his eyes, was old. Yet Stefan admired him. "I'd like to write the letter K like you do," he said. It reminded Korczak of how the orphans used to copy the way he wrote the letters of the alphabet. And of how long it had taken him to master writing the capital W like his father.

Trying to follow the logic of many of Stefan's questions forced Korczak to consider how differently children perceive things from adults. When Stefan asked: "What is a poppy seed made of?" "Why is it black? "Can you get enough poppy seeds from one garden to fill a plate?" Korczak realized that the boy's conception of a garden covered four, perhaps five, ideas, while his own covered a hundred, even a thousand. "The roots of many seemingly illogical questions asked by children are to be found here," he noted. "We have difficulty finding a common language with children because even though they use the same words we do, they fill them with an entirely different content. 'Garden,' 'father,' 'death' mean something different to Stefan than to me." He concluded that adults and children only pretend to understand each other.

* * *

It was evening. Stefan had said his prayers and "pecked a kiss" on Korczak's hand—a Polish custom that Korczak didn't approve of in his orphanage, but allowed now because he knew it reminded the boy of a family ritual. Stefan lay quietly, his eyes wide open.

"Tell me, please, is it true that if you shave, hair won't grow again?"

Korczak knew the boy didn't want to offend him by making a direct reference to his bald head.

"It's not true. One shaves the chin and hair still grows."

"Some soldiers have beards reaching right down to their waists—like the Jews," Stefan continued. "Why?"

"It's a custom," Korczak explained. "On the other hand, Englishmen are clean-shaven."

"Is it true that there are a lot of Jews among the Germans?"

"There are some. There are also Russian Jews and Polish Jews."

"What do you mean, Polish Jews? Are the Poles Jews?"

"No, the Poles are Catholics," Korczak replied. "But if anyone speaks Polish, desires the well-being of the Polish people, wishes them well, then he is also a Pole."

It was the belief, relayed to him by his own family, that he had passed on to his orphans in Warsaw.

As Stefan lay with his eyes open, still wide awake, Korczak was reminded that bedtime evoked reminiscences and quiet reflection in the orphanage, too.

"How old is your father?" he asked Stefan.

"He was forty-two. Now he's forty-five."

"Your father might not know you, you've grown so much."

"I don't know if I would know him."

"Haven't you got a photograph?"

"Where would I get one from?" Another silence. "A lot of the soldiers look like him."

On their seventh day together, supper was delayed because Walenty was on duty in the mess hall. This made Korczak late to his card game in another billet and he was still in a bad mood when he returned at midnight. Switching on the light, he was startled to discover that Stefan was not there. He rushed outside and saw the boy running toward him.

"Where have you been?"

"In the kitchen. I was watching from the window there to see when you'd be finished. Then I looked up, and you were gone. I ran to catch up with you."

"Were you afraid?"

"What would I be afraid of?"

Realizing that it was not fear but affection that had motivated Stefan, Korczak was filled with "overwhelming gratitude to the lad." He tried to analyze the strange hold the boy had over him:

"There is nothing special about him, nothing to attract attention. An ordinary face, uncoordinated body, average mind, little imagination, absolute lack of tenderness—nothing of what makes children adorable. But it is nature, its eternal laws, God, speaking through this unspectacular child just as through any scrub bush growing by the roadside. Thank you, for being just as you are—just ordinary."

"My son," he added with tenderness. "How can I ever thank you?"

On the eighth day, he was standing by the stove thinking about that day's lesson when Stefan, who was already in bed, said: "You promised me something."

"What was it?"

"A fairy tale."

It was the first time the boy had actually requested a story.

"Should I tell you a new one?"

"No, I want the one about Aladdin."

Korczak noted that of the three fairy tales he had been told—"Cinderella," "Puss in Boots," and "Aladdin"—Stefan had chosen the one that seemed closest to his own life at that time: "A wizard comes to a poor boy and changes his fortunes by means of a wonderful lamp. Here an unknown doctor (officer) suddenly appears and rescues him from the institution. In the tale, slaves carry succulent dishes on plates of gold—here, Walenty carries in the buns."

On the eleventh day, Stefan said: "I never think about my brother now."

"A pity," Korczak replied. "You should think of your father and brother." That night he jotted in his notebook: "This wicked war."

Their situation might have gone on indefinitely had Korczak's right eye not become inflamed. At first he ignored it, but Stefan prodded him to go to the eye clinic. When he came back with blue lenses, Stefan asked in a hushed voice: "Does it hurt much?"

Stefan wept when his genie was taken to the hospital because of the eye infection. Determined to maintain a professional distance, rather than believe the boy was genuinely concerned, Korczak noted: "I assume he is reminded of his family—someone who goes to the hospital dies."

Stefan came to visit with Walenty.

"Tell me, are those other officers ill, too?"

"Yes."

"Eyes?"

"No, various complaints."

"And are they playing cards for money?"

When Korczak decided to work with *one* child, he asked his journal: "What will it amount to?"—a question he never attempted to answer. His warm feelings for Stefan (and for all of the mischievous boys he favored at the orphanage) may seem as suspect to the Freudian-oriented reader as Lewis Carroll's for Alice Liddell, or James Barrie's for the Llewellyn Davies boys who inspired Peter Pan. The intimacy of being with Stefan in close quarters might have reminded Korczak of himself as a child—as some of his reflections suggest—or brought out paternalistic longings for the child he had decided never to have, or revealed an actual attraction to young boys which he kept repressed all of his life. Or possibly included elements of all three. In any case, he recorded their experience together as a pedagogical experiment: "I found that observing one child provides as much harassment and satisfaction as observing a large number. One can see in a single child much more, one can feel things more subtly, consider every fact more thoroughly. A weary educator of a group has the right, even the duty, to apply this kind of 'crop rotation' in his work."

He concluded the piece with the brief statement: "I spent only two weeks with him. I fell sick and had to leave, but the boy stayed on for some time. Then the battlefront began to move—my orderly sent him back to the institution."

11

The Sad Madame

*Life never gives more than partial liberation. Achievement can
never be more than fragmentary.*
—Educational Moments

It was not only Stefan with whom Korczak parted that March of
1917, but also Walenty, who moved on with the field hospital. When his
eyes recovered, Korczak asked for and was granted an assignment with
a regiment in Kiev, a place he had been thinking about from the time he
had taken a three-day furlough there two years before.

Kiev, the ancient capital of the Ukraine, had not been part of Poland
since the late seventeenth century, but it still had a large Polish colony.
Arriving there the day before Christmas in 1915, Korczak had gone straight
from the train with a letter of introduction to the founder of the first
Polish *gymnasium* for girls, Waclawa Peretiakowicz. She had opened the
door suspiciously, fearing it might be the police for her daughter, Janina.
Instead she found a slight man in a Russian officer's uniform, whose jacket,
she noted, was too long for him. He introduced himself as Henryk Goldszmit, but the two women soon discovered he was Janusz Korczak, the
famous writer and educator.

Madame Peretiakowicz was able to direct Korczak to Maryna Falska,
a Polish woman, who had just become director of a Red Cross home for
sixty Polish boys evacuated from Warsaw before the Germans took the
city. Korczak rushed over to Bogontowska Street, expecting to find a
tenement in a poor area of town, and was astonished to arrive at a large
dacha surrounded by trees on a slope overlooking the Dnieper River.
Despite the placid setting, the interior was in total disarray. The boys,

confused by their dislocation, had run rampant over everything, including their new directress. Overwhelmed by her own personal tragedies as well as those of her charges, Maryna Falska could hardly have guessed that the nimble military doctor who stepped unannounced into the orphanage that day would both change and anchor her life.

A crisis was occurring even as he entered the house. A welfare officer had just arrived to remove a thirteen-year-old boy accused of stealing a watch. Asking for time to question the child and to do a little investigation on his own, Korczak soon proved the boy's innocence. The children quieted down immediately, sensing an ally in this authoritative male stranger.

In the two remaining days of that Christmas leave in 1915, Korczak managed to infuse the boys with enthusiasm for self government, a court of peers, and a handwritten newspaper for which he wrote the lead article. As the moment neared for him to return to his unit in Tarnopol, Maryna Falska, shy and private by nature, did not know how to express her gratitude other than to assure her new friend that she would carry on his work. Korczak, with his charm and humor, had been one of the few people ever to break through her formidable reserve.

The Sad Madame, as some maliciously referred to Maryna, had inspired many rumors in the Polish émigré community, where everyone had some kind of complicated past but few veiled in such mystery. It was said that the loss of her husband a few years earlier accounted for the sorrow in the Sad Madame's eyes, the severity of her tightly pressed thin lips, and her long black dresses.

Born Maria Rogowska into a landed gentry family in Dubno Podlanskie in southeastern Poland on February 7, 1877, Maryna had studied to be a teacher before following her brothers into underground activities. Taking "Hilda" as an alias, she was frequently arrested for operating an illegal printing shop for the Polish Socialist party, and once shared a jail cell with Jozef Pilsudski, the future Marshal of free Poland.

Maryna told no one how or when she met her husband, Leon Falski, a Polish doctor, but it is believed that it was in London, where they both had fled to escape arrest for their political activities. Upon their return to Poland, she concealed her pregnancy as long as she could. When Falski took his first medical post in the poor Lithuanian town of Volozhyn, famous for its century-old yeshiva, he enjoyed a busy medical practice that included Poles, Lithuanians, and Jews alike. He treated poor yeshiva students without charge, discussed philosophy with the rabbis, and hunted with the landowners. Yet when Maryna insisted they move to a city where she could be politically active, he agreed to relocate. While they were making plans, a typhus epidemic broke out. Maryna would suffer guilt for the rest of her life that she had inadvertently caused her husband's death: she insisted he accompany an old woman who appeared at their door late one night seeking help for a sick relative. He contracted typhus from the patient, and died within a few days.

Maryna's sense of guilt, however, did not prevent her from boycotting her husband's funeral. A staunch atheist who had broken with her devoutly Catholic mother over religious issues, she objected to a priest, rabbi, and minister officiating jointly at the burial in spite of her protests. While gentry, peasants, and Jews turned out in an unprecedented show of unity to pay their respects to the revered doctor who had served them so selflessly, the widow and her two-year-old daughter remained at home behind closed shutters.

Maryna left with her child for Moscow, where she had friends, but the severity of the winter and her inability to provide her daughter with adequate nourishment took their toll. Within two years, the child was dead. Unable to return to Warsaw because of the war, Maryna applied for a Red Cross job running an orphanage for homeless Polish boys in Kiev.

When Korczak returned to the Red Cross Home in Kiev in 1917, two years after his first visit, he found Maryna operating it along the lines he had set down. She was as happy to see him as the boys were, and proudly showed him around the new workshops in shoemaking, tailoring, bookbinding, plumbing, and sewing. The orphanage now included several young girls who, like the boys, had become separated from their families, as well as a few women volunteers from the university.

Korczak was to have little time to spend with Maryna and her orphans. Through the influence of a Polish intellectual who worked for the local Russian administration, he had been assigned as assistant pediatrician in three municipal shelters for Ukrainian children. Moving into a basement room, he often went hungry, like so many others in that beleaguered city. The markets had only kasha and leaden bread whose dough was often mixed with sand. Should Maryna Falska's children bring over a loaf of bread they had baked, he'd send it back rather than take any food from their mouths. Once, when he ate tripe at a cheap restaurant, he "cried his eyes out" because it reminded him of home.

It was a difficult, lonely life, made even more frustrating by conditions in the Ukrainian shelters, which proved to be even worse than the "refuse bin" where he had encountered Stefan. The orphans were covered with ulcers and scabs; their eyes were infected; they were hungry. They were suffering from malnutrition and maltreatment. He did what he could, often sleeping over to comfort them with his presence. His indignant protests about the incompetent way the shelters were being run enraged the corrupt directors (who were no more qualified for the job than an "instructress of embroidery"). He saw himself as "saving the children"; the directors saw him as threatening their authority. "The same revolver that was used to shoot sick horses was pointed at me as a warning that I was in the wrong place at the wrong time. Graft! Infamy! Human language has not invented terms strong enough to denounce the situation."

Still, it was better to be in Kiev trying to rescue children than in the thick of battle with a field unit. And there was the comfort of the natural beauty of this "greenest of cities" with its old churches and palaces built on hills over the steep banks of the Dnieper. Parts of Kiev resembled Warsaw, especially the poor workers' district along the river that must have reminded Korczak of his beloved Vistula. The Jewish quarter, known as Podol, was teeming with Orthodox Jews with their sidelocks and long gaberdines, much like those who lived at the lower end of Krochmalna.

Sometimes in his walks about the city he dropped in at the cafés filled with Polish and Jewish writers and intellectuals who had been drawn to Kiev by its Polish university, established after the 1905 revolution. There were people of every political persuasion gathered at the tables, including spies working for one side or another. The early German offensive in the Ukraine had driven hundreds of thousands of Polish refugees eastward, many of whom had joined the revolutionaries and counter-revolutionaries who made up Kiev's polyglot émigré community. Everyone was careful about voicing opinions because murders were an everyday affair, accepted without comment. One faction wanted Kiev to be the capital of an independent Ukraine, another to see the Ukraine merged with Russia, and still another to have it become part of Poland once again.

Every day brought artillery bombardments and fights in the streets. Horsecarts filled with corpses were common sights. "Kiev—chaos," was how Korczak described it. "Yesterday the Bolsheviks. Today the Ukrainians. The Germans come nearer and nearer, and the whole of Russia is believed to be in turmoil."

Through all the chaos he was still working on *How to Love a Child* "absolutely every day." When Madame Peretiakowicz asked him as a favor to evaluate the Montessori school that had just opened, he made time for that, too. It was an opportunity to learn about this Italian educator whose work teaching young children to read and write had already spread to the major European cities. Although they were never to meet, Janusz Korczak and Maria Montessori had much in common. Both were medical doctors who spoke of the child's soul; both put great stress on the importance of the child's early experiences; and both were influenced by Pestalozzi's ideas about sense training—helping an individual child develop through the use of his hands, eyes, ears. But there the similarity ended. Montessori concentrated on her educational kit with its specific learning materials, while Korczak was primarily concerned with the social interaction of children.

Korczak agreed to observe at the Montessori kindergarten in two- or three-hour intervals over the course of two days. He arrived with his own equipment: a pencil and paper. His plan was to use this opportunity to develop a note-taking technique for schools of education. The ability to record what one saw was, in his opinion, an essential skill for every teacher: "In notes are the seeds from which forests and cornfields grow, the drops which become springs. . . . Notes are the entries with which you draw up the balance sheet of life, and the documentary evidence that it has not been wasted."

Scouting his "observation site"—a large room with a piano in the corner, six tables with four chairs each, a chest of toys, and Montessori blocks and kits—he was ready for action. Surely no intelligence agent in Kiev was taking notes as assiduously as this educator for whom the political scenario outside was nothing compared to the drama unfolding in there. Had his papers been seized by the police, they might have been suspected of being in code, formatted as they were like a script:

THE CAST: The charming heroine, three-and-a-half-year-old Helcia, used to being admired for her intelligence and allure, has to match wits with several costars: Jurek, a three-year-old tyrant with a bad reputation, having once tried to take a whip to his mother; roguish five-year-old Hanna, who has her head screwed on right, knows exactly how far she can go; and six-year-old Nini, a typical child intriguer who defies characterization, prefers the company of younger children.

SCENE ONE: *What are they up to?*
Helcia: (looking at a picture) The dog has a red tongue. Why?

Nini: Because it's a dog.
Helcia: Do dogs have red tongues—sometimes?

Observer: I can understand that a child looking at the picture would examine the tail, ears, tongue, and teeth separately, details that an adult would pass over, although the same adult would give paintings in an art gallery similarly detailed attention. If we are constantly astonished at children's perceptiveness—which means that we do not take them seriously—we are, in fact, astonished that they are human beings and not puppets.

I take Helcia's question about dogs' tongues to mean that she wants to converse on any subject with Nini, who, being older, is higher on the social scale. The clue for me was the word *sometimes* inserted at random. In the same way, a simple person meeting someone of a higher social class will throw in an unrelated or farfetched word to prove he is not a fool.

S C E N E   T W O: Jurek and Hanna are grabbing the blocks from Helcia. She pleads with them timidly because she knows that life is cruel, and she will not get through unscathed. Still, she does not want to run away. It is not the words she used that matter now, but the calm, utterly sad voice, the expression on her face, the posture. No actress could plead so convincingly for help, indulgence, and pity . . . And the words? So straightforward. "Please, Hanna, don't take my blocks."

Hanna—life knows nothing of compassion—grabs. Helcia hits her on the head with her last block. She fears retaliation. Note the dramatic force in her treble "Take it!" as she presses the block into Jurek's hand. In just this way, a dying standard-bearer passes the colors to the nearest man in order to keep them from falling into the hands of the enemy.

Jurek, a passive witness of the scene, turns to me in a voice thick with emotion. He pleads for the girl deprived of her all, wronged—while he himself, holding the last block, is at a loss. In turning to me, he communicates to Helcia his understanding and support, and his condemnation of Hanna.

Hanna understood. Hit on the head with the block, she only rubs the spot gently—no thought of retaliation. A sense of guilt—she gives back more than she took, and asks Jurek's pardon.

At the end of the first day, Korczak noted that "children are much richer in the realm of feeling, for they think with their emotions." Finding it impossible to record the children's movements and gestures, he had taken down only words, "wonderful in their simplicity, gathering force by repetition." When Helcia handed the block to Jurek, she said "Take it" three times. Jurek pointed out twice that Helcia had nothing to build with, and Hanna also repeated that she had returned the blocks. "It seems to me that, in a highly dramatic situation, a writer or actor might achieve a more powerful effect by repetition than by a lengthy tirade."

Stressing the importance of observing, rather than interfering in their play, Korczak was critical of himself for missing some essential details, such as how the block box suddenly appeared on Helcia's desk. Furthermore, he felt that some of his comments, which were in the "style of a theater review," lacked clarity: "When reading an essay on a play by Shakespeare or Sophocles, one has the advantage of knowing Hamlet or Antigone, but here the reader knows neither the leading lady—Helcia—nor the actual play."

Somehow the plan for a note-taking technique never materialized, but Korczak did inadvertently happen on a teaching "formula" for himself—a technique of passing from a minor detail he had observed to a larger frame of reference which allowed him to illustrate a general problem. This and the manuscript for *How to Love a Child* were the booty that he brought back to Warsaw after the war.

When, on January 8, 1918, Woodrow Wilson made a free and independent Poland one of his fourteen points, the Poles who had taken refuge in Kiev were exhilarated. And in March, after the Brest Litovsk treaty between Russia and the Central Powers recognized Ukrainian independence, Korczak's friends offered to help him obtain travel documents that would enable him to return to Warsaw. The papers came through in the late spring.

As he said goodbye to Maryna and the boys, the twinkle in Korczak's eyes, the lightness of his step showed everyone how much it meant to him to be going home. Korczak assured the children that they would be leaving soon. Madame Maryna, as they called her, was waiting for papers that would enable her to escort them back to Warsaw, where they would be reunited with their remaining relatives. She couldn't be sure of her future, of what kind of work she could find in the city that had once been her home. But one thing was certain—there would be no lack of homeless children.

PART TWO

1919–1930

12

Independence

Poland—not just fields, coal mines, forests, or munitions fac-
tories but—above all—her children.
                                        —Child Care

Korczak's mother had told everyone that she was living only "for the day Henryk arrives." Now, after four years, here he was, looking lean and muscular, even healthy, in spite of the ordeal he had been through. His pale elongated face was set off by a fringe of reddish whiskers which ended in a neat mustache and goatee. His bloodshot eyes, not yet completely healed, were still filled with irony. He was still her Henryk.

The Germans had not yet left Warsaw, but it was only a matter of months before the Armistice would be declared and the occupying troops sent home in defeat.

The orphans at 92 Krochmalna could not sleep the night before Korczak was to return to them, even those who had only the dimmest memory of him, or none at all. That morning they lined up with Stefa and the teachers in the courtyard to await the arrival of both Korczak and Dr. Eliasberg, the president of the Orphans Aid Society, who had also just returned from the Eastern front. When they saw the two men enter— one tall with dark hair and mustache, and the other slight, bald, with a reddish mustache and goatee—many of the orphans were not sure who was who. Not until the second man peered at them mischievously over his spectacles could they be certain he was Korczak. With whoops of glee, they started toward him.

"How they ran to me, crowded around me upon my return from the war," he reported in his journal. And with the sly, self-deprecating humor of a man who knows children, he added: "But would they not have been

even more delighted if white mice or guinea pigs had suddenly appeared
in my place?" Hardly able to restrain his emotions, he held them, swung
them, tickled them, patted them, bantered with them.

We have no record of how he greeted Stefa as she stood there in
her familiar black dress with its white collar and cuffs, her short hair
brushed to one side. By sheer force of will, Stefa had managed to get the
children through those long, hard years of hunger, typhus, and general
misery, and now she had the home ready for him as if it were only
yesterday that he had set off.

That night, the four Eliasberg daughters rushed to the door to greet
the special friend whose bald head they had decorated with colored pencils
before the war. They may have changed outwardly in those four years—
Helena was now eighteen, Irena sixteen, Anna thirteen, and Marta nine—
but inwardly their feelings toward Korczak had remained the same. Expecting that he would sweep them up into his arms in his old playful way
when he entered the hallway, the two oldest girls, Helena and Irena,
were shocked when he addressed them formally as Miss, with a casual
handshake, and paid little attention to them for the rest of the evening.
"We didn't interest him anymore," Helena would recall. They were no
longer children. The sisters wept that night.

On November 11, 1918, the orphans, together with all their neighbors, hung out red-and-white Polish flags in honor of independence. They
listened as Korczak told the most magical of his tales: after 120 years of
subjugation, their country was free again, and Jozef Pilsudski, the tireless
patriot who had been working for independence all his life, was the new
head of state.

Knowing that some parents would not bother to explain all that was
happening to their children, Korczak began writing a column, "What's
Going On in the World?" for *In the Sunshine*. He wanted children to
understand what independence meant, how their country had been gob-
bled up by three greedy neighbors, what was being decided at the Peace
Conference in Paris, how elections were held and a parliament formed.
He brought world politics down to size: "It is nice to have your own
drawer or closet, for then it is absolutely your own, and a place where
no one else has the right to poke without your permission. It is nice to
have your own garden plot, your own room, and a house where you live
with your family, and where no one bothers you. But, unfortunately,

someone stronger passes by, and enters, and takes away your things, and dirties the room, and will not listen to you."

It was the first journalism of its kind for children. The column became so popular that educators soon were reading it to learn how to explain current events creatively to their young students. But no one knew better than Korczak that he couldn't give children all the answers to what was occurring, because putting Poland together again was not unlike trying to reassemble Humpty Dumpty. Just as the Poles had struggled *for* independence for more than a century, they now had to struggle *with* it. Not only had their country been ravaged by the war—the industrial plants were in ruins, half the fields lay uncultivated, inflation was even worse than during the war—but it was left severely fragmented by its former partitions. There were four different legal systems, six different currencies, and three different railroads whose separate tracks symbolized the connections that had still to be made if the country was to be truly united.

Only the joy of belonging to themselves again kept the Poles from sinking into despair over the massive rebuilding that lay ahead. Hunger and cold stared at Korczak from every corner of the orphanage. No one would give him credit, and there was no money. American relief programs, which distributed Hoover care packages, rice, flour, and cotton fabric, were keeping institutions like his afloat. But they were not enough.

And then a miracle. Winter had done no more than "place one cautious foot" on their doorstep when the miners' union from the colliery—"God bless their dirty hands and crystal-clear souls"—donated a whole train car filled with coal. This generosity—"enough to move a stone to tears"—was especially touching when he realized how poor the miners were themselves. Suddenly he felt rich: coal, because of its scarcity, was regarded as "black gold." The only obstacle was that it had to be carted away from the train station at once, and he had no means of transportation.

More miracles. Everyone in the neighborhood became involved. Horse-drawn wagons sprang out of nowhere, and the coal began to find its way into their empty basement. Children carted it off in wheelbarrows, baskets, and buckets. Even the littlest ones carried lumps "as large as their heads."

The baker down the street, hearing of their good fortune, sent over fresh bread that could be paid for with the "black gold." One of the orphans, whose legs were deformed by rickets, ate almost half a loaf himself while carrying the "precious cargo," covering the rest of it with coal dust. He raced back to the train station shouting, "I can carry a hundred baskets now!" There were no more baskets, and he was not strong enough to carry a bucket, so Korczak gave him the only empty container in sight—a chamber pot. As he watched the boy stumbling along gaily, Korczak made a mental note to get cod-liver oil somehow and straighten out those legs.

Shortly after Maryna Falska returned to Warsaw in early 1919, the Minister of Education asked Korczak to set up an orphanage for the children of Polish workers in the small town of Pruszkow, about fifteen miles to the south. He immediately thought of Maryna as the perfect director for it, and she didn't hesitate to accept the challenge of running another institution like the one in Kiev, modeled on his ideas.

They managed to find a small three-story apartment building near a government school in Pruszkow, but there wasn't enough money to furnish, let alone buy it—nor was there a sympathetic philanthropic group like the Orphans Aid Society that supported the Krochmalna Street home.

Together they hit upon the ingenious plan of seeking help from the trade unions, many of whose members, killed in the war, had left orphaned children behind. The workers were so enthusiastic about the project that they not only filled the slotted donation cans supplied to every shop and factory but chose the first fifty children to enter the orphanage. They also took charge of furnishing the home: one knew where the orphanage could borrow beds; another had access to tables and chairs; still a third, to kitchen equipment. A few even queued up for bread and potatoes and managed to find surplus flour.

The children moved into the orphanage one crisp November day that year. Our Home, as it was called, was cramped compared to the orphanage on Krochmalna, its rooms so tiny that there was not even space to walk around the beds in the dormitories, yet the children had never seen anything so grand. Never having had running water, they didn't miss it, and they took great pride in their one wooden toilet on the first floor, not knowing that it was supposed to flush. The small bathroom was better than the foul-smelling outhouses they were used to, and cleaning it was worth extra work points.

In spite of the unions' help, it was hard to put food on the table. Maryna tried to keep small squares of bread in a bowl in the kitchen for snacks; one boy kissed the bread each time he took a piece. Country people brought sacks of potatoes, but never enough. Much of Maryna's energy was consumed finding coal and potatoes at a price they could afford. "We didn't have a savings account yet," she would write later. "Not even money for toys, or colored paper to make them with." But Maryna Falska was indefatigable. Her years in Kiev had taught her how to deal with contractors and haggle with workmen over such necessary services as window repairs. She went personally to each shop to ask for inexpensive food, and carried the sacks home on her back. She dressed the children in old clothes sent from America.

Even if the Pruszkow home had room for an extra bed—and it didn't—Korczak would not have had time to stay overnight. Besides attending to his children on Krochmalna, he was busy advising welfare groups on how to set up new institutions for the thousands of war orphans roaming the streets.

He was also writing cautionary newspaper articles for adults in the *Polish Gazette*. Poland was free, but the skeptical doctor had seen too much suffering and bloodshed by now not to feel some anxiety about the future. The November 11 armistice had brought peace but not an end to the fighting. With chaos prevailing in the eastern regions after the collapse of the partitioning powers, the Jews frequently fell prey to riots, massacres, and even pogroms by some units of the Polish Army—especially those under General Haller—and armed civilian gangs. And while the Allies at Versailles debated Poland's demand that she return to the map of Europe in her ample pre-partition shape, Jozef Pilsudski was trying to contend with History in his own way. There were border clashes with the Soviets in the east, with the Ukrainians in Galicia, as well as with the Czechs and the Germans over territorial rights. Could human nature be trusted to make the world better? Korczak wondered. He had warned his readers to make lasting peace one of their national goals.

"History may be the Ruler of Nations, but she is a dishonest teacher, a bad educator, who only pretends to be orderly and making progress," he began one article. "You have to rule History rather than let her rule you; otherwise, there will be more of the same—wars and violence. The sword, poison gas, and the Devil knows what else they'll think up. For there's no trick to drawing blood—drill a little hole, and it flows by itself. Any scribbler can draw a whole basinful. It's not even enough to write articles—one has to build, to plow, to reforest; one must, my dears, feed the orphans, educate them; one must . . . need I go on!"

Of course, he did go on, because he still hadn't come to his main point: whatever it was that Polish citizens still wanted, whether a seaport or a different border, they had to learn to settle disputes by lawful means. "We are responsible to the children for the wars that have been and will be, and that tens of thousands of them have died in this past one. And so it isn't time yet to celebrate the Feast of Spring. It is still All Soul's Day—the Day of the Martyred Child."

"Remember," he warned them, "Poland is not being built for only twenty years."

Having called for national conscription in March of 1919, Marshal Pilsudski was building up his armed forces in earnest. Convinced that Poland, sandwiched as she was between Russia and Germany, had to be strong, he was bent on setting up a federated Polish-Lithuanian commonwealth, allied with the Ukraine and other small nations. This plan was threatened when the Soviets took advantage of the turmoil in Eastern Europe to absorb new territories into their Communist empire. In April, Pilsudski sent his troops to recapture Vilna, his beloved native city and the ancient capital of Lithuania, from the Soviets. Meeting little resistance, the Polish Army continued eastward, taking Minsk and other large cities during the summer of 1919, intensifying what would become known as the Polish–Soviet War.

Toward the end of the year, Korczak received orders to serve as a reserve major in the new Polish Army. Again he had to make a round of goodbyes, but at least this time he didn't have to travel further than a military hospital for infectious diseases in Lodz, a manufacturing town to the southwest of Warsaw. After a short period, he was transferred to a similar institution in Warsaw.

Whenever he left the infectious ward for his own quarters or to visit his mother and the orphans, Korczak scrupulously washed up and changed his clothes. But late one afternoon, after yielding to the pressures of members of the family of a sick lieutenant who insisted they had been unfairly quarantined along with the patient, he signed release papers for them and did not take the precaution of washing.

Not long afterward, Korczak woke up seeing double. He looked at the table—two tables. Two lamps, two desk chairs. He was drenched with perspiration. His body burned with fever. His head was pounding. He knew the symptoms—typhus. The lieutenant's family must have been infected after all. Korczak's mother insisted that he stay with her so that she could nurse him. For days he was delirious, unaware that his mother had caught his typhus. She died before he regained his senses. Her last words were a request that her body be carried out the back door so that her son would not be disturbed.

When Korczak learned that his mother was dead, he was almost mad with grief. He felt he had killed her. Not deliberately, but through carelessness. His father had been right—he was "a fool and a clod." Only this time his mother was the innocent victim. Havelock Ellis, whose mother died from scarlet fever in similar circumstances, was able to rationalize to himself: "She could never have chosen a happier way to go, *in harness* as she wished, nursing her own child." But though the same could have been said of Korczak's mother, he found no such solace. After his father's death, he had felt suicidal, and now once again he considered this solution.

"When my sister returned from Paris, I suggested to her that we should commit suicide together," he would write. "I could find no place for myself in the world or in life."

His sister seems to have been less than enthusiastic about the idea. "The plan did not materialize because of differences of opinion" was Korczak's sardonic explanation. But he began a lifelong practice of keeping mercuric chloride and morphine pills in the back of his drawer, taking them out only when he visited his mother's grave (which was situated in a remote area of the Jewish cemetery allocated for typhus victims). It is possible that he swallowed some of the pills during one of those early visits. "There is nothing more loathsome than an unsuccessful attempt at suicide," he wrote. "This sort of plan should be fully worked out so as to insure certainty of success." And with a gallows humor that has the ring of authenticity, he concluded: "Having once tried the delights and joys of committing suicide, a man lives to an advanced old age without the temptation to try again."

While he was feverish with typhus, he had had a "vision." He was giving a speech about war and hunger, orphans and misery, somewhere in America, with an interpreter rapidly translating his Polish into English. Suddenly his voice broke. There was silence. From deep in the hall, a cry was heard. Regina, an orphan who had married and come to America, was running toward him. She halted in front of the dais, throwing her watch onto the platform, as she cried out: "For you—everything!" There followed a shower of banknotes, gold, and silver. People began tossing their rings, bracelets, necklaces. Boys from the Orphans Home ran onto the stage and stuffed everything into mattresses. The audience, deeply moved, cheered, applauded, wept.

Hovering close to death, Korczak was still intent on bringing his orphans "unlimited material wealth." Even then, he knew that he was not free to commit suicide as long as there were children who needed him.

"If I kept postponing my otherwise fully thought-out plan," he would write, "it was because always, at the very last minute, some new daydream would sweep me away and could not be abandoned before I worked it out in detail. These were something like themes for short stories. I put them under a common heading, *Strange Happenings*."

These "daydreams" which Korczak would work on when in stress before falling asleep were like stories in process. When he was most powerless, they gave him power. In one, he had found the magic word, and was the Ruler of Light. But lest taking on such authority was a form of hubris, he would fall asleep agonizing: "Why me? There are others younger, wiser, more suitable for this mission. Let me remain with the children. I am not a sociologist. I'll mess everything up, disgrace both the enterprise and myself."

When even the daydreams didn't work, he turned to God. He had never been an observant Jew, but he had always been a man of faith. The God that Korczak believed in, like Spinoza's, was a free spirit, a mystical force that flowed through the universe. "It does not surprise me that God has no beginning and no end, because I see Him as unending Harmony," he had once written. "The stars, the very universe, inform me about the existence of the Creator, not the priest. I have found my own kind of faith: there is a God. The human mind cannot know what He is like. Behave decently, and do good. Pray, not to ask things of God but so as not to forget Him, because one should see Him everywhere."

Now, in his grief, Korczak felt abandoned by this God he had trusted. Unable to grasp the meaning of his mother's death, or why she had to die rather than him, he composed a book of prayers, *Alone with God: Prayers for Those Who Don't Pray*, in which he poured out his sorrow and sense of abandonment. As Martin Buber has pointed out, people who talk with God in this intimate way are very close to Him.

There are eighteen prayers in all, many written for others in need. A new mother asks God not to take away the baby He has given her; a boy bargains with God—"I'll pray if you make my father give me a bicycle"; an old man is resigned to moving on to the next mystery; an artist suggests that God was drunk when He created him (one cannot create an artist while sober); an educator asks nothing for himself, only that his children will have God's guidance and blessing. While each of the prayers is in the colloquial language of the person addressing God, one can hear the personal voice of Janusz Korczak. In the dedication to the book the young Henryk Goldszmit speaks through the author. "To My Beloved Mama and Papa: We have parted for a moment in order to meet again . . . From the stones of your anguish and pain and those of our ancestors, I want to raise a high tower to shelter others. Thank you for teaching me to hear the whispers of the dead and the living. Thank you for helping me learn the secret of life in the beautiful hour of death."

Poland was in desperate need of a special prayer in the summer of 1920 when the Russians went on the offensive in the Polish-Soviet war. Forced to evacuate Kiev, which it had taken in May, the Polish Army was pursued by the notorious General Mikhail Tukhachevsky back across its own borders right up to the suburbs of Warsaw. It looked to all the world as if Poland was doomed.

However, Jozef Pilsudski, who until then had led a charmed life—surviving Siberia, escaping from Imperial Russian insane asylums and prisons, and even pulling off a daring raid on the Czar's train, relieving it of its cache of gold and silver—had a few more lives left. When the Bolsheviks were at the gates of Warsaw on August 16, 1920, Pilsudski outwitted them by severing their rear lines in a counterattack from the south, and within two days completely encircling them. Taken by surprise in what has come to be known as the Miracle of the Vistula, the Russians fled in total confusion back to their own borders.

Poland was saved. Warsaw was spared. "Filthy, torn, neglected, and careless Warsaw, whose heart is in her Old Town and whose brain is in each stone and tile, in each little urchin selling newspapers," Korczak was to write. Never had his city seemed more dear. "Warsaw is mine, and I am hers. We are one. Together with her, I have rejoiced and I have grieved. Her weather has been my weather, her rain, her soil mine as well. We grew up together . . . Warsaw has been my workshop; here are my landmarks and my graves."

13

The Spirit of
King Matt

Worth the end of the Polish–Soviet War, Korczak was demobilized and reunited with his own little "urchins." The distance he had traveled from them had not been far, but he felt very changed. He, too, was an orphan now. "Children imagine that a grownup doesn't need a mother," he would tell his young readers. "Oh, how many times does a grownup long for his mother or father, who, it seems to him, are the only ones who would listen to him and, if need be, forgive him and feel sorry for him."

In the past, discipline had sustained him, and now Korczak used that strength to go on with his life. He moved into the garret room on the fourth floor of the orphanage on Krochmalna, and lived like a monk in his book-lined room, writing on his father's massive oak desk, sleeping on a narrow iron cot, and visited by wild sparrows who came in through a transom in the window, and an "introverted" female mouse named Penetration who lived under the cupboard. The death of his mother and the rebirth of his nation seem to have released King Matt, the imaginary child slumbering inside him. By day he was the doctor ministering to a hundred Jewish orphans and a hundred Polish ones, but at night, when he climbed up to the attic, he was the writer, designing a fantasy kingdom surrounded—as Poland had been—by three greedy neighbors.

"And so this is what happened," begins *King Matt the First*, a timeless parable about a child-king who dreams of creating a utopian society with just laws for both children and adults. It is a daydream, like the one

Henryk Goldszmit had when he was young and wanted to reform the world. So deeply did Korczak identify with this young king who (like his creator) would not live to see his dreams come true that he used his own picture as a child for the frontispiece of the book, with this explanation to his young readers:

When I was the little boy you see in the photograph, I wanted to do all the things that are in this book. But I forgot to, and now I'm old. I no longer have the time or the strength to go to war or travel to the land of the cannibals. I have included this photograph because it's important what I looked like when I truly wanted to be a king, and not when I was writing about King Matt. I think it's better to show pictures of what kings, travelers, and writers looked like before they grew up, or grew old, because otherwise it might seem that they knew everything from the start and were never young themselves. And then children will think they can't be statesmen, travelers, and writers, which wouldn't be true.

The child in the photograph—about ten years old—is the age of most of Korczak's fictional heroes. Sitting stiffly on a bench next to a potted plant, in a long Lord Fauntleroy jacket and high stiff white collar with a bow, he looks, not at us, but out past the camera into some distant space of his own—a far gaze that Korczak would take with him through life. He is both there and not there. One hand rests lightly in his lap; the other grips the corner of the bench as if the boy is waiting to take off the moment the signal comes.

This is the same boy who used to go on excursions with his family to the seventeenth-century palace of Wilanow, where the Polish kings summered during the golden age when Poland was a proud, independent kingdom whose borders stretched from the Baltic to the Black Sea, and almost to the gates of Moscow. Transported not merely beyond the city limits of Warsaw, but beyond time itself, he could feel the "cold beauty" of the stately furniture in the palace and the "ghostly presence" of the kings moving about. Perhaps it was then that he and King Matt had merged into one.

King Matt the First has been called Korczak's *Emile*. Opening with the death of the old king, which follows on the death of the queen, it traces Matt's moral development from an innocent, trusting orphan who can neither read nor write, to an idealistic young reformer who must learn the disparity between dream and reality before he can rule either his country or himself. Though it can be read as a romance about a high-spirited young king's adventures, the book is essentially a philosophical treatise about spiritual and worldly power.

Matt's sudden ascension to the throne when his father dies (not unlike Henryk's sense of being catapulted into adulthood by the death of his father) is meant to be no less confusing than Alice's fall into Wonderland: Matt is confronted by a bewildering array of grownups rushing about in much the same dither as the White Rabbit, and by a society not too different from the infant Polish Republic, where rival parties proliferated, cabinets came and went, and governments rose and fell in dizzying succession. As Matt tries to make sense of it all, the author cannot resist poking fun at the muddle to be found at the center of official circles. His satirical eye misses nothing. The young ruler learns that diplomacy means lying all the time so that your enemy has no idea of what you're really doing, and that a cabinet crisis is nothing more than a fight among the ministers. Though he lives in a mythic kingdom, Matt struggles with bitter reality, confronting the same questions that plagued Marshal Pilsudski and the ministers of the newly elected government of Poland: How do you raise money to repair trains, build factories, replace broken windows, supply an army? How do you set up schools, medical facilities, and adequate social services?

Even more important for Matt, who is, after all, a child, are questions that involve the welfare of children. How do you give them self-respect and teach them to be free? How do you fight the poverty, injustice, disease, and hunger that affect them? When Matt becomes ill trying to remedy everything at once, his old family doctor tells him that people have been trying to solve these problems for a long time, but as yet no one has come up with a lasting solution.

Korczak sends Matt off to fight incognito as a plain soldier with his friend Felek, a palace guard's son, when his country is invaded. Matt experiences the harsh reality of war. "Oh, how hard it is to be a king and fight a war," Matt tells himself. "All I thought about was leaving the capital on a white horse while people threw flowers at me. I wasn't thinking how many people would be killed."

Korczak also has Matt travel to the land of the cannibals, where he learns that savages (although certainly not noble) can be in some respects more civilized than so-called civilized people. The cannibal king, Bum Drum, and his daughter, Klu Klu, a dauntless tomboy, prove to be Matt's most loyal friends.

The author is ironic but not cynical. Matt never becomes bitter, just a little sad when things go wrong, like the Sad King in one of the three bordering countries. The Sad King, who plays his violin as if the very strings were weeping, sounds much like the old family doctor (who in turn sounds much like Janusz Korczak) as he shows Matt his parliament—"a bit like a theater, and a bit like a church"—and relates the dark side of being a reformer:

> Listen, Matt. My grandfather gave his people freedom, but it didn't turn out well. He was assassinated. And people ended up even more unhappy than before. My father built a great monument to freedom . . . but what does that matter when there are still wars, still poor people, still unhappy people. I ordered that great parliament building built. And nothing changed. Everything's still the same.

Still, the Sad King doesn't want to discourage his little guest. "You know, Matt, we always did the wrong thing by making reforms for adults. Try doing it with children, maybe you'll succeed."

The Sad King's idea that children might behave more wisely than adults if given a voice in government is a romantic one, but the side of Korczak that is the old doctor knows that one needs experience to do anything successfully—the one thing children do not have. Deciding to make himself king of the children, Matt builds a parliament for them, as well as one for adults. The two buildings are identical except that in the children's parliament the door handles and chairs are lower, as are the windows, so that the delegates can look outside when they get bored. However, it takes only a few sessions of their bickering and fighting for Matt to discover that children can behave as unreasonably as grownups.

A journalist, in reality a spy for one of the three kings (and meant to represent the treacherous adult world), brings about the downfall of Matt's kingdom by persuading Felek, who has become the Prime Minister of Children, that his young constituents can do things better than adults. The Children's Parliament orders all the grownups to go back to school while children take over their jobs. This leads to much merry confusion, but eventually to the destruction of all the vital forces of the land: the trains stop running, the phones are out of order, shops are closed, factories shut down, military supplies depleted. Taking advantage of the internal chaos, the enemy king invades Matt's country.

By the time Matt sends the adults back to work and the children back to school and rebuilds his armed forces, it is too late, but Matt is determined to go down fighting. "Victory or death!" he tells his followers. When they are overrun, he consoles Klu Klu, who, along with Felek and a few others, has retreated with him for a last stand in the lion house: "Don't cry, we'll die a beautiful death." He is in control of his own destiny as long as he can choose the spirit with which he will die. Even this is denied him when he is captured with sleeping gas and wakes to find himself in prison. Told that he has been sentenced to death by firing squad, he does not know that the Sad King has managed to convince the other two kings to grant him a last-minute reprieve.

The book ends with Matt being marched in gold chains down the streets of his kingdom to his supposed execution, an eerie foreshadowing of what was to happen to his creator: "It was a beautiful day. The sun was shining. Everyone had come out to see their king one last time. Many people had tears in their eyes. But Matt did not see those tears . . . He was looking at the sky, the sun."

Matt holds his head high to prove that he has more strength of character than the enemy. "True heroes show themselves in adversity," he tells himself. He refuses the blindfold: to die "beautifully" is still his only wish. But in these last moments he can't help being curious about the kind of funeral he will be given. Instead of expressing gratitude, Matt is furious when he is granted the reprieve and sentenced to exile on a desert island, much like Napoleon before him.

The second volume, *King Matt on the Desert Island,* is a more sober book than the first, concerned with Matt's spiritual development. He escapes from the train taking him to the ship, but decides to go to the island voluntarily when he realizes that war may break out because of him. "I am willing to go because this time it will not be as a prisoner or a slave, but of my own free will," Matt declares, further expressing Korczak's philosophy that one is not a prisoner if one chooses one's own way.

Alone on the island except for his guards, his canary, and his mother's picture, Matt now has time to organize his jumbled thoughts and discipline his mind. His favorite guard Walenty sounds much like the original Walenty as he shuffles about with such asides as "Life is bitter." Matt thinks about both life and death while throwing stones into the sea. After his canary dies, he digs a grave under a palm tree on a hilltop, and ponders whether to place a wooden cross on it, much as Henryk Goldszmit once did. He then digs two more graves for his mother and father, whom he plans to move there. Sometimes he rows out to the lighthouse to play with Ala and Alo, two small orphans rescued by the one-armed lighthouse keeper when they were cast ashore during a storm. Like his author, Matt finds solace in the company of children.

One day, while roaming about the center of his island, Matt discovers a stone tower on top of a hill. He watches as one of the stones moves, revealing seven ladders inside, one on top of the other, each with seven rungs that become increasingly wider spaced. A man wearing a long gray robe tied with a rope slides, as if flying, down the ladder. This "old wanderer with a long beard" looks at him even more sadly than the Sad King. Matt doesn't know how the thought comes to him: "This is a reformer who did not succeed."

Soon after Walenty is replaced by a sadistic guard, Matt escapes from the island with the same free spirit with which he came. He returns to his palace just long enough to persuade the young king to call off the war, even thanking this former enemy for giving him an opportunity to experience exile and to train his will. He then gives up his throne so that his people may elect a president in his place.

Much like his author, Matt renounces wealth for a modest life of service to others. He takes a job in a factory—to show his solidarity with the poor exploited workers and shame the factory owners into providing better conditions. At night, he either goes to school or sits in his attic room writing fairy tales for children. His peaceful regimen is interrupted by Felek, who, demoralized by his loss of power, appears unkempt and surly at Matt's door. Matt takes him in and arranges a job at the factory for him. But when Matt tries to break up a fight Felek has started with the factory manager, he is accidentally pushed into one of the machines. Mortally wounded, he survives long enough to forgive Felek and ask him to return with Klu Klu to her country and work for a better world.

Matt is buried alongside his canary in the cemetery on the high hill on his desert island. Ala and Alo bring flowers, and wild canaries sing over his grave. Like a true Polish romantic hero, torn between a life of action and one of spiritual transformation, Matt has won morally, even though he dies, for he has inspired others to continue his struggle.

King Matt the First is the story of "the eternal tragedy of every noble reformer." Reading the book today, one realizes that the sad and skeptical author had no illusion that he would fare much better than Matt, but the book takes on an added dimension of prophetic power now that Korczak's life has come to represent a victory of the spirit. Yet, in spite of its deep pessimism, one can also see Matt's story as a human comedy, played with humor, warmth, and compassion for the human condition.

14

One Hundred Children

A hundred children, a hundred individuals who are people— not people-to-be, not people of tomorrow, but people now, right now—today.

—*How to Love a Child*

"Why didn't King Matt form a children's army?" a boy asked one night when Korczak gave a trial reading in the dormitory.

"Because if he couldn't prevent children from breaking the palace windows with their balls, how could he hope to control them at the battlefront?" Korczak replied.

The children laughed. Not a week passed but some child managed to hit or throw a ball over the orphanage wall, right through the window of the silverware factory next door. To make matters worse, the mean German owner refused to return the balls.

"Why is Princess Klu Klu black instead of white, like Matt?" a girl wanted to know.

Korczak paused to think about that. The orphans had never seen a black person. In all of Warsaw at that time there was only one: the chauffeur of a diplomat, who had brought the man back from his last post abroad.

"Children are black in Klu Klu's part of the world," he told them, "just as the children I saw in China were yellow. But it doesn't make any difference what color you are. Klu Klu was much smarter than a lot of the white children in Matt's kingdom—and she remained faithful to him when he was attacked by others."

Whenever he came to the end of a chapter, the educator would stop reading, in spite of the children's pleas that he continue. Then the writer would return to his garret room with the manuscript to revise whatever hadn't held their interest, or to work on a new book. Soon the orphans would hear about little Jack, an American boy who set up a co-op store in his school. Jack's empire was much smaller than Matt's, but he, too, had to learn about adult affairs such as handling money and keeping accounts. When his business went bankrupt as a result of the incompetency of others, Jack also emerged much richer: he had gained self-knowledge—the most important treasure of all.

Before he retired, Korczak liked to prowl about the dormitories taking notes on the children's sleeping postures for the book he planned to write on children and the night. Sometimes Stefa joined him, but life was no longer as it had been before the war when the two of them attended the orphans sixteen hours a day. Stefa was still the stolid, all-responsible mother on duty at all times, but he had a complicated schedule that included working with Maryna Falska in Pruszkow and part-time lecturing at two pedagogical institutes, as well as his professional and creative writing.

There were one hundred and six beds in the home, fifty allocated for boys, fifty-six for girls. Children were admitted at the age of seven and stayed until the completion of elementary school, which was free and compulsory through the seventh grade. The orphans went to separate government schools for Jewish children (known as "Sabbath schools," because the Sabbath was observed on Saturday rather than Sunday). Lessons were given in Polish and, except for courses on the Jewish religion, the curriculum was much the same as in the Polish schools.

Poland may have been independent, but there was still no shortage of needy Jewish children. Although the Jews were granted equal rights in the constitution and were protected by a minorities treaty, they were affected, as were all Poles, by the depressed economy of their war-devastated country. It didn't help that the government, intent on creating a Polish middle class, had a protectionist policy toward native Polish enterprises and merchants. Barred, in effect, from employment with the civil service, post office, and railways, tens of thousands of impoverished Jewish workers found themselves competing for jobs with impoverished Poles who had migrated from the countryside—a situation that did not enhance Polish-Jewish relations.

Stella Eliasberg was moved to tears when she went with other members of the admissions committee of the Orphans Home to check the applications of destitute Jewish families. She never got used to the dank basement hovels where three or four pale sickly children would be lying on one filthy straw mat, with nothing but thin rags to wear in the coldest winter. She always felt guilty because all the children needed care to survive and they could choose only one from a family.

Even after a child was approved for the home, he or she had to be checked by a team of psychologists who were under Korczak's instructions to eliminate the retarded or emotionally disturbed. Like a gardener who is careful "to avoid weeds that will choke his flowers," Korczak was unwilling to take a chance on a child who might prove detrimental to the community. If his own personal anxieties about mental illness influenced his position, he took care to camouflage them by calling forth those unsolved mysteries of heredity that were then occupying scientists in the eugenics movement. It came down to the familiar nature-versus-nurture question: Was one doomed by bad genes, or could favorable environmental conditions save one from what was genetically determined? Was a child nervous because he had inherited this trait from his parents, or because he was brought up by them? Why did sound parents have feeble offspring, and, conversely, why did extraordinary children spring from ordinary stock? And—this was a question that child-rights advocate Ellen Key had been asking in Sweden—why didn't society require licenses for people to have children, just as it required licenses for soft-drink stands? "We need to stop breeding children thoughtlessly," he wrote. "We need to think about them before they are born. We need to start creating them."

The psychologists hired by the Orphans Aid Society were in the uncomfortable position of possibly sealing the fate of a slightly retarded child. Helena Merenholtz remembers that she and her colleagues were sometimes so moved by a child's plight that they falsified their findings: "I thought that with good food and an improved environment, a boy or girl might catch up in development." Sometimes the ruse worked, but if Korczak became suspicious, as he often did, he would have the child examined by Madame Maria Grzegorzewska, at whose Institute for Special Children he lectured twice a week. More often than not, she, in turn, would inform him that the child was perfectly normal. It became a private joke between them for him to say: "It's impossible to receive a degree in idiocy from your institute."

Although the orphanage received a fixed amount of state assistance, it was still primarily dependent on its philanthropists, some of whom infuriated Korczak by asking that a particular child be admitted. "The only right a benefactor has is the right to give money," he would say. He told the children that although some wealthy people genuinely care about the welfare of orphans, most give donations for less noble reasons: "One dies, so he doesn't need the money anymore. Another wants to find favor with God. A third wants to talk to everyone about how virtuous he is." He was adamant that the children not accept candy or run errands under any circumstances.

Korczak laid down precise rules about when the philanthropists could visit. They had to leave their carriages (and later their limousines) down the street where the children couldn't see them. Those benefactors who dropped by unannounced in their formal jackets and high stiff collars to have a look at the famous pedagogue they were supporting were taken aback by the casual green smocks that were Korczak's usual attire. In a period when it was fashionable to flaunt long titles and affect pompous airs, Korczak mocked society by not taking on any of its affectations— which meant not being a proper adult by its standards.

The children were delighted when some of the philanthropists actually mistook the doctor for the janitor. One particularly haughty man asked him to get his coat, and pressed a coin into his hand upon receiving it. Another philanthropist, encountering him in the courtyard, demanded: "Where can I find Dr. Korczak?" Whereupon Korczak went inside, took off his smock, put on his jacket, and returned with his hand extended: "Yes, what can I do for you?" The caller was so embarrassed that he fled without a word.

Some philanthropists considered such antics, no less than his refusal to mix socially, a form of arrogance. But most of them excused Korczak because they could sense that he was devoid of any personal need for power or glory. His closest friends, like the Eliasbergs and the Mortkowiczes, were amused by his pranks and understood that, rather than being aloof, their idiosyncratic friend was actually shy.

New children were admitted at two o'clock on Friday afternoons whenever there was a vacancy. Most of them were seven years of age, but they shared the background and apprehensions of nine-year-old Israel Zyngman, a streetwise ruffian whose widowed mother was unable to stop him from brawling with other boys, hanging on to the back of trams, and cutting school. When his mother informed him that he was going to live at a home run by the famous Dr. Goldszmit, his buddies were sure he was going to prison. "If you see a cop and iron bars on the door, get the hell out as fast as you can," they warned.

He still remembers the day he arrived at 92 Krochmalna with his mother:

Sure enough, there was an iron gate, but no policeman. We walked into the courtyard and a large woman dressed all in black comes toward us. I looked at her face. It had a big black mole. Suddenly I turned from a tough guy into a little boy hiding behind his mother. This woman, Miss Stefa, asked my mother, "What's his name?"

"Israel."

"That's not good," Stefa said curtly. "We already have two Israels. We'll call him Shiya."

That really threw me. I had got into a lot of street fights over my name, and now this woman comes along and wants to take it away. I already hated her. I thought, This place isn't for me. I won't go inside.

Then something unexpected happened. While my mother was trying to push me along in front of her, my cap came off.

Stefa shrieked, "He still has his hair! You didn't shave his head?"

My mother looked confused. "I wasn't told to . . ."

I remembered that my buddies told me that if they want to shave your head, that means you're going to jail.

"I'm getting out of here!" I cried, and tried to run away, but my mother grabbed me by the coattail.

"You'll like it here," she pleaded. "Everybody likes Dr. Goldszmit."

"So where is he?" I growled.

"I don't have time to waste," Stefa said impatiently. She motioned to a boy who was standing nearby to look after me, and went off.

The kid tried to convince me to go into the orphanage, but I refused until my mother said she'd come with me. I followed him reluctantly through the front door into the large dining hall, where a lot was going on. But I just stood in the entrance, holding on to my mother for dear life. A lot of kids made wisecracks as they passed. I didn't like their attitude. I was sure there was something fishy about this place.

Then a man in a long smock came up to us and said he was Dr. Goldszmit. He didn't look so special. To me he was an old man, no big deal. Just like anybody else. He told my mother that he had been expecting us, and then, looking at me, he said, "I've heard about you."

I turned to my mother. "What the hell did he hear about me?"

He said that he heard I was being difficult, and had come to see for himself. Then he began talking to my mother without looking at me. But he was stroking my head tenderly while he spoke. That made a big impression on me. His skin was soft, and the warmth of his hand felt good to me.

"Follow me," he said. He led us to a small upstairs room, and said, "Take off your clothes." When I didn't move, he repeated, "Please take your things off."

I still didn't move. I felt cold when he lifted my shirt up, but I didn't stop him. He put his ear to my chest.

"What was going on in the courtyard?" he asked.

I told him the problem with my name.

"What's your name?"

"Israel. But that woman wanted to change it to Shiya. I know a guy on the street, a real idiot, with that name. Everyone will laugh at me."

The doctor said, "We also have a problem because two other boys here have the name Israel. If one of them does anything bad, how can we know who it was?"

My mother chimed in. "Call him Sami."

"No, he wouldn't like that." And then the doctor said to me, "How about Stasiek for a nickname here?"

I really liked that—a saint's name. "What, me have a name like that?" I said.

"Yes, you."

By that act he became my best friend. I agreed that my mother could go.

"What else happened out there?" he asked.

I told him about my hair. "All kids walk around with hair. Why shouldn't I?"

"If you want to keep your hair, keep it," he replied. "But don't come to me with complaints."

"What kind of complaints?"

"You'll be different from the other new kids. They'll call you Stash the Goat, or Stash the Rooster. But don't come to me about it."

I was dumbfounded.

He took a piece of candy out of his pocket and offered it to me. I didn't want to take it. I was more concerned about my hair. I was afraid and unnerved. "Where's the barbershop?" I asked suspiciously.

"What do you need a barbershop for?" he snapped playfully.

I realized he was the barber.

"Okay, you can take off my hair," I said.

"Sit down," he told me.

He picked up a pair of clippers, and in a flash I had no more hair.

The first experience of hair cropping was more traumatic for the girls, especially those with beautiful long braids, but it was considered a necessary hygienic measure to prevent the spread of lice, the carrier of typhus, into the home. After the initial cut, children who kept themselves clean were allowed to wear their hair long.

Sara Kramer, whose father had just died, remembers her first talk with the "barber":

"How do you feel about not having a father?" he asked me.

"Sad," I whispered.

"My daughter," he said softly, and put his hand on my shoulder. Then he told me he would have to cut my hair.

"How will my mother recognize me?" I cried.

He explained that it had to be done for the sake of cleanliness, to make sure there were no lice.

Sara, like most of the new children, found that having her hair cut wasn't too stressful because Korczak made a game of it, as he did of everything. Sometimes he would pretend the first strip was Krochmalna, or an animal, or the letters of the child's name. Though the technique was intended to make the children relax, Korczak regarded the process as seriously as he would a medical procedure. He kept his instruments as clean and sharp as a surgeon's, and insisted that anyone applying to work in a boarding home should be tested in dismantling and cleaning clippers. He brought the same dedication to hair washing: "It is better to massage with just the thumb, over the forehead, behind the ears, and at the back of the head," he told his students. "That's where dirty soap collects, dries out, and causes fungus infection.

Stasiek and Sara were also weighed on their first day, as they would be every week from then on, the results meticulously recorded on their personal weight charts. Korczak valued the scale as a "sensible, level-headed, unbiased informant and advisor that does not tell lies." Weighing a child was not only a scientific procedure but also a source of pleasure, enabling him to "feel the beauty of growth." It was a time for chatting and joking—one boy even brought his plant to be weighed—but it had the fringe benefit of allowing one to look into the child's eyes, peer down his throat, put an ear or wooden stethoscope to his chest, smell his skin, and sense his mood. Sluggishness in an active child could be the harbinger of an illness.

Nothing concerning children was too trivial for Korczak's attention. He studied their dirty handkerchiefs, kept track of lost gloves (there was the danger of frostbite), and made a game out of teaching them how to shine their shoes. Speaking directly to the shoes, he explained why he was putting on a particular kind of polish, why he was using a brush, and why he needed the shoes' cooperation. Before he was finished, the child was eager to take over the job himself.

After their Friday afternoon bath, newcomers like Stasiek and Sara received clothes marked with the number that would identify all their possessions. The quality of the garments they were given subsequently would depend upon how they took care of them. While Korczak was away at war, Stefa had initiated a dubious-cleanliness scale ranging from one to four. Neat children received the best clothes that had been donated to the home or made in the sewing room, while the careless ones who always tore or stained their clothes were allotted outfits made of coarse material. Doba Borbergow still remembers the thrill she felt on receiving the first dress, undershirt, and underpants she had ever owned: "On Saturday afternoon when I went to visit my family, I kept lifting up my skirt as I walked down the street so that everyone, even the boys, could see my beautiful underpants." Hanna Dembinska, who had been a tomboy, remembers just as vividly how demoralized she felt having to go around in dark, ugly jumpers which hung on her like sacks, while the "good girls" paraded about in attractive dresses. (One could change one's category, but because it meant changing oneself, it usually took years.)

That night, sitting at the Sabbath dinner table with the white tablecloth and braided challah and strange faces, the new child was comforted by the knowledge that he would see his relatives the following day. It was still the custom for the orphans to return home every Saturday after lunch and remain until seven in the evening. Mothers, grandparents, or other family members usually escorted the children back to the orphanage, but they were allowed upstairs only during Hanukkah and Purim parties and at Passover.

During the first three months the new child was helped to adjust by a "guardian," another orphan, a few years older, who guided him through the routine of the house, answered any questions, and was responsible for his behavior. Because everyone was busy with school and other activities, the new child and his guardian were encouraged to communicate through writing. Korczak was particularly fond of one such correspondence between a nine-year-old hellion and the twelve-year-old girl assigned to him:

Boy: I talked with R. about how it was at home. I said my father was a tailor. R.'s was a shoemaker. And now we are here in a sort of prison because this isn't home. Life isn't worth anything if you don't have a father and mother. I was telling how my father used to send me to buy buttons. R.'s father sent him for nails. And so on. I have forgotten the rest.

Guardian: Write more clearly.

Boy: Please advise me . . . during lessons I have bad thoughts. To steal. But I don't want to upset everybody. I try as hard as I can to do better and to think about other things, like traveling to discover a new continent or going to America, working hard, buying a car and riding across the country.

Guardian: You did the right thing in writing to me. We'll have a talk and I'll give you advice. But don't get hurt when I tell you something.

Boy: I have already improved. I am friends with G. who is helping me. And I try very hard. But can't I go out more often than once in two weeks? . . . Everyone else does. Grannie asked me to come every week and I am ashamed to say that I'm not allowed.

Guardian: You know very well why you are not allowed to go out as often as the others. I'll ask but I doubt it will work.

By watching out for the new child, the guardian played the role of a caring parent, the first branch of a unique family tree. When a child eventually became a guardian himself, his former guardian would become a grandparent, and then later a great-grandparent. These family units were treated seriously and were photographed together each year.

Although the orphanage was radically progressive in a period when children were beaten and starved in many institutions, it appears highly structured by contemporary standards. Korczak believed that structure was therapeutic for children, as long as they had their freedom within it. The house ran like clockwork: Korczak considered the clock equal in importance to the scale and the thermometer, believing that a person who is careless about time cannot work well.

An alarm rang promptly at six each morning. There was a fifteen-minute grace period for those who needed it. Children who jumped out of bed instantly earned special merit points; the habitually tardy had that noted on their record.

After washing, dressing, and making their beds, the children went downstairs at seven for a breakfast that usually consisted of cocoa, bread, fruit, and an occasional egg. On their way out to school they walked by a large basket filled with sandwiches for their midmorning break, to tide them over until they returned for lunch at about two o'clock. They also had to pass inspection by Stefa, who stood in the doorway checking that ears as well as shoes were clean, that shoelaces were tied, and that no buttons were loose or missing.

When the children returned from school, they ate their big meal of the day: soup with a piece of meat, kasha, noodles or potatoes, and a vegetable. Stella Eliasberg was usually down in the kitchen tasting and seasoning the soup herself before it was sent upstairs to the dining room on the dumbwaiter (a wooden shelf on a pulley that as often as not had a stowaway child who couldn't resist the forbidden ride between the two floors). After the tables were cleared, the children did their homework at them, and then went on to their work duties. In the late afternoon there were a variety of activities, including sports, games, and music lessons. Hebrew and Yiddish lessons were offered, at the request of some of the philanthropists, but they were not mandatory.

If he was free, Korczak would look in on what the children were doing. He would ask, "How are you getting along?" or "Why do you look so sad?" in a seemingly casual way. He knew from his own experience that children don't like questions, that they respond with reluctance or cool reserve: "Okay" or "I'm not sad." He might touch one or another lightly in passing to show his concern, for he also knew that children don't like effusive caresses. If someone looked pale or flushed, he was sure to say: "Show me your tongue." Sometimes he joined the children in a game of jump rope or ring-around-the-rosy, going round and round, singing "Romazia, the nice boy who had a hole in his pocket." When it was his turn to be in the center, he always chose a child who was not popular or who needed encouragement.

He might just sit on a bench with the children in the courtyard, in the shade of one of the chestnut trees, to watch a race or a game. "I always wanted to be alone with him," Sabina Damm, who was fatherless, recalled. "But it was impossible, because everyone wanted him. When he sat down I would go around his chair and embrace him from the back—it was the best position. 'You're going to choke me!' he would squeal." Sometimes one of the smaller children would climb up onto his lap, caress his goatee, and eventually lean his head against Korczak's chest and fall asleep. "Don't you think I look like an old tree filled with children playing like birds in my branches?" he would ask. When the games were over, the children would gather around and tease Korczak for holding the sleeping child. "Nanny! Nanny!" they'd call. He'd screw up his face and scold them mockingly: "Shh, don't disturb us. My little one is tired. Let him rest and build up his energy for tomorrow."

Stefa seldom joined in the games—she was too consumed by daily routine. She was in her mid-thirties now, weathered rather than softened by the years. Her ample figure, upholstered in black, was in perpetual motion. Her large, serious eyes, still her best feature, were the only indicator of the warmth that her brusque manner tried to hide. Her face was as "wide as a yeast cake, with warts sprinkled like raisins over it." Children loved to touch the largest wart on the side of her nose. It wobbled when she was mad. Sometimes she kissed their hands when they reached for it. They liked to watch her glasses slide down her nose until they stopped—there. She was a strong-willed mother snapping at the heels of her 106 charges, giving occasional slaps along with kisses. When they were mad at her, the children would refuse to eat, knowing she would fret that they might lose weight. A photographer taking her picture discovered that the only way he could get her to smile was to put a child on her lap. Her face became radiant, and he clicked the shutter.

15

Taming the Beast

Life is a circus ring, with some moments more spectacular than others.

—*"Theory and Practice"*

It is morning in the orphanage. The children bow their heads for a brief prayer before breakfast and sit down excitedly. They are going to vote on a newcomer who has been in the house for a month. Korczak walks through the dining hall, handing out three cards to everyone: one is marked with a plus, another with a minus, and a third with a zero. If you like the person being voted on, you are supposed to drop the plus card into the slot of the wooden box that is being passed around; if not, the minus. If you are indifferent, you put in the zero. The number of pluses, minuses, and zeros the new child receives will determine his citizenship rating.

A child who gets along easily with others is certain to receive a majority of pluses, which will earn him the top rank of Comrade. Those with a fair number of pluses become Residents; those with only a few pluses are regarded as Indifferent Residents; and those with none, Difficult Residents. Comrades, of course, have more privileges than the others: they serve in the parliament, go to more movies, and have their pick of work assignments. The rare boy or girl who receives all pluses is called King or Queen, and has the first choice in everything.

Voting on each was another way the children could assume autonomy in their own community. Rather than being subject to adult judgment, they learned to see themselves through the eyes of their peers. They were also empowered to vote on their adult caretakers, who were expected to show respect to the young citizens of the republic.

The newcomer was voted on again in six months, and annually after that. Korczak always followed the voting with great interest. He was intrigued—as in the case of a girl named Pola—by an unusually low rating. He knew that while children might fool adults, they could never fool one another. Pola gave the impression of being well-mannered, but he often heard the children say: "Don't touch that, it's Pola's." (The equivalent of one of his own sayings: "Don't touch shit, it smells.") When he asked why everyone avoided her, he was told: "Don't you know that Pola is quiet water?" (Meaning someone who on the surface seems honest and agreeable but is actually deceitful.)

Korczak believed that children like Pola, who were stuck in a low citizenship category, wanted to be accepted by the group but didn't know how to go about it. "A child with a vice feels it as a burden, but is at a loss what to do," he wrote. "Unless he has guidance, he will make a few disastrous attempts to change, and after failing, will give up." The challenge was to make his "clinic"—as he often called the boarding home—a place of "healing." If it didn't become "a health resort of the spirit," it was in danger of becoming "a source of infection."

But even as he gave his tough street children baths and clean clothes, Korczak had no illusion that he was washing away their "dark memories, bad influences, and painful experiences." There were limits to what he could accomplish: "I can hold up standards of truthfulness, tidiness, hard work, and honesty, but I will not be able to make these children other than what they are. A birch will stay a birch, an oak an oak, a thistle a thistle. I may be able to rouse what is dormant in the soul, but I cannot create anything new."

His hope was to help the children win the battle with themselves in ways that would not undermine their pride. For example, until they learned to control the rage and frustration that had built up inside them over the years, they had to let off steam, and so fights were allowed. But with the proviso that one sign up for them in advance and that the opponents be evenly matched. "If you must hit someone, hit—but not too hard," Korczak would tell them. "Lose your temper if you must, but only once a day." He liked to say, with a touch of his usual irony, that his educational method was contained in those few sentences.

He avoided the psychoanalytical jargon being bandied about by his colleagues, which he felt reduced the child to formulas. ("I will surely provoke an indulgent smile or a wry grimace when I say that a two-volume work dealing with laundry and washerwomen would be just as dignified as one on psychoanalysis.") He had an ambivalent, even contradictory, attitude to Freud (calling him a "dangerous maniac" in a letter to a friend), for he believed that his stress on sexuality "besmirched" the child and reduced childhood to a psychosexual stage. But he did admit (in that same letter) that "heartfelt thanks" were due Freud for revealing the "unplumbable depths of the unconscious."

Korczak prided himself on being a practitioner rather than a theorist—although, paradoxically, he felt there was no difference between the two. "Thanks to theory, I know," he wrote. "Thanks to practice, I feel. Theory enriches intellect, practice deepens feeling, trains the will."

Behind his creative strategies with the children was a keen psychological understanding of their nature, which came from years of practice—experience that most doctors, including Freud, who worked with adults, did not have. "I am a doctor by education, a pedagogue by chance, a writer by passion, and a psychologist by necessity," he told a friend. He knew that in requiring two hotheads to set a date for a future fight, he gave them time to cool off, to reconsider the importance of their quarrel, and, in the process, to learn how to choose their battles. If one strategy didn't work, he pulled something else out of his "pedagogical arsenal."

It is Friday afternoon. A long line of children waits in the main hall outside the small supply room, which Korczak transforms every week into a gambling casino with one croupier—himself.

"What do you bet?" he asks Jerzy, an eight-year-old rascal who is first in line. The idea is for the children to place a bet on some bad habit with the goal of overcoming it, and winning a few candies in the bargain.

"I bet I'll have only one fight this week," Jerzy says.

"I'm not sure I can accept that," Korczak responds, without looking up from the ledger where he keeps the records. "It would be unfair to you."

"Why?"

"Because you will clearly lose. You beat up five boys this week, and six the week before, so how can you stop so suddenly?"

"I can do it."

"Why not try four fights?"

"Two," Jerzy argues.

After some more bargaining, they compromise on three. Korczak records the bet in the ledger and slips Jerzy a chocolate from the candy basket in good faith. If Jerzy manages to win, he'll collect three more candies the next Friday. If he loses, he'll receive a sympathetic look, some encouragement, and perhaps another piece of candy for consolation. Jerzy knows that however many fights he reports, Korczak will not check up on him. It is an honor system.

The next one in line is Antek.

"What's your bet?"

"That I'll swear only five times this week."

"Too little."

"Six."

"How about seven, one for each day of the week?" Korczak suggests.

Antek accepts the offer and goes off beaming, determined to win the bet.

Pola is next.

"What do you bet?"

"That I'll do my math homework every day."

"How about three days?"

She shrugs: "All right, three days."

He records the transaction, slips her a candy, and the next child steps up. The gambling casino stays open until the last child has placed his bet or the gong announcing it is time for their Sabbath bath sends everyone scurrying up to the dormitories.

A strategy that was effective with one child might not be with another. Sometimes Korczak had difficulty devising a method that would work with a particularly resistant urchin. His purpose was not so much to make the children change as to enable them to train their wills as he had once trained his own. It meant removing their compulsions, and allowing their wounds to heal. "Solutions should be sought not only in psychology but in medical books, sociology, ethnology, poetry, criminology, the prayer book, and the animal-training handbook," he wrote. He was not being facetious about the last. In fact, he credited much of his skill in disciplining the wild beast in himself to his observations of how animals were trained at the circus: "The work of an animal trainer is very straightforward and dignified. The fury of wild instincts is overcome by the force of man's unflinching will." And he added, "I do not require that a child surrender completely. I just tame his movements."

Believing that an educator should also be part actor, Korczak might pretend to lose his temper with an incorrigible child. He would shout, his face and bald pate turning bright red, but his words were not the obvious admonitions "Shame on you!" or "Don't do that!" Reaching into his "jar of strong scolding expressions," he would pull out: "You torpedo! You hurricane! You perpetual motion machine! You rat man! You lamp! You table!"

Knowing that the power of an expression was diminished if it was repeated too often, he was constantly expanding his repertoire, borrowing words from nature or the arts: "You rook! You bagpipe! You dulcimer!" He also experimented to find just the word that would get through to a particular child. There was one scamp on whom he tried everything— nothing worked. He used every kind of noun—to no effect. And then, a sudden inspiration: "Ah, you F-major!" The boy was subdued for the rest of the day.

Another strategy: he would tell a misbehaving child, "I'm angry at you till lunchtime or supper." If the crime was serious enough, he would extend the sentence until the next day, and he would not speak to the boy or girl during that period. If the child's friend acted as go-between and asked: "May he take the ball?" Korczak would reply: "Tell him he may take a small ball, but he may not kick it." The child would understand that he was being punished, but also that there was a time limit, after which he would be forgiven and could begin anew.

And so, "from grumbling, snarling, chiding, even rebuking," Korczak worked through his "pharmacopoeia." He made it a point never to say "I must have told you a hundred times!" for that was imprecise and nagging, and the child would deny it anyway. Rather, he would say: "I told you on Monday, or Tuesday, or Wednesday, and so on." Or: "I told you in January, February, and so on." Or: "I told you in the spring, summer, fall, or winter." Not only was he being precise and fair; he was accomplishing two other things at the same time: teaching the delinquent child the days of the week, the months, or the seasons of the year, and enriching his vocabulary.

In the rare case when none of his strategies worked, a child might be ordered to sit in the corner behind the piano on the podium at the far end of the main room, for anywhere from five minutes to an hour. One of the boys, Johann Nutkiewicz, remembers that he always felt "imprisoned" as he sat there watching other children playing nearby. And Hanna Dembinska, who received a sentence of one hour in that corner as punishment for being suspended from school for a week, sneaked out and bought herself a raisin bun with a few pennies her mother had given her. As she sat brazenly eating her bun, a bee that had settled among the raisins stung her. Her face swelled up to twice its size. "We'll make a human being out of you yet," Korczak said fondly as he took her off to the hospital.

No matter how incorrigible the child, Korczak never resorted to methods used by other orphanages, such as beatings or withholding food—punishments he considered "monstrous, sinful, criminal." But when nothing he tried had any effect on a child, there came the distressful moment when spanking had to be considered—distressful because Korczak believed that striking a child could become an addiction for an adult rather than an educational technique. "But if you must, never without warning, and only in necessary defense—once. And that once, without anger."

The educator spanking a child was not unlike "a surgeon grappling with an incurable disease: only a daring operation might save the patient's life—or terminate it." The risk had to be taken. Three warnings had to be given first, and only when the last one was of no avail should the spanking be administered—for one should never issue an empty threat with no intention of carrying out the punishment. During the spanking, the teacher was to be calm and deliberate, never angry.

In two instances where Korczak delivered the spanking himself, the children were "impressed, and reformed." In two others, the children continued their destructive behavior and had to leave the orphanage.

When a child improved his behavior or skills, he was awarded a picture postcard signed by Korczak. If he didn't improve, he still might get a card as an incentive to try harder. The postcard had the virtue of being colorful and inexpensive; and since it was small, it could be stashed away and treasured by the recipient. The decision as to who received cards was made by the twenty deputies of the parliament who were chosen from those who had had no court case for dishonesty against them that year. The pictures on the cards corresponded to the occasion: For rising immediately at the sounding of the morning bell in the winter months— a snowy landscape; in the spring—a spring view. For peeling a bushel of potatoes—a flower card. For fights, arguments, unruliness—a tiger card. A picture of Warsaw was given to children who conscientiously carried out their monitoring duties. (Korczak considered the Orphans Home a "district" of Warsaw and the children its "citizens.")

When a woman visitor asked: "What's so special about cards we can find anywhere for a few pennies?" Korczak snapped: "There are things that some value and others don't. I know of some people who use their mother's pictures as hot plates."

* * *

Korczak valued everything connected with his children; he even collected their baby teeth. It was a common sight to see an orphan rush up to him with a tooth that had just fallen out. Korczak would take the tooth, examine it, comment on the number of holes and its general condition, and bargain over the price he would pay for it. It was a good way of providing a child with a little spending money, while at the same time marking the important rite of passage that losing baby teeth represented. The children knew that Korczak would take his new acquisition upstairs and glue it into the tooth castle he was building. "We imagined the castle was like the one King Matt lived in," one of the orphans recalled. "We couldn't wait for a loose tooth." Sometimes the children opened their mouths and asked Korczak to jiggle a tooth and judge how soon it would be ready. If a child tried to sell one that was dangling, Korczak would say, "I don't buy a cat in a bag." He would never pay the full price for a tooth before it was out, but he might put a down payment on it. Once, when a boy tried to pass off a pebble as a tooth, Korczak asked suspiciously to see the hole it came from; the culprit burst out laughing and confessed.

Everything a child collected was also important to Korczak. Seemingly worthless items—bits of string, beads, postage stamps, feathers, pinecones, chestnuts, tramcar tickets, dry leaves, ribbons—might have a story connected to them or be emotionally priceless: "They all hold memories of the past, or yearnings for the future. A tiny shell is a dream of a trip to the seashore. A small screw and a few pieces of thin wire are an airplane and the proud dream of flying one. The eye of a doll broken a long time ago is the sole reminder of a lost love. You may also find a photograph of a child's mother, or two pennies wrapped in pink ribbon that were a gift from a grandfather now dead."

He had harsh words for the disrespectful teacher who had the nerve to throw out these treasures as if they were rubbish: "A gross abuse of power, a barbarous crime. How dare you, you boor, dispose of someone else's property? How dare you demand after such a crime that a child respect anything or love anyone? You are not burning bits of paper but cherished traditions and dreams of a beautiful life."

To protect the property of his orphans, Korczak provided everyone with a little drawer of his own, complete with a lock and key, in the main dining hall. If the children wanted to trade any of their treasures, they could post a notice on the nearby bulletin board. Covered with announcements, warnings, requests, schedules, pictures, thank-you notes, crossword puzzles, headlines from the daily paper, weather reports, weight and growth charts, the bulletin board had a life of its own. It was like a shop window for the children, who stopped to look whenever they had the time and inclination. Even the child who couldn't read learned to distinguish his name and developed an appetite for words.

Korczak also set up a lost-and-found box as a reminder that "every little thing has an owner." It gave the children a sense of security to know that their meager possessions were safe, as were they, from being permanently lost.

In 1921 Korczak's dream of a summer camp for the home came true. Dr. Eliasberg convinced a wealthy couple whose daughter, Rose, had died to donate eleven acres of land in an area known as Goclawek, ten miles south of Warsaw. The camp was called Little Rose in honor of the deceased child. Korczak asked the Orphans Aid Society to lease the adjoining land for small farming. A barn was built for a cow, two horses, a goat, and chickens. The only thing the camp lacked was a pond or river, which meant that the children had to travel by train to another town when they wanted to swim.

Life in the country was more relaxed than in the city. After breakfast, Korczak would walk around with tiny pieces of buttered bread, calling, "Ice cream! Ice cream! Who wants ice cream!" (It was an opportunity to fatten the children up.) Every day there were games, sports, and excursions into the surrounding pine and beech forests to gather wild flowers and berries. Sometimes Korczak would lie blissfully on the sandy ground and open his mouth to let the campers pop berries in. He kept track of his flock by blowing a toy trumpet, much to the children's amusement; his love of music was not matched by talent. He was fascinated with ants, and would sit with the children for hours observing them. "You can learn a lot from ants' industriousness and their skill at organization," Korczak told his small companions. There were things to learn at night, too. Often he took the children to see the phosphorescent glow on the trees emitted by tiny insects and plants, so that they would realize it was nature and not ghosts that caused the eerie lights.

During those more leisurely summer months, the little republic operated with the same structure and rules as in the city. Everyone was assigned work duties. The younger children fed the chickens and picked up litter from the grounds; the older ones were given most of the hard farm work. Flower and vegetable plots had to be fertilized, planted, and tended, as did the tomatoes and cucumber plants in the large glass greenhouse. The stable had to be cleaned, and someone had to keep the goat out of the fields. Whenever the older boys and girls complained of being too hot or too tired, Korczak would say, "Roast pigeons don't fly into your mouth by themselves, they have to be prepared."

When the children staged a sit-down strike over picking apples from the long row of trees that lined the path from the gate, Korczak called a meeting of the strikers and offered them the younger children's job of spearing litter with sharp sticks. They agreed, but then, deciding it would be beneath their dignity, they hid in the blueberry bushes, giggling and eating berries. When Korczak discovered them, he gathered them once again for a talk.

"Listen, kids, I offered you hard work. You didn't want it. I offered you easy work. You don't want that either. Now tell me what you want to do."

They didn't know. Then, noticing the gravel path in front of the veranda on which it hurt to walk with bare feet, one boy suggested they convert it into a dirt road. Korczak agreed. For the next week the strikers busied themselves digging hard clay from the surrounding fields, which they brought back in wheelbarrows and dumped where the gravel had been. They succeeded in making a soft path, easy on the feet and smooth enough for croquet games. But when it turned to mud after the first rainstorm, the strikers understood the practicality of gravel—and that there was a reason behind many of the things they took for granted.

At three o'clock one morning Korczak heard some of the older boys complaining that they couldn't sleep because of the gnats. He whispered to them to dress quickly and meet him at the potato bin. The door of the bin was locked, so he told Srulik, who was the smallest and thinnest, "Crawl through the window and let us in." They gathered potatoes and headed through the woods for a small sandy clearing where picnics were often held. After playing games and telling stories, they made a fire and roasted the potatoes. When one of the boys asked Srulik what would happen once it was discovered potatoes were missing, Korczak answered for him: "I am responsible, not Srulik, for everything we've done."

As soon as they arrived back at camp, long after breakfast, Korczak signed himself up for a court case. He confessed to leaving the grounds after hours and taking food without permission. The boys signed up as

well, since they were accomplices. The children's court, which met on
Saturday mornings there as it did in Warsaw, found them all guilty. But
the judges forgave Korczak because his motives were good, and ruled
that the boys had already been punished by having missed breakfast that
day.

16

Striving for Justice

The court does not fly off the handle. It does not shout abuse.
It speaks calmly.

—*How to Love a Child*

"One court case tells me more about a child than a month of observing him," Korczak would say. He considered the court of peers the cornerstone of his system. While he was away during the war, he had drawn up a Code of Laws that would give the judges guidelines in rendering their verdicts. It was not unlike the Napoleonic Code on which the Polish legal system was based—with the difference that Korczak's Code stressed forgiveness.

The Preamble to the Code states Korczak's philosophy of law: "If anyone has done something bad, it is best to forgive. If it was done because he did not know, he knows now. If he did it intentionally, he will be more careful in the future . . . But the court must defend the timid against the bullies, the conscientious against the careless and idle."

Korczak was still hoping to impart the idea of justice, however imperfect, to his young orphans. He wanted them to understand that there are just laws and unjust laws, even as there are just people and unjust people. "The court is not justice, but it should strive for justice," the Preamble continues. "The court is not truth, but its goal is truth." Because justice is dependent on human beings, the most central of whom is the judge, it warns: "Judges may make mistakes. They may punish for acts they themselves are guilty of. But it is shameful if a judge consciously hands down an unjust verdict."

The five judges, chosen each week from among those children who had no court cases pending against them, could cite any of the thousand articles in the Code. Articles 1 to 99, which covered minor infractions, pardoned the defendant outright: "You acted wrongly, but you did not realize it," or "It was the first time and you have promised not to do it again." Article 100 was the dividing line between forgiveness and censure. It read: "Without granting pardon, the court states that you committed the act with which you are charged." Still, the only punishment was the court's disapproval.

The articles then jumped in units of one hundred up to 1,000, becoming progressively sterner in their moral judgment. Under articles 200 to 800, the guilty child's name was published in the orphanage newspaper or posted on the bulletin board, or he was deprived of privileges for one week and his family was summoned. Article 900 carried the dire warning that the court had "abandoned hope": the accused had to find a supporter among the children willing to vouch for him. Article 1000, a dreaded verdict, meant expulsion. The guilty party had the right to apply for readmission after three months, but with little hope, for his place would have been taken by another child the day he left.

Korczak had expected the orphans to be enthusiastic about the new Code, but he found them hesitant to test it. It took a while before the corridors began ringing with "I'll sue you!" A child who felt wronged listed his case on the bulletin board in the dining hall. Stefa, acting as the Court Clerk, entered it in the court ledger. But in the period before the trial the plaintiff's anger often subsided, and by the time Stefa read the charges in court the child was ready to drop charges. During the first weeks Korczak noted that almost all the plaintiffs forgave the defendants at the hearings, and the judges cited Article 1: "Charge is withdrawn."

As many as a hundred and fifty cases might be heard by the judges during a Saturday-morning court session, with most defendants receiving an article under 100. Hearings were held in the Quiet Room (where children could go during the week to be alone), and the length of the deliberations varied according to the difficulty of the case. Charges were brought for name-calling, pushing, teasing, snatching someone else's possessions, banging doors, leaving the yard without permission, climbing a tree, breaking an inkpot, using abusive language, making faces during prayers, not returning checker and lotto games to their places. The judges might ask the plaintiff: "How many times have you done this?" or "What article did you get in your last court case?" before making their verdict.

Misdemeanors that were punished by an article over 100 were: locking someone out in the courtyard for fun, disturbing others at work, misbehaving during study hour, not washing one's hands, cheating at games. In situations where the culprit was unidentified, the case was heard anyway; if the crime disgraced the republic, a black mourning patch was placed on the bulletin board.

The court was a "psychological drama based on knowledge of child psychology," according to one educator, but Korczak's critics outside the orphanage insisted that the court would accustom the children to being litigious. Korczak responded that, on the contrary, it would teach them respect for the law and individual rights, and make them appreciate how "inconvenient, detrimental, and senseless" lawsuits are.

Still, he wasn't prepared for how quickly the worst troublemakers in the orphanage would find the court a nuisance and try to sabotage it. They'd boast: "I'm not going to let some young punk be my judge!" and "To hell with the court, I'd rather have my ears pulled or my hands slapped!" The ringleaders who constantly attacked the court were sly enough to realize that they could wriggle out of things more easily without it. They started a campaign demanding that guilty defendants be hung on the spot and threw mock tantrums when the court refused to impose the death penalty. Their behavior had the desired effect. The other children stopped suing each other rather than endure the constant bickering over the court, and the judges began conspiring to acquit the defendants or to deal leniently with them, no matter what their crime. Finally, when one judge hit another who wanted to conduct the trial according to his own conscience, Korczak was forced to acknowledge that the court, which was intended to "replace irrational arguments with calm thinking," was causing more disorder than order. He even began to suspect that it was harmful to the orphanage. The answers to questionnaires he passed out among the children proved him right: "The court is necessary, but it achieves nothing." "It is good for some kids, but not for others." "Our court may be useful in the future, but not now." "Only if the court were different would it be helpful."

Korczak still believed the court was essential (and that in fifty years all schools would have one), but he had to concede that his orphans weren't ready for it yet. "It is clear that they would rather be slaves than free," he wrote bitterly in his journal when he suspended the court indefinitely. He noticed that some of the children sighed with relief to be rid of the vigilant watchdog; others, anxious to prove that the court was unnecessary, behaved better than they had before. Although a small group kept asking when the court would be resumed, the majority—"as in all human relationships"—displayed little interest.

The court reopened four weeks after its suspension, but only when three demands of the children had been met: that they could appeal a decision after three months; that a Judicial Board made up of two judges and one adult, elected by secret ballot for a term of three months, would handle the most difficult cases; and that the children had the right to sue the adult staff. This last stipulation set Korczak's critics on him again: how could he allow a child to take an adult to court? But Korczak honored the children's demands. "There are always enough tongues to wag, but not enough heads to think," he reassured the members of his philanthropic board.

Korczak even supported the boy who sued his elementary-school teacher for tearing up his drawing. When the teacher sent word that it was beneath her dignity to appear before the court, she was tried in absentia. Korczak went to the school and posted the verdict, Article 300, in the teachers' lounge: "The court censures you for acting wrongly." The teacher tore the document from the wall, and only when the principal intervened did she send an apology to the boy.

Korczak made a point of bringing himself to court five times over one six-month period. He confessed to boxing a boy's ears, throwing a boy out of the dormitory, putting a child in the corner, insulting a judge, and accusing a girl of stealing. He submitted a written defense for each incident. The judges gave him Article 21 in the first three cases: "The court finds that you were entitled to act as you did." In the fourth, he got Article 71: "The court pardons you since you regret your action." And in the last, Article 7: "The court accepts your admission of guilt."

In one trial, which has passed into legend, the cagey pedagogue was not forgiven. One gloomy, overcast day when he returned to the orphanage, he looked around to gauge the children's mood. Finding Helenka standing off to one side in a small room, too shy to join the other children playing there, he decided to stir things up. Dashing over, he swooped her up to the top of the cupboard, then walked away. He did not so much as turn around when she started screaming, "Let me down! Let me down!"

The other children, as he had hoped, now became interested in her situation. They started encouraging her to jump. When she refused, they insisted that Korczak help her. At first he wouldn't hear of it, but when they ganged up on him, he walked back to the cupboard and lifted Helenka to the ground. She seemed satisfied, but some of the children began pestering her to sue him. Flattered by all the attention, she did.

Korczak wrote out a long defense that he presented to the court, but the judges' sympathy went to Helenka, who they felt had been embarrassed and frightened by his rash action. The verdict was Article 100. He was not forgiven. Korczak made a show of being upset, and for some time after that he was called by the nickname Setka (One Hundred).

It was rare, but it happened in a few instances that neither Korczak nor the Judicial Board could save a child bent on a destructive course from receiving Article 1,000.

Abraham Pieklo, whose last name appropriately meant Hell, was a mean, redheaded, freckle-faced boy known as Little Devil. He jeered at sick children, mocked bedwetters, and tormented the handicapped. Deciding to apply shock methods, Korczak hurled names at the troublemaker meant to be as painful as those he inflicted on others: Hell-born, Black Sheep, Pest, Plague. At first the boy talked back, then he ignored the doctor, and finally he took him to court for making him nervous. Everyone was surprised when the court gave Setka another *setka* for mistreating his accuser. As charming as he was diabolical, Little Devil even managed to soften no-nonsense Stefa when she was bandaging his leg, by asking: "How come, when I get hit on the head, it makes a bump instead of a hole?" But Little Devil's sadistic behavior eventually earned him Article 1,000. No one was sad to see him leave, not even Korczak, who felt that the well-being of the community came before any one individual.

Korczak had done his best to create a just system inside his own republic, but once his children went out to school or to visit their families, they were subject to adult whims in an unjust society.

One Saturday afternoon Stasiek (the former Israel) returned home to visit his family, with permission from Korczak to bring back his pet wild goldfinch. Stasiek was very excited as he climbed with the cage onto the trolley. Since the car was full, he had to stand on the outside platform, where he was spotted by a policeman boarding at the next stop.

"Where'd you get the bird, kid?" he asked suspiciously.

"It's mine!" Stasiek said.

"It's against the law to keep a wild bird in a cage," the policeman informed him. "I'm going to free it."

Stasiek started to cry, but the officer dragged him off the tram at the next stop. Grabbing his arm, he took Stasiek to the courtyard behind the police station, where he opened the cage door and let the bird fly away.

"Okay, kid, beat it," the policeman ordered.

When Stasiek didn't move, he took him by the arm again and led him to the orphanage. It was like the day the boy had first arrived with his mother: there was Stefa in the courtyard shouting at him.

"What's going on—a policeman with a cage?"

The officer told her that he had found the boy with a wild bird and had freed it.

"You did us a favor," Stefa said. "He's been a troublemaker here right from the start."

The policeman stood at attention and saluted her.

Just then a male voice came from the garret window above the courtyard: "Wait a minute, please!"

Stefa left. Stasiek started crying.

"Who's that?" asked the policeman.

"Dr. Janusz Korczak," Stasiek said proudly.

The policeman looked very uncomfortable as Korczak approached and asked what had happened.

"This kid was keeping a wild bird against the law, so I let it go."

Korczak looked at the officer sternly. "Which law? You're talking about laws for adults, but they don't apply to children. There are other laws and other courts for them. You, as a representative of the government, should know that. I was going to teach the boy how to set the bird free himself. Now with one rash act you've spoiled everything."

Stasiek was thrilled to see the policeman scolded by the doctor. The officer was very apologetic, mumbled something about making it up to the boy, and rushed off. Half an hour later he returned with a paper bag. Inside was another goldfinch from the bird market. Korczak and Stasiek put the new bird in the cage and placed it by a window in one of the rooms, where Stasiek was to take care of it.

"Do you think that bird is singing in his cage?" Korczak asked, as they watched it thrashing about. "He is really crying. There is an ancient Polish law in Latin that I want you to learn by heart: *Neminem captivabimus nisi jure victum*. I'll tell you what it means when you are able to repeat it twenty-five times."

After three days Stasiek was able to recite his Latin sentence. Korczak translated the old law: "We will imprison no one who has not been lawfully sentenced to lose his freedom." And he added: "Just think, that law applied to people who were able to defend themselves. Your bird is innocent and defenseless. His conscience is clear as a diamond. He has no forms of pleasure, like movies or bicycles. His freedom is his only happiness. And you took it away."

"But you said you had a canary once," Stasiek reminded him.

"Yes, I had a canary, but it's not the same," Korczak explained. "A canary is domesticated like a cat or dog. If it's freed, it cannot find friends or food. Those people who brought canaries here over five hundred years ago committed a crime. We can't change that reality. But I have a plan. This goldfinch has suffered for a long time. Let's go up to the roof and free him now. Later we can buy another bird, keep him for two weeks, and then free him, too. We can keep doing this. You can earn the money by writing articles for our newspaper."

Stasiek was quite emotional as he opened the cage door, especially when the bird just peered at him from his perch without moving. He felt an enormous sense of satisfaction when it suddenly darted through the opening and flew away. He and Korczak repeated this ritual with a bull-finch, a linnet, and a chaffinch before Stasiek decided he would like a canary. When he couldn't find one he could afford in the bird market, Korczak suggested that he buy two pigeons instead and make a coop for them under the eaves. From that time on, pigeons flew freely in and out of their roost at the orphanage.

Stasiek was to discover that learning to free birds was easier than freeing himself of the bad habits he had picked up on the streets. He was constantly brought to court by someone for using bad language, fighting, or breaking rules. That summer at Little Rose, he let himself be persuaded by four older boys to steal fruit with them from a farmer's garden. They were all caught and brought before the children's court. The other boys got Article 300, with its strong admonishment: "The court rules that you acted wrongly." But because of his previous bad record, Stasiek received the perilous Article 900: "The court requires that you find someone to vouch for you within the next two days. Otherwise, you will be expelled." The judgment was published in the court gazette.

The boy who promised to testify in his behalf backed out, and Stasiek suspected that Stefa was behind it, especially when she sent a message to his mother to come for him immediately. He couldn't appeal to Korczak, who was then back in Warsaw, where he went a few times a week to lecture and arrange for supplies. Stasiek's mother, a strong-willed woman who ran a candy store, wept and pleaded in vain with Stefa to let Stasiek stay. Stasiek had given up hope, but his mother turned to him after they had left the camp grounds and said: "Wait here. I'll try to find Dr. Korczak in Warsaw. Don't move from under this tree."

After a few hours his mother returned with the doctor, who arranged for Stasiek to have another chance to find a supporter and improve his behavior. Stasiek tried his best to avoid trouble, but his fists were too fast. When he was again sued for fighting, Stefa declared that he had violated his probation and had to leave. This time his mother couldn't turn to Korczak, who had left Warsaw for a few weeks to do some writing at a country inn. And so Stasiek was expelled. He would never forgive Stefa, who he felt was behind his downfall.

Most children stayed their full seven years in the orphanage. "I take a child from his home at seven and return him to his home," Korczak would say when it came time for one of his fledglings to leave the orphanage after finishing the seventh grade of elementary school.

It was a very different child who emerged from Korczak's cocoon at the age of fourteen—one who spoke fluent Polish, and was unprepared for the daily injustices in the world outside. Stefa and Korczak did what they could for the departing youngster setting out on that "long journey called life." After a parent or relative was called in to discuss the child's future, he was given some extra clothing to tide him over, a commemorative postcard, and the farewell message that Korczak delivered to all his children:

> Unfortunately, we can give you nothing but these few poor words. We cannot give you love of your fellowman, because there is no love without forgiveness, and to forgive is something everyone must learn to do on his own. We can give you but one thing: the longing for a better life, which may not exist now but will some day—the life of Truth and Justice. Perhaps this longing will lead you to God, Motherland, and love. Farewell, do not forget.

Some children forgot, and disappeared "like the wind." But the majority felt very attached to the home in which they had been raised with such care. A lucky few were able to stay on as helpers, or were allowed to take lunch at the orphanage, but the others could only pay a visit on Saturday mornings to listen to Korczak read the orphanage newspaper and to talk to Stefa, who they knew would always be there, ready to hear their troubles and to give them advice. They were painfully aware that a new child was sleeping in their bed. As one said: "In a real family, a bed that was yours is always there for you."

They felt not only abandoned but unprepared to cope in the outside world. Occasionally Stefa or Korczak was able to arrange an apprenticeship to a barber or carpenter, but most had to leave without knowing what the future held. The girls tried to find jobs as governesses, housekeepers, or baby-sitters. The boys usually ended up as messengers or store clerks; one of Stefa's favorites could find work only in a slaughterhouse.

"I remember how homesick I was," Itzhak Belfer, recalls. "In the evenings I would walk by the house just to see the lights inside. Some of us tried to rent a room together so that we wouldn't be alone."

When Johann Nutkiewicz left the Orphans Home on a Friday afternoon in 1929, a fourth of the population was unemployed, and anti-Semitism was on the rise. He had almost no family. His father had died of tuberculosis before he went into the orphanage, and his mother had committed suicide while he was there. At Stefa's prodding, his married sister had reluctantly agreed to take him in until he found some kind of employment, but she worked until seven every evening. Johann had no choice but to wander around the unfamiliar city until she came home.

"Finally I found a park bench by the river and fell asleep," he recalls. "I felt someone poking me roughly, and heard a policeman say, 'Hey, Jew boy, what are you doing here? Don't you know it's against the law to sleep on public benches?' I explained the situation, but the policeman was unmoved: 'Either you get up and go, or I take you straight to reform school.'

"I had been nursed on beautiful values until then, and now here I was in the cruel world. I just sat there thinking: This is something different now—reality."

Reality wasn't much better when he arrived at seven at the small room his sister shared with her husband. On hearing his request to wash his hands and face, his sister retorted: "Don't think you can act like a little prince here. If you try to wash now, you'll wake my landlady and get us thrown out."

This was the second blow that day, and others were to follow. After he was fired from his job at a box factory because he had insisted the owner pay him his two zlotys at the end of the week, as they had agreed, his sister yelled: "Don't talk about fairness! You'd better start learning what other boys your age have known all their lives about the kind of world we live in." Johann began to understand that not only was he different, he was also more vulnerable because of the "hothouse" environment in which he had been raised. Comparing experiences with other children who had been in the home, he realized that all of them were unaggressive, had little desire to compete with others if it meant "elbowing" them out, and had idealistic expectations of people they encountered as well as of themselves. He was certain that without the values he had received from Korczak and Stefa, he would never have known that there could be justice in the world.

Korczak's belief that all children should be protected by just laws extended beyond the walls of his miniature world. The stooped figure of the eminent pedagogue in his old gray suit became a familiar sight at the Juvenile District Court where he worked as a consultant once a week. The magistrates of the court were impressed not only by Korczak's earnest dedication to delinquent children, but by his casual attitude about payment. He never sent a bill, while all the other consultants could be relied upon to make an immediate beeline to the bookkeeping office. The only problem was that this famous educator seemed to place the welfare of the accused above that of the court. Once, when Korczak refused to interrogate a tired and hungry young offender until the child had been given something to eat and a few days' rest, the magistrate impatiently brought in another doctor who had no such scruples.

Always on the side of the poor slum children—arrested, for the most part, for petty thefts—he tried to prevent their being sentenced to Warsaw's grim detention center for minors. "The delinquent child is still a child," he wrote. "He is a child who has not given up yet, but does not know who he is. A punitive sentence could adversely influence his future sense of himself and his behavior. Because it is society that has failed him and made him behave this way, the court should condemn not the criminal but the social structure."

Korczak held to this view even in a murder case in 1927 when he defended Stanislaw Lampisz, a student who shot and killed his high-school principal. It was hard to say which was considered more sensational: the crime, or Dr. Janusz Korczak's testimony at the trial.

Korczak, who had spent a great deal of time examining Lampisz in prison, spoke for more than half an hour. He asked the jurors to see the boy as a loner who had come from a small village to live with his aunt while he attended high school in Warsaw. His only friend was a girl in his class. He had been looking forward to graduation, but a few days before the event, he had committed a minor offense at school for which he was suspended and ordered by the principal, Dr. Lipka, to have his head shaved. Lampisz had panicked. If that happened, he'd lose his room at his aunt's house, and his girlfriend as well—he'd have to return home in disgrace. Lampisz appealed to Lipka to change his punishment, but the principal, unwilling to respond to the young man's stress, refused.

Feeling that his world was shattered, Lampisz decided to commit suicide. He drank some vodka and was crossing a bridge over the Vistula with a gun, looking for a place to kill himself, when he chanced to run into Lipka. He tried to kiss the principal's hand, thinking to plead his cause one last time, but Lipka pulled away. Lampisz then grabbed the gun to shoot himself, but shot the principal instead. Turning the gun on himself, Lampisz fell to the ground, expecting to die. A policeman found the two men lying on the bridge and rushed them to the hospital. When Lampisz, whose wound proved superficial, learned that the principal was dead, he expressed his regret at what he had done, saying he wished it were he who had died.

"I cannot see any crime here," Korczak concluded. "Lipka died like a chemist who carelessly concocts a solution which explodes. He died like a surgeon who gets a blood infection during an operation. And, please remember, when Lampisz shot Lipka, he was at that same moment shooting himself."

The court adjourned for a brief period at noon, after which the two judges gave the verdict. Guilty. Because of Korczak's moving defense, many were surprised at the severity of the sentence: five years in a high-security prison for hardened criminals.

Korczak may have been ahead of his time in offering psychological testimony for the defense in a murder trial—and faulting the victim in the process—but he saw Lampisz as the victim in this case: a child brutalized by an uncaring adult. In his view, Lipka, as a school principal, had the responsibility to try to understand why his student was so troubled and to reach out to him. By taking this extreme stand, Korczak was demonstrating yet again his passionate belief in the right of the child to be heard and respected by the adults who have authority over them.

17

Long Live
the Herring!

Don't try to become a teacher overnight with psychological
bookkeeping in your heart and educational theory in your head.
—How to Love a Child

In the mid-twenties, when it became clear to Stefa and Korczak that they needed help in taking care of the children, Korczak thought of offering room and board and a weekly seminar to student teachers in exchange for their part-time services.

The orphanage was soon besieged by applicants eager to work with the famous Janusz Korczak. Some had already taken his courses on child psychology at one of the two pedagogical institutes in Warsaw where he taught. His method of teaching, like his strategy with children, was known to be idiosyncratic. He titled the first lecture of one seminar "The Heart of the Child" and held it in the X-ray room of the Children's Hospital. The students were surprised to see Korczak enter with a small boy clutching his hand. Without a word, Korczak took off the child's shirt, placed him behind the fluoroscope, and turned off the overhead light. Everyone could see the boy's heart beating rapidly on the screen.

"Don't ever forget this sight," Korczak told them. "Before you raise a hand to a child, before you administer any kind of punishment, remember what his frightened heart looks like." And then, heading for the door, with the boy's hand once again in his, he added, "That is all for today."

Korczak did not use textbooks in his seminars or give tests. Homework might be nothing more than writing up a childhood memory. Students were amazed to find that most of the experiences that had stayed with them were sad, and usually involved a parent or teacher who had not responded to what they were feeling. By calling forth the vulnerable child in each of his students, Korczak was able to help them understand one of his basic premises: adults are insensitive to the suffering of children.

Feiga Lipshitz, who at seventeen had just arrived in Warsaw from a small town in Russia, never forgot the excitement with which her roommates jumped out of bed on the days of his seminar, shouting "Today we have Korczak!" They would rush to be on time: latecomers had to listen from outside. When Korczak announced that he was looking for three student teachers to work as counselors at the Little Rose summer camp and, if they qualified, to become part of the training unit in his orphanage, Feiga summoned the courage to ask for an interview. She was disappointed to find Stefa rather than Korczak waiting for her. However, Stefa was immediately drawn to this younger woman who looked almost like a child in her long braids—indeed, resembled Esterka Weintraub, the orphan who died of typhus during the war—and accepted her without hesitation.

The arduous task of selecting the right apprentices for the *bursa*, as the training unit was called, was not made easier by the fact that Korczak and Stefa differed in their criteria. Stefa, who did most of the screening, was impressed by well-dressed young people who were rhapsodical in their love for children, whereas Korczak paid no attention to an applicant's appearance and was impatient with "flighty romantics," who, he believed, would flee as soon as they were exposed to the hard realities of working with deprived children. Pedagogic love, he said, was not an empty sentiment, but a true giving of the self. In his view, old nannies and construction workers were often better pedagogues than a doctor of psychology. Asked if he could spot a future educator, Korczak replied that he might not be able to predict who would make a good one, but he could certainly tell who would not. (This talent was shared by one of the orphans, Neska, who always knew during a camp season which counselors would be voted on by the children to move into the *bursa* on Krochmalna. "You won't see her in the winter," Neska would say. Or: "He won't be back with us next year.")

Training to be an educator under Korczak was not easy. (He preferred the word *educator* to *teacher*: a teacher was someone paid by the hour to drill something into the child, while an educator drew something out.) He demanded a commitment as deep as his own. His eyes, sometimes alarming in their intensity, could mask his true feelings, challenging the students to decide if he was serious or joking—not a simple task with a man whose form of irony was to say the opposite of what he really meant.

The apprentices were thrown without orientation into the daily routine of the orphanage from the moment they moved in. They soon learned that the rules of the republic were intended to serve the children, not the adults. They were given the same work duties as the orphans—mopping floors, peeling potatoes, washing windows—because Korczak expected an educator to be able to do everything that was asked of a child. They had to accept being voted on by the children, and, hardest of all, being taken to court by them.

Ida Merzan, who was from a small town near Hrubieszow in eastern Poland, remembers being shown by one of the apprentices to the room she would share with a few others and being warned not to be late to meals. Then she was left on her own. "It was really difficult those first few days," she said. "I was embarrassed when Korczak kept blocking my way—sometimes playfully, sometimes angrily—whenever I passed him in the hall. I didn't know what he meant or wanted. Later I learned that I had been breaking a rule, because the hall traffic on that floor was one-way, but no one had bothered to tell me."

When she entered the dining room her first night, the children were already seated at their tables for eight, with a teacher at each end. "I looked around helplessly," she recalled, "but Stefa just indicated with her hand a place at the ninth table. I could hear laughter when I passed Korczak's table, but he didn't look up. Later I noticed that the children who were assigned to be waiters didn't bump into each other because the traffic was regulated there also: those who served went down one row of tables, those who cleared down another."

Misha Wroblewski, an apprentice who came from Minsk, also remembers being confused his first day in the home. Told that he could do anything he wanted with the children after they returned from school, he organized a race with two teams. Bewildered by the heated banter between the opposing sides, he didn't know what to do when two boys began a fistfight. Noticing that the other children were sitting down to watch, he joined them. The two combatants soon tired, their blows trailing off into name-calling. Just as Misha was getting up to resume the race, a gong sounded calling the children to supper. They immediately scattered to wash their hands. Seeing Korczak watching from the doorway, Misha was sure he had lost his chance to train with the famous educator.

Korczak said nothing to Misha until ten that evening, when it was the custom for the apprentices to gather "under the stairs" in the back hall for a snack and coffee. "You know, it was wonderful, it was perfect," Korczak said, taking him aside. "But tell me, why did you let the boys disrupt the race with their fight? Why didn't you intervene?"

Misha felt himself flush because he didn't know what the doctor meant or how to answer. He decided to be honest: "I didn't stop them because I was as tired as the rest of the kids and was glad to sit down. And I knew the boys wouldn't kill each other."

Korczak scratched his bald head, then patted the spot absently in a characteristic gesture, as if lost in thought. "When one is close in age to children, he is able to feel as they do," he said softly, almost to himself. "Children know better than we when they've had enough. You were right not to stop the boys. If a fight breaks out spontaneously, it's best not to intervene as long as the children are evenly matched and aren't harming each other. Stopping it only forces children to continue it later in another place."

"Not interrupting the fight was my first educational coup," Misha recalls. "And it brought about my first conversation with the doctor. He told me that men make better kindergarten teachers than women because they're willing to let children fly at each other at the appropriate time." Yet, as focused as Korczak had been during that exchange, Misha would learn how absentminded the doctor could be when he was working on a book: sometimes he would repeatedly greet Misha with a hearty handshake when they passed in the hall as if it were the first time they had encountered each other that day.

Joseph Arnon was eighteen when he discovered Korczak's pedagogic writings in a library in Lvov and wrote to ask if he might train with him. Although the cordial return letter inviting him to visit the orphanage was noncommittal, Arnon packed a bag and set off for Warsaw.

Arriving at the orphanage, he encountered a large woman in black who asked brusquely if Korczak was expecting him and ordered him to wait in a small room adjoining her office near the front door. When Korczak came rushing by a half hour later with a group of children, Arnon was surprised to discover that he was the man in the green smock whom he had passed in the courtyard.

"He shook hands with me and led me into the little storeroom at the far end of the dining hall," Arnon has recalled. "We sat down at the small table there, and then he just looked at me with his intense blue eyes, saying nothing. I was wondering what to do when he began bombarding me with questions: Why did I choose to be a teacher? Why not something else? What did I want to do here? I can't remember exactly what I replied, but Korczak smiled and asked me to take off my shirt. I couldn't believe it. He was going to give me a medical examination. He put his cold ear against my chest, listened to my heart and lungs, and asked about my childhood diseases. I felt I was in a clinic. When he was finished and my shirt was back on, he said: 'Well, let's see how it all works out.' I was amazed. I had expected a deep conversation about education and the child. But this was so—ordinary."

Arnon then received the unsettling news that before a final decision could be made he would have to be interviewed by Stefa. His spirits were considerably dampened when he stepped into the office of the large woman in black. Did he have any money? she wanted to know; there was no salary. Did he realize all that would be demanded of him? Would he keep the rules of the home?

Arnon agreed to all of Stefa's conditions, only to be told that he would have to wait a month to be notified one way or the other. He had naïvely expected to begin immediately, and was now forced to find a temporary room. To his relief, he received his acceptance in only two weeks—Stefa's policy was to make most people wait for an answer so that they would appreciate getting in—but it took much longer than that before he felt comfortable with Stefa.

Like the other apprentices, he was initially confused when Korczak left it to him to decide his activity with the children. Eventually he chose to teach Hebrew to those whose relatives hoped to emigrate to Palestine. He realized that Korczak was deliberately vague with the new apprentices because he believed that it was impossible to teach pedagogics, that "everyone must find his own personal way to the child."

Arnon was fascinated that Korczak looked for nonrational reasons behind a child's behavior, and often reached a child by means of fantasy. The orphans were allowed to choose the portions of food they wanted, but could not leave any of it on their plates, so Arnon was nonplussed when Halinka, a seven-year-old girl at his table, refused to eat the crusts of her bread. Passing by at the end of a meal, Korczak would ask for the crusts and pop them into his mouth, a clownish antic that amused the other children. Later he took Arnon aside to inquire why he thought Halinka, who was usually well behaved, rejected the crusts. Trying to impress Korczak, Arnon began speculating on possible reasons, but Korczak dismissed them all. "You know, this girl may be endowing them with some special mystical powers," he told Arnon. "Let's pursue that possibility."

Korczak cajoled Halinka into confiding that she was afraid witches lived in the crusts. Her grandmother had told her so. He had to persuade her otherwise, but in a way that didn't contradict her grandmother, the only person she had left in the world. "No, Halinka, witches do not live in these crusts," he assured her. "They would never dine in such a humble place as ours. Witches eat caviar in castles in the mountains, very far from here, or in royal palaces like the ones our kings used to reside in. So now you can eat all your bread."

Although he played the seemingly detached observer, Korczak had a way of voicing an opinion when least expected. Once he came up behind an apprentice in the courtyard who was patting one child's head while talking to another: "Young lady," he said, "that is not a dog you are petting, but a person." Another time, after watching a new apprentice comply with a boy's request to untie his shoelace, he asked: "Tell me, my dear, do you plan to make education your career or just a temporary pastime?" Then he stooped down and gave her a practical lesson on how to teach a child to untie his own shoelaces. He was really teaching her how to make a child self-reliant. "I'll remove splinters from your tongues or your behinds," was his constant refrain to the children, "but never out of any place where you can do it by yourselves."

Yanka Zuk still remembers Korczak materializing out of nowhere as she was supervising a group of eighty children cooped up in a side room while the dining hall was being cleaned. She was having fun racing about with them when she saw Korczak moving toward her without a word, making it necessary for her to back up to avoid a collision. After maneuvering her into the narrow space between two cupboards, he stood with his hands in his pockets, his eyes full of mischief, and said: "Now stand quietly, my little one. Just observe. What do you see?"

When she didn't answer, he continued in the same sardonic vein: "Isn't it amazing that eighty children can play in such a small space without fighting or hitting one another? When you remain still like this, you have an opportunity to notice what is going on." He watched her watching the children interact with each other for about five minutes before he let her go.

From that experience Yanka learned firsthand that the art of observing was an essential part of her training as an educator. If the children asked for help or advice, one could give it; otherwise, one should not interfere with their natural play. "The truth about children is not to be found in books, but in life," Korczak would tell her. Yanka was also to learn that beneath Korczak's gruff exterior was a warmth that would surface once someone had gained his trust, that even his temper was part of his pedagogical strategy. "Run, run, run!" he would shout at her as she dashed by him down the hall. "How much longer are you going to exhaust yourself this way? You have to be able to work for the next thirty-five years!" But his seeming impatience with the apprentices was often no more than a theatrical act. "When I'm shouting at you, try to observe if I am only shouting with my mouth—the tongue and throat—or if I'm shouting from the heart," he wrote one of them years later. "Observe if I'm really angry, or just pretending. It's because I love you that I feel I have to scold."

Many of the apprentices came to think of Korczak as an erratic combination of father and adviser. Others were annoyed that he had the patience of an angel with the orphans but not with them. As young adults they belonged to an age group that he felt lacked trust and sincerity—unlike young children, who were open and honest. It bothered him that, no matter how much he and Stefa scolded, some of the apprentices still came late to meals and returned to the orphanage after hours. More than once he had the late-risers locked out of the dining room. An even worse fate befell them when they returned after curfew—10:00 on weeknights, 11:30 on weekends. Misha never forgot the terrible moment of finding Stefa waiting at the door. "She didn't have to say anything. Just her look was enough."

Korczak acknowledged that the *bursa* was like a monastery. It was not he and Stefa who required such strict conditions, but "faceless necessity, life itself," he told them. "We'd like to give you more. We know that you yearn to take part in Warsaw life. But if you stay out late, you'll be too tired the next day to keep up with the relentless energy of the children."

Korczak might lose his patience occasionally, but he seldom lost his sense of humor. In a skit he wrote entitled "The *Bursa* Suffers," he has

(preceding page) Janusz Korczak (Henryk Goldszmit) as a boy. "I have included this photograph because it's important what I looked like when I truly wanted to be a king." (opposite) Korczak teaching "Moshki" to read in summer camp, c. 1907. (above, top) Korczak in his medical school uniform. (above, bottom) Stefa Wilczynska about the time she met Korczak, 1909

(above) The Orphans Home, 92 Krochmalna Street. (below) The main
hall of the orphanage

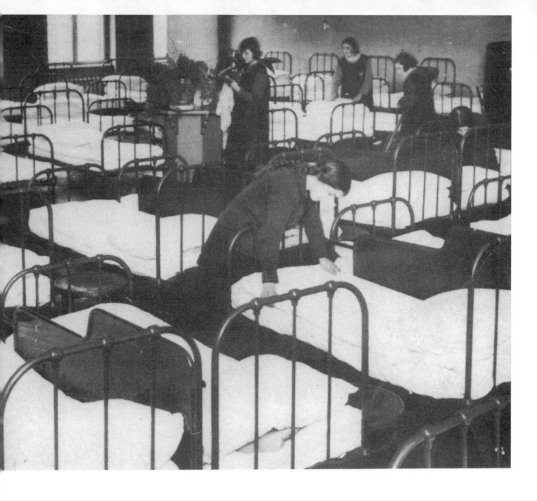

(above) The dormitory. (below, left) The kitchen. (below, right) The bath

(left) Maryna Falska, c. 1920.
(below) Falska with children in
Our Home, Pruszkow, c. 1924.
(opposite, top) A backyard
ballgame, Pruszkow. (oppo-
site, bottom) Children play in
snow behind Our Home, Bie-
lany, c. 1929

(above, top) A cottage in Little Rose summer camp. (above, bottom) Korczak at camp with teachers and children, 1927. (opposite) Korczak with children in courtyard of Orphans Home, early 1930s

(opposite) Korczak with the children of the Orphans Home, c. 1935. (above, top) Children's orchestra, Korczak conducting, c. 1930. (above, bottom) Relaxing under the chestnut tree, c. 1935

(right, top) Stefa, c. 1935. (right, bottom) Stefa with baby, Kibbutz Ein Harod, 1931. (opposite) Korczak at Kibbutz Ein Harod, 1934

(above) Korczak flanked by Hashomer Hatzair students, 1939. (below) Children peeling potatoes the last summer in Little Rose, 1940. (opposite, top) The last picture of Korczak, the Warsaw Ghetto, 1941. (opposite, below, and inset) Korczak's statue near his father's grave in Warsaw's Jewish cemetery (inset courtesy Witold Jaroslaw Szulecki)

(above, top) Unveiling of memorial stone for Korczak and the children, Treblinka, 1978. (bottom, from left) Igor Newerly (courtesy Bernd Graubner), Ida Merzan, Joseph Arnon, Michal Wroblewski

one apprentice complain: "I thought Korczak would be young and handsome. That we'd talk. If I got sick, he'd sit on my bed and read to me from his books. That wouldn't be improper because he's a doctor. But he's old and bald. I thought he'd be full of poetry. But he just prays and cleans his shoes."

Igor Newerly was Korczak's private secretary for two years before he moved into the orphanage to teach carpentry in 1928. As the son of a Russian army officer and a Polish woman of aristocratic origin, Newerly had lived in both Poland and Russia before coming to Warsaw at the age of twenty-three. He learned secretarial skills to support himself, and was grateful when a family friend introduced him to Korczak. For two hours each morning he took dictation for Korczak's private letters, articles, and stories; harboring a dream to become a writer himself, he valued watching Korczak meticulously prune each sentence down to its barest essentials. But one morning, feeling depressed over a love affair that had just ended, Newerly remained in bed, wondering if he should kill himself or leave for Abyssinia. He didn't even bother to notify Korczak that he wouldn't be at work that day, and it never occurred to him that Korczak might be worried and come by. Late that afternoon, still in his pajamas, he was horrified to find Korczak at his door, asking, "What's wrong, are you ill?"

Newerly had no sooner said yes than he remembered that his boss was a medical doctor. Korczak felt his pulse, did a cursory examination, and then asked sympathetically, "What's bothering you?" When Newerly told him about his broken heart, Korczak replied: "There's only one solution—to go to a monastery."

"A monastery?" Newerly repeated.

"Yes, the orphanage," said Korczak. "In the long run it's the same thing. You can regulate your life with gongs and schedules. And you can take classes at a university."

"I haven't the money to study," Newerly admitted.

"You'll receive free room and board, as well as 150 zlotys in exchange for teaching the children something," Korczak replied.

"But I'm not a teacher. I have no skills."

"What do you like to do?"

"Work with my hands. I'm a jack-of-all-trades."

"Very well, then," Korczak said, "you can set up a carpentry shop. We need one."

"But"—Newerly didn't know how to phrase it. He wasn't Jewish and he wasn't sure how he would fit into the orphanage. "But what if a child speaks to me in Yiddish?"

Korczak laughed. "You know the children speak Polish in the home. And, for that matter, I don't know Yiddish either."

Newerly still wasn't sure it was the answer to his problems. "But what if the children don't like me?"

"We'll know soon enough," Korczak told him. "After three months, the children vote on each new teacher. It's their decision who stays in the home."

But, of course, it was someone else's decision, too. "You'd better drop in and have a talk with Stefa as soon as possible," Korczak added.

Newerly remembered how apprehensive he had been of Stefa when he first became Korczak's secretary. They had had little to do with each other; if he thought of her at all, it was as a huge column supporting the entire house. But the interview went well. When Stefa laughed at a joke he had the inspiration to tell her, he saw that her face, though still not attractive, was actually pleasant. She was not as formidable as he had feared. He moved into the orphanage within a few days and enrolled in a course in sociology with Korczak's old friend and cellmate, Ludwik Krzywicki, at the Polish Free University. He had a hard time getting used to all the "monastery" rules, especially arriving for breakfast on time, but eventually bought himself an alarm clock. He set up a carpentry shop on the little balcony over the dining hall, and, like all apprentices, he was nervous when it came time for the children to vote on him. To his great relief, he received a majority of pluses—which meant he was one of the most popular teachers in the house.

The apprentices were instructed to keep a daily record of observations of the children in their care and to include any questions they themselves might have. Stefa went over the journals every night, writing answers in the margins. Korczak looked through their questions before the *bursa* seminars that were held each Friday night at nine, jotting down topics he wanted to refer to on small pieces of paper he carried in his pocket.

Those apprentices who hoped the famous educator would dazzle them with academic brilliance were disappointed by Korczak's low-key style. He would enter the room quietly, often lost in his own thoughts. Taking his seat at a small table, he would look attentively at the group, pull out a small piece of paper, and begin talking. He spoke extemporaneously, weaving in incidents from his own experience so freely that sometimes the thread of his thought disappeared from view until he unexpectedly retrieved it at the end of the seminar. He might devote a whole evening to one special point in a journal, or he might continue the discussion of the week before.

"To whom do Laibush's ears belong?" Korczak asked in one seminar. Yanka Zuk's face, as well as her ears, turned red as Korczak proceeded to read a note from the school nurse complaining that nine-year-old Laibush had dirty ears. Laibush, a sad child whose grandmother, his only living relative, had just died, was one of Yanka's charges. Even though a dormitory monitor saw to it that all the children washed each morning, it was her responsibility to check that he was neat and clean, dressed warmly, and took his sandwich with him when he went to school.

"Where did we make our mistake?" Korczak continued. "If everyone did his job here, what went wrong? During the course of the day, Laibush passed through many hands. Were his ears dirty when he left home, or did they become dirty in school?"

The discussion became a philosophical inquiry into who was responsible for Laibush's ears, rather than who was to blame. How had Laibush's ears escaped everyone's scrutiny? The next day Yanka overheard Korczak still talking animatedly to Stefa about Laibush's dirty ears.

Korczak prided himself on precision in everything—even the maintenance of ears. Ida Merzan remembers that he would not let the apprentices use vague words like "frequently," "seldom," "many," or "little." He would ask: "Exactly how many times did he hit that boy?" Or: "How long did he cry?" If an apprentice could not remember the first time, he always remembered after that.

Still, Korczak could be reassuring when his students were overly concerned that they had slipped up or failed. "Out of big worries you have to make small ones," he would say. "And out of small worries, you have to make nothing. It's easier that way."

One Friday night Korczak announced that a tangy piece of salted herring on a dry piece of bread is better than bland pea soup. "It is better to strive and suffer than to have everything and be bored. A difficult life, even with its suffering, has the tang of herring."

Stefa sat, as always, at the back of the room, looking through the apprentices' journals. At ten o'clock she glanced at her watch and announced: "We've been talking for about an hour. Tomorrow is going to be a busy day. We'd better end now." Taking Stefa's weekly cue, Korczak ended the session with: "Long live the herring!"

18

Madame Stefa

One morning in 1928, when she was forty-two, Stefa got up, put on her black dress with the white collar and cuffs, and went downstairs to the bulletin board. She tacked up a notice: "From now on, I am to be called Madame Stefa. It is not proper for a woman with as many children as I have to be called Miss."

The apprentices joked among themselves, Misha Wroblewski recalls: "Who was this courageous man who fathered all these children? How did she find him?" No one dared ask questions, but Stefa was adamant: she would answer to nothing but Madame Stefa. If a child cried out in the night for *Miss* Stefa, no one came. She was Madame Stefa from that time on.

She was, however, still the same Stefa. Up at six each morning, she rolled bandages before breakfast, examined wounds, and handed out medicine. Sometimes Korczak helped her: it was a good opportunity to have a private word with a child or to give a forgiving pat to one who had misbehaved. Yet the children turned to Stefa when they were sick—Korczak might be a physician, but she was their medical authority. One boy who had been told by Korczak that he could get out of bed after a bout of fever refused to leave the isolation room until he had her permission. Some children even looked forward to getting sick and having Stefa's full attention. "Being ill was a real treat," one recalls. "Stefa would prepare special dishes and fret over you. We all had a secret longing to be ill and treated by Stefa." Johann Nutkiewicz, never a favorite of Stefa's because of his mischievousness, remembers fainting when he had a high fever, and fading in and out of consciousness. Each time he opened his eyes, he saw Stefa beaming down at him.

During the day Stefa oversaw every aspect of the house's operation. It was she who made the budget; ordered coal for the winter, medicine for the infirmary, food for the kitchen; inspected the bedding; checked missing buttons, tears in clothes, soles on shoes; arranged trips to the circus or movies; recorded the court proceedings; organized the bulletin board; and kept up with the apprentices' notebooks.

Stefa walked softly, often taking the children by surprise, and slowly, as if honoring her mother's dictum: "The slower you go, the faster you get there." No one could anticipate better than she when to close the windows against the rain. The children used to say that Madame Stefa knew everything, saw everything, and heard everything. She could pick up the quietest whisper, and seemed to have eyes in the back of her head. When she returned to the home after doing errands in the city, she would run around with a pencil, making a list of those who had broken the rules.

She was never without her basket of keys. "When Stefa was passing through the house, we felt that a ship was crossing the ocean," Itzhak Belfer recalls. "It was a tight ship, with everything scrubbed and battened down." She seldom had engagements, except for her regular Wednesday-night dinner with her mother and sister, and never had visitors other than her brother Stash, an engineer, whose long legs served as a bridge for the children to run through, and whose suitcase with stickers from countries all over the world was a constant source of wonder.

For most of the orphans Stefa was "the heart, the brain, the nurse, the mother." And no one knew this better than Korczak. "I am like a father, with all the negative connotations of that word," he would say. "Always busy, lacking time, telling bedtime stories—and rarely that. While Stefa, well, she may not be right about some things, but I could not manage without her."

They were an impressive team, Stefa playing the no-nonsense mother to Korczak's more lenient father. When one scolded, the other would caress. Rarely did Korczak take the side of a child against her. But once when he came upon Sara Kramer in tears because Stefa had forbidden her to leave the dining hall until she had eaten all of her kasha, he sat down beside her, put his finger to his lips playfully, and swallowed the kasha. Stefa muttered a few words in French, as she always did when she didn't want the children to understand, and strode furiously out of the room. But later she laughed with some apprentices about the incident. "It was so like the Doctor to be sympathetic to a child in trouble," she said, as if to excuse his behavior.

"I was afraid of Stefa when I first came to the orphanage," Sara remembers. "I missed my mother very much. On Saturdays when I was home, I'd cry that I didn't want to go back to the orphanage. But my mother would say: 'Stay, it will be good for you.' And she was right. My mother was always my mother, but I developed differently than I would have if I had lived with her. She couldn't give me the knowledge and values that Stefa did." Sara recalls fondly how Stefa bathed and washed her hair with the girls. "She liked me to comb her hair. It took a long time because the part had to be straight. Now I understand that she needed someone to touch her."

"I think Stefa may have been jealous of my mother, because in spite of her limitations, she had a daughter, and Stefa didn't," Hanna Dembinska said. "Whatever Stefa did for me, she could never be my mother." As if she understood this, Stefa would not let herself believe how much she meant to the children. Even when they returned to visit every Saturday after they had left the orphanage, first bringing their troubles and their joys, then their husbands and babies, she would say: "They come because they need me."

In many ways Stefa was also like a mother to the young apprentices, especially the women, who were living far from home for the first time. "She treated us like children, while Korczak regarded us as adults," one recalls. "She would bring sausage, rolls, and halvah for our ten o'clock snack under the stairs because she worried that we weren't eating enough." Most of Stefa's communication with the apprentices was limited to her responses in their journals, but she could not resist a direct comment if she felt that they were careless with their things. Noticing a young woman hopping on one leg to keep her balance while putting on stockings, Stefa said, "I always sit down to do that. I'm not so rich that I can risk ruining my hose."

She was an inspiration to many of the apprentices, who learned organization from her, and marveled that she could get so much done. Coming upon Stefa inspecting the children's clothes one Saturday afternoon when everyone else was out, Ida Merzan asked her: "Don't you ever rest?" "There are many ways to rest," Stefa responded. "If you feel tired doing one job, switch to another. It calms you down."

* * *

Was it Korczak or the children who held Stefa to the daily grind of her life? the apprentices often wondered. "Now I realize how much bitterness there must have been behind her request to be called Madame Stefa," Ida Merzan says today. "How many hidden feelings and thoughts about life passing by and the approach of old age."

That Stefa loved Korczak no one had any doubt. When he went into town to lecture or to see his publisher, she was always at the door to check if his tie was straight, if he had a handkerchief, if he had money, if he needed an umbrella. He would wave her away impatiently with his hand—something he would never do with a child.

It bothered the female apprentices that Korczak could treat Stefa so rudely, but Stefa remained undaunted after each dismissal. Once when he went out dressed lightly on a cool day, she was overheard muttering to herself: "What shall I do with that big child? He coughs and goes without a sweater." It was a joke among the apprentices that she had a hundred and seven children—if you counted Korczak.

Ida Merzan remembers Stefa laughing about the trouble she had buying Korczak a new sweater. She had to go from shop to shop because she knew that if she didn't find one exactly like his old cardigan, he wouldn't wear it. When she finally located one, she had to contend with a saleswoman who kept insisting that pullovers were more fashionable. "I am buying this for a large child with a lot of hair," Stefa said with a straight face. "A pullover will mess it up."

That Korczak needed Stefa was also beyond anyone's doubt. She shielded him from the mundane details of orphanage management; she spared him from involvement in the flurry of activity around the annual Orphans Aid Society's ball, a gala social event whose proceeds helped keep the orphanage solvent; she put up with his moods and his frequent absences. With her he could be himself—absentminded, abstracted, remote—with no playacting necessary, no mask.

But was it enough for Stefa? When she was away on Wednesday nights, Korczak liked to tease the female apprentices during the ten o'clock snack under the stairs: "Now that Madame Stefa is out, we can flirt." But when she was there, no one ever saw them exchange so much as a gentle caress of the hand, or heard them address each other with anything but the formal *you* or their titles: Pan Doctor and Pani Stefa. Living under the same roof, they were seldom together. They sat with the children at separate dining tables. Their bedrooms were on different floors. They seldom went out together, except for the odd Sunday visit to Stefa's sister, Julia, who was the director of a fashionable summer camp for girls just outside of Warsaw.

It was rumored that there had been a tragedy in Stefa's personal life, but the stories were contradictory. A fiancé who had been killed in the war, some thought. But which war? No one knew. Stefa never spoke of it, but then Stefa never confided anything intimate, never invited anyone into her modest room, whose only adornment was tiny cactus plants. No one, that is, except her favorite apprentice, Feiga Lipshitz, and her family. Her brother, Stash, a successful engineer and now married to Irena Eliasberg, often came on Friday nights. Irena, who did not share her parents' involvement with the orphanage, or her husband's need to see Stefa, dreaded those visits because of the unpleasant smell of the floor cleaner applied just before the Sabbath. If they arrived when the children were still eating, Stefa would wave from her table, and then escort them upstairs.

"I would often think of my luxurious drapes, paintings, and brocade chairs as I sat in Stefa's bare room," Irena said. "I wondered how she could be satisfied with so little. And you couldn't give her anything. She was just like her mother—wouldn't accept gifts. I used to get really frustrated when the holidays came around. Not that her mother had anything either. She had made the mistake of selling her apartment building in the early twenties and lost her money in the subsequent financial crisis. Fortunately, she had held on to her own apartment and could take in a few boarders. When Stefa and Stash wanted to give her something, they persuaded the boarders to pay higher rent, which they subsidized from behind the scenes. Stefa could give, but she couldn't take. Still, I think she was truly happy with what she did. It got rather boring sometimes to hear how wonderful everything was with her children and the Doctor."

No letters between Stefa and Korczak have been preserved—not a scrap of paper that might reveal the measure of intimacy they had with each other when not under the scrutinizing eyes of their wards or the apprentices. There is only the dedication of an advance copy of *King Matt the First*, which Korczak inscribed to Stefa in his precise handwriting on October 25, 1922. It is witty. He takes the guise of one of her boys, the fifty-first:

To Miss Stefa:

The boy with number 51 does not have a skin disease. He lost his birth certificate in the kingdom of Bum Drum. He asks for the work duty of gathering rubbish. He is clean ("God help him!"). He is a resident of Warsaw.

Goldszmit

The jaunty style of the dedication reveals a playful rather than a romantic relationship. In the real kingdom where Stefa reigns, Korczak is one of the real boys, with a number, and work duties, and citizenship in Warsaw to prove it. But his true homeland, the land of his birth, is in the fantastic kingdom of the imagination where Stefa cannot enter.

The question has often been asked: Were Korczak and Stefa ever lovers? According to Stella Eliasberg, Korczak suspected her of trying to match him with Stefa when she first invited him to the shelter on Franciszkanska back in 1909. When he confided this to Stefa, they had a good laugh and analyzed their feelings: yes, they were both in love—but with the children.

Igor Newerly sees the situation differently: he believes that Stefa's unrequited love for Korczak was the tragedy of her life. Once, when he was alone in Korczak's garret room typing up correspondence, Stefa, knowing that Korczak was away, opened the door and walked in. Startled at seeing Newerly there, she turned and rushed out without a word. Newerly felt pity for her at that moment. "I think she must have come into his room often when he was out, probably just to look over his desk and see what he was working on, and to check that everything was in order. It was a way she had of feeling close to him."

"A few months after I moved into the orphanage, I was in my basement workshop putting together a new game for the boys when Stefa suddenly appeared at my side," Newerly continued. "She had a way of walking softly so that you never heard her approaching. 'What are you making?' she asked me, adjusting the wool shawl over her shoulders. When I explained that it was a war game, played with ships, she asked if it wasn't strange that a sociology student should be preoccupied with games. I told her that when I was twelve my mother had wondered the same thing. She smiled, as if recalling something very pleasant, and said, 'Well, Pan Doctor said he played with blocks until he was fourteen.' And then she reminded me that it was eleven o'clock and I had an exam the next day.

" 'How is it possible for you to know everything?' I asked her. 'I simply observe and remember,' she replied. 'You put a note on the bulletin board a few days ago that you would not be available on Friday because you had an exam. Please go to bed now.' When I went to sleep that night, I kept thinking of how Stefa's face lit up when she spoke of Korczak."

19

Not Every Truth
Can Be Blown
on a Trumpet

It is possible that Stefa's request to be called Madame Stefa had nothing to do with Maryna Falska being known as Madame Maryna. Yet she must have been on Stefa's mind in 1928, because that was the year the new building that Korczak had helped Maryna design for Our Home became ready for occupancy.

Maryna had attracted a powerful patron in Aleksandra Pilsudska, the second wife of Jozef Pilsudski. This resourceful woman (known for her courage in the prewar underground) had chosen social work as an arena where she would not create any "ambiguous situations" for her husband. Dissatisfied with the inadequate quarters in Pruszkow, she began raising money to build a large, modern facility for the orphans in a wooded suburb of Warsaw known as Bielany. Her excellent connections made it possible for her to acquire a state concession for a small shop selling liquor and tobacco, whose proceeds would go to Our Home. She also helped Maryna organize an annual charity ball, which, not surprisingly, was well attended.

Maryna was still the intensely private and formal person whom Korczak had met in Kiev. Like Stefa, she continued to wear only black, a style of dress that many women of their generation had chosen to commemorate the failed uprising of 1863 and had not discarded once independence had been won. Although these two women so dedicated to social welfare had much in common—including their attachment to Korczak—they seldom saw each other.

One of the few occasions they were together was the opening ceremony of Our Home, at which Aleksandra Pilsudska presided. It was a big event in Warsaw. The press called the sprawling building the "Children's Palace," because it had running water, electricity, and other amenities that were unheard of in most orphanages at that time. Designed in the shape of an airplane, it had two residence wings which fanned out at right angles from the central administrative building, and easily accommodated 120 children, ranging in age from four to fourteen.

The right-wing anti-Semitic newspapers labeled Our Home "a new nest of Masonry and potential Communism erected in the heart of the capital," and decried the lack of a chapel. "Well, it's Korczak," one journalist wrote. "What else can you expect when a Jew runs the board?" Few people knew that Korczak had tried to persuade Maryna to include a chapel in the original plans. He had set aside a room in his Jewish orphanage where children could go before breakfast to say kaddish or other prayers for their parents, because he believed that all children need to express their grief and talk with God. He often sat with the children in the room, a yarmulke on his head, a prayer book on his lap, his eyes closed in silent meditation. But there was nothing he could do to persuade Maryna, who had boycotted her own husband's funeral on atheistic principles, to yield on the chapel.

Maryna had a staff—one might call it another "regiment of women"—to do much of what Stefa took care of herself. Many of them were loyal friends who had known Maryna in Kiev: Karolina Peretiakowicz (Miss Kara), whose mother had the girls' school there, was her administrative assistant—a warm, motherly woman whom the children adored; Maria Podwysocka (Miss Maria) was in charge of finances.

"We were close, but Maryna kept her distance even with us," recalls Eugenka, another colleague from Kiev. "She would answer our professional questions but never shared her personal thoughts. Just once, at the beginning of the war when she was depressed, did she confide to me that there were moments she could feel the presence of her dead husband and friends, and that those ghosts were more real to her than living people."

Maryna's schedule was much like Stefa's. Up at five-thirty or six every morning, she never deviated from her routine. At seven she was in the kitchen supervising the children's breakfast, and was always at the door to see them off to school, checking buttons, collars, school bags. After inspecting all the rooms, she went to her office to plan menus with the cook and organize work details. At two, when the children returned for lunch, Maryna always sat at the same place at the head of the horse-shoe-shaped table where she could see everything. (The door to her office on the main floor had a glass pane through which she could observe the children passing by.) Between three and five every afternoon Maryna retired to her room, where it was understood that she was not to be disturbed.

At five o'clock on Fridays she presided over what the orphans called the "Hour of Guilt." Anyone who had committed an offense that week was to come to her room to sign a book that she kept there for that purpose. She did not invite anyone to the orphanage, but on Friday nights she went to the home of relatives, where she received old friends. On Saturday evenings after she and the children had their baths, she took bets against bad behavior in a ledger, much as Korczak did, and dispensed milk chocolates, after which she told stories by the fire.

Maryna spoke in low, measured tones, as if weighing each word. She inspired both love and fear in the orphans and apprentices. She had only to glance at whatever they were doing, and she knew what they were thinking. "She wasn't forgiving like Korczak," Igor Newerly recalled. "With Maryna, there was no hope. She held everyone responsible for their actions. If you were late, you were not excused. If she didn't like you, she made your life miserable. She was a tough woman." Maria Taboryska, one of the orphans, remembers that Maryna's blue eyes peered out of her pale face "like pieces of ice," but that she was capable of such caring gestures as reaching out to brush back a lock of a girl's hair when they passed in the hall. Only one boy, whom she always called by her pet name for him, Lomulek, was able to get close to her. He was clearly her favorite. But if he was naughty, she could reduce him to tears by calling him by his last name.

Maryna sometimes took walks with the older boys and girls through the forest behind the orphanage. They were amazed to see her roll a cigarette, since she never smoked in their company at home. She would reminisce about her former political activities, including the periods she spent in prison and exile, and would advise them never to be afraid of difficulties in life.

Igor Newerly, recalling the year he taught carpentry in Our Home, said: "Maryna would walk through the world of children in her black dress with its stiff collar and white starched cuffs, encased as if in armor against the outside world, against herself, like a nun in her habit, like a woman judge in her robes. She would smile kindly at the children who came to her with their small yet very real problems, but the smile did not look comfortable in the corners of her severe, narrow mouth. She had moments of uninhibited merriment—but she lacked a sense of humor. Her sharp, concentrated gaze would notice things unobserved by us, though she wasn't articulate like Korczak. She was the loneliest, most isolated person I have ever met."

Newerly recalls that when he stayed up late one night in the carpentry shop finishing a chest as an Easter gift for the house, Maryna became infuriated that he went to bed before sweeping up. She cleaned the room herself and was so hostile to him after that that he was forced to move out. It wasn't until a year later, when he stopped by to see the children on a day when Korczak was there, that she was willing to offer her hand and shake his as a friend once again.

The children of Our Home would wait for Korczak by the windows or down at the gate. A boy might want to sell a loose tooth; an older girl might need his help in getting permission to go to a real beauty parlor for her next haircut; others might just want to have a piggyback ride, or to look in his pockets for the candy he always carried. Some weeks Korczak came early to talk with Maryna and the staff, bragging that he had walked all the way to Bielany to save tram fare. He would sit on the front stoop to rest, recounting how he had also saved money by reading all the newspapers in a small coffee shop on the corner of Marszalkowska Street, which was on the way.

"I won't wish you good health," he would tell the caretaker, Wladyslaw Cichosz, who always waited for him as eagerly as the children. "Be a little ill, go to bed, you work too hard." And he would add, "I don't mean seriously ill, just a cold or something."

The children would hang on Korczak with the same glee as the children he had left behind on Krochmalna. He made jokes while he examined them, and with mock gallantry would kiss the hands of the youngest girls. He liked to tease them with questions like: "Have you ever seen a cow with a green tail?" He never tired of telling friends about the girl who answered: "And you? Have you ever seen a cake with a herring inside?" Although he stayed only one night a week at Our Home, he always appeared on holidays such as May Day and Easter. On Christmas Eve he danced with them around the tree.

Once when a child asked him why he had no wife, he replied he had three: "Madame Maryna, Madame Stefa, and Miss Kara." But not all of the women on the staff at Our Home felt comfortable with Korczak. "I respected him, but it is difficult to say I liked him," Eugenka said. "He was certainly unusual. When he asked me questions, I felt I had to answer cleverly."

Maria Podwysocka was reluctant to take walks with Korczak because he had a disconcerting way of digging into his pocket to oblige every beggar who approached them. "Why must you give money to these people?" she once had the courage to ask. "They probably have more than you do."

"They may," he replied. "But then again there may be one who does not have as much."

Maria never questioned Korczak's aims, and would rise to his defense if anyone else did. When a mutual friend suggested that Korczak was not preparing his orphans to face the real world, she replied indignantly: "You understand nothing. The doctor knows very well that the world is unjust; that's why he has created an oasis of goodness. He wants to raise children who will be incapable of doing evil, and who will fight it with virtue."

After Our Home moved to Bielany, there was room for twenty apprentices. Like their counterparts at Krochmalna, they had been eager to work with the eminent Janusz Korczak, but they, too, were confused by his unpredictable behavior. Stanislaw Rogolowski remembers that when he was being interviewed by Maryna Falska in her office, a "small man with a beard" sat writing in a notebook at a far table. Trying to impress the directress, Rogolowski was emphasizing his interest in working with troubled children when the bearded man pushed back his chair and shouted: "There are special institutions for that!" On his way out of the office, Rogolowski learned from one of the children that the man who had exploded at him was none other than the famous Dr. Korczak. He was amazed when he was accepted into the *bursa*.

The new apprentices at Our Home were also given very little orientation. "You either stayed afloat or went under," Henrietta Kedzierska commented, recalling her disappointment in the "slim, inconspicuous elderly man in a gray smock" who shook hands with her group, glanced indifferently from behind his wire-rimmed glasses, and went on his way. Madame Maryna spoke only a few words about what they were expected to do with the children before turning them over to an experienced apprentice to show them around. They were informed that after the children were in bed on Thursday nights they would have their seminar with Dr. Korczak.

"Whenever the doctor ran out of his office, he was immediately surrounded by children flocking to him like chickens to a mother hen," Henrietta noted in her private diary. "And that grump laughed with them, listened to their nonsensical chatter with great interest, while he didn't have even a few minutes to spare for the new apprentices." She hoped he would finally make the members of her group feel welcome when they joined the Thursday-night seminar, but "not a chance." He was completely indifferent to them, continuing a topic from the previous week as if they weren't there. That night she noted in her diary: "The so-called philosopher is a real crackpot."

Besides helping the third-graders with their homework, Henrietta was assigned to polish the corridor outside the dormitories on the third floor after it had been washed by someone else. Equipped with a cloth and a broom, she was rushing down the hall to attack her job when she encountered Korczak. Feeling self-conscious, she started sweeping the floor. He stopped, watched her for a few moments, and asked: "New?"

"A new broom—or new person?" she retorted quickly.

"Person," he replied, equally flip.

Afraid that her sharp tongue would get her into trouble, Henrietta tried to sound polite: "New person." But she added boldly: "However, since yesterday, she's lost in this jungle." She didn't know that the hearty laugh Korczak gave in response meant he was up to mischief.

"Well, what have we here?" he asked gaily. "Have you ever in all your long life polished floors before?"

"Yes," she replied, still feeling bold, "but the rooms were like matchboxes compared to these."

She felt ill at ease again as he examined her hands with their brightly painted nails. Whatever he was thinking was hidden by his pleasant "Since you are in training here, I will teach you how this work should be done. To begin with, your piece of cloth is much too small to polish this large corridor. It would be better to use a blanket." He suggested that she take one from her bed, being sure to remove its cover.

He folded the blanket she gave him lengthwise and told her to sit on one end while he grabbed the other and pulled. She rode "as if on a sleigh" back and forth a few times until the corridor shone like a mirror. When they finished, the blanket he handed her looked like an old rag.

A wicked expression came over Korczak's face as he exclaimed in mock horror: "Well, well, this is how the new staff respects an institution's property! In ten minutes a new blanket becomes a dishrag! How shocking! Disgraceful! I will inform the administrator in charge immediately!"

"But you told me to do it," Henrietta protested weakly.

Now he seemed genuinely angry. "What an innocent baby you are! What a smart aleck! There's always someone else to blame." And he rushed down the hall.

Henrietta was left standing there, completely bewildered. She resigned herself to being in Korczak's bad graces. But during the next Thursday-night seminar, he seemed to have forgotten the incident as he addressed the complaints of some apprentices about being unfairly sued by the children.

"So they sue you and take you to court," he said. "You ask why. You insist you are innocent. You blame others, not yourself." His voice was growing agitated. "You cannot make a fool out of a wise man. One needs courage to refuse."

The other apprentices couldn't follow Korczak's digression, but Henrietta understood that his remarks were directed at her. She realized that he had tested her to see how far she would go in blind obedience to authority. She had failed the test, but gained some wisdom. In the future she would think before she acted, and rely on her own judgment.

Like Stefa, Maryna communicated with the apprentices through their journals. She was capable of filling many pages when she felt strongly on a subject. In 1929 Stanislaw Zemis wrote of how furious he had been at the boys for using swear words at Scout camp. After he reprimanded them, they had asked for time to improve and were making progress, but now back in Bielany, they were cursing again. Could Madame Maryna please speak to them about this?

"It's not easy for me to answer you," Maryna replied in his journal. "I can't recall hearing the girls swear. I think they're afraid of me, so they don't quarrel in my presence. But Pan Doctor, whose room is next to the boys' dormitory, notes their swearing, and says nothing. Naturally the boys think he accepts it. Since I've started staying in the dormitory with the boys until they go to sleep, their behavior has improved. I tell them sternly to keep their things in order and not to use bad words. However, on the one night I skipped going there, I found that the boys had blocked the toilet door with a broom. It means that the boys, like the girls, are afraid of me and behave differently when I'm around. They know I'll react. One should react. Pan Doctor's habit of being just an observer doesn't change the behavior of bullies like Oleg who lord it over the weaker ones."

Maryna crossed out another page of comments, perhaps because she realized they were too critical of Korczak. Although she had written a booklet only the year before on the educational practices of Our Home (which were based on Korczak's self-government system) with a laudatory introduction by him, she was becoming increasingly impatient with his refusal to confront the more aggressive boys. She didn't agree that one should wait patiently until a troublemaker had come around to accepting the necessity of being a good citizen of the home. In fact, she disapproved of many of Korczak's ideas: that children should vote on each other and the staff (she would soon discontinue this practice and award the children merits for good behavior) and that children should be permitted to take adults to court. The apprentices often heard her quarreling with Korczak on these issues. More than once she threatened to resign and turn the orphanage over to him. "We thought he was soft-hearted," one said, referring to the way Korczak would try to placate Maryna. Yet the apprentices also noticed that Korczak did not modify any of his strategies with the children.

Stanislaw Rogolowski remembers how surprised he was at Korczak's reticence in answering some of the questions the apprentices posed. "Instead of giving a definite answer, he would say 'I don't know,' or 'Maybe,' or 'I can't answer because I've never been able to solve it.' Or: 'I could offer an interpretation, but I don't know if it would be adequate.' If he were pressed, he might say: 'Not every truth can be blown on a trumpet.' "

Yet there were seminars when Korczak surprised everyone with a definite, unqualified response. One of the apprentices confessed to losing his temper when a difficult boy challenged him with: "You wouldn't dare hit me! You know Pan Doctor would throw you out in the cold!" Grabbing the child by the collar, the apprentice had snapped: "I won't spank you, but I'll fix you so you'll never have the nerve to behave like this again." And he dragged the boy down the stairs to the basement, threatening to lock him in there where he could yell and curse all he wanted at the rats. It had the desired effect. The boy became docile immediately, and was compliant from then on.

Everyone waited for what Korczak would say. The doctor seemed to shrink before their eyes, his head disappearing into his shoulders as he spoke in a strange whisper, as if to himself: "A mischievous child is naughty because he is unhappy. Nervous. Your duty as a teacher is to find out what is bothering him. Perhaps he has a toothache and is afraid to admit it because you'll insist on calling the dentist. Perhaps he has a temperature and doesn't want to tell for fear he won't be allowed to go to tomorrow's movie. Perhaps he had a bad night because he was thinking of his mother who is dead, or living far from here. Perhaps he dreamed of her and woke up crying. Perhaps he was certain that nobody loves him. And you, the teacher, are the one he uses to get even for all those injustices, for his lost mother. Far away, sad, poor, angry, bitter—but still his own mother. You are strong, healthy, smiling—but a stranger. The mischievous child doesn't know that you really care about him, that you are trying to protect him from a cold world filled with evil. He doesn't understand that you have to protect the other children, who trust and need you, from his pranks. He doesn't realize that he is harming himself as well as you. But you know. So into that dark cellar with him! Scare the brat out of his wits! Perhaps you really hope he gets hurt. A wrong for a wrong!"

Korczak was still whispering to himself: "There are many terrible things in this world, but the worst is when a child is afraid of his father, mother, or teacher. He fears them, instead of loving and trusting them." Now Korczak's voice was full of hurt and bitterness. He closed his eyes. Minutes of uncomfortable silence followed. No one knew what to do. Was Korczak thinking? Crying? Sleeping? The apprentice who had confessed wished he hadn't. But Korczak had not fallen asleep. Suddenly he cried out: "God, please forgive him for scaring the poor child!" And without saying good night, he got up from his chair and left the room.

20

The Happiest Period

When the orphanage was asleep, Korczak lived in his garret room as "deliberately" as Thoreau did in his hut on Walden Pond. By shutting himself off in this monastic way from marriage and family, from card games, dinner parties, and balls, he left himself free to concentrate on what were to him the essentials of life. If Thoreau was an "inspector of rainstorms and snowstorms," then Korczak was an observer of the storms that swept across the landscapes of childhood.

Late one night in 1925 he was sitting at his desk, taking stock. At forty-seven, he was aware of the passage of time, that he was slipping toward the half-century mark—not a respectable age for a child. The fact that his body had betrayed him by growing into an adult shape was one of the strange ironies of his life. For walk as he might among adults in their hypocritical world, resemble them as he might with his "watch and mustache and desk full of drawers," he knew that he was really an impostor. The apprentices might be younger, but in some ways they were not as young as he. It was only the years that were on their side. If he could help them return to that earlier period when all their senses were open, if he could penetrate the defenses they erected to shut out the crying child in themselves, then he could make them sensitive to the underlying causes of a youngster's seemingly irrational behavior. But how could he make them young again—or himself?

He wrote on a piece of paper: *When I Am Little Again,* and followed it with the same first line with which he had begun *King Matt*—"And so this is what happened." However, this story was not about an imaginary young king, but about a middle-aged teacher, very much like himself, who is lying in bed daydreaming: What if he were a boy again? He'd want to remember everything that he knows now, only he wouldn't want anyone to find out that he had once been a grownup. If children only knew how unhappy adults are, they'd never want to grow up: adults have much less freedom than children, and many more responsibilities and sorrows; if they don't cry anymore, it's because there's nothing worth crying about. And here the teacher sighs deeply.

The room suddenly becomes dark. He sees an incandescent ball float into the room, becoming smaller and smaller until it lands on his head. It is a tiny man, no larger than his finger, with a long white beard and a tall red hat. He carries a lantern in one hand.

"You called me with the Sigh of Longing," the elf says. "What is it you wish?"

"I wish to be little again."

Immediately the elf swings his lantern around, blinding him for a moment, mumbles something, and is gone.

The teacher wakes the next morning in the house of his childhood. His mother is preparing breakfast for him before he leaves for school. He is a boy again, but with a difference—he still has his adult memories.

It is awkward at first, having to fool everyone into thinking that he is experiencing childhood for the first time. He has to pretend that he doesn't know how to read and write. He feels foolish when he finds himself banging a metal sign with his hand and whistling like a train. But soon the old magic of childhood becomes natural—he recovers his clear thin voice, and enjoys barking like a dog and crowing like a cock. Once again, running is like galloping on a horse, racing with the wind. When he wakes the next morning to the "white, transparent, blinding joy" of snow, he remembers that when he was a grownup, looking at newly fallen snow, he was already anticipating the slush that would follow, the damp overshoes, and the difficulty of getting coal.

When I Am Little Again is vintage Korczak, taking the reader through the playgrounds and minefields of childhood. "A child has a different clock, a different calendar, measures time differently," the teacher turned child declares. "His day is divided into brief seconds and long centuries. Children and grownups disturb one another. It would be nice if people could alternate being big and little—like summer and winter, day and night. Then children and grownups would understand each other."

This imaginative device is ideal for Korczak the writer and Korczak the educator. In the dual role of boy/man he can jump back and forth in the life cycle, explaining each side to the other. The middle-aged teacher has not been a child more than a few hours when he sheds his first tears. He realizes he has forgotten the slights and injustices he felt as a boy. A real child has never been an adult and doesn't understand why he irritates his parents and teachers, but the make-believe child who is really an adult sees quite clearly how things look from both sides. And so, after a series of misunderstandings with both adults and his young peers, the author has the boy/man implore the elf to return him once again to his grownup form as a teacher.

Because this book was written for both children and adults, Korczak wrote a separate preface for each. In the one for children he is the close friend, explaining that they will not find the usual adventure story, but rather a psychological tale about how a person thinks and feels inside. In the preface for adults, he is the didactic educator: "You are mistaken if you think we have to lower ourselves to communicate with children. On the contrary, we have to reach up to their feelings, stretch, stand on our tiptoes."

The nineteen-twenties were Korczak's most prolific period. "If one could say to the sun: stop, it would probably be at this time of life," he would write in the *Ghetto Diary*, recalling those years when the world was still the world he had known, all intact. Warsaw was still Warsaw, a cosmopolitan yet cozy city. "My city, my street, the store where I regularly shop, my tailor, and most important of all—my workshop." Equally beloved was the Vistula River, which ran through his city, changing in color and shape with the seasons, along whose shores he had strolled alone or with friends as a boy and a man: "I love you, gray Vistula. I would not exchange you for the proud Thames, the turbulent Niagara, or the magical Ganges. Those others, perhaps a hundred times more beautiful, would speak to me in a language which I could not understand."

In the fall of 1926 the Jewish children of Warsaw found out about an exciting new project in Korczak's workshop, through a letter addressed to them in their parents' newspaper, *Our Review*, a Zionist Polish-language daily. "To My Future Readers," it began, and went on to announce a newspaper for children, the *Little Review*, which would appear as a supplement every Friday. Janusz Korczak, the writer of the letter—who identified himself as the author of *King Matt the First*—explained how the idea for the newspaper had come to him: "When I stopped being a doctor, I didn't know what to do with myself, so I started writing books. But writing books takes a long time, and I don't have enough patience. It takes a lot of paper, too, and your hand aches. So I thought maybe it's better to start a newspaper, because then the readers will help you. I cannot do it alone."

He needs their assistance, he tells them. They must all become correspondents and send articles and letters regularly to the office at 7 Nowolipki, "a big building with a garden nearby, and an antenna on the roof which picks up news from all over the world." They were to write about the things that made them both happy and sad, and the problems that they needed help with. There would be twelve telephones for anyone who wanted to call in a story, an editor for boys and another for girls, and "an old one with spectacles to help see that everything gets done."

The purpose of the paper, he explained, was "to defend children." Those who didn't know how to write could come in and dictate to an editor. No one was to feel shy or fear being laughed at. Articles would be published on all kinds of topics: soccer, movies, trips, politics. The morning edition for younger children would have lots of pictures, and contests with prizes of Swiss chocolates and toys. There would be feature stories on pets, childhood illnesses, or hobbies, interviews with children who were doing unusual things, and a weekly serial, the first of which would be the diary of an orphan. The afternoon edition would take up more serious subjects, with prizes of books, watches, and movie tickets. The paper would be "nonpolitical and nonpartisan."

What Korczak did not tell his future readers was that this was an old dream coming true. He regarded a children's press as the "ABC of life." "Children are a sizable social class, have a large number of professional and family problems, needs, desires, and doubts," he had written in the *Polish Courier* the year before. When *Our Review* offered him a supplement in the Friday issue, he could not refuse.

The response surprised everyone. In the first few weeks, hundreds of letters from children all over Poland poured into the office of the *Little Review*. "There were nice and cheerful letters about birthdays and holidays, and sad and serious letters filled with dreams, troubles, and complaints," Korczak reported to his readers. One boy complained that his father had not kept his promise to give him a bicycle if he got good grades, and another that he was being ridiculed in class because of a special smock his mother made him wear over his clothes. To the boy who reported being slapped by his mother and father for sliding on the carpet, Korczak wrote: "Parents hit when they have problems and they're short of patience. Tell them not to hit you immediately, but to warn you that if you don't do as you are told, they will hit you in half an hour. That will give them time to calm down."

Korczak sent his young reporters to investigate the validity of the letters, and wrote editorials about how bad it was to give false promises to children and to be insensitive to their needs. Parents found it was embarrassing to have their child's letter in print for all the neighbors to see and gossip about. Before long, the boy with the smock wrote that he didn't have to wear it anymore, and others reported similar progress.

Nothing was too trivial to be printed in those first years of the paper. One child told of being shaken by the death of a chicken, another of seeing a small dog run over by a train. In his weekly response to letters, Korczak recalled having nightmares for weeks as a boy after seeing a cat run over. He even gave a brief account of how he and his sister buried his dead canary: "We were crying when we came back from that cemetery and the cage was empty. And later on I saw many terrible things, how people and animals suffer. Now I don't cry anymore, but I'm very, very sad. Sometimes grownups laugh when a child cries. They shouldn't do that. A child hasn't seen much suffering, and isn't used to it."

Although Korczak neglected to mention that the burial of his canary led to the traumatic realization that he was a Jew, the *Little Review* did have a special column of letters from children reporting on anti-Semitism. A boy wrote: "I am the only Jewish child in my class, and I feel like a stranger, an outsider." One girl complained that some nasty classmates used a Jewish variation of her name; another girl reported that some bullies always shouted at her: "Jews, go to Palestine!"

Korczak responded to these children: "I know how it used to be, how it is, and how it should be. Our paper will devote many articles to this subject. We can't promise that we'll solve the problem or have quick remedies, because we know it is a difficult and painful issue. But if a paper for children has a duty to defend children, then a paper for Jewish children has a duty to defend those who suffer for being born Jews."

In the afternoon edition of the paper, Korczak wrote articles on politics for the older children. Having promised that they would not be "boring or have the kind of long difficult words that adults use," he tried to explain, in language they could understand, how Jozef Pilsudski, weary of the constant change of governments, had come out of his three-year retirement and staged a coup in May of 1926. Korczak, who admired Pilsudski for his fair treatment of all minority groups, including the Jews, hoped that, with Pilsudski at the helm again, Poland would become more stable.

Because Korczak saw the newspaper as more therapeutic than literary, he was not bothered by bad grammar or misspellings. His young reporters were encouraged to write about their own experiences rather than compose poetry or fiction. Korczak the doctor wanted to give children a healthy outlet for expressing the grievances bottled up inside them; Korczak the educator wanted to gather more data on children's perceptions of their lives. The children wrote openly about their feelings because they saw the paper as a publication that spoke directly to them and through which they could speak to each other. The sales of the adult paper, *Our Review,* soared as parents bought both the morning and afternoon editions for their family.

Shortly after the *Little Review* came into being, fourteen-year-old Maja Zellinger submitted an article describing what she had seen while sailing down the Vistula on a boat with her younger brother. She was surprised to receive a letter from Janusz Korczak asking if he could come to visit. When he appeared at her house, she was disappointed to see how ordinary-looking he was, with his beard and round glasses, but she accepted his invitation to become the "official secretary" of the paper.

Maja was ill at ease at first because Korczak didn't give her any directions. If she asked a question, he would say: "I don't know" or "You'll see." He read everything that came into the office, underlining some parts with a blue pencil or writing "What to do?" in the margins. He seemed to be paying no attention to what anyone else was doing, but Maja was aware that he saw everything. He spoke slowly, and did not pass out compliments or flatter anyone. She felt honored when he assigned her to investigate the home situations of children with problems, or to counsel those who came into the office.

When letters began to arrive from very poor children, Korczak established a special fund for them. As with all new projects, he went himself to verify the situation described in the first few letters, before turning the task over to Maja. "The paper will allot you some money each week," he told her. "Read through the letters and check into how many really need help."

"But how will I know?" she asked.

"You'll know."

Soon she was traveling all over Poland, dispensing aid to needy children and writing an annual report of the cases she handled.

Within a year, the *Little Review* grew from two pages to four, and had two thousand correspondents across the country. It sponsored sports competitions, hosted four movie showings a year, and held an annual conference.

Jozef Balcerak, then eleven, managed to sneak his way into a conference at the newspaper by using his camera to pass as a reporter. He was astonished to find himself listening to a heated discussion about whether the letter of Iza of Lwowska Street describing how her father pulled out her loose tooth was too insignificant to be printed. Korczak supported it, explaining that everything a child wrote about was important. It was the first time Balcerak had ever heard an adult say that a child was a person to be respected and understood.

He began writing stories for the paper with an eagerness he didn't know he had in him. But the day came when he had to admit to Korczak that he had run out of ideas.

"Nonsense," Korczak replied. "Do you have a desk in your room?"

"Yes, but only one drawer is mine."

"Is it neat?"

"No, it's a mess. Mom's always after me."

"Well, then dump the contents on the floor and sort through them. Everything has a history, so all you have to do is write the stories connected to them."

And that was how Balcerak came up with the idea for his series *Stories from a Drawer*.

Korczak's voice was low and soft when he spoke to his reporters, Balcerak recalls. He would lean forward, as if he were whispering a secret. His hands would be busy with his cigarette, but if he thought of something, he would pull a pencil and pad out of his pocket and jot it down. He often peered over his glasses when he was questioning someone, and if they became steamed, he would painstakingly clean them with his handkerchief.

After Korczak had been given permission to read Balcerak's secret diary and learned that the boy needed a winter coat, he suggested putting him on the staff so that he could be paid like the other reporters. "Come to the orphanage on Saturday at eleven, before the reading of the newspaper, and Madame Stefa will give you something," he said. (Stefa was the business manager of this project—as of everything else.) Balcerak saw Korczak as "a man not of this earth, but of another dimension." He thought the *Little Review* was "the most democratic paper in the world"; anyone could write for it.

Alexander Ramati, who became the chief correspondent from Brest Litovsk at the age of nine, has no doubt that this experience influenced his becoming a writer. He felt very important traveling by train to Warsaw a few times a year to meet with the senior editor. The editorial room was always crowded with children of all sizes who were writing, singing, or playing games. A printer who dropped by once asked him: "What do we have here—a clinic, a club, or a bazaar?"

The brass plate on the door of Korczak's little cubicle was inscribed: OFFICE HOURS, THURSDAY 7–9. Ramati would find the doctor in his old gray suit working at his cluttered desk. "His voice was always kind, but sometimes abrupt," Ramati recalls. "He was like your father, punctual, glancing at his watch if you were late. But he gave you the feeling he was talking to a colleague, which your father did not."

Leon Harari was fifteen when he applied for a job one Thursday afternoon at five. He was amazed when Korczak told him to open his mouth, examined his teeth, and suggested he buy a toothbrush. That was the beginning of Harari's long stint on the paper writing articles about poor street children who had to use their wits to survive.

"We used Korczak as our Wailing Wall," he recalls. "We found our real father in him. We were from poor homes and our parents were overworked. There were eight kids in my family. My father came home and went to sleep. But Korczak would talk to us, understand us. Sometimes his face was that of a dreaming child, and other times, worried and drawn. He always wore the same old gray suit. I never saw him dressed like a tailor's dummy."

The *Little Review* attracted a few non-Jewish reporters. Kazimierz Debnicki came to the paper when he was fourteen. He was a rebellious boy who had been thrown out of so many schools that he had a "wolf's ticket," which meant a bad record that followed him around. He was accused of causing one teacher's heart attack because he sat with his arms folded for two hours, refusing to do his painting assignment. Through the influence of his father's brother, a bishop, he was accepted into a conservative *gymnasium* that, among other things, prided itself on not admitting Jewish students. When his biology teacher criticized him for slouching in his seat "like a Jew," he became so incensed that he went home and wrote an article, "The Teacher Who Teaches Prejudice." He was sensitive to the issue because he knew that his deceased mother had Jewish origins. His father praised the article and suggested he offer it to Janusz Korczak's *Little Review*. He warned his son that going into the Jewish quarter would be like entering a foreign country: not only did the people wear different clothes and speak a different language, but Jewish poverty smelled different from Polish poverty because of the spices in the food.

The only wall around the Jewish quarter then was the wall of custom, but once he passed beyond it, Debnicki's "great adventure" began. After his article was accepted by one of the young editors, he was advised to go to the Orphans Home and introduce himself to Dr. Korczak. He managed to find 92 Krochmalna and called out to a child playing under a chestnut tree in the courtyard: "Listen, little girl, where can I find the doctor?" She looked at him as if he were a "rotten egg," and shouted, "Go find him yourself!"

Only much later, after he had joined the *Little Review* staff, did Debnicki muster the courage to ask Korczak why the girl had been so rude. "Because you treated her badly," Korczak replied when he heard the details. "Why did you say 'little girl'? You should have addressed her as 'My very distinguished and gentle lady,' and she would have laughed because you'd said something clever. Or you might have tried 'My beautiful young mademoiselle,' and you'd have found a woman in her. But you said 'little girl,' so how could she treat you otherwise?"

Every Thursday evening after their editorial meeting, Korczak took the staff to the sausage shop around the corner. Seated at one of the few tables in this narrow restaurant, they ordered sausages and rolls with mustard. The boys drank tea, and sometimes Korczak asked for a beer. The children felt there were no barriers with Korczak. He was like "an island in the ocean" in that he was free of family attachments and was always available to them.

One Thursday night when Korczak and ten of his reporters went to the sausage shop to celebrate the repair of a light that had been out of order, he lifted his glass in a toast: "I feel that all of the correspondents of the *Little Review* are here with us tonight, even those who have gone abroad. We are like the headquarters of a large youth army."

Every three months the *Little Review* rewarded its most prolific writers with a private showing of a Hollywood movie in a theater owned by the father of one of the reporters. Korczak's favorites were those of Charlie Chaplin and Buster Keaton, but over the years he was also drawn to romantic adventure stories about children, such as *Treasure Island* and *The Prince and the Pauper*. He felt these films had educational as well as entertainment value. What child with an alcoholic father wouldn't be moved watching little Jackie Cooper running after Wallace Beery, a has-been prizefighter, defeated by drink, in *The Champ*. It was a scene that certainly moved Korczak: "I have witnessed three wars," he would say. "I've seen wounded people whose limbs were shot off, whose bellies were split open, whose intestines were hanging out. But, believe me, the worst thing one can see is a drunkard hitting his defenseless child, or a child running after his drunken father, pleading: 'Daddy, Daddy, please come home . . .' " He saw *The Champ* as a perfect vehicle for teachers to open up this painful topic in class and encourage students to express how they felt. "The child is ashamed of his drunken father, as if he, poor one, is guilty," Korczak wrote. "He is ashamed that he is hungry, his family so poor. He may even make light of his torn shoes and frayed clothes in order to hide the deep sadness in his heart."

Sometimes, after Korczak had seen a film he liked, he would stay for a second showing to observe the reactions of the young audience. He was particularly intrigued when a three-year-old sitting quietly with his mother suddenly rose and cried out: "A doggie! Oh, a doggie!" Not having noticed the dog himself, he stayed for still another showing to see if it was there. He was fascinated to discover that the dog appeared for just a few seconds in the corner of the screen while the dramatic action was focused in the center. The child could not understand the plot of the film, yet had managed to find something of interest to himself.

Not only did Korczak choose the films sponsored by the *Little Review*; he often acted as ticket taker. Zygmunt Kora, the boy who had been upset by the death of a chicken, never forgot the thrill of receiving an invitation to come to Warsaw for a showing of *The Nibelungen* at the Apollo Theater on Marszalkowska Street.

"I arrived early and strolled about, holding the postcard in my hand as an identification badge," Kora remembers. "An older man came up to me and introduced himself as Janusz Korczak. He took off my cap, kissed me on the forehead, and we began to chat as if we'd always known each other. When he learned how poor my family was, he arranged for me to be paid enough as a correspondent to continue my schooling."

It was a joke in Warsaw that the *Little Review* was a good paper with bad writers, but it disturbed Korczak when people attacked it for encouraging bad spelling and abominable grammar. "Children will become scribblers rather than develop a literary style," one critic declared.

"Scribbling is not dangerous, only illiteracy," Korczak responded. "Scribbling is a healthy phenomenon in a cultured society." Then, expressing that familiar belief of his father's generation of *maskilim* that good Polish was the glue that would hold Jews and Poles together, he added: "It is a gratifying and useful task to teach Jewish children to write well in Polish. Thanks to our newspaper whole generations of children will have learned to express themselves in this beautiful language."

Korczak printed one unusually vicious letter under the heading: "Should We Close the *Little Review?*" The critic, who claimed to be concerned with the welfare of all children, accused the paper of "producing big heads on little shoulders," while putting children into an unhealthy state of nervous excitement until they saw their letter or article printed—and all for the sole purpose of compelling them to keep buying the paper. Korczak commented wryly: "If the *Little Review* truly ruins the health of children, wouldn't it be better to terminate its existence?" He knew that no one would take him up on this.

Still, it was not outside criticism that disturbed Korczak so much as what was happening on the paper: the very young reporters were being edged out by teenagers who wrote articles on politics and issues that interested adolescents—like dating and sex. The problems of children with their parents and teachers—problems that interested Korczak—were given little space. In 1930 he asked Igor Newerly to take his place as editor. It was Korczak's style to turn a project over to others once he had launched it—and, in this case, he still planned to write an occasional article and attend conferences and film showings—but some saw his retirement as a protest at the editorial shift. He explained his action to his readers this way: "I thought: I am tired. Let the *Little Review* be run under the eye of a younger, gayer person for now."

PART THREE
1930 – 1939

21

Crossroads

"Other orphanages breed criminals, but ours breeds Communists," Korczak used to say in jest.

His humor masked his serious concern in the early 1930s that many of the apprentices were attending underground cell meetings of the illegal Communist party. The sharp increase in unemployment in Poland after the collapse of world economic markets had accelerated anti-Semitic activities by fascist right-wing groups. The young apprentices looked to international Communism, with its call for a brotherhood that transcended religious differences, as a solution to their problems. They slipped Communist literature to the children, who hid it under their pillows. When Stefa received complaints from teachers that the children were bringing political pamphlets to class, both she and Korczak feared that the orphanage would be closed down if Communist activity were reported there.

Seeking a scapegoat for the crime and prostitution bred by poverty, and fearing the small but vocal Communist movement, the government looked with suspicion on the rootless young people emerging from the orphanages. To counteract the influence of the radicals, it organized teams of volunteer orphans who were to return to their former institutions and instill proper values in the younger generation. The fallacy in this plan was that these Circles of Ex-Orphans, as they were called, more often than not took advantage of the opportunity to spread the subversive political ideas that the government was trying to eradicate.

The Communist agitators in the Circle of Ex-Orphans who returned to Krochmalna, unemployed and bitter, incited the Communist apprentices to be more outspoken with Korczak, whom they labeled a "naïve humanist" or an "enemy of the people."

"I felt he was a typical bourgeois educator who turned out people who were good, but weak," recalls Bolek Drukier, who had joined the *bursa* more out of a need for a place to live than from an interest in pedagogy. "In those days I knew what I hated more than what I liked. I was against capitalism and for a culture that benefited the masses. And I believed we had to be aggressive and cruel in the name of our idea."

Confronted by one apprentice who wanted to know why he was not sympathetic to the Party, Korczak replied: "I respect the idea, but it's like pure rainwater. When it comes down the rainspout of reality, it gets polluted." He was less patient with another apprentice who suggested he read Karl Marx: "I read him before you were born."

Sometimes he would try to tell them about his own underground activities at the turn of the century, how he had become disillusioned with ideology in general after seeing the violence of the revolutions of 1905 and 1917. "In revolutions, as in the rest of life, the clever and calculating continually reach the top, while the naïve and trusting are brushed aside," he said. Not only were revolutionary programs "self-righteous to the point of boredom," they were "a bloody and tragic attempt to alter and restructure society—a combination of madness, violence, and daring that revealed an abysmal disregard for human dignity."

It wasn't his intention to change anyone's point of view, believing as he did that one must learn from one's own experiences and trust only one's own perceptions. But Korczak could not keep silent on May 1, 1931, when the ex-orphans encouraged the apprentices to march with them and other Communists under the banner of the newly formed Teachers Union. That evening he asked the apprentices to give their first loyalty to the orphanage, which meant not endangering it through their political activities. When the apprentices announced that the union demanded an eight-hour workday at all summer camps. Korczak responded calmly that even if they had a right to make such a demand—which they didn't, because they were not on salary—it was against a teacher's calling to strike. Stefa was less controlled: "How can you dare propose a short working day when teachers have worked fourteen hours or more in orphanages without complaint?"

Hoping to alleviate the tension in the home, Maximilian Cohen, who was then president of the Orphans Aid Society, called a meeting of the ex-orphans, the *bursa,* and the management to air their differences. Korczak appeared at the session still weak from a nose-and-throat infection as well as from another bout of inflammation of the eyes. He was saddened to see some of the ex-orphans who had been his favorites being led by a hostile boy who had once received Article 1,000.

One by one Korczak's attackers rose and delivered their accusations: he ran the orphanage like a scientific laboratory rather than a loving home; he weighed and measured the children like guinea pigs; he lost interest in everyone once they left the orphanage; he hadn't prepared them for a trade to support themselves in the outside world.

Korczak stood up and tried to defend himself on each point: "It is true that this is a scientific as well as an educational institution," he began. "But it was my hope that our weight and height charts could serve as a guideline for other orphanages. If their findings did not match ours, they might learn that their children were not being fed the right diet, that their bedrooms were not being kept at the right temperature, or that there was not enough fresh air. As for not training the children for a trade, I felt it was more important for them to learn life skills, rather than vocational ones, in the few years we were able to keep them."

When some of the ex-orphans tried to interrupt him, he took the offensive. "Do you feel we were wrong to take in small, neglected plants and nurture them until they became strong and healthy, even though we were learning in the process and made mistakes? It's easy for you to find fault, but a person who is content with himself doesn't blame teachers or parents for the hardships in his life. It's unfair to attack my system at a time when even qualified workers are unable to find employment."

Most of the apprentices and ex-orphans were placated; only a few diehards muttered that he had not taken their criticism seriously enough and had spoken to them like children. The evening ended with hard feelings after the president of the Orphans Aid Society took an uncompromising stand. He reminded those with ties to the Communist party that they weren't old enough yet to run the country, and that in the meantime the Society was in charge of running the orphanage.

Shortly after that night, Korczak appeared, flushed and trembling, at Igor Newerly's apartment. Newerly, now married to Basha, an apprentice who had grown up in the Jewish orphanage, thought Korczak might have heard bad news about his sister in Paris. Not until he sat down and had coffee was Korczak able to tell them what had happened. During his lecture at the Institute of Pedagogy that afternoon, one of the former apprentices had stood up in the auditorium and denounced him. When Korczak tried to reason with him from the podium, the young man had screamed to the audience that Korczak was dangerous and should not be allowed to influence children. Newerly had never seen Korczak so upset.

Yet Korczak was not one to hold grudges. He would tease his critics: "Which lamppost are you going to hang me from after the revolution?" He even staged a mock trial in which he played the parts of three Communist functionaries who had once been Janusz Korczak's apprentices and were now assigned to judge him politically. Each wrote a large GUILTY across his file. The first functionary did so because he was afraid it would be discovered that he had worked in Korczak's home, the second after a stiff drink, and the third because he saw Korczak as a reactionary and counterrevolutionary.

In spite of his differences with his Communist apprentices, Korczak gave Bolek Drukier and others letters of reference when they left to find work. And Stefa was known to bring food packages to the young women when they were jailed for their political activities. Perhaps as an answer to their rebukes and public criticisms of his methods at the orphanage, Korczak published a follow-up study of the children who had graduated during the home's first twenty-one years. After listing their occupations and the countries to which some had emigrated—Argentina, Brazil, Canada, the U.S.A., China, England, France, Belgium, Spain, and Palestine—he concluded the report: "I hesitate to point out that, of all the children, three have been convicted of theft, two have become beggars, and two prostitutes." (He didn't mention that one of the prostitutes had tried to solicit him on the street before recognizing him.)

The apprentices who had embraced Zionism as the answer to the Jewish problem were also critical of Korczak—in their case, for not directing the children toward a life in Palestine.

Korczak's skeptical attitude toward Zionism went back to his days in medical school. While writing travel articles in Switzerland in 1899, he had stopped in "by chance" at the third Zionist Congress in Basel to see a friend who was a delegate. He found the whole atmosphere "bourgeois," he wrote, and the idea of trying to solve the problem of Eastern European Jews in the deserts of the Middle East positively "utopian." He hated the "highfalutin" speeches at the Congress, which made him realize that the only language that interested him was that of the child.

When he was invited to attend the Jewish National Fund conference in Warsaw in 1925, he refused for the same reasons, although he did acknowledge in his letter that "something very great, very courageous, and very difficult" was taking place. He urged the sponsors to consider if their plan was a "return or an escape," if it was motivated by their "grief for the past or by longing for the future." As a man "who walks his own lonely road," he was offended by their propaganda, although he knew it was necessary to their cause. In his opinion, a Messiah must be born in silence.

He boycotted the conference, but he did agree to sign the Jewish National Fund's appeal that Jews contribute the equivalent of one day's salary as an expression of their solidarity "with their brethren building a Jewish land." Still he held to his universalist position, writing to a friend in Palestine: "The problem of *Man*, his past and future on earth, somewhat overshadows the problem of the *Jew* for me." Christians and Jews were "children of the same God." In Palestine, as well as in Poland, "the noblest intentions" were being trampled by hatred and racial strife. (He was referring to the conflict with the Arabs.) Such was the human condition. And always his question: Why?

Some of Korczak's apprentices had joined the Hashomer Hatzair, the left-wing Zionist organization that was preparing young people for emigration to Palestine. Nineteen-year-old Moshe Zertal, who was in charge of inviting guest speakers, was very nervous as he made his way in dim lamplight over the broken cobblestones on Krochmalna to ask Janusz Korczak to talk on education to their group. "I imagined he would be someone with wings," Zertal recalls. "I couldn't believe that this man wearing a simple smock over work clothes was the great Dr. Korczak. He looked more like a monk."

Korczak's reserve, tinged with his usual suspiciousness toward strangers, did not put Zertal at ease. "Lecture to your group? No. Impossible. You don't need anything I could tell you." The young man wasn't sure whether the doctor meant it seriously or as a joke when he added: "You know more than I do." But Korczak left the door open, as he always did, to test the sincerity of his visitors: "If you want to come on Saturday morning for the reading of the orphanage newspaper, you are welcome."

Zertal was not the first to discover that the way to Korczak was through his children. After attending a few Saturday-morning readings, he mustered enough courage to ask Korczak if some of the orphans could join the Young Pioneers' annual boat excursion to the countryside on Lag

B'Omer, a spring holiday that is celebrated with camping trips and bon-
fires. The doctor not only gave his permission, but arrived at the Vistula
dock with the children. Zertal remembers that "he cut quite a figure in
his black hat with the wide brim, round glasses, and a cigarette that never
left his lips. He seemed the epitome of an intellectual, and a very turn-
of-the-century Polish intellectual at that."

The Hashomer Hatzair tried to make the orphans feel at ease with
the hundreds of other Jewish children assembled from all over Warsaw
for the overnight camping trip. They were given tents to carry and bags
of rice for their backpacks. Korczak stood apart, but his piercing eyes
watched as the children, weighed down with their loads, jumped from
the steep embankment onto the ship's narrow gangplank. He was the last
to board. When two drunken Poles staggered onto the dock and started
heckling the children, Korczak spoke to them calmly in a rough Polish
much like their own. The men quieted down and went their way.

On the boat trip home, Zertal noticed the change in Korczak's children. The "special stamp" that was the common badge of orphans—pale
faces, short haircuts, drab clothing—was no longer noticeable. Their
movements were proud and erect, their clothes brightened with the
flowers they had picked, their faces smiling, their cheeks rosy.

It was only natural that the children would bring the blue-and-white
flags of the Young Pioneers into the orphanage with them, as well as the
secular Hebrew songs about social justice they had learned. They brought
the dream of the homeland, too: before long, a map of Palestine appeared
on the bulletin board, and two Hebrew-speaking tables were created in
the dining hall.

Korczak was so impressed with the Lag B'Omer outing that he told
everyone he wished children of all religions could participate. Not long
after that, as a personal favor to Zertal, by then a trusted friend, he agreed
to speak to a group of nervous parents who were reluctant to allow their
children to become "Sons of the Desert." Not knowing quite what to
expect, Zertal was amazed to hear a stirring and original talk on the
importance of the youth movement from this man "who wasn't even a
part of it."

In June of 1929, Izaak Eliasberg, who had worked tirelessly for twenty
years to keep the orphanage afloat, died. Before his death, Korczak had
sat at his bedside, telling him jokes and anecdotes about the orphans to
make him laugh. In the eulogy he gave at his friend's grave, Korczak

called him an "enthusiast of responsibility": a man who chose to live not for himself but for others.

Two years later, in August of 1931, Jakub Mortkowicz, Korczak's publisher, took his life in his apartment in Warsaw. He had just returned from the International Book Fair in Paris depressed about the decline in the publishing field and his mounting debts. Always a man of shifting moods, he locked himself in his room and put a bullet through his brain. During the somber period between the loss of his two closest friends, when Poland was reeling both economically and politically from the world-wide economic crisis, Korczak had begun working on his second and last play, *Senate of Madmen*, which is set in a madhouse.

The earlier play, *Which Way?*, dealt with the madness of his father; now Korczak used the madhouse itself as a metaphor for society. He was grappling with his old themes again: insanity in the individual and in the world, man's struggle for faith and reason, and the child as the God-chosen redeemer. This time, however, the playwright was in control of the madness. Not only did he give the directorship of the asylum to a good doctor suspiciously like himself; he also resurrected and cured his father, who, when the play opens, has returned voluntarily to do carpentry work, accompanied by his son Janek, who has brought along his building blocks.

This democratic asylum, similar in spirit to the children's republic, has its own officers and a parliament that meets to judge the guilt of the human race. Who is it that is mad, the play asks: those inside the asylum—the restaurateur who wants to serve laxatives with every meal, the homosexual who thinks people should have to apply for a license to procreate, the would-be murderer who shot a woman because she was rude to him on the tram, the Sad Monk who wrestles all night, like Jacob, with a mysterious stranger, the sadistic colonel with his constant refrain of "Destroy and burn!"—or those outside?

It might be Pirandello speaking—what is illusion and what is reality? But it is also the voice of a playwright who has not come to terms with having been deserted by a mad father. "Every madman is just a pretender who couldn't cope and took the easy way out," the Jewish merchant says. And another character: "Insanity is one of the many masks one wears in life. Like Hamlet—a mad disguise." And a third, revealing that the playwright still fears inheriting his father's illness: "At least the man who has gone mad can be at peace. He doesn't have to be afraid anymore of losing his mind."

And where is God in this mad world? Perhaps He felt unneeded and has escaped. The idea of God fleeing from human stupidity germinated in the playwright's mind until it took shape as a prologue much in the style of a droll Hasidic tale. The Sad Monk (very like the Sad King) comes downstage to tell little Janek about the time God tried to withdraw from the world. People were so desperate to find Him that they put advertisements in the newspapers offering a reward for information about His whereabouts. There were no fingerprints or photographs, only rumors: He had been seen feeding birds; He had been overheard talking to prostitutes. When He was finally discovered by a little girl in a lark's nest, God agreed to appear at the gold-and-marble shrine that had just been erected for Him. He allowed Himself to be dressed in an ermine cloak and driven in an open coach drawn by four white horses through triumphal arches so that everyone could see Him. He stopped His coach once, before an old woman named Faith, who stood pressed against a wall with blind Justice and Hope, muttering: "So I've lived to see Him." It seemed that He wanted to stand up, but He merely waved His hand and fell back again on the cushions. The procession was a success, with only a few robberies and one or two people fainting in the crowd. God's long-awaited message at the shrine had the virtue of brevity—"Love each other, my children!"—but a high official from the Ministry of Foreign Affairs found it vague and unclear. That night God rose from His throne, sighed, threw off His heavy ermine cloak and escaped out the side door. It was a scandal! All the money, all the work—in vain! Once again, the chase was on. This time God turned into a blueberry to take a nap, sat in a wagon chatting with the Jewish driver, rode across a field on a wild mouse, wept at a slaughterhouse, and closed himself inside the petals of a lily of the valley. He was standing by a fence watching some children at play when an intelligence agent spotted Him. At that moment, God rose into the air and descended in a shower of pearls which landed in the hearts of the children.

When the actor Stefan Jaracz, then the Laurence Olivier of Poland, heard a reading of the play at the home of a well-known actress, he had no trouble imagining himself as the Sad Monk. The first rehearsal was held at Jaracz's theater, the Atheneum, located near the Vistula not far from the Old Town. Financed by the railway workers' union, the theater specialized in programs with social content. Korczak sat at a large round table with the actors and read all the parts in a low voice without expression, a succession of cigarettes dangling from his lips.

"We were all surprised to see Korczak dressed in a shabby jacket and high workman's boots, not like the famous writer we expected," Henryk Szletynski, one of the actors, recalls. "Even his glasses had cheap round metal frames. When he took them off, I noticed how red-rimmed his eyes were, as if he hadn't had enough sleep. After the reading, while we were discussing the script, Korczak told us that the only interesting people are madmen and children. When he got up to leave, he already had a fresh cigarette in his hand."

Most of the cast followed Korczak's suggestion that they visit the mental asylum in Tworki. The patients were outside on the grounds when they arrived. One stood like a statue with his arms outstretched; another, a boy of thirteen, sat rigidly with his head twisted to one side. Stefan Jaracz was so unnerved by the sight of real madmen that he sat without a word on the train back to Warsaw. No one knew that Korczak's father might have been an inmate there.

Rehearsals were scheduled for eleven each night, when the current production was over and the stage cleared. Jozef Balcerak remembers sitting with Korczak as long as an hour and a half in the empty, dark auditorium, waiting for Stefan Jaracz—a heavy drinker and ladies' man— to arrive a little unsteady on his feet. Korczak left at two in the morning because he had to be up early with the orphans, but Balcerak, who had never seen a rehearsal before, stayed until four.

On the opening night of the play—October 1, 1931—Korczak sat with Igor Newerly in the last row of the balcony, the better to observe the audience. The set was stark: a large papier-mâché globe under a clock with one hand in the shape of a sword. It was a static play in spite of the fact that the madmen had whimsy and wit, but everyone who knew Korczak could recognize him as the despairing Sad Monk when Jaracz came downstage to bless and forgive humankind: "Friends, distant and close, well-known and unknown, cousins, sisters, brothers, the weak, the sad, the hungry, and the yearning, you have made mistakes, but not sinned. You didn't know how else to act, but you have not gone astray. I put my warm hand on your tired heads."

At the end of the performance the audience shouted: "Author! Author!" Korczak reluctantly descended from his hiding place in the balcony and took a bow with Jaracz and the cast onstage. Many of Warsaw's intelligentsia had turned out to support Korczak in his first theater production. But in spite of the warm response that evening, the reviews were mixed, most of them preferring the prologue to the play.

Antoni Slonimski, a poet whose family had converted to Catholicism, and the most influential theater critic at that time, wrote: "Here we have a good theater troupe—the Atheneum, an exquisite actor—Jaracz, and a charming author—Korczak. However, together they have produced an unfortunate concoction. Korczak wants to solve all the questions that plague the modern world in two hours of talk. He speaks a great deal about God, but no one knows whether God is Christian, pagan, or Jewish."

Another critic, comparing the play to works by Poland's most eminent dramatists, Zygmunt Krasinski and Stanislaw Ignacy Witkiewicz, called the characters "philosophical madmen with cosmic pain, human beings who have taken on the burden of insanity to save millions of their brothers . . . If one could force these madmen to act, to do something, one could have an interesting modern play." A right-wing critic, always ready to attack a Jewish playwright, complained: "Janusz Korczak (Goldszmit) is saying that most mad people laugh at our society. He criticizes the military, and takes an antigovernment position."

Warsaw, considered by its denizens a "laughing city," was not in the mood to be amused by philosophical madmen. The play closed after fifty-one performances, and had a short run in Lvov. Asked in a newspaper interview if he wanted to publish the play, Korczak responded that he considered it an unfinished sketch and hoped to work on it further. But Igor Newerly recalls that Korczak was downcast that the public was not receptive to his ideas. Only much later would it become clear that the sanatorium mirrored the world before World War II, and the colonel who advocated burning books and hanging all inventors, idealists, Jews, and parliamentarians without pity resembled the madman who wrote *Mein Kampf*.

If writing *Senate of Madmen* was a way of trying to order a universe slipping out of control, then *Rules of Life,* which Korczak composed at the same time, was meant to give young people a way of ordering their own world. Written in haste—"I would have torn up the manuscript had I even paused"—the book gives advice on how to deal with the mixed messages one receives from parents, teachers, siblings, and friends. The idea for the book came to him when he received a letter from a boy saying: "Kids like me feel very angry and unhappy because we don't know the rules of life."

The title was probably inspired by Tolstoy's *Rules of Life.* Yet the content seems an outgrowth of a work Korczak had just finished, *The*

Child's Right to Respect, in which he explained: "The child must be seen as a foreigner who does not understand the language of the street plan, who is ignorant of the laws and customs. Occasionally he likes to go sightseeing on his own; and when up against some difficulty, asks for information and advice. Wanted—a guide to answer questions politely."

He was now creating that guide. Trust your own perceptions, he tells his young readers. "Each person carries an entire world within himself, and everything exists twice: once the way it is, the other the way he perceives it with his own eyes and feelings."

You must dream your own dreams but be ready to accept life as it is: "One day is happy, and one day is sad. Sometimes you're successful, and sometimes you're not. Sometimes the sun is shining, and sometimes it's raining. What can one do?"

And so, what are the rules of life? he asks. Each person must find out for himself. The secret is not to get discouraged about mistakes and to be honest. "He who is sincere, pursues justice, and is considerate of others is the one best loved by everyone."

A few years later Korczak published another children's book, *Kajtus the Magician,* a picaresque adventure story that he dedicated to restless boys who find it difficult to improve themselves. "Life is like a strange dream," Korczak informed them. "But for those who have strong wills and a desire to serve others, the dream can be beautiful—even if the way to the goal is winding, and one's thoughts confused."

Kajtus is one of those mischievous boys whom Korczak favored. Finding himself suddenly in possession of magic powers, he wreaks havoc by making people walk backwards, changing clocks, creating traffic jams. He has to endure many trials on his way to learning how to use power wisely. The worst ordeal is his imprisonment in the tower of an evil sorcerer's castle. One of the orphans on whom Korczak was testing the chapter grabbed his arm and cried: "It's horrible!"

"But fairy tales about sorcerers are always frightening," Korczak reassured him.

"Yeah, but this is something else," the boy said with a shudder.

Because the child had nightmares that night, Korczak crossed out everything that had scared him. The book was published with blank spaces on many pages in that chapter and an explanation of why the spooky parts had been deleted.

Kajtus's trials are not over even after he escapes the sorcerer's castle:

he has to be turned into a dog in order to learn humility. When he is worthy of regaining his human shape, he has to witness human suffering in hospitals and prisons in China and Africa. Making his way to the Land of the Eskimos, Kajtus hears a voice coming from the grave of a fearless one: "Be disciplined, be brave!" He pledges: "I will."

Kajtus was the last Polish boy to leap from Korczak's imagination: a hero who must learn to dream boldly, but prudently. After this, there would be only Polish Jewish boys—like Hershkele, in *The Three Journeys of Hershkele*—who dream of the Promised Land.

22

Palestine

If I had the means, I would like to spend half a year in Palestine in order to contemplate what has been, and half a year in Poland in order to preserve what remains.
—*Letter to Joseph Arnon, 1933*

Stefa's thoughts were filled with Palestine in 1929 because her favorite apprentice, Feiga Lipshitz, was emigrating there to live on a kibbutz. Tempted to go along for a few months to help her get settled, Stefa trained a few teachers to take over the myriad details of her work. She even prepared for the possibility that something might happen to her in the Holy Land by tacking a note to the inside of her closet door: "Children, after I die, don't cry, and go to school. I donate my body to science."

At the last minute, she decided not to accompany Feiga because her mother's condition had worsened. By a strange coincidence, Feiga's first letter from Palestine arrived the day Stefa's mother died. "I would have been very miserable if I had left with you," she wrote Feiga. "You know how much a mother means. But now I am free to make plans. My brother and sister don't need me, and the orphanage can manage very well in my absence."

The death of her mother left Stefa emotionally drained and with a heightened sense of her own mortality. "I have the courage to tell myself that forty-four is the beginning of old age," she wrote Feiga. "I am exhausted, and my nerves are still frayed from the war. I have to get some calmer work. I'm tired, and lonely." As if it were unrelated to her fatigue, Stefa added casually: "The Doctor is holed away upstairs—as a matter of fact, he's writing a new book. It's not easy without him."

Stefa could not know how troubled Feiga would be by the letter

announcing her visit. Kibbutz Ein Harod, which had been founded in
the north by three hundred young Russian Zionists eight years earlier,
was much more primitive and dangerous than Feiga had expected. She
could not imagine Stefa in that barren terrain, exposed to the relentless
sun and sporadic Arab attacks.

Those original founders had thought it romantic to settle by the spring
(*harod* in Hebrew) in the Valley of Jezreel, where Gideon had once
camped before slaying the Midianites. But they found themselves in a
malarial swamp where they were perfect targets for bands of Arabs coming
over the Gilboa Mountains. Within a year, more than a hundred of them
had died from disease, or suicide, or in armed skirmishes. Those who
had not given up and returned home had chosen another spot halfway
up the hillside facing Mount Gilboa, where they built two fortress-like
concrete buildings to protect their children.

After procuring tractors, the young settlers had planted eucalyptus
trees to drain the swamps, pine and cedar groves on the mountains to
block the winds, and a citrus grove in the Valley of Jezreel to support
themselves. By the time Feiga arrived, the original tents were being
replaced with spartan wooden cabins that had only the bare necessities.
Feiga confided to Stefa in her letters that life was so strenuous there were
times she didn't have the strength to work with the children. "Your
feelings of discouragement will pass," Stefa had hastened to reassure her,
and described her own suffering during the war when she had to shoulder
the full burden of the orphanage. "Later I didn't know if I had done the
right thing by staying," Stefa wrote, "but I had so many responsibilities
by then, I had no time to think."

For two years Feiga managed to dissuade Stefa from undertaking a
trip to Palestine, but in late 1931 Stefa sent off a letter: "I am coming!"
She arrived on the kibbutz's tenth anniversary.

Feiga's fears about her friend's stamina proved unfounded. Stefa,
who had been through so much in her life, was not one to be undone by
rugged living conditions. The first night of her visit, Feiga searched frantically for a spoon for her tea, which was taken Russian-style with jam,
only to find that Stefa, resourceful as ever, had used the other end of her
tin knife. "You didn't think I could manage, did you?" cried the triumphant Stefa.

For the three months that she was there, Stefa worked in the Children's Houses where the young were cared for from birth while their
mothers labored as equal partners with the men in the fields. She was

full of practical suggestions, such as advising the kibbutz to lower the height of the washbasins in the bathrooms, and to sew loops on both ends of the towels to make hanging them up easier for impatient little ones. Sometimes she and Feiga worked shifts together, and sometimes they alternated, the two of them teaching others Korczak's pedagogical ideas.

Stefa returned to Poland a new woman. Her face was tanned and radiant. She was amazed that in three months away "one could depart so far from one's everyday life." That summer at camp she wore short-sleeved white blouses with a few buttons open at the throat. She smiled more, appeared at peace with herself, and was almost playful with the children. But she was preoccupied with returning to Palestine and Feiga, if she could obtain a visa.

In the fall, when the children were in school, Stefa started taking Hebrew lessons in preparation for her return trip, and spoke endlessly to Korczak about the kibbutz's experimental education system. Nothing would do but that he go and see the Children's Houses for himself and give the kibbutzniks, as they were called, some much needed advice.

Korczak listened politely, but he was not looking for a new homeland. He already had one. He had said as much in his correspondence with Ester Budko, a former apprentice, who had settled in a kibbutz in the late twenties. "Palestine is still a legend to the children," he wrote—and, he might have added, to himself as well. Those who spoke to him of emigrating seemed embittered and filled with longings—rebels, as opposed to those who were resigned to life in Poland. The difficulties that the émigrés experienced in adapting to their new life only confirmed his suspicion that bitter disappointment as well as youthful illusion were connected with that land—that it was too late for Europeans to try to recover a lost past: "We have acclimated ourselves to a land of pines and snow, physically and mentally. The effort required to tie together the two ends that were broken two thousand years ago is enormous." He himself had too little time left to "sacrifice" the ten years it would take to adjust not only physically but spiritually to the new conditions.

Stefa scoffed at Korczak's argument that without Hebrew he wouldn't be able to communicate with the children. He could concentrate on the infants, she said, and use sign language with the toddlers. When he countered that he wouldn't be able to speak to adults either, she reminded him that most of the settlers were Russian or Polish immigrants. In response to his claim that there was nothing he could contribute anyway, she cited the stream of visitors from various kibbutzim who were always stopping by the orphanage to consult with him. And it was true—so many kibbutzniks came and went all the time that Korczak often quipped that Warsaw was turning into a suburb of Palestine.

It may have been Stefa's influence, or his own increasing pain at seeing the orphans taunted and beaten up as they made their way through Christian neighborhoods, that prompted Korczak to write in late 1932 to Joseph Arnon, the former apprentice, who had emigrated to Palestine: "If there is one country where the child is honestly given a chance to express his dreams and fears, his longings and perplexities—it might well be Palestine. A monument should be erected there to the unknown orphan." And he added, "I have not given up hope that I shall be able to spend the last years left to me in Palestine, and from there long for Poland . . . Longing strengthens and deepens the soul."

The following spring, a journey to Palestine was still no more than a vague possibility. "If fate were to decree that I go to Palestine, I would not be going to the people, but to the thoughts that would be born to me there," he wrote to Arnon. "What would Mount Sinai tell me? Or the Jordan? The tomb of Jesus, the university, the cave of the Maccabees, the Galilee? I would be reliving two thousand years of European history, of Polish history, of Jewish wanderings. . . . The world is not in need of labor and oranges, but of a new faith. Faith in the child who is the source of all hope."

In the fall of 1933, upset by "cheap gossip" in a right-wing newspaper that he would be going to Palestine, Korczak decided to leave as quickly as possible during the winter.

Stefa lost no time in getting a letter off to Ein Harod: "Please consider having Dr. Korczak stay with you for a few weeks. He would like to work in the nursery, with the newborns, or with older infants, and is willing to do whatever work is required of him. What he doesn't know, he'll learn on the spot. He'd prefer not to be assigned to the Children's Houses since he is unable to speak the language. He wants to learn about kibbutz life, and all that he asks for in return is a bed, a table, and a chair. He is even willing to wash floors."

The reply came back as expected: the kibbutz would be honored to have Dr. Janusz Korczak as its guest.

Korczak did make a change in his life at that time, but one unrelated to Palestine. He moved out of the Orphans Home and into the apartment of his sister Anna at No. 8 Zlota Street, on the edge of the Jewish quarter.

"I felt tired, old, and superfluous in the orphanage, and that is why I left, or to be more precise, I was driven away," he wrote to Arnon. "You will find it difficult to understand and I shall not try to explain again." It had obviously been a wrenching decision. "All I have left are my thoughts, and faith in the future, which I doubt whether I shall live to see."

It was not only the conflicts in the Orphans Home that caused his despair: "We are in the midst of a hundred years' war, still in the Dark Ages," he continued. "Unbelievable injustice is being done to the human race, and especially the child . . . For years I have been observing sensitive children, watching their helplessness, and their silent sadness, and the frantic insolence of *homo rapax* as well." It seemed that "everything fine and delicate was being indiscriminately destroyed, that sheep were being torn to pieces by wolves." He admitted to "trying to flee from the world of thoughts" by losing himself in work: he sought relief in cutting hair and washing heads, but found even this no longer effective.

During this period when he was fluctuating between hope and despair, Korczak was deeply absorbed in a new project. For the past year he had been supervising a temporary experimental school he had set up for the first- and second-graders in Our Home who could not find places in the overcrowded public schools in Bielany. Dispensing with school bells, assigned seating, and other conventional rituals that regulated a child's day, Korczak created a progressive curriculum in which each child was treated as an individual, given the freedom to choose his own activity and to stay at it as long as he wished, be it reading, math, arts and crafts, or music. There were no grades, just points that were added up like a game score. Once a week the children took trips with their teachers to factories or farms to see how things were made or grown. Although Korczak didn't teach at the school, he stopped in during the week when he had time to tell stories and to observe.

Korczak's spirits were lifted at the end of 1933 when he was awarded the Silver Cross of the Polonia Restituta, a decoration given only to a select few for their contribution to Polish society. The ceremony was conducted in the dining hall of the Krochmalna Street orphanage with great solemnity by the Minister of Social Affairs, Dr. Stefan Hubnicki, before an invited audience of prominent health officials and press. The Minister, who had been a classmate of Korczak's at medical school, had no sooner begun reminiscing about his colleague's outstanding work with poor slum children than Korczak walked out of the room. The surprised dignitaries had no way of knowing if this was another example of Korczak's well-known eccentricity or a deliberate insult. Reappearing only after he heard the polite applause at the close of the Minister's speech, Korczak apologized. He explained that he could not listen to so much praise because he did not deserve it. He would accept the distinguished award of the Polish Republic, not as a personal tribute, but as a command to work harder. The Minister embraced him warmly.

The trip to Palestine was still unscheduled but Korczak was reading about ancient Greece and Rome and studying the Bible in preparation for it. "One cannot focus on just one generation of children in that ancient land," he wrote Arnon, "one has to span centuries." When Arnon, who had been waiting impatiently for Korczak's arrival, asked if he was hesitant because of the unstable conditions in Palestine, Korczak answered by return post that his doubts were not dependent upon outside circumstances, but were rather within him. At fifty-six, he was "too old to rush around the world without a purpose or merely to satisfy his normal human curiosity." He had to mull over what he would tell the settlers about Poland, and what he wanted to bring back to the people here. "I am not idle, or indifferent. It is just that this is my clime, where I grew up. I am acquainted with the traditions of the people. I know the language proficiently—there everything will be strange and difficult." But he assured Arnon that he would see him by the middle of August, unless he had to postpone the trip again.

As summer approached, Stefa managed to pin Korczak down to a definite date: he would travel to Palestine during the month of July, a time when the children were at camp and he had no teaching responsibilities. However, just before departure, he insisted that he could spare only three weeks.

"The purpose of a man's journey can be the search for himself or for God," Korczak would write toward the end of his life. When he found himself on the ship sailing from Athens to Palestine, he still could not have said what his real purpose was. Adolf Hitler was now the Chancellor of Germany, and a few months earlier the Polish–German nonaggression pact had been signed. Hitler's emissary Joseph Goebbels had just received the red-carpet treatment in Warsaw. Korczak knew that the situation of the Jews in Poland could only worsen: was this trip he was making an "escape," as he had once wondered about those early Zionists, or a "return?"

He arrived in Haifa on July 24, 1934, two days after his fifty-sixth birthday. David Simchoni, whose wife worked with Feiga in the Children's Houses, had been selected by the kibbutz to be his host and to meet the boat. While the two men were waiting for the bus to Ein Harod, they walked about the old quarter of Haifa. Korczak was full of energy and curiosity in spite of the heat, and could not resist buying Oriental sweetmeats from the Arab vendors. After a taste, he gave what was left to an Arab boy passing by.

Korczak placed his well-marked Bible on his lap and checked historical spots as the bus made its way north from Haifa, past Mount Carmel and on into the Valley of Jezreel. Trying to maintain his objectivity as flowering orchards and plowed fields appeared through the window, he jotted in his notebook: "So what? Haven't similar things been achieved in the Australian desert? What about Holland's struggle with the encroaching sea, or Japan's with volcanic eruptions? They only have swamps and mosquitoes to contend with here."

He was tired when they arrived at the kibbutz late in the afternoon, but deeply moved by the exuberant welcome he was given by the pioneers. His first question upon seeing his tiny room was: "How can you offer such fine accommodations to visitors without making them pay?" When he was advised to shed his coat and tie if he wanted to return to Warsaw alive, he quipped: "But if I take them off, what will remain of Korczak?" He soon removed them. At first he couldn't understand why everyone was wearing shorts rather than protecting their legs from the burning sun, but he had to admit how comfortable he felt when he rolled up his pants.

Early the next morning, Simchoni was alarmed not to find Korczak in his room. He looked all over the kibbutz, searched the Children's Houses, and finally discovered him in the kitchen, peeling potatoes with some of the elderly parents of kibbutz members. Korczak explained that the smell of freshly baked bread, which filled his room at dawn, had taken him back to his childhood home next to a bakery. He had gone to chat with the baker and then, hearing the pots and pans begin to rattle, had joined the kitchen crew.

Dismissing Simchoni's protestations that he needed his rest, Korczak said, "I want to earn my keep." But Korczak had ulterior motives in gravitating to those old potato peelers who could speak to him in Polish or Russian while they worked. He listened to their anecdotes about kibbutz life, but he was also aware of what was left unspoken. From such facetious comments as "What kind of country is this that doesn't have raspberries?" or "My one dream is to eat a plate of strawberries before I die!" he could calculate the emotional price of transplanting oneself to this "old-new homeland." "Yes, it is a difficult country," the kitchen crew would say. "But our children like it here."

As Stefa suspected, Korczak couldn't help being fascinated by the kibbutz, which, like his own children's republic, replaced the conventional family unit with a responsible community that stressed social justice, the importance of the child, and the dignity of human labor. He was amazed to see the Jew in the role of the peasant, toiling under the relentless sun to bring forth olive and grape arbors and acres of potatoes and corn from the inhospitable soil. "Jewish brains are resting," he observed. "Here the saw and ax have replaced European intellectual snobbery."

As he watched the children helping adults in the fields, Korczak could see that they moved differently from his orphans in Warsaw, who cringed at the invectives and stones hurled at them. These children, who had grown up with "the heat of the sun in their soul" and the "burning wind in their blood," belonged to this land in a "biological sense" that their parents, with their roots in other soil, did not. They were a new breed, these Sabras, tough and resilient as the native cactus after which they were named.

Korczak prowled about the Children's Houses "with the enthusiasm of a young detective on his first case," asking endless questions of the caretakers, but he was shy with the children because of the language barrier. To ease the situation, he soon devised strategies for making nonverbal contact. Entering one classroom, he shouted: "*Sheket!*" ("Silence," in Hebrew), which he had memorized for the occasion. "*Sheket!*" The children were surprised, but then, seeing his mischievous smile, they realized it was a joke. This amusing stranger walked up and down the aisles while they were drawing, using his pen to add buttons to a jacket, lengthen a cat's tail, give horns to a goat. The children were comfortable with him; one boy offered Korczak his artwork as a souvenir.

The seven-year-olds in another class had been prepared in advance by their teachers that a guest as famous as the British High Commissioner was coming to have lunch with them. Twenty-seven pairs of eyes watched in trepidation as Korczak entered and took his assigned place at the teachers' table. Twenty-seven young bodies sat stiffly, hardly daring to breathe. Wanting to stir things up a bit, Korczak motioned to a boy near him to turn around, and then stole his plate of meatballs. The boy immediately suspected his neighbor, and soon voices as well as fists were raised. Just as a fight was about to break out, Korczak, with masterful timing, produced the missing plate. It broke the tension: twenty-seven children burst out laughing, and were at ease from then on.

Every other night, tired as they were, members of the kibbutz would gather in the dining hall to hear the famous educator from Warsaw lecture on the child. He stood before them, slightly stooped, his short-sleeved shirt open at the throat, his fair skin mottled from the sun, insisting modestly through his Hebrew interpreter that, as a stranger to their language and customs, he could not give them answers to the many questions they had asked him since his arrival. He could offer only suggestions based on his own experience.

His talks covered his usual subjects: children's sleep patterns, heredity, nutrition, types of children, learning disabilities, childhood sexuality, and the task of the educator. The necessity of respect for the child was such an insistent refrain that years later the kibbutzniks would say that Korczak left them with five commandments: Love *the child,* not just your own. Observe the child. Do not pressure the child. Be honest with yourself in order to be honest with the child. Know yourself so that you do not take advantage of a defenseless child.

No matter how late it grew, some parents stayed behind to ask questions about the best way to run the Children's Houses. Ein Harod was one of the few kibbutzim to have its children sleep at home, rather than in the Children's Houses, after they reached the first grade. But still unresolved was the question of who should be assigned to care for the children's groups during the day: specially trained educators, or any women who volunteered. Feiga maintained that only professionals should be in charge of the children. What did the doctor think?

Korczak responded that, ideally, men as well as women should work in the Children's Houses (an idea never followed up), but that it was best to train a few experts in child care, rather than bewilder the youngsters with the cultural bias of each individual caretaker. It was also essential to coordinate the rules in the parental home with those in the Children's Houses, so that the child did not become confused.

Unable to resist a little mischief, he left his most important advice—

a dose of humor for every problem—in a letter to the kibbutz to be read after his departure:

Knowing that you are dissatisfied that the children are always late to school, let me propose five solutions:

1) Put a rooster in a coop in every room. When he crows, the children will awake on time. If not, I suggest:

2) Firing a cannon. But if, after waking, the children walk so slowly that they are still late, I suggest:

3) Spraying them with cold water from an airplane. But if they enjoy that too much, I suggest:

4) Writing down the names of those who are late. But if the children don't care, since everyone knows anyway, I suggest:

5) Putting a notice in a big city newspaper. But the children may say, "Who cares, nobody knows us!" And so on.

If these proposals do not meet with your approval, I suggest that someone propose something better.

I give my consent to exhibiting this letter on the bulletin board on condition that the kibbutz members add the following statement: We are always on time, and want our children to follow our example.

During his brief three weeks at Ein Harod, Korczak often sat with his Bible in the late afternoon under the newly planted palm trees, waiting for the rare breeze to blow in over the mountains from Haifa. He knew that Mount Gilboa had been arid from the time David had cursed it: Saul had fallen on his sword there in grief that Jonathan had been slain by the Philistines. David (whose childhood he planned to write about) had lamented: "Fallen, fallen are the men of war; and their armor left in the field." Ancient history was now intertwined with the present; many of the early kibbutz settlers had fallen on that very same ground.

Just before dawn one morning, Korczak groped his way by flashlight for two miles across the stony hillside to the kibbutz graveyard. The cobbler, who accompanied him, pointed out the monuments erected for Joseph Trumpeldor and others who had become legendary heroes in battles with the Arabs. Korczak was disturbed to see that most of the dead lay in anonymity. "It's a distortion of justice that some should be remembered and others not," he said. He scooped up some soil from that graveyard of forgotten pioneers to carry back to Poland.

Toward the end of his stay, when Simchoni offered to guide him around Palestine, Korczak refused. "It's more important to get a thorough knowledge of life here," he said. "I can always buy picture postcards of Tel Aviv for people who are interested in that city." But he did agree to a tour of the Jordan Valley and the Galilee. He was fascinated by Nazareth and spent some time interviewing an old Polish priest he found living in Tiberias. Only a few hours remained for Jerusalem, but time enough for him to wander through the narrow alleyways, and stop by the Wailing Wall and the Dome of the Rock, and to know that if he was ever to return to Palestine it would be to this old, eternal city, rather than to the kibbutz.

As he packed to leave Ein Harod, Korczak refused to take the bedsheets, scissors, and razor he had brought with him. It was his way of leaving some gifts for the Simchoni family, little knowing that they would treat them like relics. "You are sleeping on the sheets that Korczak slept on," Simchoni would tell guests. "Look, here are Korczak's scissors."

Joseph Arnon, who had to travel from another kibbutz, arranged to see Korczak off in Haifa. "Who knows, I may come back if I can collect a thousand zlotys," Korczak confided to him. "But for now, what do you think I should tell everyone in Warsaw about Palestine?"

Arnon answered without hesitation: "Tell the Poles that this country is by no means a hell for those Jews they told 'Go to Palestine!' And tell the Jews that a new world is being built here, that it's worthwhile for them to take a risk."

"Joseph, I can't tell them such things," Korczak replied. "I can speak only about what I have seen."

23

The Old Doctor

Korczak may have gone to Palestine for the "thoughts" that would
be born to him there, but as the ship plowed its way toward Greece on
the first leg home, he was still thinking of his new friends. Waking suddenly just before dawn on the first day out, he felt impelled to go up on
deck and begin a letter to them. It was not the marvelously alive and
impatient foam that held him in thrall on this starless night, he wrote,
but the smoke rising from their bakery, the silhouette of Mount Gilboa
where their dead lay, and the green of Lake Kinerett.

Back in Warsaw, he was so determined not to cut the thread that
bound them, he set aside one day a month for correspondence, addressing
as many as thirty envelopes at a time, though seldom filling them all. In
a letter to the Simchonis' little daughter, Mia, Korczak described the
busy schedule that made his "weeks fly by." On Monday, he examined
children in juvenile court; Tuesday and Wednesday, he lectured at pedagogic institutes; Thursday through Friday noon, he was at Our Home
in Bielany; Friday afternoon through Saturday, he was at the Orphans
Home; Sunday, he allotted to writing.

To an adult friend he wrote, "I am so tightly programmed here, how
could I even consider a different life in a different land?"—as if an excuse
were necessary. Even as he urged Stefan Jaracz and other friends to go
and see this "courageous and sincere experiment" for themselves, he
knew he had yet to evaluate the whole experience. "I have been waiting
for a moment of total silence to conclude what my stay in Palestine gave

me," he told one of his correspondents. "The task is difficult, and I keep wondering: Was I sincere in my feelings?"

That moment of "total silence" had to wait: shortly after he returned to Warsaw, Korczak was offered his own radio show. He couldn't refuse. Ever since he had adapted some of his stories for radio in the late twenties he had been fascinated by its educational possibilities. Here was the chance to reach thousands of children at a time, instead of just one hundred. "Radio will never replace the book," he told an interviewer, "but it is a new language." Radio had made it possible for nothing ever to be lost, for everything to become "immortal"; yet this new medium also brought awesome responsibilities in its ability to steal "into the home, into the intimate areas of life, and into the human heart."

Korczak's friends in children's programming had been able to arrange his show on the condition that he assume yet another pseudonym to placate higher officials who did not want to be accused of allowing a Jewish educator to shape the minds of Polish children. (It was already common knowledge by then that Janusz Korczak was a pseudonym for Henryk Goldszmit.) Korczak deliberated for a while, and then made the pragmatic decision that it was better to influence people anonymously than not at all. He agreed to call himself the "Old Doctor," which he ironically referred to as his underground name.

Before long the warm, intimate voice of the Old Doctor became famous in Poland. People hurried home from their offices on Thursday afternoons to be on time for the fifteen-minute program. In contrast to the formal tone of other broadcasters, the wry and compassionate voice of the Old Doctor made each listener feel he was being spoken to personally. Korczak's radio style was similar to that of his writing: the usual rules of syntax were dropped, and words and ideas juxtaposed in creative disarray until, like a magician, he pulled everything together at the end. The originality of his method was so provocative that one listener, tuning in to the middle of the show, called the station to complain that the speaker sounded drunk.

Whenever he needed a convincing pig's snort or cock's crow, Korczak would ask his orphans to try out for the part. During auditions, the two homes sounded like barnyards. Adam Dembinski, a Jewish orphan, recalls being chosen to go down to the studio along with a Gentile boy, who was a tailor's apprentice: "My job was to bark like a dog. I gave a loud bark, and got five zlotys. It was wonderful!"

The Old Doctor's fans never knew what to expect when they tuned in: he might be interviewing young patients in a hospital or poor orphans in a summer camp; he might be ruminating about children and airplanes, analyzing children's relationships to adults and each other, or speculating about current events. Or he might simply tell a fairy tale. The proper timing of "Puss in Boots" proved such a difficult challenge that he devoted three shows to it in the fall of 1935 before he was satisfied.

"If I'm with a group of children I can always pace myself, I know instinctively when they are going to laugh, cry, or ask questions," he admitted to an interviewer. "But alone there in that little room with the clock ticking away, I worry if I am talking clearly enough and when the music is scheduled to come in. As soon as the red light says 'Speak,' I feel like someone who doesn't know how to swim being pushed into the water. It's the same panic you feel in war when someone levels a gun at you, or when you're about to go down on a sinking ship."

The analogy to a sinking ship was one that Polish Jews would use often from the mid-thirties on. A wave of fear had gone through Poland's many ethnic communities (the Jews were the second-largest minority after the Ukrainians) when in September of 1934 the government abrogated the minorities treaty, which had guaranteed them equal rights. As long as Jozef Pilsudski, officially only the Minister of War and Inspector General of the Armed Forces, unofficially ruled the country, they had felt safe. The Marshal had become increasingly repressive and disillusioned with the Poles' aptitude for democracy in his later years, shocking many by establishing a special camp for his political enemies after the assassination of the Minister of the Interior; but he had never abandoned his vision of Poland as a multinational federation. When on May 12, 1935, Pilsudski succumbed to stomach cancer at the age of sixty-seven, a great number of Jews feared that the future of Polish Jewry would be buried with him.

Many rabbis were among the mourners in the funeral procession that escorted Pilsudski's embalmed body, dressed in full uniform, from St. John's Cathedral, where it lay in state for two days. It was then taken on a railway flatcar with an honor guard of generals past hundreds of thousands of Poles who lined the two hundred miles of track to Cracow. A hundred Jewish delegations from every part of Poland attended the funeral at Wawel Castle, the historic burial place of Polish kings.

Korczak had never met Pilsudski (years before, for lack of time, he had turned down a request to write his biography), but wanting to pay homage to him, he prepared a tender script, "A Pole Does Not Cry," for his next broadcast. It was true that Polish heroes were not supposed to cry, he planned to tell his listeners, but did they know that their beloved Jozef Pilsudski actually cried twice in his life—once when his army was surrounded by Cossacks in Lvov, and again when his favorite chestnut mare died. The Old Doctor wanted to comfort his audience with the knowledge that Pilsudski, like all courageous leaders, was human too and capable of weeping, even as they were now at his death. But the censors, who had come to power with the nationalization of radio the year before, rejected this portrayal of Pilsudski as a man of tears. In spite of the appeals of a number of Korczak's influential friends, the Old Doctor was forced to replace the script with one innocuously titled "A Story about Children."

Korczak decided to take some of his orphans to the unveiling of the Marshal's memorial in Cracow when he heard that the railroad was offering four free children's tickets to every adult traveling there during the month of July. Shimon Agassi, one of the four lucky Jewish orphans chosen to go, remembers that they slept the night before at the apartment Korczak shared with his sister. They stayed up late, packing foodstuffs and giggling over Korczak's silly contingency plans for the various things that might happen to them. If they couldn't find seats together, one of the boys was to dash into Korczak's compartment moaning that he had just been bitten by a rabid dog. The occupants would flee to avoid him, and they would have the entire compartment to themselves. However, on the train the next morning, the boy chosen for the role burst out laughing in the middle of his story, and none of the passengers were fooled. The children had to take turns sitting in the one seat next to Korczak. They passed the time playing with a portable chessboard and helping Korczak roll his cigarettes. The six-hour trip south through the flat green fields of the Polish countryside to the old royal city flew by quickly.

Korczak picked a room at random from a list at the station information desk and off they went by tram. Depositing their bags at the boarding house, they proceeded to a restaurant, where for the first time in their lives the four orphans were allowed to choose their own food. They ordered all kinds of dishes, but not meatballs, which they knew only too well from the orphanage leftovers. The next day they walked the cobblestone streets of the lovely Renaissance city that had once been the capital, visiting the Municipal Museum, the square where Kosciuszko had taken an oath to free his people from the partitioning powers, the statue of the great romantic poet Adam Mickiewicz, and then Wawel Castle, where Jozef Pilsudski was buried alongside the Polish kings. At the ceremony for the unveiling of the memorial, the children finally understood why Korczak had brought a large stone from the orphanage yard when he motioned them to join him in placing it by the monument.

A few hours before they were to return by train to Warsaw, Korczak took his young companions to the airport. There, with the same straight face he had managed to keep on the train during the abortive rabid-dog scheme, he asked the man at the counter for four free tickets for the children accompanying him. Informed that this was impossible, Korczak replied innocently that since the airline, like the railroad, was owned by the government, he felt the same offer should hold for both. The clerk consulted a few other employees, who went into a huddle with still others, but the answer that came back was no. Korczak and the children were still laughing when they jumped onto the last train to Warsaw that night.

After Madame Pilsudska intervened for him at the radio station, Korczak was permitted to read "A Pole Does Not Cry" over the air on December 5 of that year. But right-wing newspapers had uncovered the identity of the Old Doctor and now accused him of being part of a Jewish plot to ruin Polish children. Soon after, the Old Doctor was informed that the show scheduled for December 26 would be canceled because of special holiday programming that week. Humiliated by this last-minute directive—the station was obviously reluctant to put a Jew on the air during the Christmas season—Korczak reminded his superiors that his contract was not binding after the end of February. His threat was clear, but futile. In spite of his popularity, the Old Doctor's contract was not renewed. Following his last broadcast on February 27, 1936, the Old Doctor disappeared from the lives of his loyal fans as mysteriously as he had appeared.

Although he tried to hide his pain over what was happening at the radio station—and in all of Poland, for that matter—Korczak confided his anguish and self-doubts in his letters to Joseph Arnon. On February 7, 1936, shortly before his program was terminated, he wrote: "When you are overtaken by a feeling of numbness, when you see yourself as superfluous and your whole life as useless, when you feel like hiding in a secret corner to contemplate things for the last time, when you feel like no longer existing—then from somewhere a kind word reaches you, a friendly echo from the past. You change your mind impatiently: 'What nonsense!' And then you hesitate: 'Perhaps after all! . . .' Every person wants to contribute one more thing! You write that I am wrong about having failed. My failure lies in the fact that all that brought me joy in the past has turned into crushing toil, everything that seemed worthwhile and feasible now produces doubt, apprehension, shame. What little I've achieved seems unimportant. I took a vow to uphold the child and to defend his rights, but all that I can do is offer a prayer or wishful blessing to support his insecure steps."

Arnon was still urging Korczak to emigrate to Palestine, and he was still deliberating on it: "Where is there a more suitable place to defend (in words) the small and weak, if not the land of Israel? That is why I am filled with yearning. But, to my sorrow, I am bound (and overloaded) here by my real work, which is at the point of decline." Yet, in closing, Korczak assured Arnon that he would consider coming to Palestine if he could be certain that he wouldn't be "a burden on the country."

Stefa was in Palestine visiting Feiga and her new husband (a teacher who had emigrated from Russia) during the difficult period that Korczak's show went off the air. By April, when Stefa was scheduled to return, Korczak found himself waiting impatiently. But he didn't hear from her on the day she was due back, nor the day after. It wasn't like her not to be in touch with him. He asked a number of people if they'd seen her; no one had.

"Stefa doesn't seem to have arrived yet," he told Natalia Wislicka, who, together with her philanthropist husband, had become a confidant over the years. It was not unusual for Korczak to come by for a chat in between engagements, or to have a quiet dinner in their home. "I don't know what could have happened to her."

While they were having tea in the garden, Natalia's young son, Alfred, kept running out of his room to check that she was still there.

"It's a sign he really loves you," Korczak commented.

"It's not love—it's the fear of loss," she said, with a shrug.

"Well, what is love but fear of loss?" he replied.

It was fear of loss that Natalia Wislicka detected in his voice when he complained about not hearing from Stefa. For the first time she realized how successfully he masked his deep attachment to Stefa from her.

A few days later Stefa finally appeared, explaining that she had been exhausted by her trip, which took seven days and seven sleepless nights with a stopover in Athens; she'd gone directly to her brother's home, taken a bath, slept for twenty-four hours, and then given herself another three days before facing the orphanage again.

Stefa was already planning an exhibit at the orphanage of the colorful scarfs, straw pen-cases, olive-wood rulers, seashells, and other treasures she had brought back. As she and Korczak pored over the photo album the kibbutz had presented to her on her departure, she began to speak of Palestine as a future for both of them. She was amazed that he was so open to her suggestions, although he questioned how the orphanage could survive with both of them away. She began exploring the options with him, and wrote excitedly to Feiga in one letter about his idea that they rotate trips, alternating six months in Palestine with six months in Poland, so that one of them would always be on call for the Orphans Home. "Things are becoming more agitated every day on both the national and the religious front," Stefa added in that letter, alluding to the Jewish labor strikes protesting the government's anti-Semitic policies. "The evil permeating the atmosphere here is worse than the economic crisis. And there doesn't seem to be anything one can do."

When Korczak agreed to go to Palestine for six weeks that summer of 1936 as a prelude to a more extended stay, Stefa again took paper and pen to notify Feiga. This time Korczak jocularly added in his own precise handwriting at the bottom of her letter: "I already speak Hebrew—*Netzyan Hetzyan* [Excellently]. *Shalom*, Korczak."

Korczak flew from Athens to Palestine on his second trip. As enthusiastic about aviation as about radio and film, he had been one of the first in Warsaw to take sightseeing excursions by plane in the late twenties. "It makes you realize how small man is in the universe when you look down on him from up there," he would tell his friends. Now, looking down on the coast near Haifa, he was struck that this was "where exile ends." Once again he was "privileged to live to see the Promised Land," and once again he was mystified by the emotional hold it had on him.

As Korczak's skepticism receded on this second trip, he was able to acknowledge that Palestine was a promised land in more ways than one: it promised a place where people who were Jews could live and work without stigma and dislocation, promised sun and healthy growth for children, promised the security of a genuine community. But this time he became even more aware of the promises it had made to the Arabs, who saw it as their land. If Palestine was to be the solution to the Jewish question, he understood, as did Martin Buber and others, that the Arab question had to be solved. When he heard that a new port was being created in Tel Aviv because the Arabs were protesting against Jews working in Jaffa, Korczak had startled his friends with: "But what about the Arab children?" Would they go hungry if the Jaffa port were closed?

Palestine was unusually tense that summer after a year of Arab rioting across the country. Just before his arrival, marauding bands of Arabs had set fire to Ein Harod's wheat fields, cut down the grapefruit trees, and shot at the settlers from the top of the mountain. Korczak was surprised to find that the kibbutz looked like an armed stockade. He volunteered to take his turn standing guard duty at night and was insulted when he was refused.

"Don't you know that I'm a Polish officer who has served in three wars?" he asked his hosts. When that bit of information didn't alter their decision, he related his theory of chance: one should face danger head on, with the attitude that fate might have your number, but then again it might not. He was willing to take that chance. But the kibbutzniks were not willing to risk losing their special guest.

Korczak was more successful in testing his theory a few days later while visiting one of his former orphans, Moses Sadek, in Haifa. When Sadek urged him not to return to the kibbutz the following day because there were rumors of shooting along the bus route, Korczak responded: "Who says that tomorrow when I go the Arabs will start shooting? And if they do, who says it will be on my road? And if it is, who says it will be at my bus? And if it is, who says they'll hit anyone? And if they do, who says it will be me?" Having rendered Sadek speechless, Korczak declared: "Since there are so few risks, I'm going."

Though they refused to permit him to perform guard duty, Korczak urged the kibbutzniks to allow the older children to share this dangerous task with them, just as they shared the food shortages and exhausting manual labor. "You shouldn't wrap the children in cotton," Korczak said. "The struggle to create a life here is their destiny."

He spent less time at Ein Harod on this trip, making a conscious effort to lecture at other kibbutzim so that he could broaden his observations. Everyone noticed that the doctor seemed more at ease with himself, no longer smiling in a self-deprecatory way when he spoke the few sentences he had mastered in Hebrew before his interpreter took over.

He was particularly interested in the *moshavim*, those agricultural settlements based on free enterprise, where he could see the initiative of the individual farmer on his own plot of land. The transformation of the young men and women he had known into people of the soil was a constant source of amazement, although he saw it as more a spiritual than a physical change. The success of one of his orphans who had never received warmth from his mother was especially gratifying to him. Korczak thought the boy would be handicapped all his life, but he had obviously found a constructive outlet for his emotions here. It made Korczak realize that a specialist cannot predict a child's ultimate destiny; a place like Palestine had liberated this orphan's hidden potential in ways that he could never have imagined back in Warsaw.

He had a desire to keep moving on this trip, as if some premonition told him that he would not be given a chance again. When he met Hillman, a mechanic from Siberia who was a "veteran wanderer," he was tempted to "grab a knapsack" and ask if they could hike through the whole country together. Out of this might come a *Robinson Crusoe*-like book for children—only the hero would be an "Eretz Yisrael Robinson."

He even imagined hiking in the mountains with "old Gilson," a kibbutz friend, as his guide. Every great deed occurred in the mountains—Ararat, Sinai, and now Mount Scopus (the site of Hebrew University), he wrote Arnon. He had the solution to the Arab–Jewish problem: "Let the Arabs keep the fertile valleys and the sea, and the mountains will sustain the Jews."

Some of Korczak's rapture must have spilled over into his letters to Stefa, for he told a friend wryly: "Because of my enthusiasm, Stefa is afraid I may never return—but I think she will come here before me, and stay forever."

Whenever possible, Korczak avoided meeting officials. He refused to visit Tel Aviv, which he felt did not represent the dream of Palestine. He considered it an "unhealthy" city, controlled by "ambitious tricksters." Jerusalem attracted him most—Jerusalem with its timelessness, its pink light reflecting off the limestone buildings set against the Judean hills. He felt at home in this city where it was natural for one to have dreams of ascending to heaven. He explored the narrow streets of the Jewish quarter of the Old City, mingling with Orthodox Jews, who looked not too different from the poor Jews at the other end of Krochmalna but who lived in even worse squalor. He could not forget the medieval conditions at one of the Orthodox Jewish orphanages that he visited in that "city of grace."

Despite warnings that it was dangerous, Korczak wandered through all of Jerusalem, visiting sites sacred to Christianity, especially those connected with the life of Jesus. Bible in hand, he might one day stroll with Franciscan monks in an effort to re-create the world of Jesus, and on another walk beyond Dung Gate and the Wailing Wall so that he could look out on the Arab village of Silwan, which was once the city of David, whose life he was also trying to re-create.

Korczak spent his last few days in Palestine with his Young Pioneer friend Moshe Zertal, who had emigrated a few years before. From the last letter he had received from Korczak—"I am an old man, not creating anymore, just observing from the sidelines"—Zertal had not known what to expect. He was relieved to see the doctor looking younger than ever, as if Palestine agreed with him. The two men checked into a small hotel in Haifa, then strolled leisurely through the city as they waited for the ship that would take Korczak to Greece, the first stop on his journey home. Korczak was amazed when Zertal suggested they leave the small package he was carrying in a store and come back for it later. He couldn't believe the package would still be there. Although he was perspiring from the heat and clearly fatigued, Korczak was his old humorous, ironic self. Spotting a FOR RENT sign on one of the houses near the sea, he couldn't resist a little fun and knocked on the door. Using Zertal as his bemused interpreter, he pretended to be a new immigrant in search of a room, questioning the landlady carefully about the routine of the household, checking out the bathroom, and examining the porch.

After they retreated to the beach, they "laughed like children," but Zertal understood that Korczak had been trying to imagine an alternative way of life there. As they sat in silence, listening to the voices of children playing nearby and watching the waves breaking on the shore, Zertal wondered if Korczak would ever return to test that life for himself.

24

The Hard Truth
of Moses

Learn to know life, little Moses, because it is difficult, my child.
—Moses

"One needs time to absorb an experience until he understands not only with his head, but with his heart," Korczak told an audience in a talk on his Palestine trip at the Institute of Judaic Sciences in early October.

In seemingly unrelated vignettes, much in the style of the Old Doctor, he spoke of watching an Arab mother and son saunter nonchalantly into a Jewish village at six in the morning with two donkeys and four dogs to draw water from a well, "as if the area had been theirs in the past and would be in the future"; of his surprise at the uniform price of bus tickets no matter what the distance between cities; of the nuisance of mosquitoes (he counted forty bites his first night); of the disparity in living standards from one region to another, some settlers enjoying fruits, vegetables, and beautiful flowers, while others were starving; of his disappointment on learning that the black spots he found on the stones he collected were tar from paved roads rather than the blood of the fallen. Like all other places, Palestine had its good and its bad features, he said, cautioning his audience not to think they could escape their problems by going there, because life is difficult everywhere.

"The doctor gave a wonderful lecture," Stefa wrote Feiga, "though it's a pity he had to read it. He was very excited. I shall send it to you."

Those who had attended Korczak's lecture to hear a political analysis of what was happening in Palestine must have been disappointed. Only once did the famous educator touch on the political situation: "Palestine is like a long rope, one end of which is held by the Jews, and the other by the Arabs," he said. "They both pull, in the process coming closer and closer. But just when they are about to touch, a third party appears and cuts the rope. And then the whole thing starts over again."

The same analogy could have been drawn about the Poles and the Jews, whose relationship was continuing to deteriorate with the acceleration of fascist influences from the Third Reich. The Nuremberg Laws, which in 1935 had declared the Jews an inferior race, further encouraged Polish extreme-nationalist groups (like the National Radical Camp and the All-Polish Youth) to push for economic boycotts of Jewish businesses and for segregated seats at the university (known as ghetto benches) for Jewish students.

The right-wing press used Korczak's talk on Palestine as an excuse to vilify him in a series of articles that once again identified the Old Doctor as Janusz Korczak, the so-called Pole, who was really Henryk Goldszmit, the Jew. Why had Korczak decided to go to Palestine? the papers wanted to know. Why was he allowed to educate Polish children?

If Korczak was saddened by the viciousness of the press attacks on his Palestine trip, he was devastated by what awaited him at the next meeting of the board of Our Home in Bielany. To this day little has been said publicly about what happened that afternoon in the late fall of 1936 to make Korczak resign from his work with Maryna Falska. Their fundamental differences in educational philosophy are cited as the cause. Korczak wanted to give the children the security of being raised in a family atmosphere, while Maryna, more ideological in her approach, believed that Our Home should serve the needs of the progressive working class. Over Korczak's objections, she had opened the library and playground to the neighborhood children, and given space to community projects.

Maryna could never have been accused of anti-Semitism—she was once about to expel an orphan for making an offensive remark when Korczak intervened—but she was known to be under criticism from anti-Semitic groups for allowing a Jew to educate Polish children. She had remained silent that fateful day when a member of the board confronted Korczak with: "Are you a Zionist?"

Korczak had looked at the group in disbelief. He walked out of the room, feeling betrayed that those with whom he had worked for so many years should ask him in effect: Are you loyal to Palestine rather than to Poland? Most of the board accepted Korczak's resignation with a philosophical shrug—as assimilated as he was, he was still a Jew. To prevent a scandal, his name was not dropped from the board roster. The orphans were told only that Pan Doctor would not be able to come around as often as before.

In her memoir written after the war, Madame Pilsudska discreetly omitted anti-Semitism as the reason for Korczak's break with the orphanage: "Some of his methods seemed strange to us. For instance, Dr. Korczak would ask the children their opinions of the young teachers, and base his own judgment on what they said. The staff lost all authority with the children, which resulted in chaos. So we had to part with Dr. Korczak the educator, with the greatest regret. However, he still remained a member of the board."

Korczak not only lost his radio program and his affiliation with the Polish orphanage that year; he also lost his consulting post at the juvenile court. One of the lawyers who witnessed his dismissal was to write years later: "I still cannot forgive myself for my silence at that time. Those officials who represented Polish law and justice informed Korczak: 'No Jew can be in charge of our juvenile offenders.' "

The loss of so much that gave meaning to both his professional and personal life revived the anguish of Korczak's earlier childhood losses. "I have never felt closely attached to life—it just flowed by me," he wrote Ester Budko. "Since my youth I have felt myself both old and superfluous. Is it any wonder that this feeling has become more intense now? I am not counting the days, but the hours left to me. The trip to Palestine was probably my last effort. And now nothing." Alternating as he always did between hope and despair, Korczak added: "I believe in humanity's future. If I had kept an innocent faith in God, I would probably pray for the salvation of this world where children are the first to suffer. The child will have the leading role in man's spiritual renewal—it was my intention to play some part in it, but I didn't know how."

Palestine could not be his own personal salvation, Korczak told another correspondent, because he did not have "forty years to spend in the desert." Yet he remained ambivalent about emigrating.

"The doctor is so depressed that he is indifferent to everything around him," Stefa wrote to Feiga. "Imagine, he wanted to go to Jerusalem this month. Just take off suddenly. Don't mention this to anyone because people who don't know him may get the wrong idea. He intended to live in Jerusalem rather than on the kibbutz. He is miserable, and makes others miserable."

The indecision of their lives—hers and Korczak's—was too much for Stefa. At the age of fifty, she decided to take Feiga's advice to leave Poland. On November 4, 1936, she requested her to ask the kibbutz if she could become a member. If the answer was affirmative, could they help her apply for papers? She knew it would take some time, but she wanted to set things in motion—now.

Stefa's resolution seems to have deepened Korczak's depressed state, but it may have been that same "fear of loss" he had experienced over her absence earlier that eventually propelled him into action. On March 29, 1937, he confided to a friend in Jerusalem: "After a depression of a few months, I have finally made my decision to spend my last years in Palestine. I will go first to Jerusalem to study Hebrew in preparation for living on a kibbutz. The only family I have here is my sister, who is able to support herself as a translator. But since I have so little saved up, I wonder if it will be possible for me to manage there." Korczak was quite definite: he would be leaving within the month because he was no longer able to bear "the insecure situation in Poland."

On March 30 he wrote more letters to Palestine. Congratulating Moshe Zertal on the birth of his baby—"It is good that you have a child"— Korczak revealed his doubts about his decision to spend his life serving children and defending their rights, rather than marrying and having children of his own. Now that he had failed to protect his orphans against the onslaught of anti-Semitism or to put enough food on their table, he saw how naïve he had been. They (the dark forces) had power, while he had only justice on his side. When he watched his orphans hurrying down the street to school, he was overwhelmed by his inability to protect them from attacks by children who threw rocks and beat them up. He felt "responsible for all the evil done to them."

He tried to hold on to his faith—"Despite everything, I do believe in the future of humankind, the Jews, the land of Israel"—but the present reality had to be seen in a more universal perspective. While taking a compulsory course for physicians on gas warfare, he was reminded of "the Middle Ages—plague and disease—fear of the end of the world." Now there was gas and fear of world war. "Even if our rockets reach the moon, even if we go further and further in splitting the atom and discover the secrets of the living cell, will there still not be something beyond those mysteries?"

But always he arrived where he had started: grappling with his ambivalence about emigrating to Palestine. "I'm not trying to save myself
but my thoughts," he wrote. He could not easily cut himself off from
contact with Polish reality. "I shall be awake for every call and every
sound. I want to link what was with what is. I cannot be otherwise." He
intended to leave as soon as he decided whether to apply for a tourist
visa or a residence permit, and had solved the problem of money. He
had only a thousand zlotys to his name, but he wasn't going to let that
bother him. "Only the small things disturb." The most difficult part had
been making the decision, and that done, he was impatient to come. "I
would like to be in Jerusalem tomorrow, sitting alone in my small, narrow
room with a Bible, some study books, a Hebrew dictionary, paper and
pencil—so that I can say: a new page, the last chapter."

In another letter he wrote: "I called for respect for the child, but
someone has rightly asked me who respects adults these days. Maybe I
am deluding myself that it will be easier to call for justice from Palestine,
or at least for pity." And then he added, alluding to the Japanese war
against China, the Italian invasion of Ethiopia, and the Spanish Civil War:
"China, Ethiopia, Spain, these are the stations of my misery."

In his letter to friends at Ein Harod, Korczak explained that only his
lack of Hebrew prevented him from settling immediately in the kibbutz.
Once he had mastered the language in Jerusalem, breathed some fresh
air, stretched his bones, and regained his sense of humor, he would come
to them. But he added with a mystical turn of thought, as if he had a
premonition that this would never be: "It may not sound comprehensible,
but I believe that if I don't come as a weary, tortured old man to share
what is left of my talents, I shall come to you as a child again, starting
his life wanderings anew."

Only to Arnon did he admit his lack of conviction about "permanent
settlement" in Palestine. He would have to adapt himself to a different
life, climate, language, and surroundings. "When you are sixty, it is
impossible to approach it any other way, it is forbidden. A man is responsible to his own spirit, to his own mode of thought—that is his
workshop."

What gave him comfort was that he was finally going. "I have asked
myself: Is it too late? No. Had I gone earlier I would have felt like a
deserter. One has to remain at his post until the very last moment."

This "last pilgrimage" on which he was embarking carried an ethical
burden as heavy as the one he was putting down. He saw the Jews as

having a "moral responsibility" to aid the oppressed races of China, South Africa, America, and India. Palestine should become a second League of Nations. Just as Geneva served as a parliament to oversee such mundane affairs as war, world health, and education, so Jerusalem should represent the rights of the individual to a spiritual life.

He was to depart in May, yet took no action, writing Zertal that conscience did not permit him to leave the children at that moment. With his usual irony he wrote the poet Zerubavel Gilead that one reason he still hesitated to come to Palestine was the language. "I'm old. My teeth are falling out, and so is my hair. This Hebrew of yours is a tough nut to crack. It requires young, strong teeth."

Like Julian Tuwim, the Polish-Jewish poet, he felt that the Polish language was his "homeland." One's mother tongue was "not a set of rules and moral precepts, but the very air which one's soul inhales."

Instead of preparing for his departure that summer, Korczak arranged to spend June and July in the Polish mountains, "to remind me of the ones in Palestine." There on a remote farm he would have time to think and write. His conflicting needs—to stay in Poland and struggle for what he believed; to retreat to Palestine into a life of quiet meditation—were reflected in the two slim volumes he produced, one on Louis Pasteur, the other on Moses.

"The lives of great men are like legends—difficult, but beautiful," he wrote in the Pasteur book, which he intended as the first in a series of mini-biographies whose subjects would include Pestalozzi, Leonardo da Vinci, Pilsudski, Fabre, Ruskin, Mendel, Waclaw Nalkowski, and Jan Dawid. (It was a project similar in spirit to the one his father and uncle had undertaken seventy years before.)

Korczak clearly identified with Pasteur, "whose beautiful life was spent in the struggle for truth," and whose attitude toward children was so much like his own. "When I approach a child, I have two feelings— affection for what he is today, and respect for what he can become," Pasteur had written. He taught the world many of the same things that Korczak taught his children: to wash their hands, drink boiled water, open the windows to let in good fresh air. He dared to say "I don't know" while doing his experiments, and never gave up, even when he was the most discouraged.

Korczak dedicated the Pasteur book to his sister, Anna Lui, but he told friends that he had written it for children living in a time when the "Hitler madness" had seized power over everything decent. He wanted them to know there were people in the world who devoted their lives to enriching the human condition.

If Korczak had looked to Pasteur, the scientist-healer who stubbornly went his own lonely way against all opposition, for strength to endure in those difficult times, he looked to "the hard truth of Moses" the lawgiver for spiritual strength. The book on Moses was to be the first in another series he planned to write, this one on the early years of biblical heroes. David, Solomon, and Jeremiah were on his list, as well as Jesus, but it is not surprising that he chose to begin with Moses, the foundling who had been forced to dwell among strangers until he eventually made his way back to his own people.

Like Freud, Korczak wrote his book on Moses toward the end of his life. His purpose was not to question Moses' origins, as Freud had, but, like a good storyteller, to ask the questions that would fill in the pieces omitted in the original tale. Why did Moses' mother decide to hide him after three months, rather than after two or four? What did his mother and father say to each other before he was born, and after?

One can understand Moses, although he lived four thousand years before, because he is no different from children today, Korczak told his readers. If we can recall our own childhoods, we can become Moses, and if we recall our experiences as adults, we can begin to understand how Moses' parents made that most difficult of decisions: to give up their baby.

Korczak saw Moses as a child living in terrifying times, under a death sentence. He saw him lost in the bulrushes, then found and reared in the enemy's palace. He saw him dreaming nostalgically of his lost home, having nightmares. He knew children, and so he knew Moses—because Moses was a child before he was a lawgiver, and had experienced the universal emotions of childhood.

"As he sleeps," Korczak wrote of Moses, "he does not know that his mother will have him put on the riverbank. . . . He does not know that the sea will part before him, and that he will become a leader, also a lawgiver. He does not know that he will complain to God in the desert— 'Why did you dislike me so much that you gave me the burden of an entire people? . . . I cannot carry it all because it is too much for me. Please kill me.' "

When Korczak returned to Warsaw with his two manuscripts that August, it was as if his spirits had been lifted by his communion with

Pasteur and Moses. For the rest of the year he made "feeble attempts" to reach Palestine. Money and language were still the stumbling blocks, he wrote Joseph Arnon, but he also had to "cleanse" himself from within, exclude everything temporal from his thoughts, and relive all that he had ever experienced "through the silence within silence." There were times he felt his head was "bursting." At other times he heard a stern accusation: "You cannot leave the world the way it is." Again his thoughts returned to the child he did not have: "Fate has so ordained that everything I have done has been for the benefit of an orphanage, not of a family. Is this why it is so difficult for me now? This too is an endless subject." He apologizes for his "wild" thoughts. He should be writing about his encounters with Zertal, about Stefa, about concrete day-to-day affairs. Yet he still imagines that someday in a letter such as this he will chance upon the "magic word that will create a shelter for homeless humanity."

On November 4, 1937, the Polish Academy of Literature awarded Janusz Korczak the Golden Laurel for outstanding literary achievement. It was gratifying to know that he was still valued as a Polish writer.

He felt this same sense of connectedness to Polish culture and history the following month when he spoke at the funeral of Andrzej Strug, a leading socialist and a novelist friend from Flying University days. Strug's funeral was attended by thousands of the political left whose struggle in the underground socialist movement against the czarist empire was immortalized in his book *Underground People*.

"The times were cruel, gloomy, and dangerous in a different way when Nalkowski died," Korczak began his graveside eulogy for Strug. "Our first reaction then was—what now?" Paraphrasing the words that the protagonist in *Underground People* had said over the grave of his fallen comrade, Korczak continued: "Why did he leave us like orphans? He went calmly to sleep when we needed him most. He shouldn't have. What about us?"

It would be more difficult now that this man who had "kept vigilance with his thoughts, his breath, and the pulse of his blood" was gone. The world would be a "colder place" without him.

25

Loneliness

When does the loneliness of old age begin?
—Radio talk, 1938

"There is little of me outside the orphanage," Stefa had written Feiga after Korczak moved into his sister's apartment. For a while she initiated new policies—children were sent out for job training after the fifth or sixth grade, prayers were dropped before breakfast and after dinner—but still everything seemed routine. The young teachers she had trained to take over her work while she was away could manage quite well without her. She no longer felt challenged or needed. And so, in January of 1937, while she was waiting for her visa to Palestine, Stefa decided to give up her position in the orphanage and take a room of her own.

Temperamentally unable to remain idle, she accepted a part-time arrangement with CENTOS, a social welfare organization that sponsored a hundred and eighty progressive orphanages in Poland. She was to travel three days a week around the country, inspecting their various institutions.

The advisability of Stefa's cutting herself off from work with children seems to have been questioned by Feiga. Stefa reassured her: "Of course, I will still keep an office on Krochmalna." She would never give up a place to meet with her "children," who still brought their families to see her every week, just as she would never stop corresponding with those who wrote from all over the world, but she needed space of her own now, needed a change. "I can admit to you in a selfish way that I'm learning to appreciate my modest, quiet, and sunny room. I can be alone—at last! No one knocks at my door, no one comes when I do not invite them. I don't have to dispense good advice, make telephone calls, answer questions. I can go to bed when I like, and come home as late as I want. I know I will renounce my newly gained freedom after a year or so, but right now, after twenty-five years in harness, I enjoy it immensely."

Stefa's one-room apartment with kitchen and bath was small and simple, according to Misha Wroblewski, who visited her there. It looked very much like her room at the orphanage, with few personal touches other than her cactus plants. Having tea with Stefa, Misha realized that he had never seen her sit still, had never really talked to her before. "How can you bear to leave the orphanage after all this time?" he had asked her.

And she had replied in that blunt, straightforward way of hers: "Look, every few years the children change. After a while, one cannot relate to the new ones as ardently as one did before. And to work without loving them intensely is something one should never do." She did not say what many believed to be closer to the truth: that the home was not the same without Korczak living there.

Stefa was not committed to CENTOS as she had been to the Orphans Home; she was working only to pay her rent and make enough money to buy necessities and little presents for her "children and grandchildren" until her visa came through. Like Korczak, she had taken very little salary over the years and had almost no savings.

In spite of her lack of enthusiasm, Stefa was good at her job. She revealed much of her character in the way she evaluated the CENTOS orphanages. She was fair. She never dropped in on a home unexpectedly, but notified the directors in advance that she would be arriving, to give them time to fix up the place if necessary. She was astute. She stayed at each orphanage for a few days, rather than for just a few hours. She observed not only what the children ate but also how they handled their food. If they wolfed it down, she knew they had been hungry the day before. When they left for school, she walked through their dormitories, examining the sheets to estimate how frequently they were washed. The condition of the bathrooms also revealed the quality of the orphanage.

When Stefa returned to Warsaw, she told stories that revealed her sense of the absurd. In one home a philanthropist had given the girls brooches that another philanthropist disapproved of as frivolous. A sentry had to be posted at the window each day to signal which philanthropist was approaching so that the girls would know whether or not to put on the brooches.

Stefa always defended the personnel when she could. She saw that their rooms were as cold as the children's and that they were as hungry. But her experiences only increased the disillusionment she had felt with boarding homes ever since returning from Ein Harod. Observing how a child lived in the Children's House, while sharing activities with his family and community, had changed her outlook. She now believed that Poland's orphanages should be transformed into halfway houses that allowed children to have greater contact with their relatives. If that were not possible, the children should be cared for in small, family-size units.

In her application for membership in the kibbutz, Stefa had written: "I am a dishonest person. I have been clearly against boarding homes of our kind for six years, but I have stayed through the law of inertia." She often joked with friends in Warsaw: "Before I die, I want to write one book, *Abolish the Boarding Home.*"

Stefa was ecstatic to hear that Feiga had given birth to a boy in August. (Years before she had advised Feiga to have a baby even if she never married.) Though her lack of a visa prevented her from rushing to the new mother and baby in Ein Harod, she wrote constantly over the next few months to encourage Feiga, who was suffering from postpartum depression. "You think one goes through this experience without problems," Stefa wrote when the baby was two months old. "I am not surprised your nerves failed you. Only in books are the 'blessings' of motherhood and 'sacred feelings' so poetic. I happen to know a great many sensitive women who were not able to deal with the shock of having a first child—especially if they had been married for five to ten years." But Stefa needed reassuring, too: "And I am certain, my darling, that you will feel less lonely and need me less and less."

Stefa worried about Ein Harod whenever she read in the Warsaw papers about Arab attacks on Jewish settlements. "I fear you are hiding something from me" or "I feel you are keeping secrets just to spare me" was a constant refrain. "For my peace of mind, write me, even if it is just a postcard." Feiga reacted like a rebellious daughter, withholding letters at times and accusing Stefa of being overbearing. Many of Stefa's letters were prefaced with "And don't you dare be mad at me!" or "You may get mad at me, but . . ." before she revealed some action she had taken, or some gift she had sent. In one package with three blouses, Feiga found a typical note: "I am sure you will not be satisfied with them—the first because of the color, the second because of the style, and the third because of the buttons."

Stefa could speak of nothing but Feiga's baby to Korczak, although he didn't share her attachment to Feiga—who openly voiced her resentment that Stefa did not get enough credit for the success of the Orphans Home. While she waited for her visa, Stefa often volunteered to babysit for Romcia, the daughter of two *bursa* members, Roza and Jozef Sztokman. Born the same month as Feiga's son, Romcia lived with her parents in the garret room that had once been Korczak's study. Her mother, Roza, who had been raised in the orphanage, was in charge of the kitchen. When Romcia was born, the apprentices had called out to each other: "We have a baby!" Korczak was fascinated with the child and always took time to play with her on the days he spent at the home. He and Stefa found themselves comparing notes like doting grandparents whenever they got together on what they knew was a most unlikely project. "Don't burst out laughing, but I am teaching the Doctor Hebrew," Stefa reported to Feiga. "I write words out as they sound in Polish, he repeats the sound and jots them down phonetically by his own method."

In March of 1938, when she was losing hope that it would ever come through, Stefa received her certificate of immigration to Palestine. It was, she said, the highest Jewish award she had ever been given. She immediately wrote to ask Feiga if she should mark her linens, and how. She couldn't study Hebrew because her head was "spinning" with too many things. And Feiga "shouldn't be mad"—she hadn't requested a room of her own, but just a corner in someone else's place.

Still, once she had the certificate, Stefa felt uneasy. "It's so difficult to leave the Doctor here," she told Feiga. She was trying to convince him to follow her. "If he had a different character, he could get a plot of land in a *moshav* from the Jewish National Fund, because he recently became a deputy member. But now he is depressed again and indifferent."

The imminence of Stefa's departure probably had something to do with Korczak's depression. He warned her that she wasn't used to the relentless heat in Palestine, that at fifty-two she might be too old for such hardships. Stefa's resolution to emigrate faltered. She wrote Feiga: "I am not like your old ladies who come to the land of Israel to die, but I can't help worrying how the weather and other conditions there will affect me."

Conflicted though she might be, Stefa pulled everything together and arranged for her departure. She quit her post at CENTOS, promised to write all her children at the Orphans Home and agreed to send articles about her life in Palestine to the *Little Review*, where she had worked briefly as an editor with Newerly after Korczak resigned. It was especially difficult for her to part with little Romcia, but she had Feiga's infant son waiting for her. The actual moment of departure was what she dreaded most. "I am afraid of goodbyes and embarrassed at the welcomes that await me," she admitted to Feiga.

Stefa was gone, and still Korczak remained in Warsaw. The political situation might be bleak, but Korczak held on to his belief in the liberal stratum of Polish society as the true face of Poland. His faith was sustained by the many Poles who still esteemed him and abhorred anti-Semitism. Close friends at the radio station had been able to negotiate some air time for him if he wanted to do another Old Doctor series. At first he hesitated, for fear "things might end harshly again," but finally he allowed himself to be persuaded. He chose loneliness as the theme of his first three radio talks: "The Loneliness of the Child," "The Loneliness of Youth," and "The Loneliness of the Old Man."

Like Henry James, Korczak might have said that his loneliness was the "deepest thing" about him: the port from which he set out and the port to which his course was finally directing itself. All his adult life, he had exposed the loneliness of the child in an alien, adult society, and occasionally the "impatient, strange loneliness" of the adolescent; but now it was the loneliness of the old man he confronted with the most passion, because it was his loneliness. It is one thing to call oneself the Old Doctor, and another to come to terms with approaching old age.

"When does the loneliness of old age begin?" the Old Doctor asked an ancient linden tree which he recognized as his double. "With the first gray hair? The first extracted tooth which will never grow back again? When you have your first grandchild?" This chat with the tree was his "diary, confession, balance sheet, last will." He asked the question he had been asking himself all his life.

Who are you? Pilgrim, wanderer, castaway, deserter, bankrupt, outcast? . . . How have you lived? How much land did you till? How many loaves of bread did you bake for others? How much did you sow? How many trees did you plant? How many bricks did you lay before taking leave? How many buttons have you sewn? How many garments have you patched? How many socks have you darned?

. . . While you lived, did you just observe languidly as life flowed by? Did you steer the course, or were you carried along?

The lonely people of the nation revealed themselves in the thousands of letters to the Old Doctor that poured into the station. But even as the Old Doctor spoke as a tree rooted firmly in Polish soil, he was investigating ways of being transplanted elsewhere. "Nothing is new here since Madame Stefa's departure," he wrote a former apprentice in Tel Aviv, before asking him if he knew a boarding house where he might rent a room for a few months.

After he completed his loneliness series, the Old Doctor was given another program, which he called "My Vacation." In June of 1938 he was on the air every Monday and Thursday at 3:45, recalling his experiences with children he had encountered during his travels to the mountains and countryside over the course of his life.

One show, a lyrical account of a day's boat excursion with some of his little friends, had much of the magic of that immortal voyage taken by Lewis Carroll with Alice and her two sisters half a century before. "When I'm with children—I accompany them," the Old Doctor began. "And they accompany me. We talk or we don't. No one is the leader. It is my hour and theirs at the dock, when we are together; our shared good hour of life. It won't come back."

The children, ranging in age from five to fourteen, arrived at the dock accompanied by nervous mothers.

"Will you take a preschool child?"

"I won't, but the boat will."

The boat seemed stable and balanced, the fisherman experienced in rowing . . . So only: the question of weather, a sweater, cheese, seasickness, to take or not to take sun hats, a football, a Scout knife, a dog, and if they can be home in time for dinner because mothers are anxious.

A whistle. They set sail. They wave. Silence. "Views, landscapes change. Splash. The water sparkles blue."

This storyteller is not a fantasist taking his children down rabbit holes, but rather a scientist, dealing skeptically with matters of the real world:

"Is there such a thing as dragons?"

"I don't think so."

"Were there ever?"

"Historians don't mention them. There were prehistoric animals . . ."

After considering such other questions as "Can a frog have a runny

nose?" and "Are there any poisonous trees?" they decide to form a scientific society back at the inn. "Attendance will not be obligatory. They
can meet after lunch or in the evening. Mother permitting. They are
right to fall asleep even during this planning. (I, too, often fell asleep at
scientific meetings.)"

So they returned, no one having got lost during a picnic on shore,
nothing exceptional having happened other than one girl discovering how
wonderful leaves look with a bouquet of flowers, and one boy learning
not to cover an ant with earth. "And who knows but at this very moment
the ant may be home telling the story of how it survived to all of its
friends," the Old Doctor concluded his radio tale.

The Old Doctor was the greatest humanist and intellectual on the
air in Poland, according to his friend, Jan Piotrowski, the editor of the
radio magazine, *Antenna:* "He spoke to children as if they were adults,
and to adults as if they were children . . . He would understand us, but
still place a stethoscope over each heart and soul. Carefully, he would
reach his diagnosis, and before you noticed, the kind Old Doctor had
vanished. But on your table he had left a prescription and a coin, for he
knew that you, his patient, were poorer than he."

In the slim volume he wrote on Korczak after the war, Piotrowski
tells of receiving permission from his friend to publish his "beautiful
triptych on loneliness" in *Antenna*. After writing on the proofs: "Here we
conclude the third talk of the Old Doctor," Piotrowski added: "When
shall we hear the Old Doctor again?"; it was an appeal to both Korczak
and the head of programming at Polish Radio to come to some agreement
about future shows. He was particularly hopeful that high officials at the
station would be so moved by the loneliness talks that they would not
submit to pressure from right-wing groups, "who could not forgive the
non-Aryan origin of such a remarkable man." Piotrowski's appeal did not
succeed. Once again the station was under fire from anti-Semites, and
once again the Old Doctor disappeared from the air waves. A few months
later Piotrowski received a "formal and definite injunction" from the head
of the radio's programming department not to print any more material
on the Old Doctor in the magazine, and to cancel plans for a book of his
radio talks.

As the Polish world continued to push Janusz Korczak out, the Jewish
world gathered him in. He received invitations to speak at Jewish com-

munity centers all over Poland, which he accepted because, as he wrote a friend, it would be like visiting small settlements in Palestine. Perhaps he would learn something; perhaps he could lift the spirits of poor, honest people by explaining to them what was happening in the country.

Rachel Bustan, who was ten in 1938, remembers the excitement when the Old Doctor arrived in her little town, near Oswiecim (which would soon become known as Auschwitz), to speak at the Jewish community center. He didn't look at all important as he sat quietly on the podium, his hands folded on his lap, telling the story of "Puss in Boots."

Korczak was also giving lectures in Warsaw to the Young Pioneers who were on waiting lists for visas to Palestine. He was concerned not with preparing them for life in that country, but with inspiring them to remain intellectually curious about the world. "We must attempt to find answers that cannot be found in books, for we are searching for the larger truths about man and the universe," he said in a lecture titled "We Do Not Know." Reminding them that great scientists are not ashamed to admit their ignorance about the earth's mysteries, he quoted a Talmudic scholar: "I have learned a great deal from my teachers and colleagues, but I have learned most of all from my students."

After the lectures, the Young Pioneers often accompanied him home, surrounding him on all sides to prevent possible street attacks. Incidents in which Jewish pedestrians were shoved or spat on by Polish thugs were becoming more frequent, but Korczak would never acknowledge that he was in any danger or allow himself to be intimidated. Once when he was traveling with one of his Jewish orphans on a crowded tramcar, another passenger, spotting the Semitic features of the boy, pointed a free seat out to Korczak: "Would the old Jew like to sit down?" Korczak responded icily: "The army major cannot sit down because he has a boil on his ass." Terrified of the consequences of insulting a Polish Army officer, the anti-Semitic passenger got off quickly at the next stop.

Korczak encouraged his friends visiting from Palestine to wander freely with him about the city. Walking with Moshe Zertal, who had just arrived in Warsaw with his wife and young child on Hashomer Hatzair business, he said: "We are having a wonderful autumn in Poland. You will never find such colorful foliage anywhere, not even in Palestine." But Korczak's good spirits vanished when they passed a large poster: DON'T BUY FROM JEWS! He paused for a moment to take in its message and moved away, muttering, "Stupid idiots! They don't know what they're doing. They are ruining our country!" After this outburst, he was silent for a while, then continued: "It's not good, my friend, not good. Human values are being eroded. The earth is trembling."

Shock waves continued to reverberate from the Third Reich. On September 29, 1938, Germany annexed the Sudetenland. And then, in response to Poland's revocation of the passports of Polish nationals who had lived abroad for more than five years, the Nazis rounded up and transported to the Polish border eighteen thousand Polish Jews who had been living in Germany, many from families that had been there for generations. Unable to obtain the special reentry consular stamp that Poland required, the Jews languished in terrible conditions in a no-man's-land between the two countries. When Hershl Grynszpan, a Polish-Jewish student in Paris, heard that his parents had just been expelled from Germany, he shot and killed a third secretary in the German Embassy in Paris. The Nazis retaliated by destroying synagogues and Jewish businesses all over Germany in a violent outburst in which ninety-one Jews died. It would go down in history as *Kristallnacht* (The Night of Broken Glass).

Helpless as the earth continued to tremble, Korczak began writing stories about heroic Jewish boys who wielded unlimited power. In one tale called "Reveries," an unnamed boy dreams of saving the Jewish people from persecution. Smuggling himself onto a plane bound for England, he manages to gain permission from the King for all Jews to emigrate to Palestine. When the boy's discovery of a cache of buried gold makes him world-famous, Hitler regrets having expelled the Jews and invites them back. But the boy informs Hitler that the Jews have had enough of being invited and uprooted all the time, and will stay in their own homeland. In the spirit of King Matt, the boy ignores Hitler's request for a loan, but buys milk and butter for the starving German children.

This plucky boy was not the first Jewish child that Korczak had created. In the early nineteen-twenties he had drafted a story about a boy named Hershkele, a four-year-old orphan who dreamed of becoming the Messiah King. But Hershkele had been supplanted by King Matt, the universal king of children, and had to wait until the late nineteen-thirties to reemerge in *The Three Journeys of Hershkele*.

Hershkele—a diminutive of Hirsh, the Hebrew for Henryk—dreams of seeing the Holy Land and sets out from his village three times in an attempt to make his way there. Unlike Matt, who dwelled in a palace, Hershkele lives in an attic room without glass in the window. Instead of royal tutors, he has only two teachers: his older brother, Lieb, who talks constantly of the Promised Land where everyone has honey, figs, and fish with noodle soup; and a crippled madman who tells him that each person must conduct his own search for God.

Wishing to bring order to the world, Hershkele swaggers about with a big stick as his sword, and looks for the sun and moon in the garbage dump. He becomes Moses, and climbs mounds of garbage to receive the Ten Commandments. Malka, his little friend, becomes the Jewish people. She stands at the bottom of the dump and will not listen to God. Hershkele hits her with his sword, and Malka runs home crying. After being scolded by Malka's mother, Hershkele/Moses continues to dream of leading poor Jews across the desert to a land where "there is bread, honey, and grapes."

Gray-haired Abraham tells Hershkele: "Who knows, maybe you'll be famous in the land of Israel." Then he adds: "But Palestine is far away. It isn't time yet."

Hershkele never makes it to Palestine, although in his first attempt he manages to get as far as the marketplace, and beyond:

He is already outside the town. He is already in the desert. He walks all by himself. He sees unfamiliar countries. He sees a river, a bridge. He sees a boat. And over there woods, small houses, small cows and small horses. He hadn't known that everything in Palestine was so small.

He keeps walking until he can't walk anymore.

In a moment he will fall down.

He strikes the ground with his sword expecting water to spout up. And then everything goes blank.

He wakes to find himself at home with rich Sarah giving him sweet, white milk.

Esther says: "He has measles. But he'll get well."

The would-be Messiah makes two more attempts, but he never reaches Palestine.

One gloomy day in late November 1938, when Korczak entered the orphanage "in low spirits," the children surprised him with a movie they had prepared with a waxed paper box and an electric bulb. "It was naïve, primitive, and moving," he wrote Joseph Arnon. "Their enthusiasm and their anxiety that it might not succeed, the excitement of the others waiting for the show to begin, the accompaniment of an accordion—all beautiful. A tremendous experience for me. The labor, the effort, the risk, all ending in triumph."

In answer to Arnon's question about his plans, he added: "I am eager to spend the winter in Palestine, since I've already experienced summer and early fall. Lot Air Line has agreed to let me have a ticket for half price, but I still cannot manage it."

There was always some excuse that prevented Korczak from going to Palestine. For him, as for Hershkele, it wasn't time yet. And time was running out.

26

The Religion of
the Child

I watch baby sleep.
Eyes sleep, lips sleep,
Nose is sleeping too.
Now little eyes are tired.
Eyes say goodnight, lips say goodnight,
I say goodnight, sleep, baby, sleep.
                    —*Lullaby*

In early 1939, while right-wing groups were busy agitating against the Jews, Korczak was "busy with Krochmalna." He was also trying, unsuccessfully, to compose lullabies—for "one needs silence to write for children, and a calm mood," both of which were in short supply in Poland those days. To Sabina Damm's inquiry about when she would see him in Palestine, he replied with his usual: "Who knows? Who knows?" But he assured her that he still wanted to come. "At least there the worst will not spit in the face of the best because he is Jewish." As for the insomnia she experienced the night before her lectures, he offered her encouraging advice that reveals his own philosophy of creativity: "What comes easily has little worth. Anxiety, lack of confidence, hesitation, suffering—these are necessary until you write or say something of value."

In March 1939, one year after Stefa arrived at Ein Harod, Germany marched into Prague, and Czechoslovakia ceased to exist as a state. People returning to the kibbutz from Europe were full of rumors of impending war, causing Stefa to worry about Korczak. When she made the decision to emigrate, she was sure he would follow. Now that he hadn't, she decided that she had better return to organize his departure. Feiga tried to dissuade her, but once Stefa made up her mind to something, she followed her course like an arrow to its target. She would go back to Warsaw to help Korczak with whatever problems were standing in his way.

Life had not been without problems for Stefa on the kibbutz. She had discovered that being a guest at Ein Harod and living there were not the same. Once she became a member of the communal family, she was treated with the lack of consideration that people often show their relatives. She who had for twenty-five years moved through the Orphans Home "like a ship crossing the ocean" found that she had no real authority here. Everything had to be decided in turbulent meetings which were as inconclusive as they were interminable. "It takes three hundred years to change anything on a kibbutz," Stefa would complain.

Not a few settlers thought this "unattractive newcomer with her faulty Hebrew and thick Polish accent" had a lot of nerve demanding things be done her way. It was not enough that she was dedicated and punctual, and had worked with Korczak: her timing, as well as her style, was different from theirs. Sometimes the kibbutzniks felt that Stefa and Feiga were allied against them. Feiga's unsmiling, severe personality often seemed as abrasive as Stefa's, as if the two women were joined by blood as well as pedagogic theory. They were equally dogmatic about how the children should be raised. "Give me a child of five or six," Feiga would say, "and I will see that he learns to dress himself quickly."

Stefa couldn't help but be aware of the resentment against her, especially when some of the settlers made a point of avoiding her in the dining hall. Eight months after her arrival, she tried to defuse the situation by asking to have the floor at a kibbutz meeting. "I feel I'm not needed here," she announced honestly. She sensed she was treating the children one way, they another; that they didn't even notice the children except to complain about them making noise and disturbing their afternoon siestas. "I left Europe because I thought I'd be able to contribute something here," she reminded them. "But without your support, I cannot be effective." Stefa's heartfelt plea cleared the air. Such outspoken confrontations were not unusual on the kibbutz, where everyone was under some kind of tension. Life went on, with personal problems subsumed by the larger ones of survival.

In her letters to the Orphans Home in Warsaw and to the *Little Review*, we glimpse Stefa's innovations. She installs a lost-and-found box in the northeast corner of the dining hall, chamber pots in lighted, accessible areas for children who have to get up at night, bed lamps for those who wake up with stomachaches or nightmares, and a note-taking system that enables caretakers on one shift to leave messages for the next. She quarrels with the builder about placing the light switches and toilet chains so high that the children are always breaking things in their efforts to reach them. "It's more difficult to explain to these adults how to do things than to children," she writes. "I told the builder that in our home on Krochmalna only one chair out of a hundred and ten was broken over a twenty-five-year period. And that one, even without its legs, is still in service in the sewing room."

Not until Stefa had departed for Poland on April 22, 1939, did the settlers appreciate the diversity of her contributions to the Children's Houses. She left a letter thanking the kibbutz for its hospitality and for teaching her so many things. "Maybe I will see you again," was the way she phrased it, leaving her future plans unclear. She left with sorrow, but with no illusions. "The kibbutzniks don't want someone to teach them how to behave with their children," she told Zerubavel Gilead, who had come to the kibbutz as a child from Russia.

"The kibbutz wasn't ready for Stefa," Gilead would say years later.

When Stefa returned to Warsaw, she brought another album from Ein Harod to share with Korczak. He was still intent on going to Jerusalem, but she insisted it would be safer for him to live on the kibbutz. The subject became such a charged one between them that, whenever they saw a friend off for Palestine, Korczak would make a point of saying: "See what you can do about finding me a room in the Old City in Jerusalem." And Stefa, with the same stubborn persistence, would take that person aside and say: "Don't look too hard, it's dangerous for him there."

Moshe Zertal, arriving with his family for a short stay in Warsaw, remembers not wanting to disturb Korczak because he knew the doctor was at a "crossroads" in his life and going through a period of "great soul-searching." But as soon as Korczak heard that Zertal's young son had fallen ill, he called to say he was coming that afternoon to examine him.

"At the appointed hour the doctor appeared," Zertal recalls. "He was tired, having been out on a trip with the children that morning, but in good spirits. He went straight to my son's bed, gave him a cursory check, and began to play with him. The language the two used was not very recognizable—one having no vocabulary, the other only pidgin Hebrew—but there was a definite conversation between them. As he was leaving, Korczak said, 'Don't worry, it will pass. Keep him in bed, and put a big pan of boiling water in the room to supply moisture.' Then spotting my mother, with whom we were staying, he added with a smile, 'You'll see, Grandma won't be happy there's no prescription. She'll get another doctor the minute I leave.' "

Zertal discovered that Korczak was right. The next day a doctor "like all other doctors" arrived, and left behind two real prescriptions like all other doctors.

When Zerubavel Gilead came to Warsaw that spring in search of new stories to publish in Palestine, he made Korczak's apartment one of his first stops. He was surprised that Korczak's sister, Anna, a thin woman in a prim black dress, opened the door herself. He had expected an important man like Korczak to have a servant.

"Welcome, welcome," she greeted him warmly, and called down the long hallway, "Doctor, a guest from Palestine."

Anna, who worked at home as a legal translator, retreated as soon as Korczak came walking sprightly down the corridor in his long green smock, a woolen cap on his head, to escort Gilead to his quarters.

Gilead took in the details of Korczak's simple room: the piles of books and papers strewn on the desk, the bust of Pilsudski that Korczak had received with an award, the tall wardrobe, the iron cot covered with a rough military blanket, the face of his mother peering out from her photograph on the wall.

When Korczak saw him glancing at the open Polish Bible, which had fresh notes in the margins, he said: "This is the novel I read daily like a serial. I'm working on a Children of the Bible series, and I'm always discovering something new. But why are you standing? Please sit down. Help yourself to what's in front of you." A few oranges, dates, and almonds had been set out on a small table for his visitor. "To keep you from being homesick," Korczak said, "and to keep your spirits up."

Korczak offered Gilead his short stories about Jewish children that the Hashomer Hatzair hadn't already translated into Hebrew for its magazine. The young poet was soon in the habit of dropping by regularly to see if the doctor had anything new for him. Their conversations covered a wide range of subjects, and once Gilead asked him shyly what he thought love was.

In one of his books, Korczak had explored love from a child's point of view: "What is love? Does it always depend on something else? Is it always given to those who deserve it? What is the difference between liking a lot and loving? How can we know whom we love more?" But, of course, he knew that Gilead was asking about adult love.

"My dear friend, I am now over sixty, but to your question 'What is love?' I must say I don't know," he replied. "It is a mystery. I know aspects of it, not its essence. But I do know what mother love and father love are."

He told Gilead about a dreamlike experience he'd had as a medical officer in the Balkans during the war: "Our unit was stationed in a mountain village. I was working in my hut until very late one night and I became thirsty. Stepping outside to the water barrel, I was stunned by the brilliance of the moonlight. The mountains above me were dark, but the village was illuminated in a dreamlike haze. And there, in the hut across from mine, I saw a young woman leaning in the doorway, her dress stretched tight across her body, and her head, crowned with heavy braids, resting on her bare arm. As I stood watching her, my heart told me: 'She is the one! The mother of your child. What could be a more perfect combination: a man of the plains and a woman of the mountains!' All of this happened in just a moment. The woman disappeared into the darkness of her hut, but I remember her to this day. I don't know if that was love, but it was a kind of love—a desire for fatherhood."

Korczak did not reveal to Gilead anything about the close call he had with fatherhood to which he would allude in a baffling entry in the *Ghetto Diary*. Setting up an imaginary dialogue between two "old codgers" reviewing their lives, he has one, who is clearly himself, tell the other, who is married with many children: "I had no time for girls—it's not only that they're a greedy lot and take up all your nights, they also get pregnant . . . A nasty habit. It happened to me once. Left a sour taste in my mouth for life. I had enough of it, the threats and the tears . . ." The full exchange between the two old men is Korczak at his most sardonic, but the rough locker-room talk about women and pregnancy seems oddly out of character. One senses a fear of and aversion to women under the male bravado of this man who always had time for children—and a secret at last confessed. (Whether a child was ever conceived, born, or aborted, is not known; the mystery of that diary entry remains.)

The main topic of conversation in Warsaw that spring was the threat of war in Europe. Partial mobilization had begun in Poland. In the cafés it was said that Hitler would not attack because of Poland's mutual-assistance pact with France and Britain, but should he be so bold, the Polish Army would hold out until the Allies intervened. Despite the uncertain atmosphere, Warsaw went about business as usual. Gilead noticed that Korczak never mentioned the trepidation that everyone, including himself, was feeling.

"You seem preoccupied," Korczak observed during one of his visits. "What's the matter with you? Homesickness?"

Gilead, who was scheduled to remain in Poland another six months, tried to make light of his nervousness. "Well, I think I should return to the kibbutz soon. I may not have long to live if there's a war."

Korczak surprised him with the vehemence of his response: "Don't talk nonsense, young man. This is no time for jokes. People die only when they want to. I've been in three wars and, thank God, I'm still alive and kicking."

He told Gilead about a fearless officer who had been with him on the Eastern front. When the shells were raining down on the trenches, he would casually lift the collar of his coat as a shield. But one night the officer returned from leave very depressed because he'd learned that his wife had been cheating on him. He was killed the next day.

"So go to your flat, young man, take an aspirin, and put yourself to bed," Korczak ordered. "You'll perspire nicely, and all the nonsense will evaporate. If you feel badly after that, go back to Palestine. But don't go in defeat."

It would have taken more than aspirin to keep Gilead in Poland. He came to say goodbye the following week. Korczak's sister Anna opened the door—only this time, before withdrawing, she snapped at him, "Why don't you ever speak to me?" Fortunately, Korczak came down the hall just then, full of good spirits, and ushered him into his room. For the first time, he pulled out a bottle of Mount Carmel wine.

"Let's have a little fun," Korczak said, ignoring their last conversation. "We are parting, maybe not for long, but still there will be a considerable distance between us. You know, even though I'm used to traveling by ship, I always feel queasy at first. I have to wait a while until I get my sea legs. Maybe it's because I am the son of a land which is far from water. I don't know, but let's drink—*l'chaim*, my friend, *l'chaim!*"

In the midst of their chatting about future plans, Korczak stood up, crossed over to the cupboard, and removed a wooden box containing stacks of long, narrow notebooks filled with his distinct, minuscule handwriting. "This is my life's work," he said in a tremulous voice. "Ten years of material on my experiences with children, my research, conflicts, failures, and successes. I'm going to call it *The Religion of the Child.*"

When Korczak came to the station to see Gilead off, he handed him an envelope. "This is just a token for you," he said. "Fragments of the preface to the book I intend to write. I'll finish the last chapter in the land of Israel. Have a safe trip. I shall follow you." And he pulled Gilead to him warmly, hugging and kissing him.

On the train Gilead read the pages that Korczak had given him: the preface was to be a philosophical discussion between an old doctor and his son during a camping trip at the foot of Mount Gilboa in Palestine. Until then, the two had never been able to communicate. The son's little daughter (whose mother, a mountain woman, has just died) is playing nearby. As the son tells his father of his childhood love for him and of his grievances, his daughter comes running toward them. She puts one tiny hand on her father's hand and the other on her grandfather's. She says nothing, but father and son know what she means: they have to reach out to each other.

In this unfinished story Korczak seems to be creating the dialogue he never had with his own father. The reconciliation he seeks can only come at a moment of mutual forgiveness which is made possible by the healing power of a child. We recognize the fantasy child the army doctor imagined having with the mountain woman in the Balkans—the child who might have been.

Before he joined Stefa and the children at summer camp, Korczak followed her advice that he spend the month of June working on his book while taking salt baths at a nearby spa. From his window in the country inn, he could see newly conscripted young soldiers being trained for duty on the German–Polish border.

Little Rose, the summer camp, proved to be a stronger tonic than the salt baths. "July was enchanting," Korczak wrote to Joseph Arnon. "Twenty new children whom you have to discover like twenty books written in a little-known language, books that are somewhat damaged, pages missing, a riddle, a puzzle. It was like old times—all that mattered were lost sandals, a thorn in the foot, a quarrel near the swing, a broken branch. I slept in the isolation room with the children who came down with measles. When I caught myself dozing, I would think: Don't fall asleep, listen for another ten minutes to their breathing, coughing, sighing. What wisdom there is in their coughing while they sleep—a constant struggle goes on with the infection, the fever, the scratching, the flies."

It was a tradition that each camp season end with Olympic Games in which there were competitions in running, jumping, throwing, and other sports, as well as music and singing. But that last summer before the invasion the children wanted to replace their Olympics with War Games—Poles against Germans. A large sandy area was prepared for the battlefield, fortifications built, bunkers dug. Shotguns were carved out of wood and chestnuts became bullets. Any boy hit by a chestnut fell down, played dead, and was out of the game. The girls, acting as nurses, helped the wounded from the field.

It didn't dampen anyone's spirits when the Poles lost the war—it was only a game—but a pall fell over the children as they passed a brick works on their way to the forest for their last campfire. Korczak realized that it reminded them, as it did him, of the two drunks who had threatened them at that spot the first day of camp by shouting: "Give me the pistol! Call Hitler!" But everyone relaxed that night as they sang songs and told stories under the full moon until long after midnight. He was able to report to Joseph Arnon that he returned to Warsaw "very excited and jubilant—if it is proper to describe oneself so at the age of sixty-one."

In late August of 1939, Korczak was preoccupied with finding a way to provide squirrels for the children of Ein Harod. During his last trip to Palestine, he had begged the Polish consul to have a dozen red squirrels shipped from Poland, but the consul had not understood that it was a matter of great consequence—that, "without squirrels, trees are sad and motionless." His new plan was to have the children of Ein Harod write directly to the British authorities requesting that gray squirrels be shipped from India. The reason he was optimistic, he wrote Gilead, was that after World War I he had asked the British consul for napkins for the orphanage, and eight months later, when he had given up hope, a crate had arrived with enough napkins to last ten years.

Squirrels were uppermost in Korczak's mind at this time because he had finally decided to visit Palestine for four months in October to gather material for the "last chapter" of *The Religion of the Child*. With the usual reservation—"If I have enough money"—he wrote Arnon: "I intend to spend two months in Old Jerusalem (at an interesting cheder I saw there) and two in a seminary in Tiberias. I am afraid of rheumatism, bugs, and even a little of the Arabs, in that order."

On September 1, 1939, the Germans invaded Poland.

On September 2, the letter that Sabina Damm had written to Korczak in reply to his inquiry about a room in Jerusalem came back to her, stamped: "This item is being returned to the sender due to the suspension of all communication between Palestine and Poland."

PART FOUR
1939–1942

27

September 1939

I am well versed in reading the pages of war.
—"Appeal: To the Jews!"

The ambivalence and depression that Korczak struggled with in the late thirties—"those wicked; shameful, destructive prewar years"—lifted with the German invasion. He was galvanized into action: at last there was something he could do. He took out the musty Polish uniform that he had worn as a medical officer during the Polish–Soviet War in 1920, and volunteered for duty. Disqualified because of age, he moved out of his sister's apartment and back into his garret room at the orphanage on Krochmalna, like a captain taking over his ship's command again.

When his friend from Polish Radio, Jan Piotrowski, offered him a position with the newly formed radio information agency called Warsaw II, he accepted without hesitation. Soon the reassuring voice of the Old Doctor could be heard encouraging the population to keep their spirits up. "Yesterday I was an old man," he told his audience. "Today I am ten years younger—maybe even twenty." It was satisfying to return as a Polish patriot to the air waves from which he had been dismissed as a Jew. Then, life may not have been "worth living," but now the "storm had cleared the air, made breathing easier."

For the first few days, while the Germans were bombing the outlying districts of Warsaw, it was possible to believe that everything might go on as usual if the citizens took the necessary precautions of digging ditches and erecting barricades. On September 2, a Saturday, Korczak allowed the orphans to visit their families. He even took time to reply to the complaint of a boy published in *Our Review* that adults were treating young people as nuisances during this crisis. "You mustn't give in to gloomy feelings," Korczak advised, "but draw strength from the advantage that youth gives you."

On the air, the Old Doctor encouraged young people to make themselves useful. "Don't stay inside cowering and crying about what might happen. Go out into the streets and help dig fire lanes. Go to the Tomb of the Unknown Soldier who died for Poland and put flowers on his grave." He told his orphans that it was all right to continue playing, as long as they did it quietly. "Every moment soldiers are dying as they defend Warsaw. It's hard for their mothers and fathers who live nearby to hear you laughing and singing when they've just lost their own children. Have respect for their suffering."

Because of their mutual-assistance pact with France and Britain, the Poles were waiting for their allies to come to their rescue. When Great Britain entered the war on September 3, Korczak joined the excited crowd gathered outside the British Embassy. He didn't know which made him happier: the hope that England would help Poland push back the Germans, or the sight of Poles and Jews once again "rubbing shoulders like brothers," as they had during the uprisings against Czarist Russia and in the First World War. Tears filled his eyes when he heard the singing of Poland's national anthem, "Poland Is Not Yet Lost," followed by the Zionist song "Hatikvah."

Two days later the government left the city, after ordering all young men to go East to be mobilized. The few remaining members of the Orphans Aid Society urged Korczak to send the children back to their relatives because of the difficulty of providing for them, but he would not consider disbanding the home. The children were safer remaining together with him and Stefa, he insisted. Somehow he would manage to find the necessary food and supplies.

Korczak even took on the task of bringing food to Maryna Falska and the orphans in Bielany, who had been temporarily evacuated to another building because Our Home was on the front lines. As soon as the children saw him standing in the corridor in his uniform, they cried, "Oh, there's Pan Doctor!" and ran up and grabbed him, and begged for candy as they showered him with kisses. Antoni Chojdynski, a former apprentice, remembers the children clinging to him on all sides, and how happy he looked. "He called them by name, saying: 'How are you?' 'Are you all right?' 'What's happening?' "

As he pulled herring out of his sack, Korczak apologized that there was no bread to eat it with: he'd brought canned cucumber instead. A few days later he reappeared with a sackful of lentils, a popular Jewish dish, which these children had never tasted before. "We thought of it as biblical food," Chojdynski recalled. "Pan Doctor told us that he'd asked a storekeeper to donate the lentils to hungry Polish orphans, since the Germans would probably confiscate them anyway."

On the eighth day of the invasion, the Germans were at the gates of Warsaw. The city was like a besieged fortress: many streets had been reduced to rubble by incendiary bombs; fires burned everywhere; buildings were gutted; dead horses lay rotting on the ground. There was no bread, gas, electricity, or water for its citizens or the thousands of refugees and demoralized soldiers who had streamed in from other parts of the country where the Polish cavalry and infantry were being decimated by German tanks and planes.

Korczak dashed about the blazing city, rescuing frightened children, giving aid to the injured and comfort to the dying. A few times a day, he checked in at the radio station to bring news or encouragement to the apprehensive populace. A coworker remembers him "slightly bent, enlivening the bomb-shattered quarters with his humor."

Although seven shells hit the orphanage in the course of the next three weeks, morale remained high. Whenever the air-raid sirens sounded, the children, whose number had swelled to one hundred and fifty, would rush down the stairs to the basement shelter, where sandbags had been piled up against the windows. Even an injured boy whose father was missing and whose mother and sister had been killed by a shell in front of him managed the stairs quickly, though neither his leg nor his one remaining eye had healed. "We'll bring a smile to his battered face yet," the Old Doctor told his radio audience.

The older children took turns standing guard near the roof during incendiary attacks. They had only a second or so after a fire bomb landed to douse it with sand or water to prevent it from bursting into flame. There was one terrifying moment when a shell exploded right outside the dining hall, smashing all the windowpanes. No sooner had Korczak gone out to investigate than the whole house shook from another explosion. The children dove under the tables with the young teachers, not even daring to run down to the shelter. They were certain their beloved Pan Doctor had been killed. But a few moments later he ducked back inside sheepishly without his hat, explaining that the blast had blown it off. "I had to make a quick retreat," he said with an impish grin. "My bald head would be a perfect target for those planes."

But not everything turned out well. Romcia's father, Jozef Sztokman, died of pulmonary complications after struggling to put out a fire on the roof. The whole orphanage went to the cemetery for the funeral. Over his grave they vowed in both Polish and Hebrew that they would honor "Truth, Work, and Peace."

Korczak tried to keep a smiling face with the orphans and staff, but Ida Merzan remembers one night when he let down his guard. She was being cared for at the orphanage after receiving a head wound in a bombing attack outside Warsaw. During one of the air raids she got up to follow the children down to the shelter and encountered Korczak on the stairs.

"What are you doing out of bed?" he demanded when he saw her.

"I don't want to be alone," she replied. "I feel sad."

"My God, who isn't sad," he said quietly. "The whole world is one great sadness."

During this period, many of the former apprentices and orphans came to Korczak for advice about whether or not to flee to the Russian zone. "No one knows what will happen," he would say, in keeping with his policy of never giving direct advice, but he did not discourage them from going.

On September 23, after a night of unusually heavy bombardment when the whole of Warsaw shook as if the earth might open up and swallow it even before the Germans could, Mayor Stefan Starzynski delivered his now famous radio address: "Warsaw may be in flames, but we are proud to die bravely!" Rachmaninoff's Second Piano Concerto, which followed, was interrupted when German bombs hit a power plant and the station went dead. It was four in the afternoon. From that moment, the guttural sounds of German would command the air waves.

Five days later Poland fell to the Nazis. For three weeks her people had struggled valiantly together against impossible odds, and now it was over. The day after the siege ended, Stefa's sister-in-law, Irena, encountered Korczak hurrying through the ruins of the once bustling Marszalkowska Street, carrying a young boy in his arms.

"What are you doing here?" she asked.

"Looking for a shoe store," was his reply.

"But all the shops are destroyed or closed," she reminded him, looking around at the desolation.

"Then I'll find a shoemaker," he said. "This boy can't walk on all this glass without shoes."

"Who is he?" she inquired.

"I don't know. I just found him crying in the street. I have to carry him until I find something for his feet."

He moved past her, continuing down the street with the boy to the Old Town, where he rang the bell of Hanna Olczak, the daughter of his publisher, Mortkowicz. He often dropped in unannounced to have a cup of hot sweet tea with her and reminisce about her father while her little girl Joanna played at their feet with the brown spaniel. "How beautiful," he would say, before pulling himself out of the soft armchair and forcing himself back on his rounds. Hanna was not surprised to have him come by with the barefoot child that day. She gave them both tea, and took care of the boy while Korczak continued his search for shoes.

The Nazis were orderly when they entered the city: they set up soup kitchens and distributed free bread. For a while it was a relief just to be done with the bombings. Things were bad, but people hoped that the worst was over, that this German occupation would end, like the last one, in German defeat.

As he wandered through the "enforced misery" of Warsaw, Korczak marveled at the resiliency of the young when he heard noisy, mischievous children's laughter erupting out of heaps of burned rubble. "Despite the carnage, despite the power of man's destructiveness, the mighty life force goes on," he wrote. "After this war, no one will dare to hit a child for breaking a window. Adults will pass children with their heads bent in shame."

The brief period of calm was shattered when a new kind of German terror was unleashed on both Poles and Jews: sadistic attacks in the streets, imprisonments, and executions. The Jews were rounded up for work details and the Poles shipped as forced labor to Germany. Jewish businesses and factories were appropriated, Jewish schools were closed. When the Russians unexpectedly invaded on September 17, once again Poland was partitioned—the Soviets taking the Eastern part, the Germans the West—as had been secretly agreed upon in the Molotov–Ribbentrop Non-Aggression Pact.

Most of the philanthropists of the Orphans Aid Society had either fled Poland or had their businesses confiscated and their bank accounts frozen. In spite of the increasingly sinister atmosphere of the city, and fears for his safety, Korczak continued to wear his Polish uniform, without insignia, on his daily rounds to procure food and supplies for the orphanage. He became a familiar figure at the offices of the Judenrat, the Jewish council set up by the Germans to act as intermediary between them and the Jewish community. He also stopped by regularly at the American Joint Distribution Committee and at CENTOS, the Jewish welfare agency for children where Stefa had worked. With everyone trying his best to keep a low profile, it was unnerving to have Korczak come by in his uniform. Abraham Berman, the director of CENTOS, recalled: "We were so startled by his appearance, we couldn't help asking what he thought he was doing dressed like that. 'As far as I am concerned, there is no German occupation,' he replied. 'I am proud to be a Polish officer and I shall go about as I wish.' He was unconvinced when we argued that it was not a matter of our personal feelings, but that we were a social institution with very crucial aims that would be jeopardized if he were found here like that."

When Newerly expressed surprise to see him in uniform, Korczak said that he was no more enamored of uniforms than he had ever been, but had decided to wear his as a symbol of protest. He was equally adamant about *not* wearing the white armband with the blue Star of David which was made mandatory for all Jews over eleven years of age on December 1, 1939. Not only did he feel it was demeaning to the Jewish star to wear it as a badge of shame, but he would not let the Germans erase his Polishness by branding him only a Jew. "As a teacher, I value eternal laws above transitory human ones," he had once written, and he still held to that position.

Korczak loved to regale his friends with stories about how he dealt with German officers who eyed him suspiciously on the streets. "I'd start singing at the top of my lungs, reel back and forth as if I'd lost my wits, and they'd look at me with disgust and move on." If they stared at him in a café when he stopped for coffee, he'd begin "mumbling incoherently" to himself until they turned away. But all the while he was watching the Germans, too, as they patrolled the streets, observing them with a clinician's eye, trying to make a diagnosis of their aberrant behavior. He didn't believe in stereotyping people (during his year in Berlin it had amused him that the one German student in his lecture course was always late, while the Slavs were always on time), but the Germans did seem true to form as they strode about the city, efficient, detached bureaucrats, concerned with order and small details. And yet they were not the Germans he had known. There was a brutal edge to their behavior that made their previous occupation of Warsaw seem almost benign.

One cold night in January 1940—wasted by "adhesions, ruptures, scars, but alive and still kicking pretty hard"—Korczak began the memoir that he had been putting off for years. "Reminiscences make a sad and depressing literature," he wrote, aware that he would discover, like ambitious artists, scholars, and statesmen before him, that life was not what he had meant it to be, that all he had achieved was graying hair, wrinkles, failing eyesight, and slower circulation: in short, old age. Still, as a writer, he intended to make the story of his life something different, just as he had made the living of it. Writing his memoir would be "like digging a well," not starting at the deepest point but breaking up the top layers, shovelful after shovelful, until he reached "subterranean streams."

As he wrote, the Nazis were outside patrolling Warsaw. They might curtail his freedom of movement, but they could not restrain his free spirit and his faith in a higher order than theirs: "For in the hour of reckoning, I am not inside a solitary cell of the saddest hospital in the world, but surrounded by butterflies, grasshoppers, and glowworms; and I hear a concert of crickets and a soloist high in the sky—the skylark. Merciful Lord!"

Korczak struggled to keep inviolable that deep quiet place within him even as he struggled for food for his children; yet he did not make another diary entry for the next two years. With his energies completely absorbed in finding the funds and essentials he needed to keep his children alive, he wrote only appeals to the public for help, a genre that necessity had forced him to refine. Just eight months before the war, Korczak had deliberately provoked the Jewish community with an ethnic announcement in *Our Review*:

It's bad to be an old man, but it's worse to be an old Jew.
Could there be anything worse?
Oy, oy, oy—and what if that same old Jew is penniless?
And what if he is both penniless and unresourceful?
Isn't that the worst of all?
No. What if the old Jew who is unresourceful bears the yoke of a large family

of children, and his heart aches, and his legs and his hips, while his eyes perceive that his strength is ebbing away?

As Korczak expected, some found his new style less than amusing, but it did bring in donations. After the Germans occupied Warsaw, he once again used his writer's skill—which any professional fund-raiser might envy—to move the most obdurate heart. Addressing "the Jews," the petitioner declares: "One cannot flee from history. Extraordinary circumstances demand an extraordinary effort of the mind and the senses, will power, and action." Crediting God with saving the orphanage, he demands "a loan of 2,000 zlotys, which will be returned sooner than you think." (This last has the familiar touch of King Matt, who demanded a loan from the three defeated kings, saying, "Don't be piggy.") Not only was the future of his orphanage at stake, but the "entire tradition of aid to the child." Anyone who failed to respond would suffer "moral decay," and destroy a tradition of two thousand years. It was Jewish "honor" he was upholding, and who would want the burden of discrediting that?

His strategy must have been successful, for a few months later he appended a postscript: "I am happy to note that but for a few exceptions, man is a reasonable and ethical being. There are now 150 children in the orphanage."

In his next appeal, Korczak recommended that people give something to him before they were forced to give everything to the Germans. He wanted not only financial assistance but addresses of well-to-do acquaintances when he came to call. The two documents were signed: "Dr. Henryk Goldszmit / Janusz Korczak / the Old Doctor from the Radio."

As he pounded the pavements making those promised calls, Korczak was still in his Polish uniform, still without the Star of David armband, still "playing the clown," for he knew that people "don't like gloomy faces." Sometimes he would stand in front of a café where his friends gathered, shouting like a beggar: "Is there someone here with a bag of potatoes to get my children through the winter?" Waiting on line for kasha, he would tease the woman behind the counter that she reminded him of his elder granddaughter, so that she might add a little extra to the purchase. And once, wanting to get off the tramcar before the usual stop, he whispered to the conductor: "If I were a young girl, I would hug you for slowing down so that I could jump off at the next corner." Much to his delight, the rattled conductor snapped: "You don't have to kiss me, sir," and slowed down to get rid of him. And, even if only to revive his own flagging spirits before facing Stefa and the children each evening, he would make his way through the streets singing bawdy songs from his military days.

Adam Czerniakow, the Chairman of the Judenrat, recorded in his diary some of the clownish exploits Korczak, an old friend, had related to him. Although Czerniakow was a civil engineer by training, he had always had a passionate interest in children's welfare. Korczak's visits were obviously a welcome relief from Czerniakow's otherwise grim activities.

Not all of Korczak's friends were comfortable with him in the role of buffoon. Leon Rygier remembered his alarm one night when the bell in his partially bombed-out apartment rang just before curfew, and his relief upon seeing it was Korczak.

"It's so good to be here with you," Korczak exclaimed, throwing himself onto a chair and trying to be lighthearted about his difficulties soliciting money that day. "Some people are generous, but not everyone. If they're difficult, I just undo my coat and reveal my Polish uniform. They get so nervous about having someone in uniform in their place that they give me something just to make me leave."

Rygier listened in pained silence, knowing how reticent Korczak was with strangers and how contrary to his nature this kind of begging was. Their eyes met, and he was sure that Korczak knew what he was thinking.

"It's difficult," Korczak admitted. "But one can't be squeamish in these matters. I am so tired." And then he rushed off to get back to the orphanage before the nine o'clock curfew.

That first winter of the German occupation was bitterly cold, the temperature falling some days to thirteen below. Korczak had coal, but he couldn't use it effectively until he replaced the glass in the bombed-out windows. Fortunately, Igor Newerly passed his exam as a glazier and, with the help of the older boys, soon had the orphanage comfortable again. Other former apprentices and orphans also came to the rescue, volunteering their time, donating mattresses, sweaters, and underwear, or performing services such as dental care and repair work.

Clothing the children adequately was an acute problem for Stefa, since the cost of textiles and tailoring of any kind was prohibitive. Resourceful as ever, she set up a sewing school in the orphanage funded by ORT, a relief agency with which Stella Eliasberg was active. The twenty students, ex-orphans from Krochmalna or other institutions, came six days

a week from nine in the morning until two in the afternoon. ORT supplied
the instructor, as well as two sewing machines, an electric iron, and thirty
chairs. Stefa was proud to report that in one month they managed to
make seventy-eight dresses, twenty pairs of trousers, thirty pairs of boys'
pants, and thirteen shirts.

April 1940 was the deadline for anyone with a foreign passport or
entry visa to another country to get out of Poland. When Stefa was notified
by the International Red Cross that Kibbutz Ein Harod had arranged the
necessary papers for her to return to Palestine, she replied by telegraph
through its Geneva office: "My dears, we are well. I am working a bit,
but Korczak a lot. I cannot leave without the children. Be patient. I bless
you all. Stefa."

That spring, Korczak, along with many others, clung to the hope that
the Allies might defeat the Germans quickly. It was a blow when the
Nazis invaded Norway and Denmark that April, Holland and Belgium a
month later, and France in June, forcing the British to evacuate at Dun-
kirk.

When an American delegation charged with arranging relief con-
signments with the German occupation authorities asked to visit the orphanage with their Nazi escort, Korczak at first refused. Only after being
pressured by Stefa and Jewish welfare officials did he give his reason: he
always wore his Polish officer's uniform under his smock, and he would
not remove it. Not until Stefa thought of putting a scarf around his neck
to hide the uniform did Korczak agree to receive the delegation. He did
so with his usual ironic charm, directing his remarks to the Americans
and pointedly ignoring the Germans. The children, who had not been
told there would be visitors, were involved in a game of soldiers, some
of them decked out in paper helmets and brandishing wooden sticks.
"Obviously the war hasn't upset them too much," some of the Americans
remarked. They told Korczak how impressed they were by the orphanage,
but he couldn't help noticing their disappointment that "things were not
that bad." Convinced that they expected "corpses and skeletons," he
decided that nothing is easier to get used to than the misfortune of others.

The strain of keeping the children in the good condition that impressed the Americans was beginning to show on Korczak. He developed
a painful condition of boils on his neck. Encountering him on the street
with a sack of potatoes slung over one shoulder, Ida Merzan was surprised
that he winced when she embraced him. "My dear, would you push my

suspender back for me?" he asked. As she gently put her hand under his coat and moved the suspender, he sighed with relief, "There, that's much better." She noticed that, though he strode off briskly, he was hunched over like an old man.

When the boils began to abscess, causing a high fever, Stefa urged Korczak to see a doctor. He waved her away in his usual fashion. Fearing blood poisoning, she called in a doctor, who ordered him to the hospital without delay to have them lanced. Korczak refused: "If I am to be operated on, it will be here, and no place else." A well-known surgeon was sent for, but he warned Stefa that because of the depth of the incisions he had to make, there was a risk of hemorrhage. At the first sign of bleeding, Korczak was to be rushed to the hospital. After twenty minutes, bleeding started, and Stefa bundled Korczak into the carriage that the surgeon had left waiting outside, just in case.

For the past eleven years, on June 1, the anniversary of Izaak Elias-berg's death, it had been Korczak's custom to accompany Stella Eliasberg and her daughters to the Jewish cemetery, where he said kaddish for his friend. This year, because of his weakened condition, Korczak had to postpone the observance until June 10. He arrived with bandages on his neck and his arm in a sling, accompanied by a group of older orphans walking in pairs and carrying King Matt's large green banner—which had the blue Star of David on a field of white sewn onto one side. Korczak led the children down the main path, past his father's grave, to a small embankment on the left where Eliasberg was buried under a modest tombstone.

The high death rate had filled the cemetery with mourners, many of whom joined the gravediggers in listening to the orphans sing. Korczak invited those children who so desired to place a hand on the Bible he was carrying and swear to live as Dr. Eliasberg had in the spirit of love for all mankind and in devotion to justice, truth, and work. All the children took the oath. The acacia were in bloom, and their branches, alive with birdsong, belied the tragedy that was unfolding beyond the cemetery grounds. A few birds flew down onto Korczak's shoulder while he was reciting kaddish. Helena Eliasberg thought he looked like St. Francis.

Despite all the obstacles, Korczak was able to arrange for the children to go to Little Rose that summer. The fate of the camp had been very much on his mind following the German occupation, and shortly after the first snow he had gone out there to take inventory. Train travel being forbidden to Jews, he had walked the twenty miles in the bitter cold, accompanied by two of the older boys. They found nothing left but the buildings. German soldiers had looted the camp, and neighbors had chopped down many of the trees for firewood.

Cold and exhausted, Korczak sat with the boys on some stumps in the yard, staring at the desolate scene. No longer up to such exertion, he sat with his eyes closed for some time. The two boys hesitated to disturb him, but they were frightened. They knew that he wanted to return to Warsaw before dark.

"Pan Doctor," they said softly.

Korczak opened his eyes, and jumped up. "We will go to German headquarters and complain about this," he told them.

They went first to see the mayor of the district, who greeted them cordially. Together with him, they paid a call on the German commandant, Captain Stephens, who turned out to be an engineer of Swedish descent. Speaking with Korczak in German, Stephens not only agreed that the camp could open for July and August but promised to replace some of the equipment and to allow provisions to be sent in.

That summer of 1940, the children were able to forget for a time the world outside Little Rose, but Korczak got little rest. He had to go into Warsaw a few times a week to check on food supplies, and was in a good or bad mood depending on his success and what he encountered in the city. Witold Kaczanowski, the son of the director of Tworki, remembers stopping by Korczak's camp with his father in a horsecart filled with grain that the inmates had raised on the asylum's land. His father greeted Korczak as if he knew him, but Witold was too young to know if the grain was part of a business transaction or a donation.

At night Korczak always took a few of the younger children who were ill into his room, in case they wanted water or to use the chamber pot; he worried that the young teachers, needing their own sleep, might not hear the children call. When Ida Merzan came out to visit the camp, she saw Korczak standing near the children, but speaking as if to himself. Or was he praying? She wasn't sure which.

When Korczak returned with the orphans to Warsaw in September, he found that Saxon Square had been renamed Adolf Hitler Square, and that all parks were closed to Jews. Jewish doctors, officially forbidden to treat Aryan patients, were ordered to register with the Gestapo. Korczak filled out the form straightforwardly: his permanent address, No. 8 Zlota Street, Apartment 4; his professional one, 92 Krochmalna; his rank in the

First World War, captain; his rank in the Polish Army, major; his religion, Mosaic faith; his area of specialty, pedagogue-pediatrician; his academic work, the study of children. But Korczak's nervousness revealed itself in the mistake he made in his already bungled birthdate, escalating it by a century: 22 VII 1978 (1979?). He signed the document Dr. H. Goldszmit.

There was new optimism in Warsaw when Britain began air raids on Berlin. Many believed the war would be over in two or three months. In mid-September, Korczak stopped by to chat with Adam Czerniakow, whose authority as Chairman of the Judenrat extended to every aspect of Jewish life in occupied Warsaw. At a time when the Chairman's diary was filled with entries about Jews being thrown out of their apartments, the rise in the number of suicides, mothers weeping for sons in forced-labor camps, and complaints about the bread tax, he took time to note how amused he was by how Korczak dealt with Wedel, the chocolate maker. When Wedel complained that he could not sell him 120 pounds of grain because sales to Jews were forbidden, Korczak had retorted, "Then give it to us as a gift."

A few weeks later the Chairman recorded Korczak's droll fund-raising plan: the Judenrat should tax each person who left a plea for help on the grave of a tzaddik (holy man) and use the money for the poor.

28

Arrest

There had never been walled ghettos in Poland, as there had been in other European countries in the Middle Ages, but rumors that there was to be a Warsaw Ghetto had been circulating from the early days of the German occupation.

The Nazis had managed to keep Czerniakow in a state of confusion with their arbitrary instructions. At first the Judenrat was ordered to close off a "quarantined" portion of the Jewish quarter with barbed wire, and then it was directed to wall the area off. Czerniakow had argued the virtual impossibility of building a wall—it would damage water installations, and electric and telephone cables—but he lost the battle. The Judenrat had to supply both the money and the labor to construct one. In July of 1940, after twenty sections of the wall were standing, Czerniakow heard reports that the Germans had decided against a ghetto; when he met with Korczak in mid-September, he was once again resigned to its probability—by then there were small ghettos in the provinces, and a large one in the city of Lodz that was sealed off with barbed wire.

The German technique, in setting up their ghettos, was to take everyone by surprise with a sudden announcement (which gave them an opportunity to confiscate hastily abandoned Jewish property). On Yom Kippur, the most sacred of the Jewish holy days—October 12, 1940—they announced the creation of a special "quarter" for Warsaw Jews. Despite the previous rumors, Korczak, like everyone else, was caught off guard. Examining the ghetto map posted in his area, he was startled to see that the western border cut through Krochmalna Street: the upper section, where the orphanage stood, was not included within the ghetto limits, but was on the Aryan side—as the rest of the city was now called. To add to the confusion, a number of conflicting maps had been posted throughout the city, each showing different boundary lines.

It seemed impossible to Korczak that he and his children would be expected to move from their famous institution into another building within the ghetto zone. The Germans knew his work: their educators had visited him and written about his experimental methods. The Nazis might hate the Jew Henryk Goldszmit, but they would have to respect the educator Janusz Korczak. Realizing that there was no time to lose, Korczak hurried up to his room and began a letter to the German command, based in Cracow, which Judenrat officials would deliver along with similar appeals from other institutions. Writing "Petition" across the top of the paper, Korczak sought to impress the Germans with the orphanage's self-sufficiency in its present location.

"During the current year, the German authorities have neither harmed nor troubled us," he began. "Nevertheless, we have suffered many deprivations and hardships. We have lived off donations and managed with great effort to make ends meet in this our 28th year of communal living." Korczak pointed out that his diligent staff—a cook, assistant cook, dishwasher, and two teachers—had all been raised in the orphanage. One staff member had even sacrificed his life during the siege of Warsaw trying to put out a fire on the roof. The children had helped repair the doors and windows shattered in the bombardments, whitewashed the shower room, and kept the orphanage so clean that there were no contagious diseases that might have necessitated their being placed under quarantine. Enclosing financial and other reports, Korczak ended his petition with: "Fully trusting in your understanding, we request your support in allowing the children to remain in this building, with which it would be difficult for us to part." He signed it: "Respectfully yours, Director of the Orphanage and *Bursa*, Dr. H. Goldszmit, J. Korczak."

The petition was worth the gamble, but while he was waiting for a response, Korczak began to look around within the ghetto area for alternative lodging for his children. He was negotiating an exchange with a high school of commerce a few blocks away at 33 Chlodna Street which, though not comparable, would fit their needs, when he received the refusal from Cracow. Having no other alternative, Korczak rushed over to complete arrangements with the high-school principal. The two institutions agreed to maintain each other's property with care until they could take possession again.

Korczak kept his sense of humor even then. When Czerniakow's appeal to remain in his apartment on the Aryan side was also refused, Korczak said he could give him the name of an official in the Judenrat who, for a bribe, would find the Chairman a good address in the ghetto.

During this chaotic period when Poles and Jews alike were rushing about to find or exchange apartments on their designated sides of the wall, many of Korczak's Gentile friends visited the orphanage to try to convince him to go into hiding. Igor Newerly was one of the first to appear. In spite of their close friendship, Newerly was not confident that he could persuade his stubborn mentor to do anything that he was not ready to do. As they climbed up to the garret room, Newerly noticed that Korczak was breathing with difficulty, and he realized that this once youthful man, so quick and nimble in the past, was growing increasingly debilitated. He waited while Korczak knocked to warn the sparrows of their arrival, and, as usual, was forced to accept the deep armchair while his host took the less comfortable one.

As Newerly sat down nervously, thinking about how to begin, Korczak lit a cigarette and asked about his wife and child and all their mutual friends, as if their well-being were all that mattered to him.

"Everyone's worried about your going into the ghetto with the children," Newerly told him. "Just say the word and we'll get you false identity papers to live on our side."

"And the children?"

"We'll try to hide as many as we can in monasteries and private homes."

Korczak put down his cigarette, took off his glasses in their cheap round metal frames, and began wiping them with his handkerchief as he always did when he was stalling for time. Finally, he asked: "Do you realize how difficult it would be to hide one hundred and seventy Jewish children—that's how many we have now."

"We'd try," Newerly repeated.

"But can you guarantee me that every child will be safe?"

Newerly shook his head sadly: "I'm afraid that's impossible. We can't guarantee anything"—he paused—"even for ourselves."

Now Korczak was in the position of trying to console Newerly. "My friend," he said, "it's almost impossible to hide anything so well that the person who is after it cannot find it." He had expressed this belief earlier in his story about Moses being concealed in the bulrushes. He knew that the Germans would look for Jewish children as surely as the Egyptians had looked for the babies hidden by the Hebrew slaves. "It is hard for a person to speak lies to those who question him," he had written. "The hands shake, the eyes are full of fear, the face blushes or turns pale." And he had added: "I have never hidden a child from enemy soldiers."

Newerly understood Korczak's reluctance to jeopardize the welfare of any of the orphans. Just as he could not bear the thought of a child being punished in a dark closet or cellar, so now he could not bear to imagine the children being hidden from the Nazis in dark places. Their hearts would pound with terror that they might be discovered. He was a father who did not abandon his children. "My friend, it is best that I keep the children with me." Korczak told Newerly, extending his arm for that firm handshake that had sealed so many agreements in years past and now asked for approval.

At that time no one could say that the ghetto might not be the safest place for Jewish children. What would come to be known as the "Final Solution" was still in the future, beyond the imagination of the darkest pessimist. "Don't worry, the Germans won't harm us," Korczak tried to reassure him. "They wouldn't dare. I'm much too well known here and abroad."

As the November 30 deadline for the Jewish population to move into the ghetto approached, the city was in an uproar: 138,000 Jews, hauling their meager belongings in pushcarts or on their backs, streamed through the twenty-eight gates of the ghetto to the apartments left by 113,000 Poles who were moving out in much the same demented frenzy. In losing homes located above their shops and the shops as well, many in both groups were losing their main source of livelihood.

Korczak gave a great deal of thought to how he would relocate the orphanage. He didn't want the children to experience going into the ghetto as something fearful, but rather as a new kind of challenge that they would all meet together.

Jona Bocian, who was an apprentice teacher that year, remembers the painstaking care with which Korczak and Stefa organized everything down to the smallest detail. There were daily meetings to decide who would be responsible for what. Christian friends who wanted to contribute something were asked for colorful pictures or rugs to decorate the children's rooms, or red geraniums for the window boxes. When Hanna Olczak stopped by, Korczak told her that he wanted to move the household "as if it were a large theatrical troupe." The procession would be like an advertisement for a performance, "a kind of parade in which the children will carry lamps, paintings, bedding, cages with pet birds and small animals."

On the day they were scheduled to depart, November 29, the children lined up in the courtyard as rehearsed, while Korczak made a final inspection of the wagons filled with the coal and potatoes that he had so arduously procured on his daily rounds. The children waved goodbye sadly to the Polish janitor, Piotr Zalewski, who was staying behind to care for the house. His face was swollen almost beyond recognition from the beating he had received the day before when he and the laundress had applied to the Nazi police for permission to go into the ghetto with the orphans. The Germans had thrown the laundress out, but detained Zalewski for questioning. Didn't he know that Aryans were no longer allowed to work for Jews? When the janitor replied that after twenty years of service he considered the orphanage his home, the Germans thrashed him with whips and rifle butts.

Zalewski, a tall, beardless man of erect bearing, had been a grenadier in the Czar's army before being hired at the orphanage. Every year on Zalewski's name day, Korczak had dropped in at the gatehouse for a few glasses of vodka, which always inspired the two men to swap scatological war stories and compete to see who knew the most swearwords. (Korczak had been able to hold his own with the janitor on both counts.) The orphans had loved working in Zalewski's carpentry shop in the basement, where they were allowed to get as dirty as they wanted. Often they had poured their hearts out to him as they were hammering and sawing away, or trailing after him as he shoveled coal and swept the courtyard. If, in jest, he occasionally tweaked their noses too hard with his powerful fingers, he had always been forgiven.

The orphans tried to sing as they marched out of the courtyard and into the street, clutching their few possessions. The green flag of King Matt, with a Jewish star on one side, flew over the little parade as it made its way through the teeming streets the short distance to 33 Chlodna Street. When they reached the place where the wall cut along Chlodna, slicing its "Aryan" half off from the ghetto, they found German and Polish police at the gate demanding identification, as if they were crossing a foreign border.

While they were passing through, a German policeman confiscated their last wagon, which was filled with potatoes. Korczak shouted at the

German to release the potatoes or he would report the incident to his superiors. When the sentry stood firm, Korczak had no choice but to continue with Stefa and the group to their new home. That night, while the children dashed about the schoolhouse exclaiming over the different windows and doors and their new sleeping quarters, Korczak decided to protest to the Gestapo the first thing in the morning.

When Korczak arrived at Gestapo headquarters the next day, the officer on duty was at first bemused by the highly agitated man in the remnants of a Polish uniform who introduced himself in flawless German as Dr. Janusz Korczak. He offered his visitor a chair. But on hearing Korczak's tirade about potatoes being confiscated at the ghetto gate, the German began wondering why this Pole was so concerned about the Jews.

Becoming suspicious, he asked, "You're not a Jew, are you?"

"I am," Korczak replied.

"Then where is your armband?" The German was angry by now. "Don't you know you are breaking the law?"

Korczak drew himself up and started to explain as he had so often: "There are human laws which are transitory, and higher laws which are eternal . . ."—but he didn't finish.

Infuriated by the impertinence of this Jew, the German officer ordered him seized by the guards. He was beaten and thrown into a cell.

The ghetto was soon buzzing with rumors about what had happened to Janusz Korczak: he had been tortured and killed during interrogations at Gestapo headquarters; he had been taken to a forest and shot; he had been transported to a camp in Lublin where he lay dying. It was no consolation to Stefa and his friends when they learned that Korczak was only a few blocks away in Pawiak. That massive red-brick compound built in Czarist times for political offenders was the most notorious of all the German prisons. Situated in the heart of the ghetto, it was now a walled city within a walled city. Commitment there by the new conquerors was the equivalent of a death sentence.

During the day Stefa put on a brave face: it was not for nothing that she had been nicknamed Minister of the Interior by those who worked under her. When she found herself suddenly without Korczak at their new quarters on Chlodna Street, she did what she had done during World War I while he was away for four years: she rolled up her sleeves and, with the aid of the teachers and older children, she put things into working order. She had already decided that the classrooms of this former state secondary school would be used for activities during the day and double as bedrooms at night. The outside world might be unjust, but this just society would remain in operation. She turned the basement into an isolation ward for the sick, not wanting to risk sending the children out to a ghetto hospital where they might become infected with typhus or cholera. She had only a syringe and one vial of morphine, but having nursed generations of orphans, she had her own methods: treat throat inflammations with salt water, use a sock filled with heated sand for relief of pain, apply your own big warm hand for comfort when all else fails. Only at night, when everyone was asleep, did Stefa allow herself the privilege of tears.

It was still possible to bribe one's way out of Pawiak. Stefa was in touch with Korczak's friends, but the problem was not so much money as how to make contact with the Gestapo. "Harry" Kaliszer, a resourceful young man who had been one of Korczak's favorite orphans, finally arranged a ransom through the notorious Nazi collaborator Abraham Gancwajch—a mysterious figure with great power in the ghetto. The total sum was set at thirty thousand zlotys, part of which was to be paid on release, the rest over a period of time.

Korczak may have survived his month in Pawiak only because he was fortunate enough to have been thrown in with common criminals rather than political prisoners, who were usually executed. He arrived pale and debilitated at the ghetto orphanage in late December to find the children lined up to greet him, just as they had been when he returned from World War I. After listening to one of the girls deliver a brief welcome speech, he retired quickly to his room—but not before promising to tell them about his experiences at the Saturday-morning meeting.

That Saturday, the children and teachers were joined by many of Korczak's friends who were eager to hear what had happened to him. He gave no hint of his ordeal in front of the children, and was his usual witty and ironic self in answering their questions.

"How did you dare scream at the Germans? Weren't you scared?"

"On the contrary, they were afraid of me. The Germans are always afraid of anyone who yells louder than them."

"What was it like in prison?"

"Wonderful." And, with that, he did the little jig they knew so well.

In spite of the overcrowding in the cell—which, he assured them, made their new quarters look like King Matt's palace—he had managed to eat like a horse, sleep soundly, and exercise vigorously during the short time allowed in the prison yard. Not once, he bragged, did he have to report sick.

The children loved hearing about Korczak's cellmates. One of them, in for murder, thought that the title of doctor meant surgeon, and suggested they both be called Mac the Knife. When they learned that he was the Old Doctor of the popular radio show, they made a place for him on the dirty pile of straw that served as their bed and pleaded for stories. He told them about the cat with white boots and a feather in his cap who managed to acquire fine clothes and a palace for his Prince without stealing them, and about a boy with a magic lamp that produced a genie who granted all his wishes. And they wept, those hardened criminals, remembering the stories their mothers had told them when they were young and still could dream that a cat or genie might change their destiny.

Korczak may have convinced the children that he had kept his sense of humor throughout his imprisonment—he had them in hysterics over how he trained his cellmates to catch the fleas that were plaguing them— but Stefa and the other adults saw how wasted he was. He hadn't burdened them with the details of what he suffered—or the screaming, the moaning, and the shots of the firing squads that went on day and night—yet he could not conceal his nervousness and depression.

The first thing he did on returning was insist that the street entrance be sealed so that the only access to the orphanage was through the courtyard. He also checked the blackout shades each night so that no sliver of light would catch the attention of the German patrol stationed at the nearby gate in the wall.

Stefa didn't know which she found more alarming, Korczak's emotional or physical deterioration: he had difficulty breathing and swelling in his legs. Ignoring his protests, she bundled him off to the hospital for a thorough checkup in the care of a staff member. The admissions doctor noted that though Korczak's cheeks and eyes were burning with fever, he strode into the examining room in his military jacket and high boots with the flair of "an aristocratic Pole." The doctor had difficulty persuading him to get X-rayed. Informed he had fluid in his lungs—a sign of heart failure—he had asked quietly: How much? Hearing that it was below the fourth rib, he declared that it was not enough to keep him from collecting supplies for his children.

Still, for all his bravado, it would be some time before Korczak was ready to venture out into the streets alone—and then it would be with a walking stick.

29

The Ghetto

"There was no natural evolution of life in the thirties that led into ghetto life," Misha Wroblewski, the only teacher in Korczak's ghetto orphanage to survive, would say. "They were two separate worlds—pre-ghetto and ghetto. Just a total, sudden break. You can't shove half a million people on top of each other into a small walled-off area without adequate food, housing, or heat and expect them to lead normal lives. In the beginning you might have felt normal, but after a while you were no longer sane. The ghetto was a mad world, and we behaved madly."

For the first few weeks after getting out of prison, Korczak saw very few people. When an occasional German militiaman came to the door with a vagrant child who needed shelter, he asked someone else to attend to the matter. The only new friend he spent time with during that period was Michael Zylberberg, a teacher who lived with his wife, Henrietta, in the block of flats that shared the courtyard with the orphanage. Zylberberg had taught Jewish literature and history in a Hebrew high school before the war, and had encountered Korczak in educational circles. In those first weeks of Korczak's recuperation, he often dropped into the orphanage to talk. The two men pored over the map of the eleven square miles of the ghetto which Zylberberg, unemployed because the schools were closed, had taken time to explore.

The sealed-off area which they were studying was divided into two zones, known as the Large Ghetto and the Small Ghetto. Chlodna Street, where the orphanage was located, was in the small one. Once a wealthy residential area, it had attracted prosperous Jews uprooted from their exclusive dwellings on the other side of the wall. It was much less congested than the larger district to the north, where the majority of the population lived crowded in unheated, inadequate quarters, as many as nine to a room.

Acting as Korczak's guide when he was strong enough to venture out, Zylberberg led him first to the Large Ghetto. They could hardly make their way through the swarming mass of human life which had turned the streets into a macabre bazaar—beggars stood side by side with desperate people bartering or selling their possessions, old clothes and underwear, doughy half-baked bread, saccharine, anything—even Star of David armbands, whose price varied according to the quality of the material. The two men had to step over impoverished refugee families from the provinces, wrapped in tattered blankets, huddled together for warmth. (Before the bitterly cold winter was over, their naked corpses, covered with newspapers, would lie in the same streets, waiting to be carted away to a mass grave, only to be replaced by a new batch of refugees and beggars whose fate would be the same.)

It occurred to Zylberberg that Korczak, leaning for support on his walking stick, blended right in with the poor people of the ghetto. Nobody would have thought for a moment that this was the famous Old Doctor. But, for that matter, it was impossible to recognize anyone's status: stripped of work and meaningful activity, unprotected by law, the ghetto Jews had become what the historian Emmanuel Ringelblum called "superfluous men." Those with musical or acting talents were hawking them on the streets like all the other vendors.

Zylberberg took Korczak to Leszno Street to hear the blind accordion player who had been famous in the twenties for his wrenching songs about the pogroms of Czarist days and the attacks on Jews by the Poles during the early days of independence. Now he was becoming known for his equally poignant lyrics about the ghetto. They found a large crowd gathered around the blind musician, who was assisted by an attractive blonde woman who darted in and out of the crowd selling the words and music to the song he was singing:

> *Where shall I go?*
> *Where shall I go?*
> *The shame and pain have become too hard.*
> *Every road is closed and barred.*

> *Great is my suffering, and great is my woe,*
> *My heart weeps and my tears flow.*
> *Where shall I go, Jews,*
> *Where shall I go?*

Moving on, they saw a paralyzed young woman with dark flashing eyes who was crawling on all fours in the middle of the muddy road. Her powerful voice, which woke the residents each morning with a Yiddish song, was now shrieking "The Three Seamstresses" by the famous writer I. L. Peretz:

> *Their eyes are red, their lips are blue,*
> *No drop of blood in the cheek shows through.*
> *On their pale faces the sweat beads lie.*
> *Their breath is hot, their tongue is dry.*
> *Three girls sit sewing.*

At the corner a half-crazed man came leaping toward them, flailing his arms and crying: "Look lively, Jews, we've lost all shame! Rich and poor are now the same!"

"It's Rubinstein, the self-appointed jester of the Warsaw Ghetto," Zylberberg said. "No one knows anything about him except that he's a refugee from the provinces. He always runs wild through the streets like this, shouting some ditty he's made up."

It was as difficult to make their way back to the Small Ghetto as it had been to advance forward. Not only did they have to push once more past the thousands of peddlers and beggars, but they had to climb back over those inert refugee families. Turning a corner, they were again accosted by Rubinstein, who sprang at them this time with a threat: "Give me a penny and you may go! If you don't, I'll start screaming!"

"It's his form of blackmail," Zylberberg explained. "Everyone knows that if he doesn't get his coin, he'll begin shouting: 'Down with the Führer! Down with Hitler!' And the Germans will start shooting everyone in sight."

Korczak handed Rubinstein a coin.

Exploring the Small Ghetto a few days later was not as strenuous, but just as disturbing. There were fewer refugees from the provinces in this more exclusive section, but the streets here were also filled with children hawking anything they could find from trays strapped to their shoulders, and with hundreds of musicians, who had staked out their turf.

Near the Judenrat building on Grzybowska, Korczak was taken with a young violinist from Jerusalem who had been trapped while visiting relatives in Poland. Leaning on his walking stick, he watched this delicate, fair-haired youth from the city he had thought to live in, noting how he kept his blue eyes closed while playing Bloch's "Ba'al Shem Tov" and other Hebrew melodies, and opened them only to look for tossed coins.

As Korczak and Zylberberg continued on down Panska to Sliska, they encountered groups of roving musicians—including members of the Warsaw Philharmonic, who drew a large crowd whenever they stopped. Stars of the opera accompanied them, singing arias that the people requested. Korczak took off his glasses to study their faces and then to look closely at the bystanders who were carried away by the music.

A short while later, they came across renowned cantors from all over Poland, unemployed now that the synagogues, like the schools, were closed. The bitter reality of the ghetto had reduced them to fierce competitiveness with each other: one, who was forced to wheel his paralyzed wife propped up in a child's stroller as he sang, was ostracized by the others for trying to play on the public's sympathy. The crowd here, just as avid as the opera fans, had not lost its sardonic sense of humor. When one man mumbled that he had heard Cantor Rosenblatt sing the same songs much better, another quipped: "Well, if you don't like these renditions, you can book passage to New York and hear Cantor Rosenblatt there."

In the course of their wanderings, the two educators chanced upon many people they had known in what now seemed another life. An assimilated philanthropist, well over eighty, reminded Zylberberg of their meeting years before. He explained that he was alone because his two daughters had converted and were living on the Aryan side with their Gentile husbands.

"Why did you come into the ghetto, then?" Korczak asked curiously. "In my case, I have no family, and my children are all here, but it's different for you. Can't your daughters arrange to get you out?"

"I could have joined them if that's what I wanted," the old man replied. "I have chosen to be in the ghetto with my fellow Jews who are suffering."

Zylberberg noticed that this answer pleased Korczak, who said he felt the same way. They began discussing the Yiddish writer Peretz, who was a relative of the philanthropist, and whom Korczak had met at literary gatherings before the First World War.

Their conversation about Peretz was cut short by Rubinstein, who came rushing by:

> Give me one cent—it's nothing!
> Two cents—that's nothing too!
> Three cents—forget it! But four—
> Four cents, or else it's Gesia for you!

Then, spotting a funeral procession on its way to the very Gesia Street cemetery to which he had been referring, Rubinstein went tearing off to join it, screaming: "Rich and poor are all the same!"

"The Jews are a strange people," Korczak said, shaking his head.

At eleven one night, as they were getting ready for bed, Zylberberg and his wife were startled to hear the thud of heavy boots coming up the wooden stairs, an alarming sound since no one in the building ventured out after the seven o'clock curfew. Instinctively, they rushed to turn off the lights, as if the darkness would protect them. But the footsteps came closer and closer until they stopped right outside their apartment. The doorbell rang.

"Who is it?" Zylberberg called.

"Dr. Korczak. Please open up," came the familiar voice.

Zylberberg looked at his wife with relief as he unlatched the door. There stood his famous walking companion in the old army boots that seemed never to leave his feet.

Apologizing for having frightened them, Korczak said that he had waited until the orphanage quieted down. After glancing over the books on Zylberberg's table, he explained the reason for his late call. Since his release from prison, he had realized that they were living in a bizarre society in which everyone had to adapt in some way to survive. Because it was too dangerous for the children to go out, he wanted to invite people in each week to talk about what they were doing. He had already lined up some Judenrat officials, representatives from soup kitchens and other institutions, as well as the historian Emmanuel Ringelblum, and a philosopher. He was also hoping to schedule a lawyer who was now a policeman, and a scholar who was a janitor. If Zylberberg liked the project, would he, as a teacher and neighbor, be willing to help him organize the series? And would he give the first talk?

Zylberberg agreed to both, but wanted time to think about his topic. Urged by Korczak to decide right then, Zylberberg suggested that he tell the children about Peretz, who, before becoming a famous writer, had worked as a teacher and even set up orphanages. Korczak was pleased. "Peretz is just the right subject at this time. He belongs to Warsaw."

The orphanage was "buzzing like a hive" when Zylberberg arrived the following week. Having just finished their midday meal, the children filed out of the dining room into the large hall that had been the school auditorium. Stefa and the teachers helped everyone get settled. Korczak sat among the children.

"The man I am going to tell you about, the ever youthful Peretz, lived not far from here," Zylberberg said. "He wrote in Polish in the early days of his career. But though he spent a lot of time teaching poor Jewish children, he wanted to find a way to help all Jews who were suffering from poverty and fleeing from Russian pogroms. When he discovered the warm, joyful faith of the Hasidim, which gave his people pride in themselves and made each man a king in his own home on the Sabbath, he began writing in Yiddish so that he could reach them."

Zylberberg spoke in Polish to his young audience, but after he had recited Peretz's poem "Brothers" (which is engraved on the poet's tombstone), he repeated it in the original Yiddish. He noticed Korczak nodding in recognition, for it had been made into a popular song and expressed a philosophy close to his own.

> *White and brown, black and yellow,*
> *Mix the colors with one another.*
> *We are all sisters and brothers*
> *Of one father and one mother,*
> *And God created us all.*
> *The whole world is our Fatherland.*
> *We are all sisters and brothers,*
> *This is what we must understand.*

When Zylberberg followed this with the monologue from Peretz's famous play, *The Golden Chain*, which had also become a song, the children began clapping their hands, tapping their feet, and singing along with him:

> *And so*
> *We go*
> *Singing and dancing . . .*
> *We great, great Jews.*

Souls aflame!
For us clouds divide!
Heaven flings open its door!
To clouds of glory we rise,
Toward the Throne of Glory!
And we do not pray,
We do not beg.
We are great, proud Jews,
Seed of Abraham,
Isaac and Jacob!
Longer we cannot wait!
Song of songs we sing!
Singing and dancing we go!

As soon as they finished accompanying Zylberberg in that song, the children spontaneously broke into the earlier "Brothers." They sang it over and over, joining hands and swaying as brothers and sisters, until Stefa reminded them that they had kept their guest long enough. In closing the program, Korczak suggested that "Brothers" become the orphanage anthem, a proposal that the children seconded by singing it exuberantly as they left the hall.

When the room was silent once again, Korczak and Zylberberg could hear the German patrols marching back and forth by the wall that cut through Chlodna Street just a few doors away.

Those who visited the orphanage found it an oasis in the midst of hell. Its daily routine carried Korczak along with it, restoring his equilibrium. Classes were held surreptitiously in morning and afternoon shifts, with Hebrew one of the main subjects in order to prepare everyone for a possible new life in Palestine when the war was over. Just as on Krochmalna, the vital center of the home was held together for the children by the court of peers and parliament. Every Saturday morning Korczak still read aloud the column he had prepared for the orphanage newspaper, but the dangers he had so wittily warned the children of in the past—such as putting their fingers in the ironing machine—seemed mild compared to those of the present. "A machine does not understand, it is indifferent," he had written in those prewar days. "You put your finger in, it will cut it off. Put your head in, it will cut that off too. Life is a machine, it does not give any warning or delay punishment."

The Germans now embodied that machine, as the children knew, especially the newcomers who had seen their parents killed before their eyes or watched them die of hunger or disease. No one who went out to visit relatives on Saturday afternoons, or just to get air, could avoid witnessing some brutal street scene. Nothing Korczak wrote could spare them, nor could he spare himself. He had to accept that he could not prevent the children from living in constant uncertainty and fear. All he could do was to continue to keep them adequately fed and sheltered, and to give them some hope for the future.

Each building compound in the ghetto had a House Committee that was responsible for raising the funds needed for the building's maintenance, as well as for the payment of taxes and for contributions to the thousands of destitute refugees arriving from other countries. As a member of the House Committee at 33 Chlodna (which was one of the cleanest and best-run compounds in the ghetto), Korczak suggested raising money through a concert at the orphanage between Purim and Passover. A special meeting to discuss arrangements was convened in the orphanage one evening at nine.

The participants in this eclectic group, made up of Jews of all persuasions, were united more by their common fate than by religious affinity. Among them were a member of the Polish Socialist party, a Talmudic scholar, an assimilated industrialist, an agnostic pediatrician, a few observant engineers, and a convert. After a lengthy discussion, it was decided that the concert program should include both professional musicians and street performers. But the question of which language the evening would be conducted in sparked a heated debate. The assimilated Jews insisted on Polish, the Zionists on Hebrew, while the Bundists and Orthodox Jews were equally vehement about Yiddish.

Korczak sat there, as he did at all House Committee meetings, leaning forward on his walking stick, his eyes closed as if asleep. But everyone knew from past experience that he was aware of all that was being discussed, and was waiting to give his opinion at the appropriate moment. When a stalemate threatened further progress, one of the assimilationists passed a note to Zylberberg, who was chairing the meeting, to request Korczak's opinion. He assumed that Korczak would vote for Polish.

Upon being asked to speak, Korczak slowly removed his glasses, as he always did when he wished to concentrate, looked solemnly around at everyone, and then said mildly that he was surprised there should be any argument, that intelligent people could waste so much time on such an obvious issue.

"And what is that?" the other committee members wanted to know.

"Just this," said Korczak. "When one argues against the use of a particular language, one also argues against those who use it. Can you deny that the majority of people in the ghetto speak and think in Yiddish, even die with it on their lips?"

Those who had been arguing the most tenaciously against Yiddish were silent.

"And so Yiddish must be the language of the concert—otherwise, the performance will have no soul."

Korczak's words had an immediate effect on the group. A motion was made in favor of Yiddish and seconded, and the concert scheduled for two weeks later. Once again Zylberberg was struck by the "fascinating and enigmatic" way that Korczak revealed himself as a Jew.

The three hundred people who attended, for the most part prominent and wealthy, had not been asked to buy tickets. Korczak had convinced the committee that the guests would give more money if it were left to their conscience to make a contribution. Some of the professional actors and musicians had agreed to perform without a fee, but a small honorarium was given to the stranded blue-eyed violinist from Jerusalem, as well as to a few of the folksingers Korczak had befriended on the street.

"Music is the religion of the future and you are its priests," Korczak told the performers in opening the program. "Artists such as you lead the way."

A few Polish and Hebrew pieces had been included in the program, but the Yiddish songs drew the most spirited response from the predominantly assimilated audience. Korczak was so moved by the street performers from all over Europe whom "fate had cast into this ghetto," that he wept unashamedly while they performed.

A professional singer, Romana Lilienstein, who, together with her accompanist, had chosen a selection of light music appropriate for children, was one of the few who would live to recall that event: "Even though the home was clean and orderly, to this day I am haunted by the air of poverty that pervaded the corridors and auditorium. The children, dressed, like everyone else, in their best clothes, were obviously ecstatic as they sat waiting under the watchful eyes of Stefa Wilczynska. They listened attentively as Dr. Korczak made a few comforting and humorous remarks in his opening speech. We knew they were as hungry as we were, as everyone in the audience was, yet I'll never forget the intensity of those hundreds of eyes fixed on us. It is difficult to explain what such a concert meant at that time."

However, the evening was to end on a discordant note. After the applause had quieted down and people were getting up to leave, Korczak unexpectedly announced that he wanted to share some brief poems he had recently composed. He drew a few cards from his pocket and started to read.

The bitterly satiric poems mentioned no names, but ridiculed a small black mustache, a large fat belly, a hunchback, and, finally, an elegant dandy, all of whom were able to hold the fate of millions of people in their hands. The audience stirred uneasily when it became obvious that Korczak was referring to Hitler, Goering, Goebbels, and their own "hangman," Hans Frank, who was in charge of the "New Order" in Poland; there was an agitated dash for the exit when he openly called those Nazis murderers and outcasts of society.

Korczak continued reading to the few house tenants who had remained out of deference to him. Zylberberg stayed on after everyone had retired to ask Korczak why he dared take such a chance. Didn't he realize the danger to all of them if the Nazis heard about his poems?

Korczak merely smiled and said: "The people who left are fools. What is there to be afraid of? Surely Jews can say what they think among themselves. There were no spies here, or anyone who would give me away—we are all in this together."

Korczak was asserting his right to autonomy in his own territory. Zylberberg realized that his new friend's nervous behavior after his imprisonment had been a temporary lapse. He felt he was seeing the real man this night, an assimilated Jew of wit and talent who had great trust in his own people. But still he found Korczak, with his unique combination of Polish defiance and Jewish irony, an enigma.

30
All Are Equal

Korczak could be satiric about the Germans, but not about the hunger that was affecting his children. Each day found him getting up and slinging a sack over his shoulder. It was as bottomless as the sack of the old man who demanded coins from him after the puppet show in his childhood: "Not enough, young gentleman, not enough! A bit more!" He had no choice but to beg as relentlessly as the old man had begged from him. And he was just as insatiable. "Not enough," he would say, no matter what was offered. "Not enough!" Those people who had managed to hold on to their money dreaded his calls. "Moral blackmail," one man called them. Even his friends at the social service bureaus of the Judenrat and at CENTOS found him difficult to deal with. "We were embarrassed by his demands, which were beyond our capacities," Abraham Berman was to write. "To be honest, it was easier to work with his partner, Stefa Wilczynska. We were always relieved when we saw her come in rather than Korczak."

The once formidable Stefa now seemed the voice of reason. In spite of the deprivations of the past year, friends noticed little physical change in her, while Korczak seemed to be shrinking, becoming more and more like a "shriveled raisin." He had always been a little wrinkled, but since his prison experience there were deep furrows at the corners of his eyes and mouth; his skin, like his teeth, had a yellowish cast now that he was relying on cigarettes, coffee, and what little vodka he was able to come by to keep him going.

One of Korczak's routine stops was the post office, where he collected damaged packages marked UNDELIVERABLE because their address labels had been torn off or because no one was alive to claim them. The Nazis allowed food packages until December of 1941, but deliveries were uneven, and German soldiers were free to rummage through them. Those packages that made it to the post office might have bread, flour, cooking fat, and grains from relatives who had fled to Soviet-occupied territory at the outbreak of the war, or coffee, chocolate, rice, sardines, and condensed milk from family and friends who had emigrated to neutral countries like Spain and Portugal. But often the contents were spoiled from sitting in way stations for long periods of time. Having persuaded the Judenrat to allow the unclaimed packages to be released to children's institutions, Korczak checked in regularly. There was no parcel, however damaged, that he wouldn't take in case it contained something salvageable. He and Stefa were at the same time sending postcards to everyone they knew overseas. In November of 1941, Leon Gluzman, who had been an orphan in the home in the twenties before emigrating to Canada, received a typed card signed by both Korczak and Stefa: "Please, if possible, send food packages to the Orphans Home at 33 Chlodna Street for our sick children (and those recuperating from recent illness). And please alert others to our need, in particular those who remember their youth." The card was addressed to Gluzman in Ottawa, Ont., U.S.A. / America, and stamped by the Nazi censor with the German eagle.

John Auerbach, an eighteen-year-old who had been lucky enough to get a post-office job through his father's contacts, was sitting on a bench with other postmen waiting for the mail to be sorted one gray April morning in 1941 when Janusz Korczak entered with his empty sack.

"Sit down, Doctor, relax, they haven't started yet," one of the postmen said, jumping up to give him his seat.

"I can stand," Korczak protested. "Your legs are more tired than mine."

When the postman insisted, Korczak lowered himself onto the bench, his chin propped on one hand over his walking stick, his eyes scanning the faces of the crowd that was sloshing melted snow across the sagging plank floor and making the air acrid with the smell of unwashed bodies. Auerbach, who admired Korczak's work and wanted to be a writer himself, noticed how old and shrunken he looked, though his eyes, despite their deep bags, were piercing and alive.

"Are you a student?" Korczak asked, suddenly turning to him.

Auerbach shrugged. "I probably would have been one, but I am a postman now. Nothing more."

Still looking at Auerbach, but seeming to talk to himself, Korczak commented: "There are three beautiful professions. Which would you choose to be—a doctor, a teacher, or a judge?"

Watching the counter for his number to come up, Auerbach answered: "I'm not sure I understand. I can see the importance of being a teacher or a doctor, but what's so special about being a judge?"

"My dear young man," Korczak replied patiently. "A doctor takes charge of a man's body, a teacher of his mind. And a judge—isn't he in charge of a man's conscience?"

Auerbach considered this, but still the point escaped him. "Does a man need a judge in the same way he needs a doctor and a teacher?"

Korczak nodded slowly as if both surprised and disappointed by this response.

"You are still very young," he said quietly. "Yes, every man needs a judge, unless he is his own judge. And that, too, is a very difficult, and very beautiful, profession."

Spotting his number at that moment, Auerbach rushed to the counter. Later in the morning he caught a glimpse of the "strange, bearded man" he so admired departing with his sack now full of rotting packages.

The following month Auerbach was asked by his superior to deliver an unclaimed parcel to Korczak's orphanage. It was an experience which to this day he does not want to judge: "A boy of six or seven with a shaved head and oversize smock opened the door, looked at me with large burning black eyes, and ran off shouting: 'The mail's here!' I took the knapsack off my shoulder and was searching for the package when I heard Korczak's steps in the dark corridor. He didn't seem to recognize me as the young man he had talked with at the post office. I gave him the paper to sign, and as he took it with a trembling hand, I was surprised to catch a strong whiff of vodka. He must have sensed my reaction, for he stiffened, and we confronted each other silently, how long I still don't know. Then he stepped toward me, and made a broad gesture with both arms, a movement that seemed to encompass the world, time, life, and his hungry children, to whom he was doctor, teacher, and judge. 'One . . . one must still try to live . . . somehow,' he said, placing a hand on my shoulder. And with that he turned and disappeared into the darkness with the battered package."

* * *

That spring Korczak was in contact with anyone who could help him feed his hungry children, even the suspected Nazi collaborator, Abraham Gancwajch, who had arranged the ransom that bought his release from Pawiak.

Gancwajch and his infamous network—known as "the Thirteen" because of their base at 13 Leszno Street—operated in the ghetto like an alternate Judenrat (much to Chairman Czerniakow's consternation) and were believed to report to one of the Nazi factions. Originally set up in December of 1940 as the Office to Combat Usury and Profiteering in the Jewish Quarter of Warsaw, the network, which would number between 300 and 400 men, had its own police force, first-aid station, and ambulance service.

"What a despicable, ugly creature," Czerniakow wrote of Gancwajch in his diary. Little is known of the man except that he materialized from somewhere outside of Warsaw. A talented orator, with a command of Yiddish and Hebrew as well as Polish, he preached the wisdom of working with the German conquerors—a pragmatic position that some compared to the Judenrat's. Whatever they thought of Gancwajch's motives—opportunistic or altruistic—many of the ghetto leaders, out of dread or need, accepted his invitations to conferences on social welfare projects. One such meeting in early May lasted well past curfew, forcing its participants to spend the night in the Thirteen's headquarters. Czerniakow noted in his diary a few names of those who attended the "tea party," with exclamation marks after Korczak's. According to Ringelblum, Korczak agreed to head a Children's Aid Commission, but what that involved, or indeed whether it ever came into being, is not known.

In early June of 1941, Korczak and Stefa spent much of the night with the Zylberbergs and other tenants in their compound peering through cracks in the shutters of the orphanage as German troops marched through the deserted ghetto streets—through Chlodna, Elektoralna, and Senatorska—and over the Vistula bridge on their way to the Soviet frontier. *Stalin, wir kommen* was written across the tanks.

Korczak was elated by the impending German attack on Russia. Like so many others, he had no doubt that the Russians would repel Hitler's troops as they had once held off Napoleon's. It was only a matter of time and Poland would be free. But the months that followed the outbreak of hostilities brought disheartening news of German victories over the Russians, and reports of the slaughter of Jewish communities in captured areas. And in the ghetto there was another outbreak of typhus that took the lives of thousands already weakened by hunger.

The Jews held on to their sardonic wit as a way of surviving. Nothing that happened inside or outside the walls was too insignificant to be recycled into gallows humor. People would greet each other with: "Why should the Germans bomb London, and the English Berlin? All that flying back and forth is a waste of gas. The Germans ought to bomb Berlin and the English London." Or: "Horowitz [Hitler] comes to the Other World, sees Jesus in Paradise. 'Hey, what's a Jew doing without an armband?' 'Let him be,' answers St. Peter. 'He's the Boss's son.' " Rubinstein, the mad jester, was still making absurd pronouncements: "The rich are dissolving!" "We're going to have some fat!" People were so amused by his chant "All are equal! In the ghetto all are equal!" (a parody of the Judenrat slogan that was intended to convince the population that everyone was being treated fairly) that a revue, *All Are Equal,* opened at the Melody Palace, one of the popular music halls.

There was no predicting Nazi tactics. Late that summer the Gestapo unexpectedly gave permission for the Judenrat to establish twenty Jewish schools with courses in Polish, Yiddish, or Hebrew. As the Jews rushed about in search of classroom space—most available public rooms had been turned into soup kitchens—they did not know that Hitler had already appointed Reinhard Heydrich, chief of the Reich Central Security Office, to carry out the "Final Solution," and that the first experiments with cyanide gas as an efficient method of extermination were being made even then at Auschwitz.

Korczak kept his children in the orphanage classes rather than risk their catching typhus outside, but he held pedagogic seminars for the teachers and directors of the new schools, which served six thousand of the ghetto's fifty thousand children of elementary-school age. It was decided that the school season should open with a theater contest in which all three language groups would compete. The Hebrew-speaking schools were planning sketches of Jewish life in Palestine from ancient to modern times, the Yiddish schools pieces stressing social justice and labor, and the Polish schools dramatizations of scenes from Polish literature that portrayed Jews and Poles living side by side in harmony.

When he visited Michael Zylberberg's Hebrew Day School, Korczak found three hundred students there speaking, singing, and playing in

Hebrew, just as if they were in Palestine. He tried to make time to drop in at rehearsals of their play, *Masada* (whose title was changed to *Fireflies* at the last moment to avoid German notice). Based on the three-year resistance of the Jews under Roman siege at a mountain stronghold known as Masada—which ended with the Jews committing suicide rather than accepting defeat—the play was meant to remind the audience that Jews do not go down passively. Zylberberg noted that Korczak particularly liked the poem with which the play ended:

> *The chain has not been broken,*
> *The chain continues on,*
> *From parents to children,*
> *From father to son.*
>
> *This is how our parents danced,*
> *One hand on the next man's back,*
> *And in the other a Sepher Torah,*
> *Bringing light where all was black.*
>
> *So we, too, will keep on dancing,*
> *With our spirits all awake.*
> *We will keep on dancing, dancing,*
> *And the chain will never break.*

Encouraged by the opening of the schools, Adam Czerniakow officially inaugurated Children's Month in the Femina Theater at noon on September 20, the day before Rosh Hashanah, the Jewish New Year.

As head of the powerful Judenrat, the Chairman was well aware that he had many critics who accused him and his Council members of graft and corruption. (A popular chant about him went: "Czerniakow's belly is big and round. Gulps broth and meatballs by the pound!") But whatever Czerniakow's ethical ambiguities, his interest in children's welfare was genuine. As the Chairman's job became increasingly difficult—he noted in his diary that the face looking out at him from a recent portrait was "very old and tired and bitter"—he became increasingly involved in special projects for children. He was also seeking to relieve his loneliness and worry over his only son, Jas. Nothing had been heard from Jas since June when the Germans captured Lvov, where he had fled after the invasion of Poland.

That day at the Femina Theater, Czerniakow, along with his wife and several other speakers, asked the audience to open their purses as well as their hearts to help the hungry and homeless children. They managed to raise a hundred thousand zlotys, some of which went for posters that read: OUR CHILDREN, OUR CHILDREN MUST LIVE and A CHILD IS THE HOLIEST OF ALL BEINGS.

Korczak decided to hold services in the orphanage for his children and the community on both Rosh Hashanah and Yom Kippur. "You shouldn't be surprised," he told Zylberberg, whom he asked to help with arrangements. "In troubled times, prayer is important. It will give the children strength, and us too. No one is required to come—only those who feel the need for it. And it will help bring in funds for the House Committee."

Whether it was their need for prayer or the excitement of celebrating a holiday, the children threw themselves into transforming the orphanage assembly hall into a synagogue. They laid down carpets and arranged flowers smuggled in by Korczak's Gentile friends. An ark containing two Torah scrolls in richly embroidered coverings, flanked by two silver candlesticks, was placed at one end of the room, and benches arranged in rows before it.

Zylberberg invited a cantor who had been deported from a small town to officiate. But, as it turned out, there were few in attendance other than fellow tenants in the compound and the orphanage children and staff. Fearing that a large crowd would bring typhus into the home, Korczak had put a high price on tickets for the services; and then at the last minute the Germans had allowed synagogues to open for the first time in two years.

Korczak stood in the back of the hall in his old gray suit and high military boots, a silk yarmulke on his head, completely absorbed, as if in meditation. No one stirred as the cantor sang out:

> *On Rosh Hashanah it is inscribed,*
> *And on Yom Kippur it is sealed,*
> *How many shall pass away,*
> *And how many shall be born,*
> *Who shall live and who shall die.*

In the sermon he gave on Yom Kippur, ten days later, Korczak tried to reassure the children that they would live to see happier times. But even as he led them in calling out together at the end of the service "Next year in Jerusalem!"—as had generations before them—he did not succeed in alleviating his own anxieties. Zylberberg, who wanted to hurry back to his apartment to break his fast, lingered at his friend's request.

"It is important that the children not be worried," Korczak told him. "But I am afraid of what lies ahead. The Germans are capable of anything."

31

Our Children
Must Live

Once again during the High Holy Days the Germans unveiled a malevolent plan—as if "the scoundrels get restless at the approach of winter," historian Emmanuel Ringelblum noted in his diary. The previous year they had established the ghetto; this year they announced their intention to reduce it in size, even as they brought in an increasing number of Jews from other countries.

In mid-October 1941, Korczak and Stefa learned that residents of 33 Chlodna and adjoining streets would have to relocate within four days because that area had been zoned out of the ghetto. It was almost as much of a blow to have to vacate this building as it had been to lose their original quarters on Krochmalna. Worn down by hunger and fatigue, they had less energy for this move. But, as always, they got on with the task at hand. Korczak managed to find a former businessmen's club at 16 Sienna Street in the Small Ghetto. It had once been an exclusive address but now it faced a recently erected wall that ran down the middle of the street to form the southernmost border of the ghetto. The new quarters were even smaller than the previous ones, but, luckily, Korczak was also able to take possession of a little house behind the club, at 7 Sliska Street, as a dormitory for the staff.

Stefa organized the limited space at the Sienna Street house to accommodate the orphanage's many activities. Using wooden chests and cupboards, she partitioned the large room on the first floor into dining, study, and play units during the day, and sleeping quarters at night. The routine of the home was established immediately. Classes were held in shifts as before, as were meals. Each child had work assignments—kitchen duty, or a cleaning detail, for which he received points. There was an active choir, a drama and sewing circle, a doll corner, and puppet work-shop.

Just before the orphanage moved to its new location, Michael Zyl-berberg's wife, Henrietta, came down with typhus. From the moment she entered the ghetto, she had repeatedly told Stefa that everyone would die of hunger, and had spent most of her days bartering possessions for food for her husband and herself. Now it seemed that she would die of typhus rather than starvation.

During the ten days that his wife lay semiconscious in their apart-ment, Zylberberg stayed away from the orphanage for fear of infecting the children. He managed to pay a few doctors to see her, but they had little medicine and her condition worsened. Late one afternoon, when Zylberberg was certain she would die, Korczak appeared at his door with his medical bag. After examining the patient, he gave her a shot of precious serum he had brought with him. He returned frequently during the next few days to give her further shots. As she battled for life, she could hear his voice testing her consciousness: "Do you know your name?" And encouraging her: "Don't give up. Don't let Hitler have another victory." One night, after sitting with her for hours, he told her husband: "It looks as if the fever will break and she will live." He proved to be right.

Henrietta didn't accompany her husband on his visit to the new orphanage because she feared that the streets had become too dangerous. Zylberberg found the atmosphere in the home heavy and the facilities not as adequate as those on Chlodna. The kitchen was tiny, and there was only one bathroom for the hundred and fifty children and staff. However, Korczak greeted him with his usual smile, and the children were so excited to see him that they burst spontaneously into their an-them:

> *White and brown and black and yellow,*
> *Mix the colors with one another.*
> *People are still brothers and sisters*
> *Of one father and one mother!*

As the ghetto closed ever more tightly around the Jews, the absence of their Polish "brothers and sisters" on the other side of the wall became an almost physical deprivation. Even the Hebraist Chaim Kaplan complained to his diary: "Our souls yearn for the sight of a Gentile face." He listed the only five Gentiles one could see: the tax collector, the bill collectors for monthly payments of electricity and gas, and the two conductors on the Jewish tram. If one was unfortunate enough to be taken to court, one saw a sixth—the judge.

Feeling the same sense of loss as the Jews, Korczak's Christian friends began devising schemes to visit him. On one of those gloomy November days when the skies were overcast and everything was covered with dirty snow, Maria Czapska managed to borrow someone's pass to get into the ghetto. Since the only tramcars that went through the ghetto didn't stop inside, she got off at the station just before the gate, showing her pass to the German and Polish police at the checkpoint outside, and to their Jewish counterparts inside. Darkness was falling, although it was still afternoon, as she made her way through the crowded streets, past vendors hawking cigarettes and sunflower seeds, past beggars exhibiting frozen limbs, past half-naked children ignored by passersby as if they were "rags of humanity."

When Korczak greeted her at the door of the orphanage, Maria was taken aback by how rapidly he had aged in the ghetto. As a student who admired his work in the early nineteen-twenties, she had sought him out, and become a social worker through his influence. Neither of them said anything as they made their way to his office through a line of children standing in the dark hallway waiting to exchange books at the library corner. She was struck by the mature and thoughtful expressions on their faces.

After they were settled in his small upstairs office, Korczak began talking about the Hanukkah program the children were preparing. He intended to write some prayers for it, as well as for a Christmas pageant. Since he wanted to compose an invocation for two choruses that would use material from both religions, he asked her to send him a litany to the Virgin Mary. Korczak looked sad as he spoke about previous years when he wrote Hanukkah plays for his Jewish orphans and danced around the Christmas tree with his Christian ones. As the darkness of the afternoon deepened, so did their silences. She could hear a tramcar speeding nonstop across the ghetto from one Aryan district to another, as well as hurried footsteps in the snow and low voices outside speaking Yiddish.

As she was leaving, Czapska hesitated at the door, knowing she might never see her friend again. "How are you feeling, really?" she asked.

"Like a butterfly," he said. "A butterfly who will soon fly away to a better world." After a pause, he gave that half-sardonic smile she knew so well. "It's either a vision—or sclerosis of the brain."

Kazimierz Debnicki also managed to get hold of someone else's pass into the ghetto. He was never to forget the shock of coming from a part of the city that was still green and where there was air to breathe into this frozen world where crowds of people were stepping over corpses as casually as they might over mounds of snow. Once he managed to find the orphanage at Sienna and Sliska, he was relieved to see it functioning in an orderly way, but he could not control his rage at the Germans as he and Korczak sat down to talk.

"This ghetto is like a prison," he blurted out.

"There are two prisons," Korczak responded quietly. "One larger than the other. One may have more trees and flowers, but the same fate awaits everyone." And then he added wryly: "When a man condemned to death leaves his cell, it makes no difference if the cell was large or small."

Debnicki couldn't help noticing how emaciated Korczak had become. His voice said one thing, but his wild, red-rimmed eyes, like those of a madman, belied his words. He was trying to keep his balance by speaking rationally about an irrational situation. He was an old military doctor, he reminded Debnicki, and with all the danger in the ghetto, he never forgot that it was still more dangerous on the front lines.

Korczak sounded like the Old Doctor as he kept steering the conversation to a philosophical level that transcended the immediate moment. Finding himself yet again in the position of having to comfort those who had come to comfort him, he tried to stress the optimistic side of things, to talk about the future. "Hitler's movement will not last because the vast majority of German people will not put up with these atrocities," he said. When Debnicki repeated his outrage at the way some Poles were behaving—informing on the Jews, turning them in to the Gestapo— Korczak responded: "Remember, for each one who acts like that, there are many who behave decently. Basically, people are good."

Yet Korczak was deeply saddened that the bridge he and his family had devoted themselves to building between the Jews and the Poles could be so effectively sabotaged by the Germans. He wrote in his diary: "How easy it is for two criminals to team up for nefarious purposes, but how impossible for a collaboration between two peoples who share the same values but are separated from each other by different histories."

Typhus was decimating the community at such an alarming rate that there was no longer space in the cemetery to hold all the victims. They were lowered naked, without even newspaper to cover them, into mass graves.

Korczak was more and more overwhelmed by a sense of helplessness as he passed emaciated boys and girls with bare arms and legs begging in the wintry streets one day and frozen to death in the gutters the next. They were usually children of refugees who had already succumbed to typhus, hunger, or cold, or sick children put out on the street just before death by parents who could not afford to pay for a burial wagon to take them away. Often someone had covered their little bodies with a decorative Children's Month poster: OUR CHILDREN, OUR CHILDREN MUST LIVE.

Sometimes Korczak knelt beside the dying children, trying to transmit some warmth from his hand to their emaciated bodies, whispering a few words of encouragement, but most of them were already beyond response. In their advanced stage of starvation, they could not get up, but lay curled in a fetal position, as if sleeping with their eyes open. One of the children's rights that he had espoused was the right to die with dignity, but there was no dignity in the way these children lived or died.

For some time Korczak had been hounding CENTOS to provide more shelters so that the street children would have some chance, however minimal, for life. When nothing came of this, or of a plan for the Jewish police to make some provisions, he decided to try to set up on his own a modest place where the dying children would at least have a sense that someone cared for them.

Having exhausted all other channels, Korczak thought of eliciting the help of Colonel Mieczyslaw Kowalski, a member of the Health Department of the Judenrat. The Colonel, who had been a professional military doctor in the Polish Army, occasionally supplied Korczak with soap, linens, fuel, and even food. Since they rarely exchanged anything but formalities, the Colonel was surprised when Korczak began speaking animatedly about his plan to help the street children die with dignity: "The hospitals are too crowded to admit them, even if there were a chance of recovery. What I have in mind wouldn't take a great deal of space or money. It could just be some empty store, like a fabric shop, with shelves to place the children on. We wouldn't have to have a large staff—one person with the skills of an orderly would be enough."

In recognizing the need for a place where dying children could be comforted and pass their last hours in peace, Korczak anticipated the hospice movement. But in the ghetto, where the living required as much comforting as the dying, the Colonel had demands that took priority. The project never materialized.

Still, Colonel Kowalski was able to help Korczak in a way that neither of them could have foreseen. One day word reached Kowalski that Janusz Korczak had been picked up by the police for not wearing an armband and was about to be sent to Pawiak again. The Colonel immediately got in touch with the chief doctor of the German division of health, Dr. Wilhelm Hagen (known as a "good German"), who owed him a favor. Kowalski had recently set the leg of Hagen's Jewish friend from medical school days; now he asked Hagen a favor in return: a medical certificate that would exempt Korczak from Pawiak. Hagen agreed to issue one, but only after he had examined Korczak. The plan almost backfired. When Korczak was brought to Kowalski's office by the police, he refused to be examined by Hagen. Pretending not to know German, he protested that he was healthy and would not undress. It took some time for Kowalski to persuade Korczak to take off his clothes. "I was shocked by how emaciated he was," Kowalski said. "He had a congested lung, a ruptured hernia, and badly swollen legs, to mention just a few of the things wrong with him." After writing the certificate, Hagen told Korczak: "I hope you'll wear the armband in the future because this is the last time I can help you." This time Korczak replied directly in German: "I can promise you that I'll never wear it."

On November 1, All Souls' Day, when the Poles visit graveyards to place flowers and candles on the graves of their dead, Korczak bribed a guard at the gate to let him leave the ghetto. He was on his way to Bielany to see how Maryna Falska and the children were faring. He arrived about noon, cold and exhausted from the long walk. Maryna and the other staff members, shocked to see how badly he looked, scurried about to make him comfortable. The children came running when they heard that Pan Doctor was there. One boy opened his mouth to show that he'd lost a tooth and asked for some coins. "No payment without the tooth," Korczak replied merrily.

After he had looked the children over and talked with them for a while, Maryna suggested that Korczak come to her room to rest and have tea. Once they were alone, she revealed that she was hiding three Jewish children. She had been able to take them because they spoke perfect Polish, but she had not confided the secret of their identity to the other children, lest they inadvertently reveal it.

Korczak didn't have to be told that life on this side of the wall was perilous, too: the Poles suffered shortages of food and fuel, and tens of thousands of them were rounded up each month for forced labor in Germany. Many of them had been killed by the Germans, including Jan Piecinski, a former *bursa* member, whom Maryna had been grooming to take over as director of the orphanage.

A few hours later when Korczak rose to leave in order to return to the ghetto before curfew, Maryna sent the caretaker, Wladyslaw Cichosz, to accompany him. As they walked along, Korczak asked him not to abandon Maryna and the children during the war (a request that Cichosz honored), and kissed him on the forehead when they were nearing the ghetto walls. Cichosz watched from a distance as the doctor disappeared through the gate.

Ten days after Korczak visited Bielany, Gestapo wall posters announced that any Jew leaving the ghetto without an official permit would be taken to the Jewish detention facility and shot. One week later, eight people caught trying to smuggle food into the ghetto from the Aryan side were given the death penalty. The Judenrat pleaded for mercy for the prisoners and a "legal trial." But at seven-thirty on the morning of November 17, the Germans ordered the Polish police to carry out the executions in the prison yard. Six of the "criminals" were women—one, a sixteen-year-old girl, asked God to regard her death as a sacrifice for her people so that no one else would have to die. Thousands of people outside the prison wall wept; the Polish police are reported to have wept, too, as they fired on command.

Despite what was happening in the ghetto, people clung to the hope that the war would soon end with the defeat of the Germans. Chaim Kaplan wrote in his diary that the Jews were waiting for that day with such anticipation that they wouldn't even commit suicide for fear of missing it. By mid-December there did seem to be reason for hope: after three months of sweeping through Russia, the Germans finally met resistance at the gates of Moscow; and America had entered the war against both Germany and Japan after the Japanese attack on Pearl Harbor on December 7. What was not yet known was that the Germans had just set up their first extermination camp in Chelmno, which would eliminate the need for guns such as those used to massacre the 34,000 Jews in Kiev, the 28,000 in Riga, and the 25,000 in Vilna during this period.

Hanukkah, the Festival of Lights, which fell on December 15, found the community once again deep in gloom after the execution of seventeen more victims caught smuggling. Because of Russian air raids, the quarter had to be kept dark; but even so, few had the price of Hanukkah candles or kerosene. Having spent the previous Hanukkah in Pawiak prison away from the children, Korczak wanted this one to be festive for them. The house hummed as the orphans made menorahs for the tables and presents for each other, and rehearsed one of the Hanukkah plays that Korczak had written years before. The holiday had a special meaning for Korczak: "an old man with a gray beard," he called it. He admired Judas Maccabaeus for his toughness in sending his sons on the daring mission to recapture the Temple from the Syrians, as well as for his shrewd ability to foresee victory. Korczak, too, would need a miracle: his meager supply of candles would have to last eight days.

In Korczak's play, *The Time Will Come,* the candle advises a brother and sister not to quarrel, because there is already too much conflict in the world: "One must begin the path to peace within one's own home. After that, the time will come when peace will prevail everywhere in the world." Each generation of Korczak's children had believed the candle's promise: "Though we still have a long road ahead of us, I will return to you next year."

A few days before the holiday, the children were surprised to see a garbage truck from the Aryan side pull up to the orphanage with presents for them concealed beneath the trash. The three garbagemen, contacted by the Polish underground, were delivering food and toys from Korczak's friends. On their way to the ghetto, they had even cut down a small pine tree as their own personal gift.

One of the men has described that day: "Korczak asked the children to gather round the tree, which he set up on a table in the middle of the room. Our parcels were lying under it. The children stood quietly, just staring. What surprised me was that they were not like children, but like smiling old people. Their eyes were full of sorrow, even though they were happy. I started to cry as we serenaded them with a Christmas carol: 'And God please give peace to people of good will.' "

The Poles explained to Korczak that, on the two days a week they were assigned to collect garbage inside the ghetto, they always smuggled in letters and food. Sometimes they were even able to smuggle people out. As they left, Korczak slipped them a postcard while shaking hands. They read it when they were back on the Aryan side: "The Jews will never forget their brothers and sisters on the other side of the wall."

That severe winter of 1941 brought yet another blow for the ghetto. The day after Christmas, notices were posted ordering the Jews to turn over to the Nazis via the Judenrat every scrap of fur they possessed. They had three days—the penalty was death.

"I would not care to be born a second time," Czerniakow had confided to his diary on his birthday the month before. Watching from his office window as thousands lined up in the freezing cold to hand over the only source of warmth they had, he may have wondered if he should have been born at all.

32

The Last Seder

On January 7, 1942, the *Jewish Gazette*, the only Polish-language paper allowed in the ghetto, printed a letter to the editor in response to an article that had praised the orphanage of Dr. Janusz Korczak: "The Orphans Home has never been, and never will be, Korczak's orphanage. That man is too small, too weak, too poor, and too dimwitted to gather almost two hundred children, house, clothe, and feed them, and give them training for life . . . This great task has been accomplished by the joint efforts of hundreds of good-willed people with enlightened minds and insight into the problems of the orphaned child . . . Wilcyznska, Pozowna, Korczak (if you need names) are merely the custodians of precious property." The letter was signed J. Korczak.

Once having caught the reader's attention, Korczak inserted his real message in the postscript: "In a Paris cemetery there is an impressive gravestone bearing the inscription 'To the memory of those who have left us.' On the initiative of our patrons, we are going to hold a memorial service for friends of the Orphans Home as well as former orphans and teachers who have passed away. We also invite you to a puppet show of charming tales narrated by Dr. Janusz Korczak on Saturday, January 10, at twelve noon at the Orphans Home, 9 Sliska Street. Tickets for both children and adults are available for two zlotys."

The following month, using the same ironic style, Korczak wrote a letter of application to the Judenrat, requesting the directorship of the public shelter that housed a thousand children at 39 Dzielna Street. He had joked with Czerniakow that he was spreading rumors about himself being a thief so that he would qualify for the job, which was now held by scoundrels who had turned the shelter into a "slaughterhouse and morgue." Describing himself in the application as an unbalanced, excitable scatterbrain who only by laboriously developed self-control was able to engage in teamwork, he listed his qualifications:

> I am sixty-four. As for my health, it passed the test in prison last year. Despite exacting conditions there, not once did I report sick, not once did I go to the doctor, not once did I absent myself from exercise in the yard, dreaded even by my younger colleagues. I eat like a horse, sleep soundly; recently, after drinking ten shots of vodka, I returned home at a brisk pace from Rymarska Street to Sienna—late at night. I get up twice during the night to empty ten large bedpans.
>
> I smoke, do not overindulge in liquor; for everyday purposes my mental faculties—passable.
>
> Experience has endowed me with a considerable ability to coexist and collaborate even with criminal types and born imbeciles. Ambitious, obstinate fools cross me off their visiting list—though I do not return the compliment. I anticipate that the criminal characters among the staff of the Dzielna Street orphanage will voluntarily resign from the hated work to which they are tied by cowardice and inertia alone.

The petitioner suggested a trial period of four weeks, which, because of the urgency, should start that week with a room and two meals daily. "By a room I mean a place to sleep; meals if there are any, and if not— I can do without." He signed the application: Goldszmit-Korczak. February 9, 1942.

Of course, the application was meant to be amusing—who on the Judenrat would refuse Janusz Korczak the thankless job of rescuing a thousand sickly orphans who were lying in filth and dying untended at the rate of ten and twelve a day? He was granted the position, but given only one thousand of the twenty thousand zlotys he requested for the institution.

As Korczak expected, the corrupt staff members at the Dzielna Street shelter did everything they could to frustrate him during the few days a week he spent there trying to prevent their siphoning off the provisions meant for the children. His efforts made him feel "all smeared, bloodstained, stinking. And crafty, since I am alive—I sleep, eat, occasionally joke." But it became impossible to joke when he realized that he could not save most of the orphans. In spite of his efforts to see that they got the provisions intended for them, the mortality rate was sixty percent. There was simply not enough food or medical supplies. He felt guilty about eating anything there, no matter how weak from hunger he might be. He wrote in his diary: "Long after the war, men will not be able to look each other in the eye without reading the question: How is it you happened to survive? How did you do it?"

He sought help everywhere.

Across the street from his own orphanage was a small relief station called A Drop of Milk, where starving mothers brought their babies. He often went there alone or with Stefa to talk to the director, Anna Margolis, and to observe how babies developed without sufficient milk or food. He presented his findings to a group of doctors studying the effects of hunger on child development, deriving some small and painful satisfaction from the thought that all this misery might at least contribute to medical knowledge. Because Margolis also worked as the head of the tuberculosis ward at the Children's Hospital, Korczak asked her if she could arrange admission for some of the children from Dzielna. She was able to allocate five beds, which he filled with the most serious cases of dysentery, pneumonia, and angina—all diseases directly related to starvation. One boy clutched his mandolin as he was carried into the ward; it was placed on a shelf above his bed, but he died before he could play it.

Every detail of the operations at the Dzielna Street orphanage came under Korczak's scrutiny. Noticing that the children's underwear never looked clean no matter how many times it was scrubbed, he prevailed on a Polish acquaintance, Witold Gora, who worked as a plumber and furnace man in a German laundry on Pawia Street, to do the clothes during his night break. Every week Korczak delivered a heavy bag of underwear to Gora's apartment, and every week Gora carried it secretly to the laundry and brought it back clean to his apartment. Gora offered to pick the clothes up at the shelter to save the doctor the trip to his place, but Korczak wouldn't hear of it. "You're taking a serious risk doing this for us," he said. "And, besides, carrying the bags is good for my health."

The "long, green Polish spring," which Korczak had always seen as a metaphor for renewal, was somewhere beyond the ghetto walls. Inside, everything green shriveled and died, as if even trees and grass could not survive the unnatural conditions. It was said that birds would not fly over the quarter. Rubinstein, the self-proclaimed jester of the Warsaw Ghetto, was silent. After recovering from typhus, he still stared wildly at everyone on the streets, but did not sing his inane ditties, as if knowing that his madness could no longer match the madness around him.

Meanwhile, the Nazis, like crazed city planners, continued to shrink the ghetto, lopping off one street here, dividing another down the middle there. If the Judenrat couldn't get the necessary brick walls up fast enough, the Germans made do with barbed wire on wooden fences.

"A beautiful hour of life" was promised everyone who received an invitation to the Passover seder at the Sliska Street orphanage on the first of April.

Many of the guests could remember the prewar seders on Krochmalna Street, a popular annual event for which as many as three hundred people competed to buy tickets. Not knowing Hebrew, Korczak always had one of the observant teachers conduct the service, but he would help the children dip their eggs and bitter herbs into salt water to remember the sadness of being slaves in Egypt. Never had the children waited more eagerly for soup than at those Passover seders, because Stefa would hide nuts in some of the matzoh balls. (The usual custom of hiding matzohs for children to find would have created bedlam in an orphanage.) The child who found a nut in his matzoh ball received a prize. But the best prize of all was the nut itself, which many orphans kept as a special treasure.

We don't know if there were nuts, or matzoh balls, or even soup at that last seder, but we have a report on its "charm" in an account written in the *Jewish Gazette* by one of the guests, Herman Czerwinski.

The long tables, covered with spotless tablecloths, were lit by the "beaming" faces of one hundred and eighty orphans, who were "not abandoned, but joined by the spirits of their mothers and fathers." Korczak sat at the head table with sixteen of the older choir members, who burst into a Zionist song whenever something in the Haggadah referred to Palestine. The seder guests were seated in the rear. When the youngest child asked: "And how is this night different from all other nights?" Korczak responded with a few words that "moved" everyone. After the service, "plates, mugs, bowls chimed. Women came with food from all directions. Joy reigned at this Passover celebration."

Czerwinski may have omitted Korczak's moving words about how that night differed from all others lest the Nazis read them. For the same reason, he may have felt it best not to report that, during the Haggadah reading, Korczak walked to the window and raised his fist, as if crying out to God in rage and despair to account for the suffering of his children.

Just before midnight on April 17 (which would come to be known as Bloody Friday), small contingents of SS, each guided by a German-speaking Jewish policeman, went about knocking on the doors of apartments throughout the ghetto. Each occupant was greeted politely with "Good evening," and asked to step outside for a moment. In the courtyard, he was placed against a wall and shot. His body was left where it fell, and the courteous death squad moved on to the next address on the list. If a victim's wife cried out or followed him down the stairs, her body was found in a pool of blood next to his.

The victims—lawyers, bakers, merchants, butchers, business people, former officials—seemingly bore no relationship to each other. How was the list drawn up? everyone asked fearfully. Who would be next? Only later was it learned that the murdered men had been putting out the illegal political bulletin *Das Blettl*, originated by the socialist Jewish Labor Bund.

Although Chairman Czerniakow was assured by the Gestapo that those not involved in underground activities did not have to fear for their own safety, two days later seven more men were shot down in the street, this time in broad daylight. After that, shots could be heard night and day in the ghetto. Again there were rumors that there would be deportations from Warsaw. In Lublin—it was said—forty thousand people had been sent away on freight cars, their destination unknown. People were terrified to leave their homes. They spoke in whispers, dreading a knock at the door.

33

The Ghetto Diary:
May 1942

*Are decent people in positions of leadership eternally con-
demned to Calvary?*

—*Ghetto Diary*

A few weeks after Bloody Friday, Janusz Korczak sat up in bed and
turned to the diary that he had begun shortly after the German occupation
of Warsaw and then abandoned.

"The month of May is cold this year," he wrote. "And tonight is the
quietest of all nights. It is five in the morning. The little ones are asleep.
There are actually two hundred of them. In the east wing—Madame Stefa,
and I in the west—in the so-called 'isolation ward.' "

His bed was in the middle of the room. Under it, the last drops of
the bottle of vodka he had been savoring; next to it, a night table with
black bread and a jug of water. All around were the beds of the sick
children: Monius the youngest (there were four with the same name),
Albert, and Jerzyk on one side; on the other, against the wall, Felunia,
Giena, and Haneczka. There was also the old tailor, Azrylewicz, Romcia's
grandfather, who was suffering from heart disease and kept Korczak awake
with his groans.

Almost every night, for what would be the last three months of his
life, Korczak would write while the children slept. His notations were
often no more than a terse shorthand. His body, now wasted from fatigue
and hunger, told him that death was near, but he did not yet suspect in
what form. As a Jewish doctor in a Catholic country, he had always
respected the "curative power of the whispered confession" to the priest,
and now he found himself yearning for "a confessor, an advisor, an understanding ear to hear his lament."

The diary he was keeping would serve those roles, and that of judge. It would not be a historical chronicle of life in the Warsaw Ghetto—like the diaries of Emmanuel Ringelblum, Chaim Kaplan, and Adam Czerniakow—but a subjective memoir of the journey inward that he had interrupted two years before. He felt responsible not to Jewish history but to his own history as a Polish Jew. On those lonely nights, when all of his personal furies became entangled with the very real furies outside, he would write of the terror of his father's madness, the fear of his own, and his regret that he had given up medical work in the Children's Hospital—"an ugly desertion." Only occasionally did his pen rest for a moment or two on some ghetto scene, illuminating that terrible world with a bright flare that would fade rapidly back into the stream of consciousness of his past. At one point he comments wryly: "Oh, yes, I almost forgot to mention there is a war going on."

The orphans commandeered some of the pages, just as they had the years of his life, springing up here and there with their coughs, their own diaries, their need for trees and flowers. Not until the carbide lamp stopped burning, or the pen ran dry, or his energy ran out did he stop. In the morning Henryk, an apprentice and the son of the old tailor, typed the pages, just as Walenty had in that other war.

An early entry reads:

It is half past six.

In the dormitory someone shouts:

"Boys, time for a bath, get up!"

I put away my pen. Should I get up or not? It is a long time since I have had a bath. Yesterday I killed a louse I found on myself without batting an eye—with one dexterous squeeze of the nail—a louse.

If I have time, I shall write a eulogy to a louse. For our attitude toward this fine insect is unjust and unfitting.

An embittered Russian peasant once declared: "A louse is not like a man, it will not suck up every last drop of blood."

For a few moments Korczak sat on his bed enjoying the "unforgettable sight of the dormitory coming awake." He was still fascinated by "a sleepy gaze, languid motions, or a sudden leaping out of bed." He watched as one child rubbed his eyes, another wiped the corners of his mouth with the sleeve of his nightshirt, and still another stroked his ear, stretched, or, holding an article of clothing in his hand, stared motionless into space.

The Old Doctor could still predict at a glance who would have a good or difficult day.

Before the "beehive began to hum," he would assess his strategy like a military commander: the calls to be made, letters to be written, supplies to be procured. Or he might review the day that had passed, with its victories and defeats.

Take Saturday, May 23, 1942.

It began with great excitement as the children lined up to be weighed. He noted on his graphs that though they were showing a steady decline, it was not yet alarming. Breakfast had been welcome, but in its own way it was work. The food reminded him of the struggle to get it on the table— the sausage, ham, and buns they had that week were the result of a "nasty" letter he had written to a dignitary. Not enough when divided among all the children, but something. True, there was that surprise in the form of two hundred kilograms of potatoes—"a real diplomatic victory"—but he couldn't rest on his laurels or relax his vigilance. The children were unaware of the history of each morsel they put into their mouths as he sat there, tortured, wondering: "Have I done right or wrong?"

After breakfast a meeting had been held to discuss which teachers could take a leave, and how to find substitutes. It would have been convenient to keep to last year's schedules, but too much had happened since then—too many newcomers and departures. "Things are—why keep on about it—different."

This being Saturday, everyone gathered for the reading of the orphanage newspaper and reports on the court trials. He was aware that the paper had lost its hold over the children, although the new ones were always interested. No one really cared any more who did well that week and who badly. (It was easier now to turn a blind eye to some problems— for example, to the fact that there was so much theft and unrest in the orphanage.) The older children knew that they would not learn from the paper the one thing they wanted to know: what was going to happen to them. They were listening for what he was not going to say. He didn't want to worry them—or to admit that even he could not be sure what the future held.

The gong sounded for lunch while he was brooding over his afternoon schedule. Three calls to be made. At the first house, an elderly supporter who had been ill was not at home; Korczak left his belated greetings with the family, embarrassed to have put off the visit for so long. The second appointment was for him to give an hour's lecture on yeast and nutrition at a nearby building. He heard himself droning on about the differences between brewer's and baker's, active and inactive, how long it should set, how much should be taken, how often, and the importance of vitamin B. But all the while he was thinking: How? Through whom? From where?

The third call was at a party welcoming some returnees from the East. The janitor pulled him aside at the entrance, extremely nervous that the Gestapo would investigate. "Help, Almighty! Don't let them question us!" Once inside, Korczak noted wryly that the guests were clearly relieved to have come back "from hell to this Warsaw paradise."

As he made his way home to the orphanage that day, Korczak noticed a scene that he would refer to a few times in his diary:

A young boy, still alive or perhaps dead already, is lying across the sidewalk. Three boys are playing horses and drivers there; their reins have become entangled. They are trying every which way to disentangle them. In their impatience they stumble over the boy lying on the ground. Finally one of them says: "Let's move on, he's getting in the way!" They gallop a few steps away and continue to struggle with the reins.

Sunday at dawn, he lay in bed thinking of the letters to be written and the seven calls to be made. But he did not stir. His will had kept him going until then, but now his body would no longer obey. He tried not to notice the odors in the room: the smell of ammonia from the urine in the chamber pots he rinsed now only every other day was mixed with the garlic stench of carbide from the lamp. There was also the occasional odor of one of his seven roommates. Bedbugs, those "infrequent enemies," were back, and now there were moths to contend with.

He lay there thinking: "To get up is to sit on the bed, reach for my underpants, button up, if not all the buttons, then at least one. Struggle into my shirt. Bend down to put on my socks. The suspenders . . ."

With great effort he forced himself to dress, to get on his way. He ignored his persistent cough, the sharp tooth cutting into his tongue. He forced his legs to step from the sidewalk down to the street, and then to climb up again. When someone accidentally pushed him, he staggered to one side and leaned against the wall. Now it was no longer his body but his will that was collapsing. He felt like "a sleepwalker—a morphine addict." For a moment he couldn't remember where he was going. And when he reached the building, he had to stop on the stairs: "What did I come to see him about?"

It had been happening a lot lately. He was perceiving things through a haze, only dimly aware of the revolting scenes all around him, of hearing things that should shock him. He could easily have postponed or canceled any of these meetings:

A shrug. It's all the same to me.

Indolence. Poverty of feeling, that eternal Jewish resignation. So what? And what's next?

What if my tongue is sore? What if someone has been shot? He already knew he must die. And what next? Surely you cannot die more than once.

He realized that he was not the only one experiencing a sense of unreality when he overheard a shopkeeper respond to a customer's complaint: "My good woman—these are not goods, and this is not a store, you are not a customer, nor I a vendor. I don't sell to you, nor do you pay me, because these scraps of paper are not money. You don't lose, and I don't profit. Who would bother to cheat nowadays—for what? Only one's got to do something. Well, am I not right?"

On another occasion, the proprietress of a butcher shop was too numbed to respond to Korczak's black humor: "Tell me, dear lady, is it possible that this sausage is made from human flesh? It's too cheap for horsemeat."

"How should I know?" she replied. "I wasn't there when it was being made."

Sometimes, when he was stirred by something like a chance meeting with someone he had not seen in years, he was relieved to know that he could still experience a clear emotion. But in the ravished features of that friend he could read how different he himself must appear from the person he had been.

He was utterly exhausted when he returned to the orphanage at midday, sometimes having nothing more for all his trouble than fifty zlotys, and a promise from someone else of five zlotys a month. "To provide for two hundred people." After lunch he would throw himself on the bed with his clothes on, to rest for two hours. When the vodka was gone, five shots of raw alcohol mixed with an equal amount of water, with a little candy for sweetener, gave him "inspiration," a blissful feeling of weariness without the pain of aching leg muscles, sore eyes, and the burning in his scrotum. He felt "content, calm, and safe." Occasionally someone might burst into the room and, seeing him stretched out there, withdraw. Or the "tranquility" might be disturbed by Stefa coming in with a "piece of news, a problem, a desperate decision."

As a doctor, Korczak was well aware that his fatigue and apathy were symptoms of malnutrition from subsisting on eight hundred calories a day. But the doctor who tried to fall asleep at night was also a hungry man. He had never cared about food in the past, but now he lay there conjuring up dishes that he could eat without the slightest difficulty: succulent raspberries from his Aunt Magda's garden, the buckwheat groats his father liked, the tripe he had savored in Kiev, the kidneys he ate in Paris, the vinegar-soaked dishes he had in Palestine. For something really soothing, he imagined champagne (which he'd drunk only three times in his life) with dry biscuits like the ones he had when he was ill as a child. Then there was the ice cream that his mother had forbidden him to have, and red wine.

Sometimes he planned a menu:

> Perhaps fish with tartar sauce?
> A Wiener schnitzel?
> Pâté, rabbit marinated in Malaga with red cabbage?
> No! A thousand times no!
> Why?
> Odd: eating is work, and I am tired.

To take on more than was humanly possible was Korczak's way of spiritual resistance. He held to his principle that if he kept the order of his house, the ritual of his day, he would succeed. Perhaps the war would end, and the Germans would be defeated. Until then, the fact that his children were well and active, did not get typhus or tuberculosis, that the orphanage did not have to be disinfected, was a point for life against death, for good against evil.

When there weren't enough helpers to investigate applications of children for admission to the orphanage, he did it himself.

At 57 Smocza Street he found a mother stretched out on the couch, dying of an ulcerated intestine, while her young son was out scrounging for food.

"He's a good boy," a neighbor told Korczak. "But I don't know if he'll be willing to go to an institution before his mother dies."

"And I can't die before he is settled somewhere," the mother said. "Such a wonderful child. He tells me not to sleep in the daytime so I'll be able to sleep at night. And at night he says: 'What are you moaning for, that won't help. You'd better go to sleep.' "

On Thursdays, when the admissions committee met to review the new applicants, Korczak was dimly aware that others were experiencing the same sense of detachment that he felt—even Stefa, who could still express her worry that refusing a child was sentencing him to certain death. The continuity of the discussion was easily broken. Someone had only to interrupt with a remark, and they'd all go off on a tangent:

> What was it we were talking about?
> Someone says: Firstly . . .
> You wait in vain for: Secondly.
> Of course, some of us are long-winded, anyway.
> There is a motion:
> The child should be admitted.
> Recorded: Admit. We ought to pass on to the next application. No. Not one but three speakers support the motion. At times it is necessary to intervene more than once.
> The discussions keep on skidding like a car out of control.
> Wearing, irritating.
> Enough!

Many of the children who were admitted, like nine-year-old Giena, were full orphans. But even Giena, who had only her seventeen-year-old brother Samuel, might not have been accepted if her brother hadn't been lucky enough to know someone who knew Stefa.

Giena had been a clever, happy child before the war. She was very close to her mother, whose long, narrow face and dark eyes she had inherited. Her father, a chemist, had worked for a factory that was closed by the Germans when they took over Warsaw, and died shortly afterwards of tuberculosis. Within a year, her older sister and mother were dead of typhus.

Before she died, the mother had told Samuel to take care of Giena, and for a while he did the best he could. During the day, while he went to work in a furniture factory, he left her with an aunt whose family shared their apartment. But before long his aunt began to complain that she had too many mouths to feed, that he would have to make other arrangements for Giena. By chance, Samuel had made friends with the wife of Abraham

Gepner—an influential member of the Judenrat and a former philan-thropist of the Orphans Home—when he went to their apartment with Hashomer Hatzair material. She invited him for lunch there once a week. Learning of his problem in caring for his sister, she offered to speak to Stefa about taking her.

When Stefa saw the gaunt child, her grief-stricken dark eyes sunken into her face, her hand clutching her brother's, she couldn't help em-bracing Giena. She assured Samuel that Giena would thrive at the or-phanage, where she'd have playmates and a regular routine. Giena clung to her brother as he left, and cried and had nightmares for weeks. But then she adjusted to her new home and made friends. She was especially close to Stefa but seldom saw Korczak, who was out most of the day.

Every Saturday, Samuel came to visit Giena, bringing some little present or food. Sometimes they'd walk through the ghetto back to his room, and once she even invited another girl to join them. He noticed that she was developing both mentally and physically that year, was more serious and better dressed than the other ghetto children. She told him about her friends, the games they played. And she wanted to hear about him—she was worried because he looked thin. How was his work going? Occasionally they talked about what it would be like after the war. She didn't understand the danger, but sensed that people did not have too much hope. "If we are still alive," she would preface her remarks, as if it were natural for a child to use such a qualification for future plans.

Time, like everything else in the ghetto, had run amok. The past was intruding into the present. The only public transportation now was horse-drawn trams like those Korczak had ridden in his youth. Carriages and automobiles had been replaced by pedicabs—bicycles with small seats attached for passengers.

At first Korczak had avoided the pedicabs, which reminded him of the rickshaws he'd seen in Harbin during the Russo–Japanese War. He had used a rickshaw only once, and then under orders. He knew that an emaciated pedicab man could not live more than three years—a strong one, perhaps five. But as it became more difficult for him to get around on his swollen legs, he began to rationalize: "One must help the pedicab men make a living. Better I than two fat profiteers with packages in the bargain." He never got over his discomfort when he tried to pick out the healthier, stronger-looking ones, and hated himself for his "noble superiority" when he gave them fifty groszy extra. Unlike the "quarrelsome, noisy, and spiteful" droshky drivers of prewar days, the pedicab men were "gentle and quiet, like horses or oxen."

Four months after taking over the directorship of the Dzielna Street orphanage, Korczak was still struggling with the staff. He incurred everyone's "shock and disgust" by pointedly shaking hands with the charwoman while she was scrubbing the stairs, and frequently "forgetting" to shake hands with them. No matter how much they hated each other, when it came to a vote on anything he wanted, they closed ranks against him. Their implicit message: Don't meddle in our affairs. You're a stranger, an enemy. Even if you suggest something useful, it won't work, and will ultimately do more harm than good.

They proved formidable opponents, going so far as to inform the Gestapo that Janusz Korczak had not reported a case of typhus—a crime that carried the death penalty. He had to rush around to high contacts to clear himself. When one of the devoted nurses, Miss Wittlin, died of tuberculosis during that period, he reflected that "the salt of the earth dissolves—the manure remains."

One day in late May, Korczak had to collect a donation at No. 1 Gryzbowska, the last building before the ghetto wall. A Jewish policeman had been killed there by the Germans only the day before while signaling to smugglers. "That's not a place for wholesale business," a neighbor commented. The stores were closed. People were scared.

Just as Korczak was about to enter the building, he was stopped by the janitor's assistant.

"Pan Doctor, don't you remember me?"

Korczak paused—his visual recall, always poor, was almost nonexistent those days. "Wait, of course, Bula Szulc."

"You do remember . . ."

"Ah, only too well. Come over here and tell me about yourself."

They sat down on the steps of the All Saints Church, which served the converts in the ghetto.

"Szulc is forty by now," Korczak was thinking. "Not long ago, he was ten." Like so many others on this street, he was engaged in smuggling.

"I have a child," Szulc said proudly. "Come and have some cabbage soup with us. You can see him."

"I'm tired. I'm just on my way home."

As they sat there talking for about half an hour, Korczak was aware of the "discreet glances" of the "shocked" Catholic converts who recognized him. Critical as they were of Jews—the converts, though themselves forced to wear armbands, were known to be anti-Semitic—he could imagine what they were thinking: "There's Korczak sitting on the church steps in broad daylight with a smuggler. The children must need money badly. But why so openly and, however you look at it, shamelessly? It's a provocation. What would the Germans think if they saw this? Yes, the Jews are brazen and irritating."

Meanwhile, Szulc was bragging about how well he could feed his child.

"In the morning he has half a pint of milk, a roll and butter. That costs a pretty penny."

"Why do you do it?"

"So he'll know he has a father."

"Is he a rascal?"

"Why not? He's my son."

"And your wife?"

"A wonderful woman."

"Do you quarrel?"

"We've been together five years and I haven't raised my voice to her once."

"Do you still remember us?"

A trace of a smile passed over Szulc's face. "I think about the Orphans Home often. Sometimes I dream of you and Miss Stefa."

"Why didn't you ever visit during all those years?"

"When I was well off, I had no time. When I was down and out, how could I come—ragged and dirty?"

Szulc helped Korczak to his feet. As they kissed heartily, Korczak was thinking: "He's too honest for a crook. Perhaps the orphanage sowed some good seed in him, or trimmed something down."

The following day most of "the Thirteen" were liquidated. The reasons were never clear. One Gestapo unit was believed to be wiping out the agents of its rival; somehow Gancwajch escaped. Smugglers like Szulc would be targeted the following month.

34

Strange

Happenings

It was the beginning of what Zylberberg would call "that dreadful summer." There were children in the ghetto who could not remember ever having seen a tree or a flower. On the rare occasions when Korczak's Christian friends were able to send emissaries to find out what he needed, he always requested plants. "The children need something to be absorbed in," he would explain. "Taking care of geranium or petunia seedlings will help them forget their troubles."

For Korczak, nature was a spiritual as well as a physical restorative. When the orphans began pining for the good old days at summer camp, he thought of the patch of green he had noticed in the garden of the All Saints Church while he sat on the steps with Szulc. Deciding that the priest might respond to an appeal from children to play there, he helped little Sami compose a letter—a poignant document that might well have been drafted by King Matt:

We kindly request the Reverend Father to grant us permission to come a few times to the church garden on Saturday mornings, early if possible (6:30–10 a.m.).

We long for a little air and greenery. It is stuffy and crowded where we are. We want to get to know and make friends with nature.

We shall not damage the plants.

Please don't refuse us.

Zygmus, Sami, Abrasha, Hanka, Aronek

The priest, Marceli Godlewski, an outspoken anti-Semite before the war, had once told Korczak: "We are a weak lot. For a glass of vodka, we sell ourselves into Jewish bondage." After the German occupation, he had a change of heart: he helped the converts who belonged to his church—which was just inside the ghetto border—and did what he could to assist Jews. There is no record as to how he responded to the children's request.

Although Korczak and Czerniakow do not mention it in their diaries, these two men (whose friendship had grown out of their work in children's welfare in prewar days) must have discussed the need for all children to have some special place in which to let out pent-up emotions. And what is such a place but a playground? In May of 1942 the Chairman announced, with the same formality with which he disclosed programs for food and other means of survival, that the Judenrat would create a few small playgrounds where children could swing, slide, and do whatever children need to do. The first play area was constructed on a lot next to a bombed-out house on Grzybowska Street, across from Czerniakow's office window. The work detail, made up of teachers, factory owners, cattle dealers, and businessmen—all of them recently deported from Germany—planted grass and built swings and slides with dedication and care. Sometimes Czerniakow had cigarettes distributed during their breaks; he confided to his fellow Council members that he wished the Polish Jews worked with such efficiency.

Korczak was among the five hundred dignitaries who were invited to the opening ceremony at 9:30 on the morning of June 7. Members of the Judenrat were seated in an official box. Korczak sat with Zylberberg and the other guests in the warm sun listening to the background music of the Jewish police band while they waited for the proceedings to begin. Suddenly the band stopped; there was a hush. All eyes turned to the entrance of the playground, where Adam Czerniakow appeared in a white tropical suit and white pith helmet; everyone stood as the band broke into "Hatikvah" and the police escorted the Chairman and his wife to their seats. "What do you think of our king?" Korczak whispered to Zylberberg. "Not a bad performance."

In his impassioned speech, which interpreters rendered from the Polish into Yiddish and Hebrew, Czerniakow urged everyone to make sure that the children survived those tragic times. Life might be hard, he said, but they couldn't give up—they had to keep planning and working. This was just the beginning: he was going to create playgrounds throughout the ghetto. Not only that, he was going to open a training institute for teachers and a ballet school for girls.

When he finished, the band broke into a march and groups of school children and their teachers filed past the grandstand. Following the singing, dancing, and gymnastics display, the children were handed little bags of molasses candy made in the ghetto. "The ceremony made a great impression on those present," the Chairman reported in his diary. "Balm for the wounds. The street is smiling!"

Czerniakow also attempted to improve the deplorable conditions of thousands of young smugglers caught by the Germans and thrown into the overcrowded juvenile detention center. When the Chairman arranged for some of them to be brought to the playground, he was appalled to see that these so-called criminals, as the Nazis called them, were "living skeletons from the ranks of street beggars." Inviting a few up to his office, he was deeply moved to have "eight-year-old citizens" speak to him like grownups. He gave each a chocolate bar and a bowl of soup. After they left, he wept as he had not done in a long time. But "one cannot wind one's watch with tears"—as he often said, quoting Dickens. He quickly pulled himself together, and resumed his work.

Czerniakow wasn't disturbed that he was criticized for devoting so much energy to playgrounds at such a grim time. He could even joke about Jewish optimism: "Two Jews were standing in the shadow of the gallows. 'The situation is not hopeless,' one said, 'they have no bullets.'" But if he needed to believe that the situation wasn't completely hopeless, Czerniakow didn't deceive himself that it was good. He could identify with the ship captain in a film he had seen: "As the ship goes down, the captain, determined to keep up the spirits of his passengers, orders the orchestra to play jazz. I have made up my mind to emulate the captain."

There were periods—such as those first two weeks in June—when Korczak could not will his arm to pick up a pencil or pen to make a diary entry. He told himself that it was because Henryk was too ill to do the typing, although he knew there were others who could take his place. On the nights when he had the energy to write, the hours passed quickly. One minute it was midnight, the next it was three in the morning. Occasionally he was interrupted by a child's cry. When Mendelek had a bad dream, Korczak carried the boy over to his bed and soothed him until he fell back to sleep. By the orphanage genealogy, Mendelek, the son of one of his orphans, was his "grandson."

Korczak had his own "ghastly" dreams.

One night: "The Germans, and I without an armband after curfew in Praga [the right bank of Warsaw]. I woke up. And another dream. On a train I am being moved, a meter at a time, into a compartment where there are already several Jews. Some had died that night. Bodies of dead children. One dead child in a bucket. Another one, skinned, lying on a plank in a mortuary, clearly still breathing."

The second dream had no doubt been influenced by the persistent rumors that the Lublin Jews who had been taken away by train had been massacred. How like his own orphans those skinned children must have seemed—virtually everything having been stripped away from them, and yet still alive and breathing—and how strong his unexpressed fears must have been that such a fate awaited them.

That same night he had a third dream, about his father, which reveals his own hungers underneath his fierce commitment to nurturing the children. "I am standing high up on a wobbly ladder, and my father keeps pushing a piece of cake into my mouth, a big one with sugar frosting and raisins. Any crumbs that fall from my mouth, he stuffs into his pocket."

He woke up in a sweat after all the dreams. "Isn't death such an awakening, at a point when there is no apparent way out?" he asked his diary. And then, with bitter humor: "Every man can surely find five minutes in which to die—I read somewhere."

If he didn't try to interpret those dreams in which he was rendered helpless to save either himself or his children, neither did he let them interfere with his daily struggle to resist the Germans and keep his children alive. And he still had his "daydreams" of omnipotence to turn to for power—power to transcend reality and soar over the ghetto wall. Those daydreams, which he had been developing for decades in his notebook labeled *Strange Happenings,* were now filled with maniacal fantasies about subduing a maniacal enemy:

I invented a machine that resembled a microscope. (I even made a detailed design of the whole complicated mechanism.) The scale—100. If I turned the micrometer dial to 99, everything that did not contain at least one percent of humanity would die. The amount of work was unbelievable. I had to determine how many people (living beings) would go out of circulation each time, who would take their place, and what would be the nature of this purged new world. After a year's deliberation (at night, of course), I got halfway through the distillation. Now the only people left were half-animal. All the others had perished. How minutely, to the last detail, I planned everything—the best proof being that I, myself, was completely excluded from this peculiar system. By a mere turn of the micrometer dial of my microscope, I could have taken my own life. What then?

On reading over Part One of his diary at the end of June, Korczak was dismayed by its incoherence. It lacked the literary skill on which he had always prided himself. Although he was aware that "in reminiscing we lie unconsciously," he worried that if he couldn't make sense of what he had written, no one else could. Was the problem in him, or in the autobiographical genre itself? "Is it possible to comprehend someone else's memoirs, someone else's life? For that matter, is it possible to understand one's own remembrances?"

He thought of trying to write the second part of the diary in the form of letters to his sister. But he got no further than "My dear . . ." because he recalled that the letter he had just written in response to hers had come out "cold, strange, and detached." A "great and painful misunderstanding," which he did not elucidate, had come between them.

Anna, who remains a shadowy figure, seems not to have been living in the ghetto at that time. Her letter had accused him of making social calls and bribing the police. He, in turn, felt hurt and misunderstood. "I don't make social calls. I go to beg for money, food supplies, information, a lead," he wrote, as if to her, in the diary. "It's arduous, degrading work. In my humble opinion, I carry out my duties to the best of my ability. I never refuse anyone if I can help it. The charge about bribing the police is unjust."

Perhaps to regain her sympathy, he confided: "Reading as a form of relaxation has begun to fail me. A dangerous symptom. I am distracted, and that in itself worries me. I don't want to sink into idiocy."

The children, as always, had the power to restore him. The day after brooding about the incoherence of his diary, Korczak tried working on it in a classroom in the orphanage. He was transported by the earnestness of the two groups of students who had voluntarily given up games, entertaining books, and chats with friends to study Hebrew.

"So. *Da* in Russian, *Oui* in French, *Yes* in English, *Ken* in Hebrew," he told the diary. "Enough to fill, not one lifetime, but three."

35

The Post Office

The first of July would go down in history as the Night of Slaughter, but it was no worse than the nights that followed as smugglers were gunned down along the walls, on the streets, in the courtyards and apartment houses. The slaughter continued through the first half of July until it seemed there could not be a smuggler left alive. The acute food shortage, especially of bread, suggested that probability; smugglers had been the lifeline supplying the ghetto with basic necessities, and that line was now severed.

Shortly after the Night of Slaughter, Korczak recorded his last daydream in *Strange Happenings*. He dedicated it to one of the youngest boys in the orphanage, Szymonek Jakubowicz. If ever he needed superhuman power to save Szymonek and the other children, it was now. And so he created an auxiliary planet, called Ro, as a refuge. The astronomer who lived on it, Professor Zi, could do what the Old Doctor only dreamed of: convert heat radiation into moral power on his "astropsychomicrometer." This original contraption was a cross between a telescope and a radio—but instead of music or war communiqués, it transmitted spiritual rays. It was so advanced that it could even project pictures onto a screen and record vibrations like a seismograph.

Professor Zi could bestow order and tranquillity everywhere except—and this was his great sorrow—on "that restless spark, Planet Earth." As he sat in his laboratory brooding about the disquiet and disorder down there, he wondered "Should one put an end to this senseless, bloody game?" Earthlings were clearly incapable of finding joy in what they had or of working harmoniously in a collective effort. But to interfere would be to force them onto a road for which they were not sufficiently mature and toward a goal beyond their comprehension. To treat them like slaves, or to coerce them through violence, would be to behave as they did with each other.

Professor Zi closed his eyes and sighed. He could see what the earthlings could not—that the space above them was filled with blue, with the fragrance of the lily of the valley, the sweetness of wine, and the gentle purity of winged flickerings.

"Planet Earth is still young," he reminded himself. "And all beginnings require a painful effort."

Life went on as usual in the orphanage. The first Monday night in July, from eight to nine, Korczak gave his customary seminar, telling friends who asked to attend: "Anyone who wishes to come is welcome, as long as he doesn't interrupt. We provide food for the spirit, the only food we have."

He offered his students a rich menu to choose from:

1. The emancipation of women
2. Heredity
3. Loneliness
4. Napoleon
5. What is duty?
6. The medical profession
7. [Henri] Amiel's memoirs
8. Reminiscences of a doctor
9. London
10. Mendel
11. Leonardo da Vinci
12. [Jean Henri] Fabre
13. The senses and the mind
14. The genius and his environment (mutual impact)
15. The Encyclopedists
16. How different writers worked
17. Nationality. Nation. Cosmopolitanism
18. Symbiosis

19. Evil and malice
20. Freedom. Destiny and free will

Such a cerebral feast may have satisfied adult palates, but it had become increasingly difficult to entice the children with anything. Beneath their relatively normal appearance "lurked weariness, discouragement, anger, mutiny, mistrust, resentment, longing." The orphanage had turned into a "home for the aged" or a "sanatorium for rich, capricious patients attached to their ailments." Preoccupied with their temperatures, the children asked every morning: "What's mine today?" or "What's yours?" They competed to see who felt the worst, or had the worst night. When Leon fainted for the first time in his life, he became completely absorbed in trying to figure out the cause.

Korczak encouraged all the orphans to keep a diary like his, hoping it would help them master their feelings. He let them read his in return for reading theirs—it was a matter of mutual respect. "I share mine with them as an equal," he told his diary. "Our common experiences—theirs and mine. Mine more diluted, watered down, otherwise the same."

Yet the seriousness of their diaries hurt him. Marcel vowed to give fifteen groszy to the poor in thanks for the penknife he had found. Szlama wrote about a widow who sat home weeping as she waited for her smuggler son to bring something home from across the wall; she did not know that a German policeman "had shot him dead." Simon wrote: "My father fought every day to put bread on the table. Even though he was always busy, he loved me." Mietek wanted a binding for the prayer book that his dead brother had received from Palestine for his bar mitzvah. Sami bought some nails for twenty groszy and was counting his future expenses. Jakob had written a poem about Moses. Abus wrote: "If I sit a bit longer on the toilet, someone says I'm selfish. And I want to be liked by others."

Korczak could sympathize with Abus after suffering the same humiliation at Pawiak. Here was one problem he could try to remedy, while at the same time solving the fly problem that plagued them. He announced that he had fixed a toilet-fee scale:

1. For number one—catch five flies.
2. For number two, second class (a bucket-stool-with-a-hole combination)—ten flies.
3. First class (a toilet seat)—fifteen flies.

When one of the boys asked, "May I catch the flies later? I can't wait," another responded, "You go on and do it, I'll catch them for you."

"Does it count if a fly is hit but gets away?" another wanted to know.

Not only were the children getting rid of the flies (each one caught in the infirmary counted for two), but they were showing "the mighty force of community goodwill."

He knew he had to offer the children something more than diaries and fly-swatting to help them transcend their present suffering—something with which they could identify and take comfort. He found the solution in a play called *The Post Office* by the Indian poet and philosopher Rabindranath Tagore. The text, about a dying child named Amal, an orphan whose nature was so pure that he enriched the lives of those who came in contact with him, could have been written by Korczak himself, so close was it to his style of fantasy and his feeling for children.

Esterka Winogron, formerly a student of natural science at Warsaw University and now in the *bursa*, volunteered to direct the play. She was one of Korczak's favorites, having impressed him with her seriousness as she assisted him on his medical rounds of the orphanage. Auditions were held. The lead part of Amal was given to Abrasha, a popular boy who played the violin. Three weeks of rehearsals were scheduled, and the performance date set for Saturday, July 18.

One afternoon, while the children were improvising makeshift sets and costumes, Nina Krzywicka, a Christian friend of Stefa's brother, stopped by the orphanage on her way to deliver food packages to her Jewish husband, who had chosen to live in the ghetto. She had also brought a little something for Stefa, although she knew of her aversion to receiving gifts. Trying to engage Stefa in conversation, Nina remembered the difficulties she'd had in the past: Stefa's answers were always direct and simple, and her questions concrete; only when she spoke about her brother Stash did she become animated. She told Nina that she was concerned because she hadn't had any word from him for a long time. While they were chatting, Korczak ran out the door to scream at the employees of a neighboring restaurant who were disposing of bags of garbage in front of the orphanage. His face was beet red, his language vulgar. Embarrassed at seeing him in such a state, Nina left hastily.

When she stopped by a week later, Nina was relieved to find Stefa smiling as she helped the children with last-minute details, yet she noticed this time how gray and wrinkled she had become. Korczak wandered over cordially to invite Nina to the play. He, too, looked old and tired—only his eyes were alive. As soon as he was out of earshot, Stefa said: "The doctor doesn't feel very well. I'm worried about him." Her tone of voice made Nina realize how much Korczak meant to her.

The night before the play, disaster struck in the form of mass food poisoning that spread through the house. Korczak and Stefa stumbled about in near darkness with medicine for headaches and jugs of limewater for those who were vomiting and moaning with pain. The staff members were offered morphine—"sparingly."

The boy whose mother had not wanted to die until he agreed to enter the orphanage became so hysterical that Korczak had to administer an injection of caffeine. Inconsolable ever since his mother's death, which had occurred shortly after he arrived at the home, the boy had exhibited bizarre behavior that Korczak interpreted as "pangs of conscience"; now, almost as if he were mimicking his mother's ordeal, the boy screamed, moaned, complained of pain, of feeling hot, of dying of thirst.

Korczak paced the dormitory, afraid that this newcomer would make all the children hysterical. Although he knew that he should remain calm himself, he began shouting at the boy, even threatening to throw him out on the staircase if he didn't quiet down. "The decisive factor: he shouts; therefore, he is in command," he wrote sardonically in his diary.

He kept careful records of all gastric upsets. That one night alone, the boys lost eighty kilograms among them; the girls somewhat less—sixty kilograms. He suspected the inoculation against dysentery that he had given them five days before, or the ground pepper that was added to the stale eggs in that night's dinner. "Not that much was needed to precipitate a disaster," he noted next to the statistics.

Somehow the children were able to recover and pull themselves together in time for the performance at 4:30 the next afternoon. The large room on the first floor of the orphanage was filled with friends and colleagues intrigued by the invitations written in Korczak's unique style:

We are not in the habit of promising anything we cannot deliver. We believe that an hour's performance of an enchanting tale by one who is both a philosopher and a poet will provide an experience—of the highest order of sensibility.

Appended to the invitation, with which admission was free, were a few words by Korczak's friend, the young poet Wladyslaw Szlengel, who would gain posthumous fame after his death in the Ghetto Uprising:

It transcends the test—being a mirror of the soul.

It transcends emotion—being an experience.

It transcends mere acting—being the work of children.

The audience was riveted by the play. Amal, a gentle, imaginative boy who has been adopted by a poor couple, is confined to his room with a serious illness. Forbidden by the village doctor to go outside, he is shut in from the world of nature, like the orphans there on Sienna Street, awaiting an uncertain future. He longs to fly with time to that land which no one knows—a land, he is told by the Watchman, to which a doctor, greater than the one he has now, will lead him by the hand.

Amal believes the Village Headman when he pretends to read the letter from the King, who promises to arrive soon with the greatest doctor in the land. No one is more surprised than the Headman and Amal's adoptive father when the King's doctor suddenly appears in the darkened room. "What's this? How close it is in here!" the doctor exclaims. "Open wide all the doors and windows!"

With the shutters open and the night breeze streaming in, Amal declares that all his pain has disappeared, that he can see the stars twinkling on the other side of the darkness. He falls asleep waiting for the arrival of the King himself, as the doctor sits by his bed in the starlight. To Amal's friend Sudah, the flower girl, who stops by and asks when he will awaken, the doctor replies: "As soon as the King comes and calls him."

It was clear from the hushed silence at the end of the play that Korczak had succeeded in providing the adults as well as the children with a sense of liberation from their present lives. Whether one believed that the King whom Amal awaited was Death or the Messiah, or that Death was the Messiah (as Isaac Bashevis Singer would write in one of his novels), everyone felt momentarily lifted to some realm not only beyond the walls of the ghetto but beyond life itself.

Asked why he chose that play, Korczak is reported to have said that he wanted to help the children accept death. In his diary he makes only a short notation about the afternoon: "Applause, handshakes, smiles, efforts at cordial conversation. (The chairwoman looked through the house after the performance and announced that though we are cramped, that genius Korczak has demonstrated that he can work miracles even in a rat hole.)" Then he added: "That is why others have been allotted palaces."

The children had seemed so natural in their parts that he wondered what would happen if they were to continue in their roles the next day: If Jerzyk were to imagine he really was a fakir, Chaimek a real doctor, and Adek the lord mayor? "Perhaps illusions would be a good subject for Wednesday's dormitory talk," he wrote. "Illusions, their role in the life of mankind." Then, having pondered illusions, he set off for reality—the Dzielna Street orphanage.

A few hours before *The Post Office* was performed in Korczak's orphanage that Saturday, July 18, Chairman Czerniakow wrote in his diary: "A day full of foreboding. Rumors that the deportations will start on Monday evening." Czerniakow had been dutifully recording the expulsions by train from other ghettos, but he did not speculate on where the trains had gone. (There was no organized Jewish intelligence network to verify rumors of the shooting of old people and children, or the gassing of thousands in camps called Belzec and Sobibor outside of Lublin.) When he noted that he had been ordered to send workers to build a "labor camp" outside the village of Treblinka, sixty miles to the north, he treated it as a routine operation. Wanting to believe that he could avert disaster in the ghetto if he did what was asked of him, he complied with the German demands as best he could, while building for the future with the opening of each new playground.

Korczak could no longer find comfort in his daydreams. He woke each day to find himself in "the district of the damned." For the last few weeks he had been busy on a new scenario he titled "Euthanasia." "The right to kill as an act of mercy belongs to him who loves and suffers— and to do away with himself if he no longer wants to stay alive," he wrote. "It will be this way in a few years."

More than once "during the dark hours," Korczak had "pondered the killing (putting to sleep) of infants and old people in the ghetto." But he had abandoned the thought as "the murder of the sick and feeble, as the assassination of innocents." Medicine was still about dispensing life— not death. He recalled a nurse from a cancer ward telling him that she used to place a lethal dose of medicine by the bedside of her patients with the veiled message that if they took more than one spoonful, it would act as poison. Not a single patient had ever reached for that fatal dose.

And yet people in the ghetto took their own lives all the time, jumping from windows and slitting their wrists. The widow who had lived in the Zylberbergs' kitchen on Chlodna Street had swallowed pills, and he knew of couples who gave their parents poison to end their misery. What was needed was an acceptable system that gave one control over one's own destiny when life had lost its meaning: a plan that gave everyone the legal right to apply for death.

Endless details had to be considered in working out the rules for the Death Application: the medical examination, consultation with a psychologist, perhaps a confession, perhaps psychoanalysis, the location where death would occur. Then, too, there had to be rules for how and when death was to be administered: while asleep, in a glass of wine, while dancing, to the accompaniment of music, suddenly and unexpectedly.

Finally the moment arrived when the applicant was told: "Proceed to this or that place. There you will receive the death you applied for." Korczak couldn't decide whether there should be a rule enforcing the procedure if the person changed his mind. Should he say, "The death sentence must be carried out in one month, even against your will. You have signed an agreement, a contract with an organization, a deal with temporal life. So much the worse for you if you recant too late."

He was "not joking," in spite of the sometimes absurd tone of the plan. Although he meant to keep it within the confines of ironic speculation, the euthanasia project threatened to veer out of control. Memories of his mad father, of the unconsummated double suicide pact with his sister, and of the unpublished novel *Suicide* that he wrote at seventeen kept surfacing.

"So I am the son of a madman," he writes in this final confession. "A hereditary affliction. More than twoscore years have gone by, and to this day the thought is at times a torment to me. But I am too fond of my idiosyncrasies not to be afraid that someone may try to treat me against my will."

He took a week's break from the diary—from madness itself. But he returned to thoughts of euthanasia again and again as the events that followed threatened to drive him over the edge.

Rumors that forty railroad cars were ready and waiting to deport everyone from the ghetto caused a new wave of panic. Chairman Czerniakow drove through the streets of the entire quarter and visited three playgrounds in an effort to calm the population. "What it costs me they do not see," he wrote in his diary on July 19. "Today I took two headache powders, another pain reliever, and a sedative, but my head is still splitting. I am trying not to let the smile leave my face."

The next morning Czerniakow went from one department to another at Gestapo headquarters to investigate the rumors personally. Although he didn't have access to the top echelon, he was told by the officials he contacted that they had heard nothing. He eventually reached the deputy chief of Section III, SS First Lieutenant Scherer, who expressed surprise, as had the others, at the rumors, especially the latest: that the trains were to be loaded that very night. When Czerniakow asked if he could tell the population that their fears were groundless, Scherer assured him that he could, that all the alarm was utter nonsense. Greatly relieved, the Chairman then ordered his aide to make a public announcement through the precinct police stations that, on investigation, the Judenrat had found that there was no substance to the deportation rumors.

When word of the possible dissolution of the ghetto reached Korczak's friends on the Aryan side, they immediately took action. Maryna Falska, who was still hiding Jewish children under her roof, found a safe room for Korczak near her orphanage. Igor Newerly, who had managed to obtain an identity card with an assumed name for Korczak, went to the ghetto disguised as a water and sewer inspector, carrying papers to bring out a "locksmith" who was working there.

It had been some time since Newerly's last visit to the ghetto, and he again experienced shock on seeing this sinister quarter of people "under the sentence of death," and a deep sense of humiliation and shame at being a "so-called Aryan." He found life going on as usual in the orphanage, although the children were quieter and slower in their movements. Korczak looked "ill, wasted, and stooped."

Once again the two friends sat across from each other, and once again Newerly asked Korczak to accept his help. "I explained that this was the very last chance to save even a few from perishing," Newerly recalled. "There could be no postponement. If the doctor would close the orphanage, some of the children and teachers would perhaps have a chance to escape to the other side. He had only to give the order and come away with me at once."

Newerly would never forget Korczak's reaction. "He looked at me as though I had proposed a betrayal or an embezzlement. I wilted under his gaze, and he turned away, saying quietly, but not without reproach in his voice: 'You know, of course, why Zalewski was beaten.' "

Newerly knew what Korczak meant. If Zalewski, the Catholic janitor at the Krochmalna Street orphanage, had risked his life trying to accom-

pany Jewish orphans into the ghetto, how could Newerly propose that
Korczak, their father and their guardian, leave them in order to seek his
own safety? It was unthinkable.

By way of farewell, and as a conciliatory gesture, Korczak told Newerly that should anything happen, he would send him the diary he had
been working on for safekeeping. The two men shook hands, and parted
again.

36

Yesterday's Rainbow

On July 21, the night before his sixty-fourth birthday, Korczak was sitting up in bed writing in his diary. According to the Jewish calendar, this was the eve of the Ninth of Av, the most tragic moment in the history of the Jews, when one laments the destruction of the First and Second Temples. But if Korczak was aware of this, or that the ghetto was on the brink of ultimate disaster, he did not mention it in the diary.

He was reminiscing about his family—how annoyed his mother had been that his father had delayed registering his birth, how Grandfather Hirsh, after whom he was named, had given his father and the other children Christian as well as Hebrew names. The thought that his great-grandfather, the glazier, spread warmth and light gave him comfort now. Writing about his beginnings, he was brooding about his end: "It is a difficult thing to be born and to learn to live. Ahead of me is a much easier task: to die. After death it may be difficult again, but I'm not bothering about that. The last year, month, or hour."

After almost two years in the ghetto, Korczak's body was giving way to the physical and emotional strain. He knew that he couldn't hold out much longer, but he worried about how to take leave of the orphans, who unlike him had not been meditating on death as the natural ending to human life. He hoped that he had given them the spiritual strength to meet whatever destiny awaited them. For himself, he wrote: "I should like to die consciously, in possession of my faculties. I don't know what

I should say to the children by way of farewell. I would want to make clear to them only this—that the road is theirs to choose freely."

At ten that night he heard several shots outside his blacked-out window. But he didn't stop writing. "On the contrary: it (a single shot) concentrates the mind."

On July 22, 1942, the morning of Korczak's birthday, Chairman Czerniakow rose early as usual to arrive at his Judenrat office by seven-thirty. En route, he was surprised to see that the borders of the Small Ghetto were surrounded by units of Polish police, and by Ukrainian, Lithuanian, and Latvian support troops, in addition to regular guards.

He expected the worst by the time ten top SS officers charged into his office, led by SS Major Hermann Höfle, who had directed the liquidation of the Lublin ghetto. They ordered the telephone disconnected, and the children removed from the playground across the street. Unlike the Germans who had been giving Czerniakow the runaround the day before, Höfle was brutally frank with him and the other Council members: "Today begins the evacuation of the Jews from Warsaw. You know that there are too many Jews. To you, the Judenrat, I entrust the carrying out of the task. Should you neglect to acquit yourself satisfactorily, you will all hang from the same rope."

The Judenrat was then informed that all Jews, irrespective of sex and age—except for Council members, their families, and essential service units—were to be deported to the East. By four that afternoon, Czerniakow was to see that six thousand people were at the Umschlagplatz, a large loading area just north of the ghetto, where freight trains were waiting to transport them to their destination.

Until then, Czerniakow had complied with everything asked of him. But when the Germans told him to sign the deportation announcement to be posted in the ghetto, for the first time in his career as Chairman he refused to put his name on an official document. Realizing now that the Judenrat members (Abraham Gepner, among others) imprisoned in Pawiak the day before had been seized as hostages to make him cooperate, he requested their release. It was granted, as well as exemption for Jewish Self-Aid personnel, cemetery administrators, garbage collectors, post-office employees, and tenant committees.

However, when Czerniakow asked for the exemption of children in the orphanages and other institutions, he was told only that it would be taken under advisement. In the meantime, the Judenrat was responsible for seeing that the two thousand members of its police force delivered their required quotas to the trains every day. At the first sign of resistance, Czerniakow's wife would be shot.

As if it were an ill omen of what was to follow, Korczak woke that morning of his birthday to discover that Arzylewicz, the old tailor, was dead. He hardly had time to react when a message came that the Gestapo had ordered the hospital adjoining the Umschlagplatz evacuated. Over fifty convalescent children were to be transported to the already over-crowded Dzielna Street orphanage. He rushed out, determined to prevent it.

By noon the ghetto was in turmoil—cattle cars had been sighted on the railroad sidings down by Stawki Street, next to the Umschlagplatz. Refugee centers and prisons were being closed, their emaciated inhabitants carried away, screaming and wailing, along with the street beggars, in the horse-drawn carts that would come to be known as death wagons. "The rumble of wagons and clopping of horses' hooves on the cobbled streets—that was how it all began!" is the way one survivor described that first day.

Deportation notices, issued from the Judenrat office, but without the Chairman's signature, appeared on wallboards throughout the ghetto. People spilled out of their apartments to read them. Resettlement in the East! What did it mean? Every deportee was permitted to carry seven pounds of luggage, including cash, valuables, and provisions for three days. Those failing to comply with this edict were liable to the death penalty.

The Jews of Warsaw read and reread the terse announcement. Nowhere did it mention their destination. The only exemptions, other than the Judenrat, its many agencies, and all hospital personnel, were those working in German factories. Immediately there was a frantic crush of people trying to find jobs in any kind of factory that issued work permits. There were, at the same time, some Jews actually relieved to be getting out of the ghetto: no place, they reasoned, could be much worse than where they were. They needed to believe that wherever they were being resettled, they might manage to survive until the war was over.

Korczak no doubt stood in the crowds reading the deportation notices, watching the wagons carry the first deportees off to the trains, but he didn't describe the hysteria in the ghetto when he turned to his diary that night. Instead, he vented his rage on a "brazen, shameless" woman doctor who had transferred fifty convalescent children from the emptied hospital next to the Umschlagplatz to his Dzielna Street shelter. A vendetta had been going on between the two of them for the past six months— she had "stooped to every conceivable outrage against the patients for the sake of convenience, through obstinacy or stupidity," and now she had overruled his objections that the overcrowding would be harmful to all the children. The young patients had been admitted on her orders when he wasn't there. "To spit on the floor and clear out," he wrote. "I've been considering this idea for a long time. More—a noose, or lead weights on the feet."

One marvels at what Korczak did *not* write in his diary. Rather than accept his powerlessness to alter the events of that day, he did battle where he could. The death of the old tailor, whose "aggressive and provocative behavior" he had tried to ignore that past year, was a footnote to things left unsaid. Looking over at the empty bed, he wrote: "Oh, how hard it is to live, how easy to die!"

By confiscating Adam Czerniakow's car on July 23, the second day of the deportation, the Gestapo effectively stripped the Chairman of still another vestige of his authority. But he was relieved to learn that his request for the exemption of vocational-school students and husbands of working wives had been granted. As for sparing orphans and pupils of craft schools, he was told to appeal directly to a higher official.

Sitting at his desk in the Judenrat that afternoon, Czerniakow ruminated on the information he had received that the deportation proceedings were to take place seven days a week. Opening his diary, he wrote what was to be his last entry: "A great rush to start new workshops throughout the ghetto. A sewing machine can save a life. It is three o'clock. So far, four thousand are ready to go. The orders are that there must be nine thousand by four o'clock."

While he was having supper at home that evening, Czerniakow was summoned back to his office to meet with two SS officers on the deportation staff. Stripped of his car, he was forced to take a pedicab for the first time. In the course of the brief meeting he was told that no exceptions would be made for orphans. Being unproductive, they had to be deported.

When the Germans left, the Chairman sat in his chair, a broken man. For almost three years he had tried to fulfill every Gestapo command, hoping that by compliance the Jews would make themselves indispensable to the Nazi war effort, however long it lasted. He had compromised more than one principle for the sake of the ghetto, but he drew the line at cooperating in the evacuation of its children. He rang for the night clerk and asked for a glass of water. She saw that he was as white as a sheet. His hands were trembling as he took the glass. Attempting a smile, he dismissed her with "Thank you"—his last words.

Like Korczak, Czerniakow kept poison available. He had twenty-four tablets of potassium cyanide locked in his drawer, one for each member of the Council should they ever be asked to do anything that went against their conscience. That moment had arrived for him. He wrote two notes. In one, he asked his wife to forgive him for leaving her, and to understand that he could not do otherwise. In the other, he explained to his fellow Judenrat members that he was unable to hand over helpless children to the Germans. He hoped that they would not see his suicide as an act of cowardice. He could no longer bear what was happening.

Shortly afterwards, the cashier, who was working in another part of the building, was surprised that no one answered the incessant ringing of the phone in the Chairman's office. Opening the door cautiously, he found Adam Czerniakow dead in his chair.

That night the Gestapo ordered an emergency meeting of the Judenrat to elect a new Chairman. In the early morning hours there was a hasty burial ceremony for Czerniakow, with only his wife, a few Council members, and close friends like Janusz Korczak in attendance. In his eulogy, Korczak said: "God gave Adam Czerniakow the important task of protecting the dignity of the Jews. Now that he is dead, he will return his body to the earth and his soul to God, along with the gift of protecting his people, knowing that he has completed his task."

The people of the ghetto, already in a state of terror, were not sure what to make of the news of Czerniakow's suicide. Many felt that the Chairman had failed the Jews by not leaving them some clear message. Marek Edelman, who would survive the Ghetto Uprising the following year, reproached Czerniakow for making his death his own private business. But others saw for the first time the heroic quality of this ordinary man (so often accused of "nonleadership") who, after the German invasion, had chosen to give up a visa to Palestine to serve his community, for no salary and at great personal risk. Chaim Kaplan, always critical of the Chairman in the past, acknowledged in his diary that while some people achieve immortality in an hour, Czerniakow achieved it in an instant.

If the Chairman's suicide was not enough to persuade the majority of Jews that resettlement meant death, it certainly made them even more apprehensive of the journey. Since the "nonproductive elements" were those slated to go, there was a new surge of people looking for jobs in the hundreds of "shops" that sprang up overnight. When not enough people took up the Nazi offer of three kilograms of bread and one kilogram of marmalade in return for volunteering for the trains, the Germans put increasing pressure on the Jewish police to see that the cattle cars were filled. The desperate Jews were now in the position of being hunted down by their own police, equally desperate to fill their quotas. Work permits were no longer enough to save one in the daily street blockades. Families were dragged from their hiding places. Anyone who resisted was shot. Stores were closed. There was no smuggling. No food. No bread. No one dared venture outside without a purpose.

During those first chaotic days, Giena's brother Samuel didn't know what to do. Hearing rumors that the orphanages would not be touched because the Germans had decided not to bother resettling children who weren't strong enough to work, he wanted to believe that his sister was safe, but his mother's pale face kept appearing in his dreams, asking: "Where's Giena?"

What could he do about his sister? If he brought her to his room, how would she manage while he was working in the furniture factory or attending underground meetings at night? He had rented a room in the apartment of an elderly couple, but he hardly knew them. What would Giena do during the day? Wouldn't she be frightened and lonely without her friends? She was clever and precocious for her ten years, but she was still only a child. And how would he feed her? Bread was scarce and expensive. He had no money left, just a few pieces of their mother's jewelry. But who would trade bread for such things now?

On July 26, the fifth day of resettlement, Samuel decided to keep Giena with him. Taking time off from work, he made his way to the orphanage warily, lest he be seized while passing through an area where an *Aktion* was taking place. He found Giena playing with two other children in the large downstairs room of the orphanage. The atmosphere of the house had changed in those few days since deportations began. The children looked grim and complained of being hungry. Giena led him to Stefa, and then slipped away to finish her game.

After hearing Samuel's request, Stefa acknowledged that he had a right to do what he thought best. But she wanted him to know that she had been discouraging family members who rushed over with the same intention. Not only did she and Korczak feel that the children were safer with them—even the Judenrat believed that the Gestapo would not touch an orphanage as famous as this one—but it was not good for the morale of the home if some children left. The staff had voted to stay no matter what. She suggested that he talk to Giena before making a final decision. Usually when a child was withdrawn, he or she could not be readmitted, but in Giena's case Stefa was willing to make an exception.

Samuel walked with Giena into the small courtyard between the two houses. Sitting on a bench there, he told her again how he had promised their mother to protect her, and wondered if they shouldn't be together now that people were being sent to an unknown destination. He admitted that he was worried about leaving her alone when he was at work.

Giena had also been wondering what to do. Two of her best friends had already been withdrawn by relatives, but she didn't want to leave the orphanage. She was afraid of the crowds of people on the street and of the thought of waiting alone for him in an unfamiliar building. Still, she gave in to Samuel's pressure that they be together during this period.

As it turned out, Samuel's fears about his sister being frightened and lonely were confirmed that next week. Giena was terrified each morning when he left for the factory, and tearful when he returned. She missed her friends, and especially Stefa. After a few days she pleaded with him to let her return to the orphanage.

Samuel was tempted to tell her that the orphanage could be in danger because the Nazis were not known for sparing children, and that some members of the underground feared that resettlement meant death. But he couldn't. What use would this information be to a child when even adults were helpless and confused? Seeing Giena's sad expression, Samuel wondered if she didn't suspect the worst. Perhaps all the children did. He took her back to the orphanage, and felt a catch in his throat as he watched her embrace Stefa. He left immediately, knowing that if he lingered he would not be able to hold back his tears. Stooping down to kiss Giena's eyes, which so resembled those of their mother, he dashed out quickly without looking back.

For three days after Czerniakow's death, Korczak avoided his diary. When he turned to it again on July 27, he did not mention the suicide of this friend who had been one of his main supports. "Yesterday's rainbow," he began the entry. "A marvelous big moon over this camp of homeless pilgrims. Why can't I calm this hapless, insane quarter?"

Even now he gave no details of the deportations: how every day whole blocks of people were forced out of their buildings, herded together, and driven with whips through the streets to the Umschlagplatz. Rather, with bitter irony, he tried to fathom this "lucid plan" of the Germans by writing a speech for someone very like the mad colonel in his play *Senate of Madmen*:

Declare yourself, make your choice. We do not offer easy roads. No bridge playing for the time being, no sunbathing, no delicious dinners paid for with the blood of smugglers . . . We're running a gigantic enterprise. Its name is war. We work in a planned, disciplined manner, methodically. Your petty interests, ambitions, sentiments, whims, claims, resentments, cravings, do not concern us.

Jews, go East. No bargaining. It is no longer a question of a Jewish grandmother, but of where you are needed most—your hands, your brains, your time, your life.

We are the Germans. It is not a question of the trademark, but of the cost, the destination of the products. We are the steam shovel . . . we may feel sorry for you at times, but we must use the whip, the big stick or pencil, because there must be order . . .

The Jews have their merits. They have talent, and Moses, and Christ, and Heine, and Spinoza, and progress, and yeast, and pioneers, and generosity, and are a hard-working ancient race. All true. But besides the Jews, there are other people, and other issues.

The Jews are important, but later—you will understand someday . . . You must listen, my friend, to History's program speech about the new chapter.

Could one ever understand this particular program? One could only hold on to the program that had informed one's own life. "WHY DO I CLEAR THE TABLE?" he now wrote in large block letters across the page:

I know that many are dissatisfied with my clearing the table after meals. Even the kitchen crew seems to dislike it. Surely they can manage. There are enough of them. If there were not, one or two could always be added . . .

Even worse, if anyone comes to see me on important business, I tell him to wait, saying: "I am occupied now."

What an occupation: picking up soup bowls, spoons, and plates.

But worse still is that I do it clumsily, get in the way while the second helping is being passed. I bump against those sitting tightly packed at the tables. Because of me, he cannot lick clean his soup plate or the tureen. Someone may even lose his second helping.

No one has asked him: "Why do you do it? Why do you get in the way?" but he decides to explain anyway:

When I collect the dishes myself, I can see the cracked plates, the bent spoons, the scratches on the bowls . . . Sometimes I watch how the extras are distributed, or who sits next to whom. And I get some ideas. For if I do something, I never do it thoughtlessly. This waiter's job is of great use to me, pleasant and interesting.

But this is not important . . . My aim is that in the Orphans Home there should be no clean or dirty work, no purely physical or purely mental workers.

To someone opening Korczak's diary at random, it might seem bizarre that this great educator went on for pages about why he cleared the table at the very moment when the Warsaw Ghetto was in the process of being swept away. But that was his way of transcending the evil around him: the rituals and order of the past were the only ballast he had to hold his little republic firmly to its moorings.

When Esterka Winogron, Korczak's devoted assistant who had directed *The Post Office,* was seized in one of the early *Aktions,* Korczak, disregarded his own safety and rushed about the ghetto trying to find someone with influence who could save her.

"Where was she picked up?" he was asked.

He didn't know. He only knew that he had to locate her among the thousands of people herded together in the Umschlagplatz before she was shoved onto one of the trains. It might already be too late.

Summoning up what little strength he had left, he made his way past German and Ukrainian soldiers, past Jewish police, past the deserted shops and apartment houses with their smashed windows, pressing himself against a wall when a German barked at him to get out of the way of the next contingent of victims being escorted past by whips and dogs. They did him a "favor," since, roaming about, he might be hit by a stray bullet. This way he could "stand safely against the wall, and observe and think—spin the web of thought. Yes, spin the web of thought."

He thought how Esterka used to confide to him that she did not want

to live frivolously or easily after the war, but "dreamed of a beautiful life."
He moved on, intent only on finding her, as if, in some magical way, by
saving her, he could save them all. When a young Pole at the police box
by the gate to the Umschlagplatz asked him kindly how he had managed
to run the blockade, Korczak turned on his old charm, and inquired if
the policeman could not possibly "do something" for Esterka. There were
instances when a bribe had persuaded a Jewish, Polish, or even German
police officer to pull someone out of the cordoned-off area to safety.

"You know very well I can't," was the polite reply.

"Thanks for the kind words," Korczak heard himself saying, knowing
that his gratitude for being spoken to humanly was the "bloodless child
of poverty and degradation."

Tormented by his inability to save Esterka, he tried to console himself
that they would meet later "somewhere else." He may have meant this
literally, or he may have been referring to that land "beyond the stars"
where Amal had gone. He was not even sure that he would be doing her
a service if he did manage to bring her back to the ghetto. "Perhaps it is
not she but we who have been caught (having stayed)," he wrote in the
diary.

A few days later he, too, was caught. Stella Eliasberg would recall
Korczak pounding on her door one afternoon and falling into the room.
When he was able to speak, he told her that he had just been seized by
an SS commando during an *Aktion* and hurled onto a death wagon. He
only escaped being taken off to the Umschlagplatz because he was recognized by a Jewish policeman, who helped him down. As he was limping
away with his cane, the German shouted at him to come back, but he
pretended not to hear. Korczak stayed at Stella's apartment for four hours,
waiting for the *Aktion* to end, apologizing all the while for boring her with
his story. And then he limped his way back to the orphanage.

The appearance of the quarter was changing from day to day, he
informed the diary:

1. A prison
2. A plague-stricken area
3. A mating ground
4. A lunatic asylum
5. A casino. Monaco. The stake—your head.

Giena's brother managed to visit her a few times in the late afternoon by waiting until the roundups were over for the day. The Germans had removed the Jewish police from this duty, and were depending on the brutal Latvian and Ukrainian troops to force the deportees to the trains. Stefa admitted she was no longer confident about the security of the orphanage, but she could still assure Samuel that, no matter what happened, the staff would not abandon the children.

During what was to be his last visit with Giena, Korczak passed by— "a bent old man with a short white beard." He scrutinized Samuel briefly, asked how he was managing, and moved on; he left communicating with family members to Stefa. Giena tried to be cheerful with her brother. She talked about the books she was reading rather than her hunger. However, when he was about to leave, she threw her arms around him, whispering, "Take care of yourself, for my sake."

On Saturday morning, August 1, Korczak's bed felt so soft and warm that he had a hard time getting up. For the first time in thirty years he was not interested in the results of weighing the children. "They ought to have put on a bit of weight," he told himself, while wondering why they were given raw carrots for supper the night before. He closed his eyes again and considered writing a monograph on the feather bed.

But he had to get up, if not to weigh the children, then to deal with Adzio, a "retarded, maliciously undisciplined" boy. Not wanting to expose the house to the "danger of his outbursts," Korczak had already written to the Jewish police to take him away. As in prewar days, the equilibrium of the community came first.

One wonders where Korczak thought the police would send Adzio other than to the Umschlagplatz for "resettlement in the East." Following his diary entry about Adzio, he records with satisfaction that he has managed to get a ton of coal for the Dzielna Street orphanage. Even as the trains were taking thousands of Jews every day to their unknown destination, he was preparing for the winter.

For the past week he had been talking to his Judenrat friend Abraham Gepner about converting his two orphanages into factories to sew German uniforms or whatever was needed. He was hoping that if the children could prove themselves useful they would be allowed to remain where they were. Gepner was still a powerful man in the ghetto—"the heart and soul of the Provisions Unit," Czerniakow had once called him—and if anyone could set up the shops, he could. "Korczak deluded himself to the end that the factories would save the children," Stella Eliasberg was to recall. "That's why he wanted everything to go on as usual, so as not to unnerve the children and create panic. But as it turned out, there was not even time to set up one shop."

Korczak may have been trying to keep one step ahead of the Germans, but he no longer had the power to ward off the demoralization that was affecting everyone. "Why, what I'm experiencing did happen," he told the diary. "It did happen. They sold their belongings—for a liter of lamp oil, a kilogram of groats, a glass of vodka." The whole ghetto had become one vast pawnshop. And everything the civilized world had always taken for granted—faith, family, motherhood—was being debased.

Each day brought so many "strange and sinister experiences" that he had completely ceased to dream. He read the memoirs of Marcus Aurelius to calm himself; he also practiced Indian meditation, which he seems to have been familiar with. One night, realizing that it had been a long time since he had "blessed the world," he tried. It didn't work. He didn't even know what went wrong. He had sat breathing deeply until he felt diffused with purifying vibrations, but when he lifted his hands for the blessing, his fingers went slack; no energy flowed through them.

Reviewing his life in those early dawn hours, it seemed that everything had ended in failure:

My share in the Japanese war. Defeat—disaster.
In the European war—defeat—disaster.
In the World War . . .
I don't know how or what a soldier of a victorious army feels . . .

Julek had taken the place of the old tailor in the bed next to his. The boy had pneumonia and breathed with difficulty like the old tailor; he moaned and thrashed about with the same "selfish and theatrical desire" to get attention. Not until Julek had his first quiet night in a week was Korczak able to get some sleep.

Korczak woke at five-thirty in the morning on August 5 to find the sky overcast. Seeing Hanna already up, he said "Good morning."

She responded with a look of surprise.

"Smile," he pleaded.

She gave him a "pale, tubercular smile."

Hanna, like all the children, was hungry. Bread, that staple of life, was nonexistent. Korczak's anger now seemed mixed with resignation and sorrow as he petitioned God:

> Our Father who art in heaven . . .
> This prayer was carved out of hunger and misery.
> Our daily bread.
> Bread.

37

The Last March:
August 6, 1942

What matters is that all of this did happen.
—Ghetto Diary

Korczak was up early, as usual, on August 6. As he leaned over the windowsill to water the parched soil of "the poor Jewish orphanage plants," he noticed that he was again being watched by the German guard posted by the wall that bisected Sienna Street. He wondered if the guard was annoyed or moved by the domestic scene, or if he was thinking that Korczak's bald head made a splendid target. The soldier had a rifle, so why did he just stand there, legs wide apart, watching calmly? He might not have orders to shoot, but that hadn't deterred any SS so far from emptying his ammunition into someone on a whim.

Korczak began speculating about the young soldier in what was to be the last entry of his diary: "Perhaps he was a village teacher in civilian life, or a notary, a street sweeper in Leipzig, a waiter in Cologne. What would he do if I nodded to him? Waved my hand in a friendly gesture? Perhaps he doesn't even know that things are—as they are? He may have arrived only yesterday, from far away . . . ."

In another part of the compound, Misha Wroblewski and three of the older boys were getting ready to leave for the jobs Korczak had been able to arrange for them at the German railway depot on the other side of the wall. Every morning they were marched out under guard and counted, and marched back again every night. It was hard work, but it gave them a chance to barter what few possessions they had for food.

They left the orphanage quietly without communicating with anyone. It seemed like just another day they had to get through.

Promptly at seven Korczak joined Stefa, the teachers, and the children for breakfast at the wooden tables, which had been pushed together once the bedding was removed from the center of the room. Perhaps they had some potato peels or an old crust of bread, perhaps there was some carefully measured ersatz coffee in each little mug. Korczak was just getting up to clear the table when two blasts of a whistle and that dread call, *"Alle Juden raus!"* ("All Jews out!"), rang through the house.

Part of the German strategy was not to announce anything in advance, but to take each area by surprise: the plan that morning was to evacuate most of the children's institutions in the Small Ghetto. The lower end of Sliska Street had already been blockaded by the SS, squads of Ukrainian militiamen, and the Jewish police.

Korczak rose quickly, as did Stefa, to still the children's fears. Now, as always, they worked intuitively together, knowing what each had to do. She signaled the teachers to help the children gather their things. He walked into the courtyard to ask one of the Jewish policemen for time to allow the children to pack up, after which they would line up outside in an orderly fashion. He was given fifteen minutes.

Korczak would have had no thought of trying to hide any children now. During the past weeks, he had seen people who had been discovered hiding in cupboards, behind false walls, under beds, flung from their windows or forced at gunpoint down to the street. There was nothing to do but lead the children and teachers straight into the unknown, and, if he was lucky, out of it. Who was to say that, if anyone had a chance of surviving out there in the East, it might not be them?

As he encouraged the children to line up quietly in rows of four, Korczak must have hoped that no matter how terrible the situation in which they found themselves, he would be able to use his charm and powers of persuasion to wheedle some bread and potatoes and perhaps even some medicine for his young charges. He would, above all, be there to keep their spirits up—to be their guide through whatever lay ahead.

He had to try to reassure the children as they lined up fearfully, clutching their little flasks of water, their favorite books, their diaries and toys. But what could he tell them, he whose credo it was that one should never spring surprises on a child—that "a long and dangerous journey requires preparation." What could he say without taking away their hope, and his own? Some have speculated that he told them they were going to their summer camp, Little Rose, but it seems probable that Korczak would not have lied to his children. Perhaps he suggested that the place where they were going might have pine and birch trees like the ones in their camp; and, surely, if there were trees, there would be birds and rabbits and squirrels.

But even a man of Korczak's vivid fantasy could not have imagined what lay in wait for him and the children. No one had yet escaped from Treblinka to reveal the truth: they were not going East, but sixty miles northeast of Warsaw to immediate extermination in gas chambers. Treblinka was not even an overnight stay.

The Germans had taken a roll call: one hundred and ninety-two children and ten adults. Korczak was at the head of this little army, the tattered remnants of the generations of moral soldiers he had raised in his children's republic. He held five-year-old Romcia in one arm, and perhaps Szymonek Jakubowicz, to whom he had dedicated the story of Planet Ro, by the other.

Stefa followed a little way back with the nine- to twelve-year-olds. There were Giena, with sad, dark eyes like her mother's; Eva Mandelblatt, whose brother had been in the orphanage before her; Halinka Pinchonson, who chose to go with Korczak rather than stay behind with her mother. There were Jakub, who wrote the poem about Moses; Leon with his polished box; Mietek with his dead brother's prayer book; and Abus, who had stayed too long on the toilet.

There were Zygmus, Sami, Hanka, and Aronek, who had signed the petition to play in the church garden; Hella, who was always restless; big Hanna, who had asthma; and little Hanna with her pale, tubercular smile; Mendelek, who had the bad dream; and the agitated boy who had not wanted to leave his dying mother. There were Abrasha, who had played Amal, with his violin; Jerzyk, the fakir; Chaimek, the doctor; Adek, the lord mayor; and the rest of the cast of *The Post Office*, all following their own Pan Doctor on their way to meet the Messiah King.

One of the older boys carried the green flag of King Matt, the blue Star of David set against a field of white on one side. The older children took turns carrying the flag during the course of their two-mile walk, perhaps remembering how King Matt had held his head high that day he was forced to march through the streets of his city to what he thought was to be his execution.

.

Among the teachers were many who had grown up in the orphanage: Roza Sztokman, Romcia's mother, with her blond hair parted in the middle and plaited into two thick braids like her daughter's; Roza's brother Henryk, who typed the diary, blond like her, a good athlete, popular with the girls. (He could have escaped to Russia before the fall of Warsaw, but he had stayed behind to be with their father, the old tailor.) There were Balbina Grzyb, whose husband Feliks (away at work that day) had been voted king of the orphanage as a boy; Henryk Asterblum, the accountant for thirty years; Dora Solnicka, the treasurer; Sabina Lejzerowicz, the popular sewing teacher who was also a gymnast; Roza Lipiec-Jakubowska, who grew up in the orphanage; and Natalia Poz, who worked in the office for twenty years, limping as a result of polio contracted as a child just before she came under Korczak's care.

The sidewalks were packed with people from neighboring houses, who were required to stand in front of their homes when an *Aktion* was taking place. As the children followed Korczak away from the orphanage, one of the teachers started singing a marching song, and everyone joined in: "Though the storm howls around us, let us keep our heads high."

They walked past the Children's Hospital, a few blocks down on Sliska Street, where Korczak had spent seven years as a young doctor, past Panska, and Twarda, where he had gone at night to see his poor Jewish patients. The streets here were empty, but many people watched from behind closed curtains. When Jozef Balcerak, who had moved into the ghetto the year before to be with his parents, caught sight of the little procession from his window, he gasped, "My God, they've got Korczak!"

The orphans marched half a mile to the All Saints Church on Grzybowska Square (where they had once asked to play in the garden), joining up with thousands of others, many of them children from institutions that had also been evacuated that morning. They continued on together through the Small Ghetto to the Chlodna Street bridge that crossed over to the Large Ghetto. Witnesses say that the youngest children stumbled on the uneven cobblestones and were shoved up the steps of the bridge; many fell or were pushed down to the other side. Below the bridge some Poles were shouting: "Goodbye, good riddance, Jews!"

Korczak led his children down Karmelicka Street, past Nowolipki, home of the *Little Review,* and past the sausage shop where he used to take his reporters on Thursday nights. Michael Zylberberg and his wife Henrietta, living in the basement of a house on the corner of Nowolipki and Smocza, happened to look out as the orphans passed by. He was relieved to see that the police were not beating and shoving them as they did with other groups.

The little procession walked past Dzielna Street, past the Pawiak prison, and up Zamenhofa toward the northernmost wall of the ghetto. The younger ones were wilting by now in the intense heat; they dragged their feet; they moaned that they wanted to rest, that they were thirsty, that they were hot, that they had to go to the bathroom. But the Jewish police, who were escorting them, kept the group moving forward.

Joanna Swadosh, a nurse, saw the orphans as they were approaching their destination. She was helping her mother set up a small infirmary in the evacuated hospital next to the Umschlagplatz. It was no use asking why the Germans, so intent on killing, were bothering to open such a unit. There was no apparent logic in anything they did. She no longer dwelled on such questions, but went numbly about her routine. Not until later would she understand that the infirmary was just a cover to allay any suspicion about resettlement.

She was unpacking a crate when someone glanced through a window and called, "Dr. Korczak is coming!" It could mean only one thing, she thought—they had Korczak. If Korczak had to go, so would they all.

The Jewish police were walking on both sides, cordoning them off from the rest of the street. She saw that Korczak was carrying one child, and had another by the hand. He seemed to be talking to them quietly, occasionally turning his head to encourage the children behind.

Word that Korczak's orphanage had been taken spread quickly through the ghetto. When Giena's brother, Samuel, heard the news, he rushed out of the furniture factory, two friends following in fast pursuit to prevent him from trying to join Giena. He ran first to the Judenrat office to ask Abraham Gepner if it was really true. Gepner, who had always seemed so powerful, sat slumped in his chair as he acknowledged it was.

"Can you help me get Giena out of the Umschlagplatz?" Samuel pleaded.

"It's impossible," Gepner said, almost inaudibly. "Yesterday they took my daughter's best friend—remember, I called her my adopted daughter. I couldn't save her."

As Samuel turned to leave, Gepner roused himself. "Even if I had a way of getting Giena out of there, she might refuse to go. She may be better off with Korczak and Stefa and the other children."

Samuel dashed out of the Judenrat office and headed for the Um-schlagplatz, his friends still trailing after him. But as he neared the loading area, he found that Mita Street, Niska, and part of Zamenhofa were blocked off. He tried to slip through the crowd of people also desperate to save their loved ones, but his friends held on to him and managed to drag him back to the factory.

All that night Samuel lay on his bed staring into the darkness, unable to think of anything but Giena. What was it like for her on the Um-schlagplatz? What was she thinking? Was she scared? Was she crying for him? He would take part in the Ghetto Uprising the following year, and survive Maidanek and Auschwitz, but his inability to save his sister would torment him all his life.

In spite of the pandemonium in the ghetto, one could still telephone out to the Aryan side.

Harry Kaliszer, who had arranged the bribe for Korczak's release from Pawiak two years earlier, phoned Igor Newerly with the terrible news that he had seen everyone being led away. Newerly immediately phoned Maryna Falska, who rushed over to his apartment to join him, his wife, and their nine-year-old son in their vigil. She paced back and forth for quite a while, and then sat in silence. When the telephone finally rang, Newerly leapt for it.

"They're at the Umschlagplatz," Harry told him. "It looks like this is it."

"Call us if there's any hope," Newerly said.

"We won't hear from him again," Maryna said hoarsely. Her prediction was correct.

At the gate where the ghetto ended, fresh squadrons of SS and Ukrainians were waiting with their whips, guns, and dogs. The children were pushed and shoved through the gate, across the tram tracks on the Aryan side, and through another gate, this one opening into the large dirt field by the railway siding which was the Umschlagplatz. Thousands of people—crying, screaming, praying—were already waiting there in the broiling sun. Families huddled together, their meager belongings tied up in pillowcases or sacks; mothers clung to their children; old people sat in a daze. There was no water, no food, no place to relieve oneself, no protection from the German whips and curses.

Nahum Remba, an official of the Judenrat, had set up a first-aid

station in the Umschlagplatz through which he was able to rescue a few
of those caught in the dragnets. Word that Korczak and his children were
on their way had just reached him when they arrived. He seated them
at the far end of the square against a low wall; beyond was the courtyard
of the evacuated hospital, now filled with yet more Jews waiting to be
loaded onto the trains.

Korczak's children weren't the only ones that Remba had to worry
about that day: four thousand youngsters had been gathered with their
caretakers from other institutions. But Korczak's children—well, they
were Korczak's. The trains carried from six to ten thousand people daily,
but Remba hoped that if he could hold Korczak's entourage there until
noon, he might possibly save them until the following day. In a mad world
such as this, each day counted—each hour.

Remba took Korczak aside and urged him to go with him to the
Judenrat to ask them to intervene. But Korczak wouldn't consider it; if
he left the children even for a moment in this terrifying place, they might
panic. He couldn't risk that. And there was always the danger that they
might be taken away in his absence.

"The loading of the railway cars began then," Remba wrote in his
memoirs. "I stood next to a column of ghetto policemen who were trans-
ferring the victims to the train, and watched the proceedings with a
pounding heart, hoping that my plan of delay would succeed."

The Germans and Ukrainians kicked and shoved people into the
chlorinated cars, and still there was room left. A tall, thin young man
with a violin case pleaded in perfect German with an SS officer to let him
join his mother, who had been crammed into one of the cars. The officer
laughed derisively and said: "It depends on how well you play." The
young man took out the violin and played a Mendelssohn Requiem. The
music floated over the crazed plaza. But the German, tired of his game,
signaled the violinist to get into the car with his mother and sealed the
door behind him.

Then, to Remba's dismay, Schmerling—the sadistic chief of the ghetto
police in charge of the Umschlagplatz—ordered that the orphanages be
loaded. Korczak signaled his children to rise.

There are some who say that at that moment a German officer made
his way through the crowd and handed Korczak a piece of paper. An
influential member of CENTOS had petitioned the Gestapo on his behalf
that morning, and the story goes that Korczak was offered permission to

return home—but not the children. Korczak is said to have shaken his head and waved the German away.

Remba records in his memoir that Korczak headed the first section of children and Stefa the second. Unlike the usual chaotic mass of people shrieking hysterically as they were prodded along with whips, the orphans walked in rows of four with quiet dignity. "I shall never forget this scene as long as I live," Remba wrote. "This was no march to the train cars, but rather a mute protest against this murderous regime . . . a procession the like of which no human eye has ever witnessed."

As Korczak led his children calmly toward the cattle cars, the Jewish police cordoning off a path for them saluted instinctively. Remba burst into tears when the Germans asked who that man was. A wail went up from those still left on the square. Korczak walked, head held high, holding a child by each hand, his eyes staring straight ahead with his characteristic gaze, as if seeing something far away.

Epilogue:
Treblinka and After

*Man feels and ponders death as though it were the end, when
in fact death is merely the continuation of life. It is another
life.*

   *You may not believe in the existence of the soul, yet you
must acknowledge that your body will live on as green grass,
as a cloud. For you are, after all, water and dust.*
                                        —Ghetto Diary

No one survived to tell the story of the last hours of Korczak, Stefa,
and the children after their train left the Warsaw Ghetto on August 6,
1942. All that is known is that Treblinka, the extermination camp to which
they were taken, was under the command of another doctor, the infamous
Dr. Irmfried Eberl. In spite of Eberl's experience in gassing people during
the "euthanasia" program in Germany, Treblinka was in chaos. The small
gas chambers, which spewed out carbon monoxide from engine exhaust,
functioned ceaselessly, but still could not handle the thousands of people
the trains brought each day. Many had to be shot. There were mountains
of putrefying corpses everywhere waiting to be thrown into mass graves.

   "We can't go on this way. I can't do it any longer. We have to break
off," Eberl phoned Gestapo headquarters in Lublin.

   "It's the end of the world," Franz Stengl said when he arrived at
Treblinka in late August to replace Eberl. The stench reached him from
miles away. The following April he ordered the graves dug up and all the
bodies cremated on "roasting racks". The ashes were scattered in long
trenches and covered with earth, over which evergreen trees were planted.

   When Misha returned to the orphanage late on the afternoon of
August 6, he found everything in disarray. Korczak's spectacles, with a
cracked left lens, were lying on the bed table where he had put them

the night before, and his papers were scattered about the room. Misha believes that no one suspected the orphanage would be taken that day. He survived the war and was a colonel in the Polish Army until the "anti-Zionist" purge forced him to emigrate to Sweden in the late 1960s.

"The day after Korczak and the children were taken, a red-haired boy appeared at my door with a package and ran off," Newerly recalls. "I was afraid it wouldn't be safe in my apartment and took it immediately to Maryna Falska in Bielany. We chose a spot under the eaves of the orphanage. The caretaker, Mr. Cichosz, made a hole and bricked it up."

After two years of internment as a political prisoner in Auschwitz (where he once thought he spotted that red-haired boy), Newerly started life anew in a Poland that was now part of the Soviet bloc. Korczak's diary was unearthed from its hiding place and turned over to the Polish Writers Union. It remained unpublished during the Stalinist years, when Korczak was out of favor as a "bourgeois educator" and the works of the Russian pedagogue Anton Makarenko took precedence.

Not until the thaw of 1956 was Newerly able to publish the works of Janusz Korczak, but even then the diary appeared only as part of a four-volume anthology rather than as a separate book. The original diary, typed by Henryk, a young teacher in the ghetto orphanage, has disappeared. Both the archives of the Korczak Society and the Museum of Literature in Warsaw possess immaculately typed manuscripts that are labeled as original.

Ida Merzan, one of the few surviving Jewish teachers who stayed in Poland after the war, describes the diary as having been typed, with many mistakes, on delicate blue rice paper. She and another woman mounted each page on sturdy paper in the mid-fifties so that Newerly could prepare it for publication. "The diary was issued without much editing, except that a few names were deleted and others replaced with initials," Merzan said. "Some Jews who returned to Poland from Russia after the war had power in the new government and objected to the critical things Korczak had written about their relatives. And certain Polish officials wanted to delete any mention of former patriots like Jozef Pilsudski who had been anti-Communist."

Both Merzan and Newerly maintain that except for minor details, the original diary was not tampered with. Merzan does not know who could have taken it. "I've been told to stop searching, that I'll never find it," she admits. "But I believe that it will reappear when this generation has passed on."

Maryna Falska had tried not to fall into despondency after Korczak and his orphans were taken to Treblinka. She continued to hide Jewish children. One of them remembers seeing her on the roof of her orphanage at the time of the Ghetto Uprising, watching a flame-streaked sky through which feathers from pillows and mattresses fell like snowflakes. Tears were rolling down Maryna's cheeks, but when she noticed the young Jewish girl standing there, she quickly composed herself and sent her off to bed.

During the Warsaw Uprising, in the fall of 1944—when the whole city was destroyed by the Germans while the Red Army sat watching on the other side of the Vistula—Maryna opened a hospital in the orphanage for wounded Polish fighters. She allowed the older orphanage boys to join the fighting units and sat up nights waiting for them to return. Eight did not.

Shortly before her death, Maryna was informed by a German soldier that her orphanage was to be evacuated to another part of Poland. Before leaving, he grabbed her wrist and tore off the watch that had belonged to her husband. "I saw her struggling in the corridor and cried out that she should give it to him," Eugenka, one of the teachers, recalls. "He hit her with his gun and left. She was stricken about losing the watch. She made no preparations for the move, though she said things like: 'Don't let the children carry heavy things. Please take care of the children.' As if she were giving her last instructions."

On October 7, 1944, the day before the orphanage was to be resettled, Maryna collapsed and had to be carried upstairs. Eugenka started to cry when she saw Maryna's face turning blue. The doctor said: "Why do you cry? There are so many people dying." Maryna didn't ask for confession in that last hour before her death. The children and staff were told that she had died of a heart attack, but Eugenka and others believe she took cyanide rather than leave the house. Not wanting to bury Maryna in a sack, as they did the Polish soldiers who died in their orphanage hospital, four of the teachers made a wooden coffin out of a few desks. The funeral took place in the courtyard at night to avoid detection by the Germans.

The orphans were evacuated with their teachers in an open truck that took them to a small village in southern Poland where they, and the Jewish children hidden among them, managed to survive by begging. After the war, Maryna Falska was given a proper burial and the orphanage was restored. It still operates under the system of self-government that she and Korczak initiated.

A Janusz Korczak club was formed by surviving Polish and Jewish orphans and teachers in Warsaw after the war. Over the years, it met sporadically, depending on the political climate. The Korczak legend gathered momentum in Europe as poets and playwrights re-created that last march with the children to the train. Schools, hospitals, and streets were named after him in many countries. UNESCO declared 1978–79 the Year of Korczak, to coincide with the Year of the Child and the centenary of his birth. Pope John Paul II expressed his "special support" for the Janusz Korczak Literary Competition, sponsored jointly by Polish and Jewish Americans to give awards to outstanding books about children.

In the mid-seventies, the Polish government found it politically expedient to set up the Janusz Korczak International Society to host annual conferences in Warsaw for the purpose of disseminating his educational ideas. The Minister of Education, Jerzy Kuberski (now Ambassador for Religious Affairs in the Vatican), was appointed chairman. Sometimes when I attend a Korczak conference in Warsaw, I feel that I am living a scene from *King Matt the First*. There are delegates from both the Eastern and Western blocs, many of them separated by the very political and religious ideologies that Korczak had hoped to bridge in his lifetime, but all of them deeply involved in rediscovering Korczak as writer, psychologist, and moral educator.

Israel and Poland both claim Korczak as their own. The Poles consider Korczak a martyr who, had he been born a Catholic, would have been canonized by now. The Israelis revere Korczak as one of the Thirty-six Just Men whose pure souls, according to ancient Jewish tradition, make possible the world's salvation. As if settling for joint custody, the two countries dutifully attend each other's Korczak commemorations, no small gesture considering that the Poles broke off diplomatic relations with Israel after the 1967 Arab–Israeli war. In a spirit of reconciliation at one conference in Warsaw, an Israeli delegate, a former ghetto fighter, made the motion that in Poland Korczak should be called a Jew and in Israel a Pole.

* * *

For some time after the war it was rumored that the cattle cars that took Korczak's orphans to Treblinka had been derailed and that he and Stefa and the children were saved. People claimed to have seen them in small villages throughout Poland.

Korczak wondered in his diary what he would do after the war: "Perhaps I will be invited to participate in restoring order to the world, or to Poland. This is highly improbable and I would not want it. I would have to keep an office, meaning the slavery of fixed working hours and contacts with people, a desk somewhere, a telephone, an armchair. Wasting time on trifling everyday problems, and contending with petty people with their petty ambitions, their influential friends, hierarchies, and goals. In sum, a yoke. I prefer to be on my own."

He also imagined creating an orphanage compound in the hills of northern Galilee: "It will have large barracks-like dining rooms and dormitories and small 'hermit huts.' I will have a room on the terrace of a flat roof, not too large, with transparent walls so that I will not miss a single sunrise or sunset, and so that, writing at night, I will be able to look now and again at the stars."

Treblinka, like the other former death camps which lie like dead moons outside the main cities of Poland, is kept alive by visitors from all over the world who go there to pay homage to the victims. I took the sixty-mile trip there by chartered bus with the International Korczak Association in 1983. Sitting in the front with me were Jozef Balcerak and Ida Merzan. Misha Wroblewski was there from Sweden; Leon Ha'ari, Yanka Zuk, Stasiek Zyngman, and Itzhak Belfer from Israel. Igor Newerly was too ill to join us. Joseph Arnon had died a few years before.

Our bus took the road along the Vistula, past small villages slumbering in the noon sun, past fields with cows, past towns renowned for their sheepskin coats, past trains with empty cattle cars sitting idly on the tracks.

We came at last to a sign saying TREBLINKA, the name of the small town two miles from where the camp was located, and continued on down narrow roads flanked by dense birch and pine forests, so beautiful, so primeval, it seemed that nature, too, was eager to cover up what had happened there. A few years earlier, driving by car to Treblinka with a Polish journalist, we had become lost in this very spot. Flagging down a man passing by with his grandson in a wooden horse-drawn cart filled with potatoes, we asked how to find the former death camp.

"I remember it," the man had said. "I saw it all from the hilltop above my town. I was a boy tending my cows. I saw the trains pull up. I saw the people get off. I saw them trying to escape. I saw them beaten. Shot. Oh, it was terrible. There was nothing anyone could do. When the wind was easterly, it was almost unbearable for us. But a westerly wind was tolerable. We sent our women and young children away to relatives to protect them from the drunken Ukrainian guards." He pointed in the direction where the camp had been. And then he moved on—horse, cart, grandson, potatoes.

Now, the bus with the Korczak delegation drove unerringly through those magnificent trees which formed the gateway to Treblinka. Stepping down from the bus, we were greeted by Boy Scouts and Girl Scouts of the Janusz Korczak troop, who lined the paths as honor guards. We waited, along with hundreds of other people who had come in chartered buses, for the ceremony to begin at the fake railroad station with its fake clock whose hands never moved, and its fake ticket counter that had no tickets, all of which had been meant to persuade the exhausted Jews from all over Europe that they were still in transit to resettlement in the East.

After listening to speeches by Polish officials, we walked, accompanied by martial music blaring from loudspeakers, along stone railroad tracks that symbolized the real tracks that had led to the death camp. For Treblinka is not there in the sense that Auschwitz and other camps are still there. There are no guard towers, no barbed-wire fences, no barracks, no empty suitcases and piles of children's shoes. This once huge killing center was partially burned down after its first year of operation in a rebellion by its captive Jewish workers, and then the Nazis completed the destruction to hide their traces.

Sometime after the war, the violated space that had once been Treblinka was transformed into a vast stone garden. Seventeen thousand rocks were brought in from Polish quarries to represent the villages, towns, and countries of the million men, women, and children who died there—all, except for a thousand gypsies, Jews.

The stone railroad tracks stopped at the place where Ukrainian guards and SS men brandishing whips and guns ordered the Jews out of the cattle cars—men to the right, women and children to the left—and into the "undressing barracks." The men had only to take off their clothes and tie their shoes together, but the women had to have their hair cut off as well, before they were ready for disinfection in the "showers."

We walked to the place where they had been herded, naked, in rows of five onto a narrow fenced-in path—the "Road to Heaven," as the Nazis called it—that led to the gas chambers.

We stared at the black stones over the pit where bodies were burned on the huge iron "roasting racks."

We passed a tall stone monument honoring the dead from Warsaw. The seventeen thousand rocks stood at attention like ghostly sentinels in that ghostly garden as we reached our destination, the one rock that bore a personal name:

JANUSZ KORCZAK
(HENRYK GOLDSZMIT)
AND THE CHILDREN

Appendix: Janusz Korczak's
Declaration of Children's Rights

As a children's advocate, Janusz Korczak spoke of the need for a Declaration of Children's Rights long before any such document was drawn up by the Geneva Convention (1924) or the United Nations General Assembly (1959). The Declaration he envisaged—not a plea for good will but a demand for action—was left uncompleted at the time of his death. Culling through *How to Love a Child, The Child's Right to Respect,* and other works, I have compiled the rights that Korczak considered most essential:

The child has the right to love.
> ("Love *the* child, not just your own.")

The child has the right to respect.
> ("Let us demand respect for shining eyes, smooth foreheads, youthful effort and confidence. Why should dulled eyes, a wrinkled brow, untidy gray hair, or tired resignation command greater respect?")

The child has the right to optimal conditions in which to grow and develop.
> ("We demand: do away with hunger, cold, dampness, stench, overcrowding, overpopulation.")

The child has the right to live in the present.
> ("Children are not people of tomorrow; they are people today.")

The child has the right to be himself or herself.
> ("A child is not a lottery ticket, marked to win the main prize.")

The child has the right to make mistakes.
> ("There are no more fools among children than among adults.")

The child has the right to fail.

("We renounce the deceptive longing for perfect children.")

The child has the right to be taken seriously.

("Who asks the child for his opinion and consent?")

The child has the right to be appreciated for what he is.

("The child, being small, has little market value.")

The child has the right to desire, to claim, to ask.

("As the years pass, the gap between adult demands and children's desires becomes progressively wider.")

The child has the right to have secrets.

("Respect their secrets.")

The child has the right to "*a* lie, *a* deception, *a* theft."

("He does not have the right to lie, deceive, steal.")

The child has the right to respect for his possessions and budget.

("Everyone has the right to his property, no matter how insignificant or valueless.")

The child has the right to education.

The child has the right to resist educational influence that conflicts with his or her own beliefs.

("It is fortunate for mankind that we are unable to force children to yield to assaults upon their common sense and humanity.")

The child has the right to protest an injustice.

("We must end despotism.")

The child has the right to a Children's Court where he can judge and be judged by his peers.

("We are the sole judges of the child's actions, movements, thoughts, and plans . . . I know that a Children's Court is essential, that in fifty years there will not be a single school, not a single institution without one.")

The child has the right to be defended in the juvenile-justice court system.

("The delinquent child is still a child . . . Unfortunately, suffering bred of poverty spreads like lice: sadism, crime, uncouthness, and brutality are nurtured on it.")

The child has the right to respect for his grief.

("Even though it be for the loss of a pebble.")

The child has the right to commune with God.

The child has the right to die prematurely.

("The mother's profound love for her child must give him the right to premature death, to ending his life cycle in only one or two springs . . . Not every bush grows into a tree.")

Notes

I have listed the first book publication of Janusz Korczak's major writings. The abbreviations before some books will be cited in the chapter notes. Titles are listed in English, followed by the Polish. All books are in Polish unless otherwise indicated.

Notes are keyed to page numbers.

Which Way? (*Ktoredy?*), unpublished play (1899).
Children of the Street (*Dzieci ulicy*) (Warsaw, 1901).
Stuff and Nonsense (*Koszalki opalki*) (Warsaw, 1905).

CDR *Child of the Drawing Room* (*Dziecko salonu*) (Warsaw, 1906).

MJS *Moshki, Joski, and Srule* (*Moski, Joski i Srule*) (Warsaw, 1910).
Jozki, Jaski, and Franki (*Jozki, Jaski i Franki* (Warsaw, 1911).
Glory (*Slawa*) (Warsaw, 1913).
Baby (*Bobo*) (Warsaw, 1914).

CB *Confessions of a Butterfly* (*Spowiedz motyla*), published together with *Baby* and *The Unlucky Week* under the title *Bobo* (Warsaw, 1914).
The Unlucky Week (*Feralny tydzien*) (Warsaw, 1914).

SWJK *Educational Moments: Helcia, Stefan* (*Momenty wychowawcze*) (Warsaw, 1919). In English in *Selected Works of Janusz Korczak*, ed. Martin Wolins (Warsaw, reproduced in Springfield, Virginia, 1967), trans. Jerzy Bachrach.

HTL *How to Love a Child* (*Jak kochac dzieci*) (Part I: Warsaw, 1919; Part II: Warsaw, 1920). In English in *SWJK*, 1920.
Alone with God: Prayers of Those Who Don't Pray (*Sam na sam z Bogiem: Modlitwy ludzi, ktorzy sie nie modla*) (Warsaw, 1922).

KM *King Matt the First* (*Krol Macius Pierwszy*) (Warsaw, 1922). In English, trans. Richard Lourie (New York, 1986).
King Matt on the Desert Island (*Krol Macius na wyspie bezludnej*) (Warsaw, 1923).
The Bankruptcy of Little Jack (*Bankructwo malego Dzeka*) (Warsaw, 1924).

WIALA *When I Am Little Again* (*Kiedy znow bede maly*) (Warsaw, 1926).

CRR *The Child's Right to Respect (Prawo dziecka do szacunku)* (Warsaw, 1929). In English in *SWJK*.

RL *Rules of Life (Prawidla zycia)* (Warsaw, 1930).

SM *Senate of Madmen (Senat szalencow)* (Warsaw, 1931).

Kajtus the Magician (Kajtus czarodziej) (Warsaw, 1934).

The Stubborn Boy: The Life of Louis Pasteur (Uparty chlopiec: Zycie Ludwika Pasteura) (Warsaw, 1938).

Reflections (Refleksje) (Warsaw, 1938).

Moses (Mojzesz) (Palestine, 1939).

The Three Journeys of Hershkele (Trzy wyprawy Jerszka) (Warsaw, 1939).

HP *Humorous Pedagogy (Pedagogika zartobliwa)* (Warsaw, 1939).

GD *The Ghetto Diary (Pamietnik)* (Warsaw, 1957). There are two translations in English: *Ghetto Diary* (New York: Holocaust Library, 1978), trans. Jerzy Bachrach and Barbara Krzywicka (Vedder), and *The Warsaw Ghetto Memoirs of Janusz Korczak* (Washington, D.C.: The University Press of America, 1978), trans. E. P. Kulawiec.

The following are abbreviations for the major anthologies of Korczak's works and books on Korczak in Polish. English translations will be cited.

MD *Mister Doctor: The Life of Janusz Korczak.* In English, trans. Romuald Jan Kruk and Harold Cresswell (London: Peter Davies, 1965).

CWJK *Wybor Pism (Collected Works of Janusz Korczak)*, ed. Igor Newerly (Warsaw, 1957–1958).

LL *Zywe wiazanie (Living Links)*, a memoir by Igor Newerly.

RJK *Wspomnienia O Januszu Korczaku (Reminiscences of Janusz Korczak)* (Warsaw, 1981).

JKGY *Janusz Korczak, the Ghetto Years*, by Yitzhak Perlis. In English (Israel, 1972), trans. from the Hebrew by Avner Tomaschoff.

LR *Maly Przeglad (Little Review)*.

WDAC *The Warsaw Diary of Adam Czerniakow*, eds. Raul Hilberg, Stanislaw Staron, Josef Kermisz; trans. Stanislaw Staron and the staff of Yad Vashem (New York, 1979).

MZWD *A Warsaw Diary*, Michael Zylberberg (London, 1969). Also original Yiddish manuscript not included in book. In English (Israel, Yad Vashem Archives).

I have translated passages from books not in English from the literal renderings of Polish assistants. I am grateful to Richard Lourie for going over most of the translations with me. I have, with permission, revised many of the quotations from the Wolins anthology and from *The Ghetto Diary* published by the Holocaust Library, with the help of Richard Lourie.

1 / CHILD OF THE DRAWING ROOM

13. his "bold scheme to remake the world" *GD*.
13. He never knew the exact year *GD*.

13. Poland having been partitioned The three partitions of Poland were in 1772, 1793, and 1795.

14. a letter of blessing Letter from Janusz Korczak to a baby, Dan Golding, in Palestine, 5 December 1934: "I have lost so many papers, but I still have a letter from the rabbi who blessed me when I was born." See also Hanna Mortkowicz-Olczak, *Mister Doctor: The Life of Janusz Korczak*, trans. Romuald Jan Kruk and Harold Cresswell (London: Peter Davies, 1965). Original edition: *Janusz Korczak* (Cracow, 1949).

14. "that stern regiment of women" *GD*.

14. "harbor secrets" *HTL*.

14. poor children were dirty *HTL*.

14. "A child is someone who needs to move" Janusz Korczak, "Podworko" ("The Courtyard"), *Opieka nad dzieckiem* (*Child Care*) (Warsaw), 1925, no. 3.

14. "That boy has no ambition" *GD*.

14. "The doll wasn't merely a doll" *WIALA*.

14. "Children's games aren't frivolous" *WIALA*.

15. His father flew into a rage *GD*.

15. "Feelings that have no outlet become daydreams" *HTL*.

15. "So she is going through the forest" *HTL*.

15. French governess *CB*.

16. Adam Mickiewicz 1798–1855.

16. prickly beards *HTL*.

16. He tweaked Henryk's ears *GD*.

16. Jozef exploded at him *HTL*.

17. "Mama was right to be reluctant" *GD*.

17. Nativity play *GD*.

18. Nativity puppet show *GD*.

19. "mysterious question of religion" *GD*.

19. The canary *GD*.

19. "I, too, was a Jew" *GD*.

2 / HERITAGE

20. Hirsh Goldszmit, after whom he was named *GD*. Dr. Hirsh Goldszmit (1805–72), a second-degree surgeon in the Jewish hospital (Szpital Starozakonnych) according to *The List of Physicians and Apothecaries in the Kingdom of Poland*, 1839. After the death of his first wife, Chana Ejser, in 1867, Hirsh married Sarah, and had a son, Karl (Archives of vital statistics, Hrubieszow). The Jewish settlement in Hrubieszow dated from 1444. In 1939, at the outbreak of World War II, the Jewish population was 7,500 (*Encyclopedia Judaica*). When I visited Hrubieszow in 1983, there were no Jews living there. The Jewish cemetery was gutted, with only a cement memorial plaque marking the spot. The famous wooden synagogue had been destroyed. The former Jewish hospital, a modest two-story building, operates

as a clinic. See *Hrubieszow Memorial Book* (Israel, 1962), in Yiddish and Hebrew.

20. **the Haskalah** The Jewish Enlightenment movement, based on the ideas of Moses Mendelssohn, was founded in the late eighteenth century in Berlin. See Jacob Katz, *Out of the Ghetto: The Social Background of Jewish Emancipation, 1770–1870* (New York, 1978).

20. **The Jews had been welcomed into Poland by the Polish kings** For background reading in English on the early history of the Jews, see Bernard D. Weinryb, *The Jews of Poland: A Social and Economic History of the Jewish Community in Poland from 1100–1800* (Philadelphia, 1972); Salo W. Baron, *A Social and Religious History of the Jews* (New York, 1952); S. M. Dubnow, *An Outline of Jewish History* (New York, 1925); Max I. Dimont, *Jews, God and History* (New York, 1962).

20. **but they had remained isolated in the society** The historian Aleksander Hertz believed that the Jews made up a distinct caste in Poland, much as the blacks are an example of a caste group in America. He defines caste as a closed group that has its own religious, legal, linguistic, moral, or cultural rules, and occupies a definite place in the social hierarchy. In Poland the nobility was the upper class, a caste of the privileged; the peasants, burghers, and Jews belonged to the lower classes and were of a "lower" order. Hertz qualified that this division was not completely rigid: only the Gypsies, as a group and individuals, remained at the bottom of the ladder. Aleksander Hertz, interview with author, Queens, 1983. See his book *Jews in Polish Culture* (Evanston, 1987), trans. Richard Lourie. See also Celia S. Heller, *On the Edge of Destruction: Jews of Poland Between the Two World Wars* (New York, 1977). Heller believes that the Poles considered the Jews inherently inferior and that the concept of caste is useful in understanding the situation of the Jews in interwar Poland.

21. **the regional Hebrew newspaper** The *Hamaggid* (*Herald*), February 1865, no. 7. The *maskilim* revived the Hebrew language for secular use. See also Maria Falkowska, "Social Work Traditions in the Goldszmit Family," *Bulletin of the International Janusz Korczak Society* (Warsaw), 1982.

21. **Ludwik, converted** "Ludwik Goldszmit, converted in 1849 at the age of 18." In the church book of conversions: Teodor Jeske-Choinski, *Neofici Polscy* (Warsaw, 1904).

21. **continuing to exhaust himself** GD.

21. **Jozef Goldszmit** (1844–96). Birth certificate in Archives of Vital Statistics, Lublin. (Available in Korczak Workshop Archives in Warsaw.)

21. **Jakub Goldszmit** (1848–?) Ibid. The date of Jakub's death is not known. In 1894 he traveled to Philadelphia, according to records of the Institute of Literary Research of the Polish Academy of Science in Warsaw. There is no information on his death in either the Jewish or the Polish biographical dictionaries that list his work.

21. **three great nineteenth-century Romantic poets** Adam Mickiewicz (1798–1855), Juliusz Slowacki (1809–49), Zygmunt Krasinski (1812–59).

22. **the Israelite** The *Izraelita* reported on the cultural and social life of the Jewish community, 1866–1912. Jozef's article on arriving in Warsaw is in the correspondence column, November 1866. For a photographic history of Jewish life in Poland,

1864–1939, see Lucjan Dobroszycki and Barbara Kirshenblatt-Gimlett, *Images Before My Eyes* (New York, 1977).

22. Jews who, except for a small assimilated circle   In using the terms *assimilated* and *acculturated*, I am aware that there is a thin line between the two, and that there are varying degrees within each. The historian Lucjan Dobroszycki defines an acculturated Jew as one who is educated in the culture into which he was born but retains his own religious customs. An assimilated Jew—a Jew of Mosaic faith as he was called in Poland—may be acculturated to a point of not observing religious rituals, while still retaining his Jewish identity. (Interview with author, New York, 1987.) The historian Aleksander Hertz wrote that the era of assimilation began in the second half of the nineteenth century when Jews attempted to leave the caste without changing their religion. Rejecting the rules of the caste, Jews began assimilating to the rules and ways of the world outside the caste. *Jews in Polish Culture* (Evanston, 1987).

22. Polish-language craft schools   "A Word on Craft Schools in Warsaw," *Izraelita*, 1868, no. 48; "On the Vital Necessity of Protection of Boys of the Mosaic Faith in Warsaw," *Izraelita*, 1869, no. 34.

22. *Sir Moses Montefiore*   First in a series of portraits of well-known Jews of the nineteenth century (*Wizerunki wslawionych Zydow*) (Warsaw, 1867). Second in the series was a monograph in 1869 on Achilles Fould (1799–1867), a financier who served Napoleon. Jakub published an article on famous Jews ("Zyciorysy slawnych Izraelitow") in *Izraelita*, 1867, no. 14. Jakub also wrote a monograph on Father Stanislaw Staszic (1755–1836), the philanthropist and statesman who bought Hrubieszow from the Austrian government. Although Staszic is considered by some historians to have been anti-Semitic, Jakub Goldszmit praised him for offering equal economic benefits to Poles and Jews in Hrubieszow.

23. Jozef and Jakub used writing as a tool to educate   The brothers wrote articles on little-known Jews who had lived pure lives helping the poor. Jozef published on Jewish doctors in Italy (*Izraelita*, 1869, no. 28) and on the last days of the Jews in Spain (*Izraelita*, 1869, no. 4–13). In 1868 Jakub was commissioned by the philanthropist Matias Bersohn to write a monograph on the sixteenth-century Jewish cemetery in Lublin in order to learn if it preceded the Catholic cemetery and monastery located next to it. It did, by fifty years. Jakub refers to this work in *Izraelita*, 1875, no. 30. The cemetery, the site of mass killings of Jews by the Nazis during World War II, was completely destroyed by them.

23. One has only to read their stilted novels   Jozef Goldszmit, *The Shopkeeper's Daughter* (*Corka handlarza, obrazek z czasow ostatniej epidemii w Warszawie*) (Warsaw, 1868). Permit by Censor, 7 October 1867. Written when Jozef was twenty-four, this is a sentimental love story that takes place during the 1867 cholera epidemic that killed thousands of Warsaw's impoverished Jews. It is dedicated to his mother with an equally sentimental poem, "At My Mother's Grave." Jakub Goldszmit, *The Family Drama* (*Dramat rodzinny*) (Warsaw, 1881). Written when Jakub was twenty-five, the book is a vehicle for protesting the subjugation of women, a theme that engaged liberal Western thinkers, like John Stuart Mill, whose works were familiar

to the intelligentsia in Poland. The plot centers on a wronged woman driven into prostitution to support her baby. Jakub also translated Herbert Spencer's *Physiology of Laughter* into Polish from the German edition in 1883.

23. doomed to failure   Dr. Jaakov Shatzki notes that Polish-Jewish literature did not achieve the popularity of German-Jewish literature in spite of the efforts of writers like the "two scholars, the brothers Jakub and Jozef Goldszmit." *Geshikhte fun Yidn in Warshe* (*History of the Jews in Warsaw*), vol. 3 (New York: YIVO, 1953), pp. 301–6. In Yiddish.

23. Talmudic divorce law   *Wyklad prawa rozwodowego podlug ustaw Mojzeszowo-talmudycznych z ogolnym pogladem na ich rozwoj z uwglednieniem przepisow obowiazujacych.* Introduction by Stanislaw Czarnowski (Warsaw, 1871).

23. the most famous Polish writers   The brothers went to the same *gymnasium* in Lublin as the novelist Boleslaw Prus (1847–1912). Jakub corresponded with historical novelist Jozef Ignacy Kraszewski (1812–87), who found political refuge in Dresden after the Uprising of 1863. Kraszewski wrote Jakub of his belief that someday Polish and Jewish children would go to school together.

23. Jewish *Kalendar   Kalendarz dla Israelitow na rok*, 1881–82 (*The Jewish Calendar 1881–82*) (Warsaw, 1881). Jakub also edited the *Lublin Calendar* for 1882 and the *Warsaw Family Calendar* for 1883 and 1884. Using the pen name Zlotnicki, Jakub wrote for numerous periodicals during this period.

23. Jakub infuriated the wealthy leaders   Jaakov Shatzki, op. cit., vol. 3, pp. 301–2.

24. lectured in Kalisz   Maria Falkowska, interview with author, Warsaw, 1979.

24. Adolf Gebicki   Obituary, *Izraelita*, 1877. Emilia Gebicka, obituary, *Izraelita*, 1 April 1892.

24. his "Grannie"   The Gebicki graves were not uncovered in the overgrown Jewish cemetery until Jan Jagielski, the secretary of the Social Committee of the Care of Jewish Cemeteries, discovered them, along with that of Korczak's father, in the late spring of 1986. Until then the maiden name of Korczak's maternal grandmother (Deutscher) was unknown. Korczak's family on both sides seems to have been wiped out during the war. In 1956 an elderly woman who lived in Lublin claimed to be Korczak's cousin. She was given an apartment by the Korczak Workshop in return for giving up any rights to Korczak's literary estate. (Maria Falkowska, interview with author, 1986.) It is presumed that she is no longer alive. No other heirs have surfaced.

3 / CONFESSIONS OF A BUTTERFLY

25. "Strict, boring, and oppressive"   *WIALA.* Henryk Goldszmit attended the Szmurla elementary school on Freta Street, which was to prepare him for entrance to a *gymnasium* in the fourth grade.

25. He never forgot   *WIALA.*

25. "The adult world revolves"   *HTL.*

26. his father suffered the first of the breakdowns   *GD* and *CB.*

26. reading became his salvation   *GD* and *CB.*

26. "degrade" his dignity *CB*.

27. Retaining his belief in the harmfulness of masturbation Korczak wrote that masturbation, like convulsions or a cough, should be treated by a doctor, and that a "cure" was possible. Janusz Korczak, "Obserwacja jednego przypadku, onanizm chlopca" ("A Boy's Masturbation: The Observation of One Case"), *Szkola specjalna (The Special School)*, 1936, no. 3.

27. Jozef Goldszmit's behavior There are no records as to which asylum Jozef was committed to, but Tworki seems almost certain for a man of Jozef's status. Hoping to find Jozef's records, I traveled to Tworki in 1981. However, the director, Wojciech Molzulski, informed me that in 1914 the Russians had evacuated the patients along with all hospital documents to Kazan to prevent them from falling into German hands. Neither patients nor documents were ever located after the war.

28. "condescending" smile of the psychiatrist Janusz Korczak, *Senate of Madmen (Senat szalencow)*. The play was performed in the Atheneum theater, Warsaw, 1931.

28. father's cloak Janusz Korczak in *Spoleczentwo (Society)*, January 1908, no. 3.

28. "The pawnshop is life" *Stuff and Nonsense*, in *CWJK*.

29. He soon devised a technique Note for teachers in "Stefan" in *Educational Moments*, included in *SWJAK*.

29. "The Gordian Knot" *Thorns* (Warsaw), 1896, no. 39.

29. Jozef Goldszmit died at the age of fifty-two Obituary, *Izraelita*, 23 May 1896.

29. possibly by his own hand There are a few references to suicide with guns in Korczak's early autobiographical novel, *Child of the Drawing Room*. And there was his own unpublished novel *Suicide*—all of which suggests that Jozef may have taken his life.

30. Henryk's mother obtained a license *Izraelita*, 23 September 1896. Her address is listed as Nowo Senatorska No. 6, apartment 11.

30. "son of a madman" *GD*.

30. "Ah, let me die" The editor of *Prawda* was the critic Aleksander Swietochowski. Olczak, *MD*.

30. "To wound a poet's heart" *CB*.

4 / WHICH WAY?

31. It won honorable mention *Echo muzyczne (The Musical Echo)*, 14 April 1899.

31. Legend has it *LL*.

31. *The Story of Janasz Korczak and the Swordbearer's Daughter (Historia o Janaszu Korczaku i o Pieknej Miecznikownie)* (Warsaw, 1879).

31. Jozef Ignacy Kraszewski 1812–87. He wrote 300 novels, which are included in the 700 volumes of his collected works. See Julian Krzyzanowski, *A History of Polish Literature* (Warsaw, 1978), and Czeslaw Milosz, *The History of Polish Literature* (Berkeley, 1983).

31. pseudonyms were not a contest requirement *The Musical Echo*, 14 April 1899, listed only two people with pen names—one of whom was Henryk Goldszmit.

31. "Take me under your wing, Master" It is interesting that in his *Confessions of a*

Butterfly, Korczak has his young narrator appeal to Kraszewski to take him under his wing. Korczak may have taken his title *Which Way?* from the title of Kraszewski's article "Which Way?" that appeared in the *Warsaw Review* in 1863. That same year, Kraszewski, blacklisted by the Russian authorities for political activities, emigrated to Dresden. Among his correspondents were Jakub Goldszmit (who sometimes used the pen name Zlotnicki—*zloto* meaning gold).

32. "I escaped from my youth" Radio interview, 1933.

32. Hundreds of articles and feuilletons Korczak wrote 600 articles between 1896 and 1907, from the age of eighteen to twenty-seven, for such Polish publications as *Czytelnia dla Wszystkich (Reading Room for Everyone), Kolce (Thorns), Glos (Voice), Kurier Polski (Polish Courier), Wedrowiec (Wanderer), Przeglad Pedagogiczny (Pedagogical Review), Krytyka Lekarska (Medical Critique), Przeglad Spoleczny (Social Review),* and *Swiat (World).*

32. Leon Rygier Recollections in *RJK.*

32. "Chekhov's becoming a great writer" In the ghetto Korczak would write: "As for writers, I owe most to Chekhov—a great social diagnostician and clinician. "Curriculum Vitae," in *JKGY.*

33. "Hair will grow on the palm of my hand" Martha Osnos, interview with author, New York City, 1984. Martha Osnos is the daughter of Dr. Zygmunt Bychowski.

33. Stefan Zeromski 1864–1925. Called "the conscience of Polish literature." See Czeslaw Milosz, *The History of Polish Literature* (Berkeley, 1983).

33. "Unkempt boys in run-down shoes" *CDR.*

34. "I lied when I told you" "Nikt" ("No One"), *Reading Room for Everyone,* 15 June 1899, no. 24. In Polish.

34. "I am a person concerned" *Thorns,* 1901, no. 1.

34. Jan Wladyslaw Dawid 1858–1914.

35. Jadwiga Szczawinska Dawid 1864–1910.

35. Zofia Nalkowska 1884–1954.

35. In one entry she notes 1 December, 1899.

36. Korczak considered Pestalozzi Janusz Korczak, "The Children: Development of the Idea of Love Toward One's Fellowman in the Nineteenth Century," *Reading Room for Everyone,* 1899, no. 52.

36. Waclaw Nalkowski 1856–1911.

36. Stefania Sempolowska 1870–1943.

36. the Free Lending Library The Charitable Society for Free Lending Libraries established a few libraries where people could take books out without charge. Many Poles and Jews worked together as volunteers on this project. Korczak wrote: "Several years of work in a free lending library afforded me rich observation material." "Curriculum Vitae," in *JKGY.* See also recollection of Helena Bobinska, who worked with Korczak in the library in 1902, *RJK.* Marek Jaworski, *Janusz Korczak* (Warsaw, 1978).

36. "enough time in the cooler" *GD.*

5 / MUZZLE ON THE SOUL

38. Ludwik Licinski 1874–1908.

38. She drank vodka Zofia Nalkowska, *Pamietniki (Memoirs), 1899–1905* (Warsaw, 1975). Diary entry: 1903.

38. "howling like a dog" *CDR.*

39. "I dreamed I was a poodle" *CDR.*

39. *Child of the Drawing Room Dziecko salonu* (Warsaw, 1906). Published serially in *Glos (Voice),* 1904–5.

40. medical diploma Korczak graduated from medical school in November 1904 (*Izraelita,* 1904). He received his diploma in March 1905 (Nazi document, 20 September 1940, Korczak Workship Archives, Warsaw).

40. Torn abruptly out of his life His departure was announced in "Personal Announcements," *Izraelita,* 26 June 1905 and July 1905.

40. "war helps you see" Janusz Korczak, "O wojnie. W pociagu sanitarnym" ("About the War: On the Hospital Train") *Voice,* 1905, nos. 48, 49.

41. "It was not that I came to China" *Little Review (Maly Przeglad),* 1927, no. 14.

41. After meeting four-year-old Iuo-ya *GD.*

41. a teacher, reeking of vodka *Little Review,* 1927, no. 14.

41. "Before you go to war" *LL.*

6 / LITTLE HOSPITAL

43. Critics proclaimed him a new voice Stanislaw Brzozowski wrote that the author was one of the most interesting cultural and literary voices of that time. See his "Janusz Korczak" in *Przeglad Spoleczny (Social Review),* 28 April 1906. Assessing Korczak's work in 1978, Julian Krzyzanowski writes that only his books for children are read today. His "excellent" novel *Child of the Drawing Room* paved the way for young naturalist writers to approach the social issues of their time. See Julian Krzyzanowski, *A History of Polish Literature* (Warsaw, 1978).

43. "general drudge" *GD.*

44. Children's Hospital on Sliska Street Officially known as the Bersohn and Bauman Children's Hospital. Founded 28 June 1878 by the banker and philanthropist, Matias (Majer) Bersohn (1832–1908), and his wife, Chai, who included their son-in-law, Salomon Bauman, and daughter, Pauline, in the project. It opened with twenty beds for poor Jewish children, but its emergency room, one of the largest in Warsaw, treated all children, regardless of religion, without charge. When a second floor was added in 1930, Korczak said it looked like something out of a fairy tale. It still operates today as a hospital for children. Interviews with staff at the hospital, 1981. See Henryk Korszczor, *Kartki z Historii Zydow w Warszawie XIX–XX w (Pages from the History of the Jews of Warsaw in the 19th and 20th Centuries)* (Warsaw, 1979).

44. "a good old soul" *GD.*

44. His mother was shocked *GD.*

44. "Please wait a moment, Doctor" *GD*.

45. Only to the poor   *GD*.

45. "it is written in the Talmud"   *GD*.

45. This idealistic young doctor   *GD*. Korczak also described his struggle to be an "honest" doctor in "Loose Thoughts," *Medical Critique*, 1906, nos. 10, 11, 12. The pieces are signed H. Goldszmit.

45. One mother entered the sickroom   Ada Hagari, interview with author, Israel, 1981.

45. Another knew that her sick daughter   Testimony of Miroslawa Szulcowa, Korczak Workshop Archives, Warsaw.

45. A former patient, Henryk Grynberg   Henryk Grynberg, interview with author, Warsaw, October 1981.

45. articles calling for basic hospital reforms   *Medical Critique*, 1906, nos. 7–8, 9–10; 1907, no. 2. *Wiedza (Knowledge)*, 1908, vol. 2; 1909, vol 1. See also article by Stanislaw Brzozowski on Korczak in *Social Review*, 28 April 1906.

45. "The breast does not belong to the mother"   *Pediatric Review*, 1911.

46. Casting his way "like seashells"   *GD*.

46. "Little hospital. I remember winter"   *Jednodniowka Towarzystwa Przyjaciol Dzieci (One Day Paper of the Society of Friends of Children)* (Warsaw, 1925).

46. "dignified, mature, and sensible"   Janusz Korczak's "Curriculum Vitae," his application to the personnel department on the Judenrat, 9 February 1942. Reproduced in *JKGY*.

46. "How terrible it must be to wake up"   Martha Osnos, interview with author, New York, 1984.

46. a girl named Zofia   Igor Newerly, *LL*.

47. "When the devil will we stop prescribing"   Igor Newerly in his introduction to *SWJK*.

47. "If you are so full of pity"   *HP*.

7 / SUMMER CAMPS

48. volunteered his services to the camp society   Korczak wrote about his experiences in *Izraelita*, 1904, no. 7. In 1933 he wrote in the *Little Review* (no. 41): "When I was a student I worked in summer camps. In the fall the campers visited me and that's how a children's club came to be organized in my flat."

48. The camp to which he was assigned   The camp system for poor children was established in Poland in 1882. The Jewish camp where Korczak was counselor was built in 1902 by the philanthropist Michal Endelman. In an application to the Judenrat, Korczak wrote: "I first came in touch with the Jewish child when I was a counselor at the Markiewicz summer camp in Michalowka." *JKGY*.

48. "There for the first time"   *HTL*.

49. "There I was, like someone wearing kid gloves"   *HTL*.

49. "I was not a novice"   *HTL*.

50. "In life there are two kingdoms"   *MJS*.

50. "Yesterday—a caveman"   *HTL*.

50. A peasant passing by   *MJS*.
51. "the Polish language smiles"   *MJS*.
51. The same was true for Yiddish   *MJS*.
53. "Courts of Arbitration"   Historian Stefan Woloszyn, interview with author, War-
    saw, 1981. See I. Newerly, A. Kaminski, and W. Zelazko, *Samorzad uczniowski
    w systemie wychowawczym Korczaka* (*Self-Government in Korczak's Educational
    System* (Warsaw, 1962). Also Jolanta Switalski-Ebersman, "Die politische-kulturelle
    Entwicklung Polens (1815–1939) und Janusz Korczaks Beitrag für die Erneuerung
    der Erziehung" ("The Political-Cultural Development of Poland (1815–1939) and
    Janusz Korczak's Contribution to the Development of Education," Ph.D. disser-
    tation (Stettin, Poland).
53. Bronislaw Trentowski: 1808–69.
54. "light and knowledge"   H. Goldszmit, "Wrazenia z Berlina" ("Impressions from
    Berlin"), *Medical Critique*, 1907, nos. 10, 11, 12. In his research Bernd Graubner
    found that Korczak worked with Heinrich Finkelstein at the Children's Home of
    the Schmidt-Gallish Foundations and the Municipal Orphanage; with Adolf Baginski
    at Emperor and Empress Frederick Children's Hospital. Bernd Graubner, inter-
    view with author, Warsaw, 1986. See *Janusz Korczak, Zeugnisee einer lebendigen
    Pädagogik*, ed. Friedhelm Beiner (Heinsberg, West Germany, 1982).
55. *Jozki, Jaski, and Franki*   It is interesting to note that in the 1984 edition, which
    is a fourth-grade reader, the line "Olek is crying, and each tear contains a cross on
    which Christ is very sad" has been changed to "Olek is crying, and each tear is
    holy."
56. asked him to compare Jewish and Polish children   Janusz Korczak, "Dziecko zyd-
    owskie—opinia rzeczoznawcy" ("The Jewish Child—in the Opinion of an Expert"),
    Miesiecznik Zydowski (Jewish Monthly), 1933, no. 3.
57. He was to meet Stefania (Stefa) Wilczynska   Joseph Arnon, an apprentice teacher
    in Korczak's Orphans Home who conducted a long correspondence with Korczak
    after emigrating to Palestine, believed that Stefa met Korczak while she was studying
    in Switzerland in 1908. However, Stella Eliasberg and Igor Newerly have placed
    this meeting in Warsaw.

8 / THE DECISION

58. He stood in the back watching   Stella Eliasberg's journal.
58. reciting the poems they had been rehearsing   These may have been the poems of
    Maria Konopnicka (1842–1910), a poet of the oppressed as well as a children's
    writer. She wrote fairy-tale fantasies with titles like *Little Orphan Mary and the
    Gnomes* (*O krasnoludkach i sierotce Marysi*). See Julian Krzyzanowski, *A History
    of Polish Literature* (Warsaw, 1978).
58. "rare children who bear"   *HTL*.
59. Stefa's mother   Interview with her daughter-in-law, Irena Eliasberg Wilczynska,
    October 1981.

60. "pedagogical love"   Joseph Arnon, "The Passion of Janusz Korczak," *Midstream*, May 1973.

60. Nothing is known of Lui   When I visited the Jewish cemetery in Warsaw in 1986, I was shown a piece of Jozef Lui's gravestone that had been found near Jozef Goldszmit's grave. There is no marriage certificate for Korczak's sister, Anna: her husband's name is known only because Korczak dedicated his book on Louis Pasteur to Anna Lui. Jozef Lui's obituary in the Warsaw *Courier* (24 July 1909) reads: "After brief but grievous suffering, he died on July 22 at the age of thirty-nine. He leaves a wife, sisters, mother-in-law and brothers-in-law." The absence of a father-in-law in the obituary (Jozef Goldszmit was already deceased), and the fact that Martha Eliasberg recalls that Anna was widowed early, strongly suggests Jozef Lui was her husband. Igor Newerly recalls that Korczak told him Lui had syphilis and committed suicide.

60. Ludwik Krzywicki   1859–1941. Konstantin Krzeczkowski, *Zarys zycia i pracy Ludwika Krzywickiego* (*Life and Work of Ludwik Krzywicki*) (Warsaw, 1939). In Polish. See also *LL*.

61. "feed his reformatory zeal"   Erik Erikson, *Gandhi's Truth* (New York: W. W. Norton, 1969).

61. "The reason I became an educator"   *LL*.

61. "The road I have chosen"   *HTL*.

62. not betraying medicine   *HTL*. Later, writing in the *Ghetto Diary*, Korczak felt he had betrayed medicine.

62. "What a fever, a cough, or nausea"   "Introductory Remarks" in *Educational Moments*, included in *SWJK*.

62. "sculptor of the child's soul"   *GD*.

62. School of Life   (*Szkola zycia*). This work by Janusz Korczak was published in fragments during 1907–8 in *Spoleczenstwo* (*Society*) magazine. Reconstructed as a whole in *Pisma wybrane* (*Selected Works*), ed. Aleksander Lewin (Warsaw, 1978).

63. "a deep stratum of an archaeological dig"   Isaac Bashevis Singer, *Shosha* (New York, 1978).

63. "momentous experience"   *HTL*. Later he would regret making large barrack-like dormitories with little privacy. "If an extra floor were ever to be built in the future," he wrote, "I would be in favor of a hotel layout: small rooms running off a central corridor." After the war, the orphanage was renovated with small bedrooms replacing the large dormitories.

63. The eldest of the Eliasbergs' four daughters, Helena   Helena Eliasberg Syrkus, interview with author, Warsaw, 1979.

64. He would tell friends   Recollections of Maria Czapska, *RJK*.

64. Berlin had taught him   *HTL*.

65. the suburb of Forest Hill   Janusz Korczak, "Forest Hill," *Swiatlo* (*The Light*), 1912, no. 2. Korczak does not name the orphanages he visited, but at that time there were two adjoining institutions known as "industrial homes" in Forest Hill: Shaftesbury House, founded in 1873, and the Louise Home, founded in 1881. See "Forest Hill," *Concern* magazine, Philip Veerman, March 1987.

65. "a slave who is a Polish Jew" Letter from Janusz Korczak to Moshe Zertal, 30 March 1937.

66. "idea of serving the child and his rights" Ibid.

66. "Out of a mad soul" The prayer of the artist, in Janusz Korczak, *Alone with God: Prayers of Those Who Don't Pray.*

9 / THE CHILDREN'S REPUBLIC

67. "those noisy, frozen, excited" *HTL.*

68. iron cots Joseph Arnon, "The Passion of Janusz Korczak," *Midstream*, May 1973. Also Igor Newerly and Ida Merzan, interviews with author.

68. Stefa would recall Letter from Stefa Wilczynska to Jakub Einfeld, Palestine, 1934.

68. that first year *HTL.*

69. "A clean polished table" *HTL.*

69. "For want of a foundation" *HTL.*

70. Grigori Schmukler Interview with author, Brighton Beach, N.Y., 1983.

70. "What were you talking about . . . ?" *HTL.*

70. the first in Polish literature Hana Kirschner, interview with author, Warsaw, November 1981.

71. "symphony of children's breathing" *HTL.*

71. An eight-year-old boy woke with a toothache Fragment of unpublished, undated work, written in pencil. Quoted in *Mysl pedagogiczna Janusza Korczaka Nowe Zrodla* (*The Pedagogical Thought of Janusz Korczak*), ed. Maria Falkowska (Warsaw, 1983).

71. When he heard Moishe sob *HTL.*

72. Some of the children did stray Written for the orphanage newspaper, the *Orphans Home Weekly.* It was reprinted in 1914 in *W Sloncu* (*In the Sunshine*), a weekly children's journal edited by Janina Mortkowicz (the wife of Korczak's publisher) and Stefania Sempolowska. In 1916 Sempolowska took over the editorship. *In the Sunshine* attracted many famous writers, including the poet Juliusz Tuwim and novelist Stefan Zeromski.

72. courses in educational journalism *HTL.*

72. "With a paper, we'll be able to know" *In the Sunshine*, 1913.

73. "Do you remember" Ibid.

73. he favored the old fairy tales Korczak's favorite tale was "Puss in Boots," written by the French author Charles Perrault (1628–1703) and translated into Polish in 1693 together with "Sleeping Beauty," "Little Red Riding Hood," and "Cinderella."

74. "I always thought in terms of obstacles" *WIALA.*

74. "Is it true?" *HTL.*

74. "lesson in humility" *MJS.*

75. "evil whisper of the street" *HTL.*

75. Warsaw's three hundred thousand Jews There was a 25 percent increase in number between 1900 and 1910. See Henryk Wereszycki, *Historia polityczna Polski 1864–1918* (Paris, 1979).

75. A militant nationalist   *GD.*

75. And another Polish acquaintance   *GD.*

75. "Three Currents"   Janusz Korczak, "Trzy prady," in *Spoleczentwo (Society)*, 1910, no. 42.

76. Hermann Cohen   See *Essays from Martin Buber's Journal, Der Jude, 1916–1928*, ed. Arthur A. Cohen (Tuscaloosa, Alabama, 1980).

10 / HOW TO LOVE A CHILD

77. When the bank refused   Recollections of Hanna Mortkowicz-Olczak in *RJK.*

78. Jakub Mortkowicz   1876–1931.

78. Janina Mortkowicz   1875–1960.

78. *In the Sunshine*   See notes for Chapter 9.

78. Esterka Weintraub   Her picture was placed in the Silence Room of the orphanage. Nothing is known of her origins. There were unfounded rumors that she was the daughter of Stefa and Korczak.

79. "an orgy of devils"   "Stefan," *Educational Moments*, in *SWJK.*

79. sight of a blind old Jew   *GD.*

79. "It is not only the Jews who suffer"   Janusz Korczak, "Z Wojny" ("From the War"), *Nowy Dziennik*, 15 July 1918.

79. *How to Love a Child*   It is interesting to note that this book was translated into Russian by Lenin's wife, N. K. Krupskaya, in 1922.

79. until you see him as a separate being   Korczak's fierce belief in the right of the child to respect has been echoed by modern educators; among them see John Holt, *Escape from Childhood: The Needs and Rights of Children* (New York, 1974); Alice Miller, *The Drama of the Gifted Child* (formerly *Prisoners of Childhood*) (New York, 1983). See also Patricia Anne Piziali's dissertation, "A Comparison of Janusz Korczak's Concept of the Rights of the Child with Those of Other Selected Child Advocates" (George Washington University, 1981), and Edwin Kulawiec, "Janusz Korczak: Champion of Children," *Childhood Education*, October 1979.

81. "the tight ring of bayonets"   "Stefan," *Educational Moments*, in *SWJK.*

81. A feeling of homesickness   Recollections of Stanislaw Zemis in *RJK.*

81. How did he happen to notice Stefan?   The material on Korczak's work with Stefan is taken from his essay "Stefan," *Educational Moments*, in *SWJK.*

11 / THE SAD MADAME

88. a three-day furlough   Testimony of Janina Peretiakowicz, *RJK.* Also letter from Peretiakowicz to Igor Newerly, 1963.

88. Maryna Falska (1878–1944). For information on Maryna Falska's early life I am indebted to interviews with Igor Newerly and his book *LL*, and to material supplied by Ida Merzan.

90. "cried his eyes out"   *MD.*

91. often sleeping over   Z. Przygoda, interview with author by telephone from Toronto, 1986.

91. "The same revolver"   *MD.*

91. "Kiev—chaos"   *MD.* For background on Kiev I am indebted to Jerzy Michalowski (former Polish ambassador to Washington), the late George Kistiakowsky, both of whom were in Kiev at that time, and to Bill Fuller, a military historian. See Richard W. Watt, *Bitter Glory: Poland and Its Fate, 1918–1939* (New York, 1979), and Norman Davies, *God's Playground*, vol. 2 (New York, 1982).

92. "absolutely every day"   *HTL.*

92. "In notes are the seeds"   "Introductory Remarks," in *Educational Moments, SWJK.*

92. Maria Montessori   1870–1952.

92. Montessori kindergarten   "Helcia," *Educational Moments*, in *SWJK.*

94. *How to Love a Child*   The original title was *How to Love Children.*

94. said goodbye to Maryna   *MD.*

12 / INDEPENDENCE

97. "for the day Henryk arrives"   *MD.*

97. "How they ran to me"   *HTL.*

98. "We didn't interest him anymore"   Helena Eliasberg Syrkus, interview with author, Warsaw, October 1979.

98. Jozef Pilsudski, the tireless patriot   1867–1935. For a fascinating discourse on Jozef Pilsudski by a Solidarity patriot, see Adam Michnik, *Letters from Prison and Other Essays* (Berkeley, 1985).

99. four different legal systems   See Norman Davies, *God's Playground*, vol. 2 (New York, 1982).

100. Shortly after Maryna Falska returned   For information about the Pruszkow orphanage, I am indebted to the former caretaker of Our Home, Wladyslaw Cichosz, and the postwar director of the Bielany orphanage, Zdzislaw Sieradzki. Interviews with author, Warsaw, 1979.

100. They also took charge of furnishing   Janusz Korczak, weekly orphanage newspaper in Pruszkow.

101. "We didn't have a savings account yet"   Maryna Falska, orphanage newspaper.

101. "History may be the ruler of Nations"   "Swieto wiosny" ("Feast of Spring"), *Gazeta Polska (Polish Gazette)*, 3 May 1919.

102. as a reserve major in the new Polish Army   Korczak is listed in *Rocznik oficerski (The Officer's Manual)* (Warsaw, 1924).

102. Korczak woke up seeing double   *HTL.*

103. When Korczak learned that his mother was dead   *GD.*

103. "She could never have chosen"   Phyllis Grosskurth, *Havelock Ellis: A Biography* (New York, 1980).

103. "When my sister"   *GD.*

103. a remote area of the Jewish cemetery   As of this writing, Korczak's mother's grave has not been located in the overgrown and badly neglected Jewish cemetery. Her

obituary (*Kurier Poranny*, 12 February 1920, no. 42) shows her to be buried there. According to Jan Jagielski, secretary of the Social Committee of the Jewish cemetery, who located the graves of Korczak's father and grandparents, typhus victims were buried in a separate area to avoid contamination.

103. While he was feverish with typhus   *GD*.

104. "Why me? There are others younger"   *GD*.

105. Poland was in desperate need   See Richard M. Watt, *Bitter Glory: Poland and Its Fate, 1918–1939* (New York, 1979); Norman Davies, *God's Playground*, vol. 2 (New York, 1982).

105. "Filthy, torn, neglected"   "Dziecko i Wiosna" ("The Child and Spring") in *Religia Dziecka* (*Religion of the Child*), in *CWJK*, vol. 3.

105. "Warsaw is mine"   *GD*.

13 / THE SPIRIT OF KING MATT

106. "Children imagine that a grownup"   *RL*.

107. has been called Korczak's *Emile*   Stefan Woloszyn, interview with author, Warsaw, 1981.

110. he is captured with sleeping gas   This now seems a prophetic foreshadowing of Korczak's death by gas.

110. a last-minute reprieve   This is obviously inspired by the last-minute reprieve that Dostoevsky was given in front of a firing squad.

111. "the eternal tragedy of every noble reformer"   Igor Newerly, interview with author, Warsaw, 1981.

14 / ONE HUNDRED CHILDREN

112. "Why didn't King Matt"   Igor Newerly and Ida Merzan, interviews with author, Warsaw 1979, 1981.

113. little Jack, an American boy   *The Bankruptcy of Little Jack*.

114. "to avoid weeds that will choke"   *HTL*.

114. unsolved mysteries of heredity   *HTL*.

114. "We need to stop breeding children"   Janusz Korczak, "Concern for Motherhood," *Higiena i opieka nad dzieckiem* (*Hygiene and Child Rearing*) (Warsaw), 1927, no. 5.

114. "I thought that with good food"   Helena Merenholtz, interview with author, Warsaw, 1981.

114. "It's impossible to receive"   Ibid.

115. "One dies"   *MJS*.

115. "Where can I find Dr. Korczak?"   Ida Merzan, interview with author, Warsaw, 1981.

115. Israel Zyngman   Interviews with author, Tel Aviv, 1979, 1981. See also Zyngman's book, *Janusz Korczak Wsrod Sierot* (*Janusz Korczak and His Orphans*) (Tel Aviv, 1976). In Polish.

118. Sara Kramer   Interview with author, Tel Aviv, 1979.

118. He kept his instruments as clean   Janusz Korczak, "Strzyzenie Wlosow" ("Cutting Hair"), *Opieka nad dzieckiem (Child Care)* (Warsaw), 1925, no. 5.

119. "On Saturday afternoon"   Recollections of Doba Borbergow in *RJK*.

119. Hanna Dembinska   Interview with author, Tel Aviv, 1981.

119. allowed upstairs only   Hanna and Adam Dembinski, interviews with author, Tel Aviv, 1981. They were orphans in the home together and married during World War II.

120. a nine-year-old hellion   *HTL*.

121. "How are you getting along?"   *HTL*.

121. "Show me your tongue"   Ida Merzan, interview with author, Warsaw, 1983.

121. a game of jump rope   Sara Nadiv, interview with author, Tel Aviv, 1981.

122. "Don't you think I look like an old tree?"   Ida Merzan, interview with author, Warsaw, 1983.

122. "wide as a yeast cake"   Jona Bocian, interview with author, Tel Aviv, 1981.

15 / TAMING THE BEAST

124. "Don't touch shit, it smells"   Recollection of J. Dodiuk in *RJK*. Korczak liked to use scatological expressions, many of which he had picked up in the military. He also enjoyed swapping off-color jokes with his adult friends.

124. "A child with a vice"   "On Various Types of Children," October 1928, in *SWJK*.

124. "I will surely provoke"   "The Ambitious Teacher," August 1938, in *SWJK*.

125. "dangerous maniac"   Letter to Joseph Arnon, 8 July 1938.

125. "Thanks to theory"   "Theory and Practice," *The Special School*, January 1924, in *SWJK*.

125. "I am a doctor by education"   Recollections of Zofia Zaimanska in *RJK*.

125. "What do you bet?"   Igor Newerly and Ida Merzan, interviews with author, Warsaw, 1979, 1981.

126. "Solutions should be sought"   *HTL*. For discussion of Korczak's educational system in English, see Shimon Frost, "Janusz Korczak: Friend of Children," *Moral Education Forum Magazine*, Hunter College, City University of New York, Spring 1983, no. 1, vol. 8; Moses Stambler, "Janusz Korczak: His Perspectives on the Child," *The Polish Review*, 1980, no. 1, vol. 25; see also "Janusz Korczak Symposium," with T. Bird, F. Gross, G. Z. F. Berday, E. J. Czerwinski, H. Grynberg, *The Polish Review*, 1979, no. 1, vol. 24. For a fascinating collection of articles in Polish on all aspects of Korczak's life and work, see *Janusz Korczak, zycie i dzielo* (Warsaw, 1978).

127. "Shame on you!"   *HP*.

127. Hanna Dembinska, who received a sentence   Hanna Dembinska, interview with author, Tel Aviv, 1981.

128. a surgeon grappling   *HTL*.

128. "What's so special about cards"   Ida Merzan, *Pan Doctor i Pani Stefa (Mister Doctor and Madame Stefa)* (Warsaw, 1979).

129. "They all hold memories" *HTL.*
130. Korczak's dream of a summer camp Little Rose (Rozyczka) was donated by Mr. and Mrs. Maximilian Cohn in 1921. For the first few seasons, until there was adequate housing, boys and girls went separately, one month each. Children from Korczak's Jewish and Christian orphanages attended camp together the first summer of its existence. However, because of protests from board members of both orphanages, this did not happen again. Ida Merzan, interview with author, Warsaw, 1983.
130. Korczak would lie blissfully Shimon Agassiz, interview with author, Tel Aviv, 1981.

16 / STRIVING FOR JUSTICE

133. "One court case" *HTL.*
135. "I'm not going to let" *HTL.*
137. One Saturday afternoon Stasiek Israel Zyngman, interviews with author, Tel Aviv, 1979, 1981.
140. "Unfortunately, we can give you nothing but" Reprinted from the *Orphans Home Weekly* in *In the Sunshine* (Warsaw), 1919, no. 12.
141. The girls tried to find jobs Letter from Stefa Wilczynska to Rose Zyzensztejn, 12 December 1929.
141. "I remember how homesick I was" Itzhak Belfer, interview with author, Tel Aviv, 1981.
141. "Finally I found a park bench" Johann Nutkiewicz, interview with author, Tel Aviv, 1981.
142. He never sent a bill Franek Piotrowski, article in *Tygodnik Polski* (*Polish Weekly*) (London), September 1973.
142. "The delinquent child is still a child" "Theory and Practice," *The Special School,* January 1924, in *SWJK.*
142. Janusz Korczak's testimony "The Trial of Stanislaw Lampisz," *Nasz Przeglad* (*Our Review*) (Warsaw), 25 May 1927, no. 142.

17 / LONG LIVE THE HERRING

144. "The Heart of the Child" Maria Grzegorzewska, *Listy do Mlodego nauczyciela* (*Letters to a Young Teacher*) (Warsaw, 1958).
145. Feiga Lipshitz Bieber *Memorial Book,* Kibbutz Ein Harod, 1971.
145. Pedagogic love Joseph Arnon, "Educational System of Janusz Korczak" (Teachers Union, Israel, 1971). In English.
145. In his view, old nannies *GD.*
145. Asked if he could spot Ida Merzan, interview with author, Warsaw, 1981.
146. Ida Merzan Interviews with author, Warsaw, 1981, 1983. See her book, *Pan Doctor i Pani Stefa* (*Mister Doctor and Madame Stefa*) (Warsaw, 1979).
146. Misha Wroblewski Interviews with author, Stockholm, 1979 and 1981; Warsaw, 1983.

147. Joseph Arnon   His recollections in Yad Vashem Archives (Jerusalem, July 1969).

149. "Young lady"   "The Passion of Janusz Korczak," *Midstream*, May 1973.

149. "Tell me, my dear"   Ibid.

149. Yanka Zuk   Interviews with author, Tel Aviv, 1979, 1981.

150. "When I'm shouting at you"   Letter to Sabina Damm, 5 February 1939.

150. lacked trust and sincerity   "Trzy Kwadranse & Dr. Korczakiem" ("Three Quarters of an Hour with Korczak"), article in *Our Review*, 1933, no. 11. Written by a team of writers, the article is signed: "Ludwik, etc."

150. "We'd like to give you more"   *Bursa* Lecture, no. 20, Ghetto Fighters' House Archives. Korczak's statements to the *bursa* are from the twenty lectures that he wrote for their paper in the mid-1920s. They have survived because Stefa mailed them to a friend in Palestine.

150. "The *Bursa* Suffers"   Stefa sent this Purim play along with the twenty lectures to Palestine. See above.

153. "Long live the herring!"   *Bursa* Lecture, no. 16.

18 / MADAME STEFA

154. One morning in 1928   Ida Merzan, interview with author, Warsaw, 1981.

155. "When Stefa was passing through the house"   Itzhak Belfer, interview with author, Tel Aviv, 1981. See Ronit Plotnik's dissertation, "Stefa Wilczynska: The Mother of Orphans" (Tel Aviv University, 1979), for interviews with former orphans on Krochmalna Street. In Hebrew.

158. Now married to Irena Eliasberg   Irena Eliasberg (1902–82) Wilcyznska, interview with author, Warsaw, 1981. Irena and Stash married in a civil ceremony in 1924, without the Eliasbergs' presence. Izaak Eliasberg, more religious than Stella, did not approve of converts. Irena became a devout Catholic. Information about the wedding of Stash and Irena is from a telephone interview with Marta Eliasberg Heyman, now living in Canada, 1987.

158. There is only the dedication   The book is in the Korczak Workshop Archives, Warsaw.

159. According to Stella Eliasberg   Her recollections in *RJK*.

159. "I think she must have come into his room often"   Igor Newerly, interview with author, Warsaw, 1983.

159. "Stefa suddenly appeared at my side"   Ibid.

19 / NOT EVERY TRUTH CAN BE BLOWN ON A TRUMPET

161. Aleksandra Pilsudska   *Rekolekcje (Recollections)* (London, 1960). In Polish.

162. "Well, it's Korczak"   *MD*.

162. "We were close"   Interview with Miss Eugenka, Warsaw, 1981.

163. "like pieces of ice"   Recollections of Maria Taboryska, in *SWJK*.

163. calling him by his last name   Wladyslaw Cichosz, interview with author, Warsaw, October 1979.

163. "Maryna would walk" Igor Newerly, interview with author, Warsaw, 1983.

164. "Have you ever seen a cow?" Stanislawa Gawronska, interview with author, Warsaw, 1981. Monika Zeromska, the daughter of Stefan Zeromski, the novelist, said that as a child she thought Korczak's questions were silly. She refused to reply when she met him with her father at parties. But when she grew up and could appreciate Korczak, he was no longer interested in talking to her. Interview with author, Warsaw, 1983.

165. "Why must you give money" *MD.*

165. "You understand nothing." Aleksander Hertz, *Confessions of an Old Man* (London, 1979).

165. a "small man with a beard" Recollections of Stanislaw Rogolowksi, in *SWJK.*

165. "You either stayed afloat" Recollections of Henrietta Kedzierska, in *SWJK.*

167. "It's not easy for me to answer you" Stanislaw Zemis, notebook.

168. "We thought he was soft-hearted" Gawronska, op. cit.

168. "Not every truth can be blown on a trumpet" Stefan Dziedzic, Leaflet, State Institute of Pedagogy, 1934–35.

168. "You wouldn't dare hit me!" Kedzierska, op. cit.

20 / THE HAPPIEST PERIOD

170. *When I Am Little Again* WIALA. Czeslaw Milosz writes of Korczak's "humor and humanizing philosophy in his fablelike novels." He notes that Korczak's idea of an adult magically becoming a child again appeared in Witold Gombrowicz's novel *Ferdyduke* (1938). Czeslaw Milosz, *The History of Polish Literature* (Berkeley, 1983).

172. "I love you, gray Vistula." *CB.*

173. *Polish Courier* The School Edition, 1925.

175. Maja Zellinger Interview with author, Kibbutz Givat Haim Hameuchad, 1981.

176. Jozef Balcerak This and subsequent attributions to Balcerak are from interviews conducted during my four trips to Warsaw, 1979–86.

177. Alexander Ramati Interview with author, Tel Aviv, 1981.

177. Leon Ha'ari Interview with author, Kibbutz Givat Haim Hameuchad, 1981; Warsaw, 1983.

177. Kazimierz Debnicki Interview with author, Warsaw, 1979.

178. "I feel that all of the correspondents" *LR*, October 1928.

179. Korczak's favorite movies Jozef Balcerak, interviews.

179. "I have witnessed three wars" *RL.*

179. Zygmunt Kora Testimony in *SWJK.*

180. when people attacked it M. Fuks, "Little Review," *Bulletin of the Jewish Historical Society*, January–March 1929. In Polish.

180. "Scribbling is not dangerous" M. Fuks, *Bulletin of the Jewish Historical Institute*, January–March 1978.

180. like dating and sex *GD.*

180. "I thought: I am tired" "Pamietan" ("I Remember"), in *LR*. Tenth anniversary issue, no. 1, 1937.

21 / CROSSROADS

184. "I felt he was a typical bourgeois educator" Bolek Drukier, interview with author, New York City, 1984.

184. "I respect the idea" Yitzhak Perlis, in *CWJK*.

184. Not only were revolutionary programs "self-righteous" Ibid.

184–5. Meeting of the ex-orphans Stella Eliasberg, "Historia Domu Sierot" ("The History of the Orphans Home"), a private unpublished journal. A copy was sent to the author by the youngest daughter, Marta Eliasberg Heyman, with whom Stella lived her last years in Vancouver, Canada.

186. "Which lamppost are you going to hang me from" Ida Merzan, *Pan Doktor i Pani Stefa* (*Mister Doctor and Madame Stefa*) (Warsaw, 1979).

186. He didn't mention that one of the prostitutes Recollections of Aaron and Doba Borbergow in *RJK*.

186. "by chance" Letter to Jewish National Fund, 1925, in *CWJK*.

187. "The problem of *Man*" Letter to Ester Budko, 1928.

187. "I imagined he would be someone with wings" Moshe Zertal, interview with author, Kibbutz Ein Shemer, 1981.

189. *Senate of Madmen   Senat szalencow*, performed in the Atheneum theater, Warsaw, 1931.

191. "We were all surprised" Henryk Szletynski, interview with author, Warsaw, 1981.

192. The play closed after fifty-one performances Korczak told a newspaper interviewer that he planned to revise the manuscript—see *Glos Poranny* (*The Morning Voice*), 1932, no. 293—but the script was never published. The only surviving copy of the play, the one used by the director, Stanislawa Perzanowska, had been hidden in a coal bin during the Nazi destruction of Warsaw in 1944.

192. The title was probably inspired by Tolstoy's *Rules of Life*. Korczak kept many of Tolstoy's books in his library in the orphanage, including *Diary of a School in Yasnaya Polyana*, which describes his educational experiments with the children of peasants on his land. Aleksander Lewin, interview with author, Warsaw, 1986. Lewin, a young teacher in the orphanage in the late 1930s, was in charge of the library that Korczak left behind when he went to live with his sister. See also Lewin, *Polityka*, 1975, no. 38.

22 / PALESTINE

Informants for Janusz Korczak's two trips to Palestine were: Tami Levi, Hana Lipshitz Bieber, Aza Ronen, Moshe Zertel, Zerubavel Gilead. For background, see Walter Laqueur, *A History of Zionism* (New York, 1976); Howard Morley, *The Course of Modern Jewish History* (New York, 1977); Amos Oz, *In the Land of Israel* (New York, 1983).

195. "Children, after I die"   Sara Nadiv and Sara Kramer, interviews with author, Tel Aviv, 1981.

195. "I would have been very miserable"   Letter from Stefa to Feiga, 1930. Just before her death, Feiga destroyed most of her correspondence with Stefa, which she had kept in a suitcase under her bed. The fragments of pages that have survived, some without dates, are in the Ghetto Fighters House Archives.

196. "Your feelings of discouragement will pass"   Letter to Feiga, 1933.

197. "Palestine is still a legend"   Letter to Ester Budko, December 1928.

198. "If fate were to decree"   Letter to Joseph Arnon, 15 May 1933.

198. "cheap gossip"   Letter to Joseph Arnon, 20 March 1934.

199. "I felt tired, old"   Letter to Joseph Arnon, 27 November 1933.

199. a temporary experimental school   1932–34. Wanda Wacinska, interview with author, Warsaw, 1983.

200. "too old to rush around"   Letter to Joseph Arnon, 20 March 1934.

201. "How can you offer"   Testimony of David Simchoni, Ghetto Fighters' House Archives.

202. "Jewish brains are resting"   MD.

202. "with the enthusiasm of a young detective"   Hana Bieber (Feiga's daughter), interview with author, Kibbutz Ein Harod, 1981.

202. "Silence"   Lecture of Aza Ronen, International Janusz Korczak Association, Warsaw, 1983.

203. His talks covered his usual subjects   Lila Basevitch, "The Party for Korczak" (1934), Ghetto Fighters House Archives.

204. "It's a distortion of justice"   Joseph Arnon, *Janusz Korczak: Personality, Doctrine, and Educational Work*, published by Kibbutz Ein Harod. In Hebrew.

204. "It's more important"   Ibid.

23 / THE OLD DOCTOR

206. he felt impelled to go up on deck   Letter to Kibbutz Ein Harod, August 1934.

206. "weeks fly by"   Letter to Mia Simchoni, 5 December 1935.

206. as he urged Stefan Jaracz   Letter to Ze'ev Yoskowitz and son, Benny, 17 February 1935.

207. "Was I sincere in my feelings?"   Ibid.

207. "Radio will never replace the book"   Interview in *Kukla (The Puppet)*, 1935, no. 42.

207. Korczak's friends in children's programming   They were Wanda Tatarkiewicz-Malkowska, the head of the children's division, and Jan Piotrowski, the editor of *Antena* magazine.

207. Korczak deliberated   Aleksander Hertz, interview with author, Queens, 1982. Igor Newerly, interview with author, Warsaw, 1986.

207. Korczak's radio style   Maciej Jozef Kwiatkowski, interview with author, Warsaw, 1981.

208. "Puss in Boots"   Joseph Mayen, *Radio i Literatura (Radio and Literature)* (Wiedza Powszechna, 1965).

208. "If I'm with a group of children"   *Antena*, 1935, no. 45.

208. a special camp   Bereza Kartuska has been called a concentration camp, but it did not resemble the Nazi camps. Right-wing extremists, Ukrainians, and Communists were detained, as well as some well-known political figures.

208–9. He had turned down a request   *GD*.

209. "A Pole Does Not Cry"   Aleksander Hertz, interview with author, Queens, 1982. Moshe Zertal, interview with author, Tel Aviv, 1981.

209. Shimon Agassiz   Interview with author, Tel Aviv, 1981.

211. "Stefa doesn't seem to have arrived yet"   Recollections of Natalia Wislicka in *RJK*.

212. "It makes you realize"   Ida Merzan, interview with author, Warsaw, 1983.

213. "But what about the Arab children?"   Letter to Moshe Zertal, 30 March 1937.

213. "Who says"   Moses Sadek, interview with author, Beersheba, 1981.

214. Every great deed   Letter to Joseph Arnon, 4 January, 1938.

215. "I am an old man"   Moshe Zertal, interview with author, Kibbutz Ein Shemer, 1981.

24 / THE HARD TRUTH OF MOSES

217. To this day little has been said publicly   Ida Merzan and Igor Newerly, interviews with author, Warsaw, 1981 and 1983; Ela Frydman, interview with author, Tel Aviv, 1981.

218. "Some of his methods"   Aleksandra Pilsudska, *Wspomnienia (Recollections)* (London, 1945). In Polish.

218. "I still cannot forgive myself"   Franek Piotrowski in *Tygodnik Polski (The Polish Weekly)* (London), September 1973.

218. "I have never felt closely"   Letter to Ester Budko, 9 December, 1936.

218. "forty years to spend in the desert"   Letter to Jakob Zuk, May 1936.

220. "I called for respect for the child"   Letter to Edwin Markuse, 30 March 1937.

221. "The lives of great men are like legends"   *The Stubborn Boy: The Life of Louis Pasteur*.

221. "whose beautiful life"   Letter to Edwin Markuse, 14 September 1937.

222. "Hitler madness"   Gedalyah Elkoshi, *Janusz Korczak* (Ghetto Fighters House, 1972). In Hebrew with English introduction.

222. "the hard truth of Moses"   Letter to the *Little Review* reporters in Palestine, 25 August 1936. The full quote reads: "The hard truth of Moses, the soft truth of Jesus."

222. The book on Moses   The original Polish manuscript of *Moses* is lost. The Hebrew translation was published in the journal *Omer (Word)* in 1939. Ida Merzan translated it from the Hebrew back into Polish, publishing sections in *Folkstyme* (a Yiddish-Polish newspaper) (Warsaw) in 1980, and in the *Bulletin of the International Janusz Korczak Association* (Warsaw), 1982, nos. 3 and 4. It can also be found in *CWJK*.

222. the first in another series   Letter to Dov Sadan, 8 August 1937.

223. "cleanse" himself from within   Letter to Joseph Arnon, 30 December 1937.

223. Andrzej Strug   Pseudonym of Stefan Galecki (1873–1937).

223. *Underground People   Ludzie podziemni* (1908).

25 / LONELINESS

224. "There is little of me"   Letter to Feiga, 1 October 1933.

224. "Of course, I will still keep an office"   Letter to Feiga, 10 February 1937.

225. Stefa's one-room apartment   Misha Wroblewski, interview with author, Stockholm, 1981.

226. "Before I die"   Ibid.

226. she had advised Feiga to have a baby   Hana Bieber (Feiga's daughter), interview with author, Kibbutz Ein Harod, 1981.

226. "You think one goes"   25 September 1937.

227. openly voiced her resentment   Ibid.

227. "We have a baby!"   Hanna Dembinska, interview with author, Tel Aviv, 1981.

227. "Don't burst out laughing"   Letter to Feiga, 1937.

227. "It's so difficult to leave the Doctor here"   Letter to Feiga, 1938.

227. "I am not like your old ladies"   Ibid.

228. "I am afraid of goodbyes"   Ibid.

228. "things might end harshly again"   Letter to Edwin Markuse, November 1937.

228. first three radio talks   "The Loneliness of the Child," "The Loneliness of Youth," "The Loneliness of the Old Man," *Antena*, 2 March, 7 March, 16 March 1938. Trans. from the Polish by Edwin Kulaviec.

229. "Nothing is new here"   Letter to Jakob Zuk, 22 June 1938.   •

229. One show, a lyrical account   Reprinted in *HP.*

230. "Here we conclude the third talk"   *Ojciec cudzych dzieci (The Father of Strangers' Children)* (Lodz, 1946).

230. the Jewish world gathered him in   Korczak began visiting villages in southern Poland in 1936, according to his letter to friends in Ein Harod, 30 March 1937.

231. Rachel Bustan, who was ten   Rachel Bustan, interview with author, Kibbutz Ein Hamifratz, 1981.

231. "We must attempt"   *Dror Hehalutz Hatzair*, Hashomer Hatzair newspaper (Warsaw), 1938. Printed in Yiddish, with a translation into Hebrew. After the war, the original manuscript being lost, the article was retranslated back into Polish.

231. "Would the old Jew like to sit down?"   This tramcar story, with slight variations, is told by every Korczakian in both Israel and Poland.

231. "We are having a wonderful autumn"   Moshe Zertal, interview with author, Kibbutz Ein Shemer, 1981.

232. "Reveries"   Jewish National Fund (Warsaw), 1938.

233. "In low spirits"   Letter to Joseph Arnon, 22 November 1938.

26 / THE RELIGION OF THE CHILD

235. "one needs silence to write for children" Letter to Sabina Damm, 5 February 1939.

235. "Who knows?" Ibid.

236. "like a ship crossing the ocean" Itzhak Belfer, interview with author, Tel Aviv, 1981.

236. "unattractive newcomer" Hana Bieber and Aza Ronen, interviews with author, Kibbutz Ein Harod, 1981.

237. "It's more difficult to explain" *The Little Review*, 20 January 1939, no. 20.

237. "The kibbutzniks don't want" Zerubavel Gilead, interview with author, Kibbutz Ein Harod, 1981.

237. "See what you can do" Ada Hagari, interview with author, Kibbutz Givat Hayim, 1981.

237. "At the appointed hour" Moshe Zertal, interview with author, Kibbutz Ein Shemer, 1981.

238. "Welcome, welcome" Zerubavel Gilead, interview with author, Kibbutz Ein Harod, 1981.

239. "What is love?" RL.

241. *The Religion of the Child* The unfinished manuscript is lost.

241. "July was enchanting" Letter to Joseph Arnon, 2 August 1939.

242. Olympic Games Irwin Baum, interview with author, New York, 1984. Jarek Abramov-Newerly, interview with author, New York, 1986.

242. "without squirrels" Letter to Joseph Arnon, 22 August 1939.

242. "If I have enough money" Ibid.

27 / SEPTEMBER 1939

247. "those wicked, shameful, destructive prewar years" GD.

247. He took out the musty Polish uniform Alexander Wislicki recalls accompanying Korczak to the tailor with the uniform. Letter to author, February 1987.

248. "You mustn't give in to gloomy feelings Letter in *Our Review* (Warsaw), 4 September 1939.

248. "He called them by name" Antoni Chojdynski, interview with author, Warsaw, 1981.

249. "slightly bent" Adrian Czerminski, article in *Stolica Capitol* (Warsaw), 1962, no. 45.

250. "I had to make a quick retreat" Sami Gogol, interview with author, Tel Aviv, 1981.

250. "Despite the carnage" "Wiosna Przyjdzie" ("Spring Will Come"), Korczak Workshop Archives.

251. "What are you doing here?" Irena Eliasberg Wilczynska, interview with author, Warsaw, 1981.

251. "How beautiful" MD.

252. "We were so startled by his appearance" *JKGY*.

252. "As a teacher, I value eternal laws" "The Little Brigand," *The Special School*, 1926, in *SWJK*.

253. "adhesions, ruptures, scars" *GD*.

253. "It's bad to be an old man" "Refleksje" ("Reflections"), *Our Review*, 1 January 1939.

254. "One cannot flee from history" "To the Jews!," November 1939, in *JKGY*.

254. "playing the clown" *GD*.

254. Waiting on line for kasha *WDAC*. Entry for 12 May 1940.

254. "If I were a young girl" Ibid.

255. "It's so good to be here" Recollections of Leon Rygier in *RJK*.

255. ORT The Institute for Vocational Guidance and Training, a worldwide Jewish relief agency.

255. Stefa was proud Report to ORT, May 1940, Ghetto Fighters' House Archives.

256. "Obviously the war hasn't upset them" *GD*.

257. kaddish Helena Eliasberg Syrkus, interview with author, Warsaw, 1981. Stella Eliasberg's journal.

258. "Pan Doctor" Adam Dembinski, interview with author, Tel Aviv, 1981.

258. register with the Gestapo Document signed 20 September 1940.

259. already bungled birthdate It is interesting to note that UNESCO declared 1978–79 the Year of Korczak, to coincide with the Year of the Child and the centenary of his birth.

259. "Then give it to us as a gift" *WDAC*. Entry for 16 September 1940.

259. droll fund-raising plan Ibid. Entry for 29 September 1940.

28 / ARREST

261. "During the current year" *JKGY*.

263. Jona Bocian Interview with author, Tel Aviv, 1981.

264. "as if it were a large theatrical troupe" *MD*.

264. On the day they were scheduled to depart *The Pedagogical Thought of Janusz Korczak* (Warsaw, 1983). In Polish.

264. The children waved goodbye sadly Igor Newerly, interview with author, 1983.

264. tweaked their noses Adam Dembinski, interview with author, Tel Aviv, 1981.

264–5. Korczak shouted at the German Igor Newerly, interview with author, Warsaw, 1983 and 1986. Sami Gogol, interview with author, Tel Aviv, 1981.

265. Pawiak prison One section of Pawiak was reconstructed after the war. It has a permanent exhibit of prisoners who were incarcerated and murdered there by the Germans.

266. It was still possible to bribe one's way out The details as to exactly how this bribe was arranged are not clear. Igor Newerly, interview with author, Warsaw, 1983 and 1986. See historian Emmanuel Ringelblum, *Notes from the Warsaw Ghetto* (New York, 1974). Entry for January 1942. Trans. Jacob Sloan.

266. He arrived pale and debilitated *The Pedagogical Thought of Janusz Korczak*.

266. "How did you dare" Jona Bocian, interview with author, Tel Aviv, 1981. Igor Newerly, interview with author, 1983.

267. The first thing he did *MZWD*. Also the translation of the original Yiddish manuscript which detailed the walks through the Warsaw Ghetto (Jerusalem, Yad Vashem Archives).

267. "an aristocratic Pole" Dr. M. Lenski, *Khayei hayehudim b'geto Varsha* (*Life of the Jews in the Warsaw Ghetto: Memoirs of a Physician*) (Jerusalem, 1961). In Hebrew.

29 / THE GHETTO

268. "There was no natural evolution of life" Misha Wroblewski, interview with author, Stockholm, 1981. For firsthand accounts of ghetto life not cited elsewhere, see Mary Berg, *Warsaw Ghetto: A Diary* (New York, 1945); Alexander Donat, *The Holocaust Kingdom: A Memoir* (New York, 1963); Vladka Meed, *On Both Sides of the Wall: Memoirs from the Warsaw Ghetto* (Israel, 1977); Janina Bauman, *Winter in the Morning* (New York, 1986); Abraham Shulman, *The Case of Hotel Polski* (New York, 1982). See also Uri Orlev's novel, *The Lead Soldiers* (New York, 1980).

268. Michael Zylberberg Material in this chapter is drawn from *A Warsaw Diary* by Michael Zylberberg (*MZWD*). Also from interview with his widow, Henrietta Zylberberg, London, 5 October 1986.

276. "Even though the home was clean" Personal account of Romana Lilienstein, Ghetto Fighters House Archives.

30 / ALL ARE EQUAL

278. "We were embarrassed" Personal account of Abraham (Adolf) Berman, Ghetto Fighters' House Archives.

278. "shriveled raisin" Jona Bocian, interview with author, Tel Aviv, 1981.

279. "Please, if possible" Leon Gluzman, in his talk at the fourth Janusz Korczak Literary Competition, New York, 13 November 1986.

279. "Sit down, Doctor" John Auerbach, interview with author, Kibbutz Sadat Yam, 1981, and New York, 1985. After escaping the ghetto and doing forced labor on a German tanker under the identity of a deceased Polish stoker, Auerbach made his way to Israel. He is now a prominent writer working in English.

281. A talented orator, with a command of Yiddish and Hebrew For what little material is known about Gancwajch, see Yisrael Gutman's comprehensive book on the Warsaw Ghetto, *The Jews of Warsaw, 1939–1943* (Bloomington, 1982) Trans. from the Hebrew by Ina Friedman.

281. According to Ringelblum Emmanuel Ringelblum, *Notes from the Warsaw Ghetto* (New York, 1974). Entry for June 1941. This is the only source we have for Korczak's involvement with a Children's Aid Commission set up by Gancwajch.

281. Korczak was elated *MZWD*.

282. "Why should the Germans" Emmanuel Ringelblum, *Notes from the Warsaw Ghetto*.
282. "The rich are dissolving!" Ibid. Entry for 18 March 1941 and 11 May 1941.

31 / OUR CHILDREN MUST LIVE

288. "Our souls yearn" Chaim Kaplan, *The Warsaw Ghetto of Chaim Kaplan* (New York, 1973). Originally published as *Scroll of Agony* (New York, 1965). Entry for 18 June 1942. Trans. from the Hebrew by Abraham I. Katsh. Kaplan, who had founded a pioneering elementary Hebrew school before the war, managed to smuggle his diary out of the ghetto before the total liquidation. It is believed that he and his wife perished in Treblinka in December 1942 or January 1943.

289. "How are you feeling, really?" Maria Czapska, *Tygodnik Powszechny* (*Common Weekly*), 1945, no. 15.

289. "This ghetto is like a prison" Kazimierz Debnicki, interviews with author, 1979 and 1981. In 1985, shortly before his death, Debnicki published a controversial book, *Korczak z bliska* (*Close-up of Korczak*), which was attacked by both Poles and Jews who knew Korczak. Among other things, Debnicki contradicted much of the interview material he had given to me and others about his last meeting with Korczak in the ghetto. He claimed that Korczak had promised to consider his offer to leave the ghetto without Stefa and the children.

290. Sometimes Korczak knelt beside the dying children For an account of the plight of children during the war, see Kiryl Sosnowski, *The Tragedy of Children under Nazi Rule* (Warsaw, 1962).

290. "The hospitals are too crowded" Colonel Mieczyslaw Kowalski, interview with author, Warsaw, 1983.

291. One day word reached Kowalski Ibid. Igor Newerly and others do not believe Colonel Kowalski's story that he saved Korczak from Pawiak at that time. Raul Hilberg doubts that Dr. Wilhelm Hagen, who was in charge of medical services for all of Warsaw, would have been involved. We do not have additional sources to verify Kowalski's account.

291. "No payment without the tooth" Wladyslaw Cichosz, interview with author, Warsaw, 1979.

293. "an old man with a gray beard" *Little Review*, 3 December 1926.

293. *The Time Will Come* *Little Review*, 29 November 1929.

293. "Korczak asked the children" Personal account of Teodor Niewiadomski, *Polski magazyn radiowo telewizyny* (*Polish Radio and Television Magazine*), 2 November 1980.

32 / THE LAST SEDER

295. letter of application Written on 9 February 1942. See *JKGY*.
295-6. He had joked with Czerniakow *WDAC*. Entry for 16 September 1940.
296. "all smeared, bloodstained" *GD*.
297. "Long after the war" *GD*.

297. A Drop of Milk   Testimony of Anna Margolis in *RJK*.

297. He presented his findings   Korczak was in contact with a group of doctors studying
   the effects of starvation on the human body. See *Doctors in the Ghetto: Studies
   by Jewish Physicians in the Warsaw Ghetto*, ed. Myron Winick (New York, 1979).

297. "You're taking a serious risk"   Ibid.

298. "A beautiful hour of life"   *JKGY*.

298. The child who found a nut   Shlomo Nadel, interview with author, Ramle, 1979.
   Nadel believes that the nut he found in his soup in 1930, when he was ten, brought
   him luck as he made his way through Russia during the war and to Israel.

33 / THE GHETTO DIARY

306. Giena Gutman   The story of Giena Gutman (her true name) in Korczak's ghetto
   orphanage was told to me in a series of interviews in both Jerusalem and New York,
   between 1979 and 1987, by her brother, who prefers to remain anonymous. Samuel
   is a pseudonym.

307. "One must help the pedicab men"   *GD*.

308. "That's not a place for wholesale business"   *GD*.

309. somehow Gancwajch escaped   He surfaced again during mass deportations, working, it was rumored, as an informer on the Aryan side of the city. Nothing is known
   about his fate after that. See Yisrael Gutman, *The Jews of Warsaw, 1939–1940*
   (Bloomington, 1982).

34 / STRANGE HAPPENINGS

The material quoted in this chapter is taken from Janusz Korczak, *Ghetto Diary* (*GD*), and
Adam Czerniakow, *The Warsaw Diary of Adam Czerniakow* (*WDAC*).

314. Anna, who remains a shadowy figure   It is not known whether Anna was ever in
   the ghetto. Because Korczak wrote his first letter to her at the end of June 1942,
   it would seem that she had been there and managed to escape. It is also not known
   how or when Anna met her death.

35 / THE POST OFFICE

Most of the material in this chapter is based on Janusz Korczak, *Ghetto Diary* (*GD*); Adam
Czerniakow, *The Warsaw Diary of Adam Czerniakow* (*WDAC*); and Emmanuel Ringelblum,
Notes from the Warsaw Ghetto (New York, 1974).

318. *The Post Office*   Rabindranath Tagore, *The Post Office* (London, 1968). Trans.
   Devebrata Mukerjea. (First edition: 1914.) In his preface, W. B. Yeats writes: "The
   deliverance sought and won by the dying child is the same deliverance which rose
   before his imagination, Mr. Tagore has said, when once in the early dawn he heard,
   amid the noise of the crowd returning from some festival, this line out of an old
   village song, 'Ferryman, take me to the other shore of the river.' It may come at
   any moment of life, though the child discovers it in death, for it always comes at

the moment when the 'I,' seeking no longer for gains that cannot be 'assimilated with the spirit,' is able to say, 'All my work is thine' (Sadhana, pp. 162, 163). On the stage the little play shows that it is very perfectly constructed, and conveys to the right audience an emotion of gentleness and peace."

318. Nina Krzywicka   Ida Merzan, interview with author, Warsaw, 1983.

318. when she spoke about her brother Stash   Stash was living with Irena on the Aryan side of Warsaw. He died of lung cancer in January 1943. Irena remained in Warsaw with her sister, Helena, after the war.

320. Death was the Messiah   Isaac Bashevis Singer, *The Family Moskat* (New York, 1950). Trans. from the Yiddish by A. H. Gross. The lines, which end the novel, read: "Death is the Messiah. That's the real truth."

323. disguised as a water and sewer inspector   Igor Newerly, interview with author, Warsaw, 1983 and 1986. See also Newerly introduction, *SWJK*.

36 / YESTERDAY'S RAINBOW

Much of the material from this chapter is based on Janusz Korczak, *Ghetto Diary* (*GD*); Adam Czerniakow, *The Warsaw Diary of Adam Czerniakow* (*WDAC*); Raul Hilberg, *The Destruction of the European Jews* (New York, 1985); Jacob Apenszlak (ed.), *The Black Book of Polish Jewry* (The American Federation for Polish Jews, 1943). For additional books on the Holocaust, see Nora Lewin, *The Holocaust: The Destruction of European Jewry, 1933–1945* (New York, 1973); Lucy Dawidowicz, *The War Against the Jews, 1933–1945* (New York, 1975); Martin Gilbert, *The Holocaust: A History of the Jews of Europe During the Second World War* (New York, 1985).

329. In the early morning hours   Raul Hilberg, interview with author, Wellfleet, 1983.

329. "God gave Adam Czerniakow"   Letter from Felicia Czerniakow to Jan Szoszkies, Korczak Workshop Archives. See Leonard Tushnet, *Pavement of Hell* (New York, 1971), and Nora Lewin, *The Holocaust: The Destruction of European Jewry, 1933–1945* (New York, 1973).

329. Marek Edelman   Hanna Krall, *Shielding the Flame: An Intimate Conversation with Dr. Marek Edelman, the Last Surviving Leader of the Warsaw Ghetto Uprising* (New York, 1986). Trans. Joanna Stasinska and Lawrence Weschler.

334. Korczak pounding on her door   Stella Eliasberg's recollections in *RJK*. Stella escaped from the ghetto during the deportations, walking out on the arm of a Polish friend through the Leszno Street courthouse that straddled both sides. Her third daughter, Anna Eliasberg, who had been afraid to leave the ghetto, committed suicide there in January 1943. Stella passed as a Pole in the countryside after the Warsaw Uprising of 1944. Two years after the war, she left Poland to live with the family of her youngest daughter, Marta, in Vancouver, Canada. During the last years of their lives, Irena Eliasberg Wilczynska and Helena Eliasberg Syrkus, both widowed, lived together in Warsaw.

336. "Korczak deluded himself to the end"   Ibid.

37 / THE LAST MARCH

338. In another part of the compound   Misha Wroblewski, interview with author, Stockholm, 1981.

339. Korczak would have had no thought of trying to hide   In his book *A Field of Buttercups* (Englewood Cliffs, New Jersey, 1968), Joseph Hyams reports that a Jewish policeman, who took part in the evacuation that day, saw a boy hiding in the bathroom with a bayonet in his hand.

340. Eva Mandelblatt   Hirsch Mandelblatt (brother), interviews with author, New York, 1984 and 1986.

340. There were Zygmus, Sami, Hanka, and Aronek   We do not have a list of the names of the 192 children who went with Korczak on that final march. I use only the names that were mentioned by Korczak in his diary, or given to me by surviving relatives or friends.

344. A tall, thin young man   Miriam Biederman, *Youth Under the Shadow of Death* (Tel Aviv). In Hebrew.

EPILOGUE / TREBLINKA AND AFTER

347. August 6, 1942. Three years later, August 6, 1945, the first atomic bomb would fall on Hiroshima. Having written on Hiroshima before coming to my work on Janusz Korczak, I could not help but note the tragic significance of the orphanage being taken on August 6.

347. The small gas chambers   Testimonies of Franz Suchomel, SS Unterscharführer, and Alfred Spiess, German state prosecutor at the Treblinka trial (Frankfurt, 1960), *Shoah*, text of the Claude Lanzmann film (New York, 1985). See also Gitta Sereny, *Into That Darkness* (New York, 1983).

347. "We can't go on this way"   *Shoah*.

348. immaculately typed manuscripts   I made special trips to archives that were said to have the original typed manuscript of Janusz Korczak's diary that had been hidden in Falska's orphanage during the war. The curator of the Museum of Literature expressed surprise that the manuscript in the portfolio was not the original. She said she had not looked inside when it came into the museum.

349. One of them remembers   Interview with author, Tel Aviv, 1981.

349. Shortly before her death   Miss Eugenka and Antoni Chojdynski, interviews with author, Warsaw, 1983.

350. as poets and playwrights re-created that last march   The best-known play is by German writer Edwin Sylvanus, *Dr. Korczak and the Children*, trans. Eva Boehm-Jospe (New York, 1979). Other plays are by Canadian writer Gabriel Emanuel, *Children of the Night* (Toronto, 1985); American writer Michael K. Brady, *Korczak's Children* (unpublished ms., 1981), and Polish-born Tamara Karren, *Who Was That Man?*, trans. Jacek Laskowski (New York, n.d.); I am indebted to Gary Heisserer for allowing me to read a section of his dissertation on Holocaust drama.

The best-known poems are: Jerzy Ficowski, "5.8.42.: In Memory of Janusz Korczak," trans. Keith Bosley with Krystyna Wandycz (London, 1981); Wladyslaw Szlengel, "I Saw Janusz Korczak Today: A Leaflet from a Diary, During the Action, August 1942," trans. Maria Lewitt (Szlengel perished in the Warsaw Ghetto Uprising in 1943; the poem was initially published in an underground paper under the title ". . . to watch your Westerplatte"—Westerplatte being the site of the ammunition depot bombarded for seven days by a German warship; it became the symbol of heroic endurance); Antoni Slonimski, "The Song of Janusz Korczak" ("Piesn O Januszu Korczaku"), trans. for the author by Anna Kolyszko; Stefania Ney (Grodzienska), "About Janusz Korczak" (Warsaw, 1947), trans. for the author by Anna Kolyszko.

350. In a spirit of reconciliation   Benjamin Anolik, International Janusz Korczak Association conference, Warsaw, 1979.

352. a vast stone garden   The stones were brought from quarries in southern Poland. The designers of the Treblinka monument are Franciszek Duszenko and Adam Haupt, professors of the Academy of Fine Arts in Gdansk.

353. one rock that bore a personal name   The rock was unveiled in a ceremony at Treblinka on May 31, 1978.

Suggested reading on Treblinka: Jean-François Steiner, *Treblinka* (New York, 1967); Gitta Sereny, *Into That Darkness* (New York, 1983); Tadeusz Borowski, *This Way to the Gas, Ladies and Gentlemen* (New York, 1976); Claude Lanzmann, *Shoah* (New York, 1985).

Acknowledgments

Writing this book about Janusz Korczak has been a profound experience, but it would not have been possible without the generous help of many people, especially those orphans and teachers whose lives had been enriched by his. Their warmth and generosity reflect the spirit of the educator whose values they live by.

In Warsaw: I am particularly indebted to the writer Igor Newerly, who, in spite of failing health, shared his vast knowledge of Korczak's life and work during each of my four trips to Poland—in 1979, 1981, 1983, and 1986 (or, as I sometimes date them: before Solidarity, during Solidarity, and after Solidarity); and to his son, the playwright Jarek Abramov-Newerly, who delved into his childhood memories of Korczak. The late Ida Merzan, an indefatigable source of information, was always available to answer questions, and expressed the hope she would live to see this book (to my sorrow, she died eight months before publication). Jozef Balcerak escorted me on walks about the city and through the former ghetto area, pointing out the places where everything used to be: his wry humor and mischievous eyes often made me think of the man he so vividly described.

My thanks to all the members of the International Janusz Korczak Association: Chairman Jerzy Kuberski, the Ambassador for Religious Affairs in Rome, who facilitated the way for me to obtain information and often even lodging; Aleksander Lewin, Director of the Janusz Korczak Archives, who had been a teacher in the Orphans Home in the late thirties; Helene Lecalot (France), who is dedicated to getting Korczak's work translated into many languages; Rafael Scharf (Great Britain), who brought his personal insight to bear on Polish–Jewish issues; Benjamin Anolik, of the Janusz Korczak Association in Israel; Erich Dauzenroth and Adolf Hampel (West Germany), who created a Korczak archive in Giessen; and Alicja Szlazakowa (Poland), Jozef Bogusz (Poland), Stanley Robe (Australia), Bruno Bellerate (Italy),

Jiro Kondo (Japan), Vladimir Halperin (Switzerland), and Mieczyslaw Wojcik (Poland), among others.

My deep gratitude to Michal (Misha) Wroblewski, whom I visited twice in Stockholm, where he now lives. Hanna Kirchner and Stefan Woloszyn shared their knowledge of Polish literature and education; Szymon Datner and Arthur Eisenbach gave me insights into Jewish life in pre-war Poland; Stefania Beylin supplied endless cups of tea and albums of old Warsaw; Wisna Lipszyc lent me first editions of Korczak's books; Andrzej Mencwel deepened my knowledge of Poland's great turn-of-the-century moral leaders; Ryszard Wasita shared issues of his cultural magazine, *Poland/Polen*; Eryk Lipinski parted with a caricature of Korczak from his portfolio of Polish writers. Thanks also to Helena Marenholz, Dr. Henryk Grynberg, Malgosia Szurmiej, Daniel Passent, Marek Gronski, Anna Kolyszko, Bogdan Wojdowski, Barbara Lopienska, and Elzbieta and Jerzy Ficowski.

I am especially grateful for a trip through the former ghetto with Marek Edelman—ironic, wise, and tired from living too much history on the dark side, but still vitally groping toward the light. Hanna Krall and Agnieszka Osiecka proved generous new friends. Mira and Jerzy Michalowski provided warm hospitality and good talk; Adam Michnik, just out of prison in 1986, discussed his identity as Pole and Jew; Eva Zadrzynska and Janusz Glowacki helped me understand the eternal meaning of "The Return of Daddy"—and what home and friendship are in Warsaw and New York. John Darnton and Nina Darnton of *The New York Times* were warm and helpful during my 1981 trip, as was Michael Kaufman in 1986.

I had remarkable assistance in Poland and the United States. In Warsaw: Elizabeth Swiecicka Macavoy was an enthusiastic researcher and friend, as she would later prove to be in New York as well. My thanks also to her mother, Maria Swiecicka, and to her father, the late Henryk Hirosz, whose portraits, especially of Polish clowns, reveal much of the spirit and sorrows of his country. Lillian Wysocka was a conscientious interpreter and researcher, while juggling her responsibilities for a small child. Jola Bak helped when she could with interviews or archival material. Leszek Borowski was a wonderful interpreter and friend, who introduced me to Cracow cream cake in the Europejski Hotel café, and drove me to Hrubieszow to search for traces of the Goldszmit family. Beata Pogorzelska diligently translated supplemental materials.

In America: thanks to Helena Schmuness, who helped in the early stages of the research. Nina Polin translated many sections of Korczak's novels for me; Irena Zabludowska and Wanda Jaeckel translated articles; Joana Dobroszycki translated sections of *Senate of Madmen*. Bozena Sawa helped with interviews. Jadwiga Gerould generously read through articles from *Voice* magazine. Kristine Keese, who as a young child had seen a play in Korczak's ghetto orphanage, was tremendously helpful with final materials in Wellfleet. Alicia Magal and Jonathan Schwartz translated materials from Hebrew.

I am deeply grateful to all the members of the Janusz Korczak Association in Israel who received me warmly in their homes and spent hours recalling the past: Israel (Stasiek) Zyngman, Yanka Zuk, Itzhak Belfer, Moshe Zertal, Shimon Agassi, Hanna and David Dembinski, Ela Frydman, Zerubavel Gilead, Sami Gogol, Ada Hagari, Sara Kramer, Sara Nadiv, Edwin Marcuse, Clara Maayan, Shlomo Nadel, Aryeh Sadek, Maja Zellinger, Johann Nutkiewicz, Jona Bocian, and Bilha Lewin. And special thanks to Leon Harari, who proved a warm and loyal correspondent.

My deepest gratitude to Ghela Sharfstein, both interpreter and loving friend, without whom I could not have functioned efficiently; to her husband, the philosopher Ben-Ami Sharfstein, who discussed ideas pertinent to Korczak and read my manuscript; to Ilan Steinberg for his diligent research and his tolerance of my midnight phone calls from New York to Jerusalem while he was working as an interpreter at the trial of the Treblinka guard, "Ivan the Terrible." Eugene Wiener was a true friend, helping out with an interview and discussing the psychology of the martyr, as was his wife, Anita, who shared her knowledge of child welfare in Israel.

In Kibbutz Ein Harod: Tami Levy provided shelter and a feeling for kibbutz life; Hana Bieber generously recalled stories she had heard from her mother, Feiga Lipshitz; Aza Ronen shared her interviews with elderly people who remembered Korczak's visits to the kibbutz. In Kibbutz Sdot Yam: John Auerbach, a writer, was a warm host to me and my daughter as he recounted his experience with Korczak in the ghetto post office. He and his wife, Nola Chilton, who created and directed a play about Korczak, are among the dear friends I gained during my research.

My special gratitude to the late Martin Wolins, who, together with his wife, Irene, befriended me in Jerusalem and gave me a copy of the *Selected Works of Janusz Korczak*, a translation he commissioned and edited; to the late Yitzak Perlis, who published four volumes of Korczak's work in Hebrew translation; to Joseph Schwartz for sharing his interest in children's book illustrations, especially those in *King Matt the First*; and to Shimon Sachs for his thoughts on Korczak's place in early education.

The main archival collections on Janusz Korczak are in Israel and Poland. In the Ghetto Fighters House Archives in Israel, Reuven Yatsiv generously supplied materials over the years. In the Yad Vashem Holocaust Research Center in Jerusalem, Yisrael Gutman tirelessly answered questions on both Korczak and the Warsaw Ghetto; Danuta Dabrowska was one of the first to translate materials for me; and Livia Rothkirchen's office door was always open, as was her home. In Poland: I would particularly like to thank Maria Falkowska, a director of the Janusz Korczak Workshop of the Department of Educational Microsystems, who somehow managed to answer most of my seemingly endless questions in spite of the conflict of interest with her own forthcoming publication on Korczak. Her staff was of great assistance. Maria Bronikowska was helpful in documenting Korczak's bibliography. I was also given assistance at the Warsaw University Library, the National Library, the Museum of Literature, and the Institute for Literary Research at the Polish Academy of Science. In New York: I want to thank the incredible Dina Abramowicz, director of the library at the YIVO Institute for Jewish Research, for so patiently helping me to locate materials. In Wellfleet, Massachusetts: deep thanks to Elaine McIlroy and Claire Beswick, of the superb Wellfleet library, for their invaluable assistance.

As yet, there are very few Korczakians in America. In New York: Irwin Baum, who was in the Orphans Home the last year before the war, relived his memories, as did Hirsh Mandelblatt, whose sister was among the children who died with Korczak; Elchanan Indelman, who studied with Korczak at a government school for Jewish teachers; Samuel Wasserstrug, an apprentice in the Orphans Home; and Grigori Schmukler, the only one who had been in the Orphans Home before World War I. Anna Berezowski recalled going with her grandmother to consult with Korczak in the orphanage. During annual visits from

Denmark, where he emigrated after 1968, Bolek Drukier, an apprentice in the mid-thirties, reminisced about his political differences with Korczak. Edwin Kulawiec, a dedicated Korczakian and translator of his work, was helpful in the early part of my research. Joseph Hyams recalled some of his experiences researching his book on Korczak, *A Field of Buttercups*, during the 1960s. Eleanor Ford shared her memories of her late husband, film director Alexander Ford.

I am especially grateful to Iza and Victor Erlich, who first told me about Janusz Korczak, gave a critical reading of Jozef and Jakub Goldszmit's writings, and then of my own manuscript; to Elie Wiesel for his encouragement from the very beginning; to Lucjan Dobroszycki for many insights into Polish–Jewish history; and to the late Aleksander Hertz, who shared his memories of Korczak. Raul Hilberg read the manuscript carefully and caringly, especially the ghetto section. Piotr Wandycz generously gave the manuscript his fine historical scrutiny; Stanislaw Baranczak gave sensitive attention to literary references, Eva Hoffman to cultural issues, and Frank Fox to both history and art. Aleksander Leyfell generously discussed Polish–Jewish history and read the historical sections in the manuscript; and Anna Anita Leyfell translated a few chapters of *King Matt the First* for me (before its published English translation by Richard Lourie) and in the process became a close friend. Andrzej Wirth helped me understand generations of Polish writers who, like himself, were "exile hungry." Hillel Levine shared his thoughts on Polish–Jewish life; Gershon Hundert, on assimilation. Harold Segal taught me much about Polish romantic drama and organized a conference on Poles and Jews at Columbia University at which I made one of my first presentations on Janusz Korczak.

My gratitude also to Martha Osnos, who knew Korczak when she was a child in Warsaw and who became my friend in New York and a warm, loving link between the two worlds; and to Halina Wittlin, the widow of novelist Joseph Wittlin, to whose Riverdale apartment Martha and I drove as through pre-war Warsaw landscapes. To Henrietta Zylberberg who graciously spent a Saturday afternoon in London recalling her late husband, Michael, as well as memories of the ghetto that were not easy for her. And to Marta Eliasberg Heyman, who shared memories of her family by telephone from Vancouver.

I am grateful to friends for sensitive reading of the manuscript in one or another incarnation: Daniel Berrigan, Joyce Johnson, Lisa Kuhmerker, Eleanor Munro, Carol Shookoff, Barbara Solomon, and Linda Spenser. And to Florence Falk for discussions on Janusz Korczak and Simone Weil.

The biography seminar organized by Aileen Ward, first at the New York Institute for the Humanities, and now under the auspices of the English Department of New York University, deepened my insight into the craft of biography and the concerns of dedicated biographers— among them Deirdre Bair and Patricia Bosworth (who read the manuscript), and Ann Birstein, Blanche Cook, Gloria Erlich, Richard Goldstone, Michael Hearn, Frederick R. Karl, Gail Levin, Estelle Leontieff, John Maynard, Joan Peyser, Harlow Robinson, Judith Rossner, Barbara Seaman, and Mary Anne Shea.

My warm thanks and love to Erik Erikson, who looked over sections of Korczak's writings with me, and declared him an "original" who had created his own life cycle. And to the late Lawrence Kohlberg, who, after our talks, added an epilogue about Korczak as a moral educator to his book, *The Philosophy of Moral Development*; and to his colleague, Ann Higgins.

I want to thank Roger Straus and Roger Straus III of Farrar, Straus and Giroux, and also Leon Friedman.

I am deeply grateful to novelist and translator Richard Lourie for his assistance in polishing rough translations of Korczak's work, for his creative reading of my manuscript, and for invaluable discussions over time. To Charles Strozier, psychohistorian, biographer, and friend, for insights and encouragement. To Berenice Hoffman, my agent, for wise guidance, invaluable editorial suggestions, and warm friendship.

It would have been impossible to conduct extensive research without generous assistance from both the Ford Foundation (where Felicia Gaer was very encouraging) and the Dorot Foundation, supplemented by grants from the New-Land Foundation and the Memorial Foundation for Jewish Culture. My thanks also to the Center for Independent Study in New Haven.

And then there is my loving gratitude to my son and daughter, who grew up listening to stories about Janusz Korczak, and to my daughter-in-law, Michelle, who became one of the listeners. And to my husband, Robert Jay Lifton, who was embarked on a dark voyage with the Nazi doctors, but shared much of my journey with me—always supportive, and always fired with the same fierce moral fervor as the man about whom I was writing.

Index

About the Author

Betty Jean Lifton, Ph.D., is a writer of fiction and nonfiction and an adoption counselor in New York City. Among her books on the psychology of the adopted child/adult are: *Journey of the Adopted Self: A Quest for Wholeness, Lost and Found: The Adoption Experience;* and *Twice Born: Memoirs of an Adopted Daughter.* She has written about the children of Hiroshima and Vietnam, as well as numerous books and plays for children and young adults. *The King of Children* won the Joel H. Cavior Literary Award, the International Janusz Korczak Society Literary Award, and was nominated for the Jewish National Book Award.

DATE DUE

3/5/08			

Demco, Inc. 38-293